QUICK LIT

Quick Lit

Plots, Themes, Characters, and Sample Essays
for the Most Assigned Books in English and
Literature Courses—Written by Students
for Students

Tufts Student Resources,
edited by Seth Godin

HarperPerennial
A Division of HarperCollins*Publishers*

HarperCollins books may be purchased for educational, business, or sales promotional use. For information, please write: Special Markets Department, HarperCollins Publishers, Inc., 10 East 53rd Street, New York, NY 10022.

FIRST EDITION

Library of Congress Catgaloging-in-Publication Data
  Quick Lit : plots, themes, characters, and sample essays for the most assigned books in English and literature courses—written by students for students / Tufts Student Resources : edited by Seth Godin. — 1st ed.
      p. cm.
    ISBN 0-06-461041-1 (pbk.)
    1. English literature—Outlines, syllabi, etc. 2. English literature—Examinations—Study guides. 3. American literature—Outlines, sylabi, etc. 4. American literature—Examinations—Study guides. I.   Godin, Seth. II. Tufts Student Resources.
PR87.Q5 1992
820.9dc20   92-52537

92 93 94 95 96 ❖/RRD 10 9 8 7 6 5 4 3 2 1

This book is dedicated to teachers who work a little harder to make a difference in a student's life. I was lucky. Jonathan Guillaume, Steve Greenberg, Elly Markson, Millicent Blaisdell, Al Clemow, Russ DeBerlow, Dan Dennett, and Bruce Judd taught me. Thanks.

CONTENTS

ACKNOWLEDGMENTS

This book would not have been possible without Ted Tye, who helped create TSR, and Bruce Reitman, who allowed it to flourish and has supported it for more than a decade; Steve Dennis, Tom Alperin, and Nancy Gibson, who were there at the beginning; and Mike Eldridge, president of TSR in 1990–1991, who pulled it all together.

Thanks also to John Boswell, who believed in the project; Carol Cohen and Alison Jahncke at HarperCollins, who made it happen; and Michael Cader, who has supported and helped me in a hundred ways.

Written by:
Lori Abetman, Kevin Casey, Hendi Crosby, Mike Eldridge, Scott Epstein, Jennifer Gottschalk, Charles Graeber, Samantha Honig, Laurie Jakobsen, Jamie Newland, Jill Radsken, and Terren Wein.

Editorial Assistance and Project Management:
Mike Eldridge, Heather Adriance, Bill Schwartz, and Tom Dyja.

HOW TO USE THIS BOOK

To succeed in English class, you need to understand two crucial concepts:

The story is not as important as the way it is told.

All your life you've been reading books or watching TV or movies to find out what happens in the end. The plot is what's considered important: Does the bad guy get killed? Does the good guy survive?

In Literature (with a capital "L"), however, the story is secondary. What really matters is the way the author tells the story. Fitzgerald loves symbolism, Melville weaves religion into his stories, and Dickens' main focus is social satire. If you take the time to look beyond the plot of these authors' books, you'll find that there's a lot there—and that's what makes a book "Literature."

When you read *Quick Lit*, use the chapter-by-chapter plot summaries to get the story part out of the way *before* you read the book. That way, you won't have to worry about what's going to happen next—you can concentrate on the writing instead.

The second thing that will help you do well in English is knowing the answer to the question, **"Why am I reading this book?"**

With thousands of books to choose from, teachers in the United States have settled on a body of about 100 books to teach in most introductory courses on American and English literature. The 35 most popular titles are taught by an overwhelming majority. Why?

Each of the 35 books covered in *Quick Lit* represents an important turning point in the development of literature. Books like *The Canterbury Tales* or the *Iliad* have age on their side, while books like *1984* and *Huckleberry Finn* were chosen for the unique way they deliver their message. Knowing in advance what to look for makes reading the book, writing the essay, and acing the test that much easier.

Always read the sample essay questions before you read the book. That way you can keep your eyes open for important sections, highlighting them to return to later. Whenever you get stuck, or feel like you're not getting it, just remind yourself why you're reading the book in the first place.

One last thought: if you try to get through an English course by reading *Quick Lit* without reading the books, your teachers will know. You'll probably try it anyway, at least once, but don't say we didn't warn you.

THE AENEID

ABOUT THE AUTHOR

Virgil (70–19 B.C.) was born Publius Vergilius Maro. He lived at the time of the fall of the Roman Republic and the beginning of the Roman Empire. His writing reflects that exciting period in history.

The *Aeneid* was the last of Virgil's works and certainly his most famous. In his earlier days, he devoted his writing efforts to pastoral poems and poetry about agriculture, the *Eclogues* and the *Georgics*.

The *Aeneid* was Virgil's most powerful poem. The epic was written for the Empire's new government, led by Augustus. Although the story of Aeneas and the Trojans is pure legend, it became a symbol of the new Roman nation. It illustrated where the Romans had been and looked toward a future of great achievement.

Many liken what Virgil did for the Romans to what Homer did for the Greeks. Much of the story of Aeneas is modeled after Homer's *Iliad* and *Odyssey*, and reading both authors gives one much to compare and contrast. However, Virgil's *Aeneid* is a masterpiece that can stand by itself.

THE BIG PICTURE

Virgil's epic poem is the story of the travels and adventures of Aeneas and his people. It details an historical event—the founding of Rome—with both fact and fancy; gods and myth are intertwined in the lives of men.

Why you're reading this book:
• It is a beautifully constructed poem; its poetry and meter are models for much later literature.

• The poem was written for a specific purpose—to glorify the new government of Rome—so it illustrates the feelings at the time of the inception of the Roman Empire.
• Because it is so old, it is an ancestor to many of the other works you'll read. Its influences are important to note.

Your teachers are looking for:
• The tension between the world of the gods and the world of the humans.
• Aeneas' sense of duty and responsibility.
• Suffering and grief. Who suffers most in the poem and why?
• The conflicting wills of the gods.
• Queen Dido's attitude towards love as compared to Aeneas'.
• The glorification of Rome and her people as being divinely chosen.
• Traditions and customs and the roles they play.
• The poem's emphasis on progress as a way of glorifying Augustus' new government.
• Devotion—to family, religion, the gods.

The epic is a challenge to read. The meter is tricky and much of the language (i.e., names of characters) can throw you off. But if you take it slowly, its literary value is clear.

KEY CHARACTERS

Aeneas: The hero of the story. He is a great Trojan leader who undertakes a divine mission to lead the Trojans on a long journey to found their nation (the Roman Empire). His most important characteristic is his sense of responsibility to his family, his country, and his gods.

Dido: Queen of Carthage. She is initially portrayed as a strong character, yet her love for Aeneas consumes her, leading to madness and suicide.

Ascanius: Son of Aeneas who represents the future of the Trojan people. Aeneas protects his son at all costs.

Anchises: The father of Aeneas. He dies in the middle of the journey. Anchises represents the old ways, and his death marks the break from old traditions. Aeneas meets with him in the Underworld.

Turnus: Prince of the Rutulians, a Latin tribe, who fights Aeneas for Lavinia, daughter of King Latinus. Turnus is a powerful character, but the Fates do not favor him. He dies by Aeneas' sword.

Jupiter: Father of the gods, the most powerful of all immortals. He has to mediate the other gods' wishes.

Juno: Wife of Jupiter, a goddess. She loathes the Trojans and Aeneas because she knows they are destined to overthrow her beloved city, Carthage. She causes much trouble for Aeneas on the journey.

Venus: Mother of Aeneas, a goddess. She attempts to protect her son from Juno's lashings. She watches over the Trojans throughout the trip.

ESSAY IDEAS

- What is the major theme of the epic?
- How does the epic place a heavy burden on its hero, Aeneas?
- Discuss the themes of destiny and fate. Are the gods always justified? Are they fair? Are they cruel?
- Discuss some of the rituals and ceremonies that were of interest to you in the book (i.e., sacrifices, funeral rites).
- Compare/contrast some themes in the *Aeneid* to those in the *Iliad* and the *Odyssey*.
- What is the importance of dreams in this poem? Who has them and what power do the dreams have?
- Explain Dido's madness.
- Discuss Aeneas as a hero, as a man, and as a human. Is he realistic?

A SAMPLE ESSAY IN OUTLINE FORM

Aeneas' duty in the *Aeneid*
- Aeneas' sense of duty is toward:
  - The gods—their divine command.
  - His mission, to establish Rome as A great power.
  - The past—Anchises.
  - The future—Ascanius.
  - His family.
  - The dead—especially his wife and father
  - His people.

Aeneas' sense of responsibility is one of the poem's most important themes, because it shapes Aeneas' character and defines his role as a hero. Aeneas' duty is toward things outside of himself (i.e., the gods, the Roman state, his family), so he must often deny himself in order to fulfill his duty. This denial creates one of the main conflicts in the poem.

PLOT SUMMARY

Book I The first book begins with Virgil narrating a brief summary of the story. He asks the Muse of Poetry to give him the power to tell his long and dramatic tale. His story is one of destiny and divine command, the adventures of a great man and his people who are at the mercy of an angry goddess, Juno. Virgil tells the Muse about Aeneas and the Trojans. The Trojans, driven out of their homeland by the Greeks during the Trojan War, are forced to take to the sea in search of a new home. Virgil's story begins near the end of the Trojans' journey. They have been traveling seven years since the sacking of their homeland, and Juno has constantly thwarted their journey.

We find Juno in the first scene explaining her hatred of the Trojans. Her anger stems from old wounds; she resents the destiny of the Trojans as a great people who will eventually rise up and take over her beloved city, Carthage. She goes to King Aeolius, god of the winds, in her first attempt to change the course of destiny. She asks that he "put new fury into [his] winds"(lines 96–97) and bring a violent storm to the Trojans on the sea.

Aeolius agrees and a great show of winds, thunder, and lightning begins. The ships are separated and many men are thrown overboard and drowned. Aeneas, however, survives the storm.

Neptune, god of the sea, has become aware of the excitement in his territory. Seeing his sister Juno's hand in the events, he calls the East and South winds and punishes them for their help in causing the storm. He also sends word to Aeolius that the god has made a grave error in invading the sea.

As Neptune quiets the sea and the weather, the tired ships turn toward Africa. Aeneas shows heroic qualities once the boats reach land. He tries to comfort and raise the courage of his frustrated and exhausted men. Showing intelligence and determination, he kills seven deer to satisfy their hunger.

On Mount Olympus, Venus, concerned for her son, goes to Jupiter. Jupiter assures her that the destiny of Aeneas and the Trojans will not be changed. He

reveals some of the greatness that will come to Aeneas: he will beget the founders of Rome, Romulus and Remus. Jupiter sends Venus down to Carthage to assure that the Carthaginians welcome the strangers with good will.

Meanwhile, Aeneas goes exploring in the strange African land with his close companion, Achates. Venus appears to the young men in disguise as a Spartan huntress. She tells the two Trojans the history of Dido, the queen of Carthage. She tells them of the greed of Dido's brother, Pygmalion, who killed Dido's husband, Sychaeus, and how this devastated Dido. Pygmalion offered Dido money to leave her native land, Agenor; she left and came to Carthage, where she built a great city. Venus advises Aeneas and Achates to enter the strange town and promises a warm reception. Venus makes the Trojans invisible in a mist as they enter the city.

Carthage is thriving. Virgil uses the image of busy bees to describe the healthy movement in the city. They enter the temple and are awed by its splendor.

Dido arrives at the temple. She is a beautiful, strong woman who rules her people with ease. Aeneas watches as Dido welcomes the captains of the lost Trojan ships: "The city I build is yours." (line 778) Aeneas becomes visible and gives thanks to the Queen for her hospitality.

Aeneas sends Achates to the ship for Ascanius and gifts for Dido and her city. Venus, however, replaces Ascanius with Cupid by drugging him. Worried about Juno's next move, Venus plans for Dido to fall in love with Aeneas.

Cupid, as Ascanius, smothers the kind Queen with kisses. The kisses are Cupid's arrows. The first book ends at the banquet with Dido feeling the effects of Cupid. She coaxes Aeneas into telling the story of himself and his people.

Book II With tears in his eyes, Aeneas begins his story, the famous story of the Trojan horse. During the Trojan War, the Greeks devised an ingenious plan. They built a wooden horse and gave it to the Trojans as a peace offering. However, hidden in the horse were Greek armed men. The Greeks went to Troy, the land of King Priam, and hid their ships at a nearby island. The Trojans took the horse into their city walls as a gift. Laocoön, a priest, begged the Trojans not to trust the horse, hitting it with his spear: "Even when Greeks bring gifts, I fear them, gifts and all." (lines 69–70) But Laocoön was ignored.

Sinon, a stranger found outside the city, was taken inside the walls. He fabricated a story that the Greeks were trying to kill him. The Trojans kept the stranger tied up and questioned him for days. Finally, he won their trust and they unbound his hands. One night, Sinon killed the guards that watched the horse and opened the wooden animal. The soldiers inside opened the walls of the city and let in the Greeks who were waiting at the nearby island.

As punishment for hitting the horse, the Greeks made Laocoön watch two snakes kill his two sons. As the rest of the Trojans slept, the Greeks came pouring into the city shocking and overpowering the unsuspecting Trojans.

Aeneas had an important dream during that night, in which Hector, a Trojan leader who had been killed by a Greek, spoke to him. Dressed in bloody clothes with wounds covering his body, he warned Aeneas about the city's ruin and told him to roam the sea and to find another great land.

Aeneas awoke and realized the havoc and turmoil that were upon his city. Everywhere, he saw the horror of death and spilt blood. He witnessed Cassandra, Priam's daughter, being dragged from Minerva's temple. Aeneas and some Trojan soldiers grabbed swords and helmets from the Greeks and fought in disguise.

Priam's palace had been utterly destroyed. Aeneas watched Pyrrhus, an evil Greek, stab all of Priam's family and then kill the King. On the advice of Venus, Aeneas returned to his home to rescue his family—his father, his son, and his wife.

Aeneas carried his aging father (Anchises) out of the city with his son Ascanius by his side. Creusa, his wife, walked a few steps behind. Once safely out of the city, Aeneas noticed that Creusa was no longer with them. He returned to the city to find her, but found only her ghost. Her ghost told him not to mourn, but to care for Ascanius. She told him that a new kingdom and wife awaited him in Italy. Aeneas returned to his father, his son, and a large group of men awaiting his leadership to begin their quest.

Back in the present, Dido begins to fall in love with Aeneas as he tells his story. Aeneas' actions in the story clearly illustrate his heroic personality. Only a hero could move forward from such chaos and turmoil.

Book III Aeneas continues with his story. Predestined by the will of the gods, the Trojans built a fleet and began their sea voyage the following summer. They sailed to Thrace and settled in a new town. While examining the new environment, Aeneas came upon the grave of Polydorus, a Trojan whom King Priam had sent to Thrace to give the King gold. The Thracians had killed him.

After giving Polydorus a proper burial, the Trojans decided to leave Thrace. They sailed to Delos, island home of the god Apollo. They were met by the King with open arms and went to Apollo's oracle to ask for safety. The voice of the oracle told them to return to the land of their ancient ancestors. Anchises (Aeneas' father) interpreted this homeland to be Crete. The Trojans made the appropriate sacrifices and planned to sail for Crete.

Anxious and eager, the Trojans arrived at the island of Crete. They had not been there long when they were plagued by infected air, which destroyed the crops and killed many people. One night, Aeneas had a vision. The image told him that Hesperia (or Italy), not Crete, was the land of their ancestors. Aeneas announced his vision to his father. They made sacrifices once again and sailed for Italy.

A storm during the night threw the ships off course. They first reached an island near Sparta, where they were attacked several times by Harpies (half bird/half woman creatures), who gorged themselves on their food. The leader of the Harpies, Celaeno, prophesied that the Trojans would land in Italy, but would only be able to build a city after much bloodshed.

In fear, the Trojans ran from the island and sailed for Actium, the place of Hector's tomb. Aeneas met Andromache, Hector's widow, at Hector's tomb. She had taken a second husband, Helenus, and together they ruled the small Trojan refugee kingdom. They welcomed Aeneas and his men.

Aeneas asked Helenus to give him prophecies about the future of his voyage. The oracle at the temple to Apollo told Aeneas that Fate had destined Italy to be very far away, and that Apollo would guide them to the distant land. The oracle told them which peoples and places to avoid on the trip, including the sea monsters, Scylla and Charybdis. The most important point, the oracle told Aeneas, was to remember to pray to Juno before traveling. The oracle also instructed him to consult the sibyl at Cumae for further visions.

Although they avoided Scylla and Charybdis, the Trojans faced many other trials along the way. In Sicily, they fought the man-eating Cyclops. And in Drapanum, they were attacked upon landing, and Anchises died in the battle. Aeneas, in mourning for his father's death, set sail again and got caught in yet another storm. This last storm brought the Trojans to Dido and the land of Carthage.

Book IV Aeneas has brought his story up to the present, and Queen Dido has fallen deeply in love with the Trojan hero. The next day, she confides her feelings to her sister, Anna. She is troubled because she has promised to remain faithful to her dead husband, Sychaeus. Anna persuades the Queen to follow her heart.

Dido begins a love affair with Aeneas. But in spending so much time with him, she neglects her duties in the city. Juno and Venus agree that Aeneas and Dido should unite, but for different reasons: Juno hopes that this will distract Aeneas from his course to Italy, while Venus only wants her son to be happy.

Juno decides to intervene in the love affair while the pair are on a hunt. With the help of Titan, she causes a thunderstorm. During the storm, Dido and Aeneas are thrown together in a cavern, where they consummate their love. Dido begins to view her relationship with Aeneas in marital terms.

Meanwhile, the rumor of the relationship spreads throughout Carthage. Jupiter, the most powerful of the gods, gets wind of the love affair and sends his messenger, Mercury, to tell Aeneas of his disappointment. Mercury tells Aeneas that his relationship with Dido is causing Aeneas to lose sight of his responsibility to his country and future generations. This clearly illustrates the tension between Aeneas' duty toward his mission and his needs as a human being.

Aeneas agonizes over how to tell Dido that he must leave. He decides to keep the departure a secret until he can find the best way to tell the Queen, and tells his men to prepare the ships. However, Dido senses Aeneas' change in plans.

She confronts Aeneas and begs him not to abandon her. She accuses him of breaking their marriage bond. Aeneas, however, remembering Jupiter's message, remains unemotional. He promises to remember the Queen always, but will not say that their relationship was a marriage. He tries to explain that the gods have ordered him to Italy: "I sail for Italy not of my own free will." Dido becomes enraged. She screams at him, telling him to go, and runs off.

Aeneas knows that he must now leave. His duties call him and his ships are ready. Dido sends Anna to tell Aeneas that she accepts that their bond of marriage is broken, but she asks that Aeneas at least wait for good winds to sail. The words fall on deaf ears, and the plans to sail can wait no longer.

Dido, depressed and near madness, resolves to die. She tells her sister to build a pyre in the inner court of the palace. She pretends that she is going to burn all of Aeneas' clothes and the bed. In reality, the Queen is planning her own suicide.

Meanwhile, Mercury comes again to the Trojan leader in his slumber, telling him of Dido's plans. He reminds Aeneas that a woman is "a thing forever fitful and forever changing." Aeneas awakes and immediately sets sail. Aeneas' deafness to Dido's pleas indicates that he is changing into a leader. In this book, Virgil depicts him more as a symbol of the Roman nation than as a human being.

From her palace, Dido sees the ships set sail. In her madness, she curses relations between the Trojans and the Carthaginians forever. After sending her nurse out of the room, Dido climbs the pyre, lies upon it, and dies by her own sword.

Book V Aeneas sails from Carthage and sees the flames from the palace. He knows that their origin is Dido's funeral pyre.

Because of a thunderstorm, the Trojans land in Sicily, from which they sailed one year earlier. Aeneas declares a celebration in memory of his father's death. They hold games, make sacrifices, and have a great feast.

Virgil shifts the focus in Book V from the plot to a detailed depiction of Trojan customs and traditions. Aeneas and the Trojans compete with the native King Acestes and the Sicilians in various athletic events.

The group holds a ceremony and rites for Anchises. Juno, still angry, incites the Trojan women to revolt against the long wandering and sea toils that have become their lives. The women take flames from the altars of the ceremony and set the ships afire. The women scatter when the men, led by young Ascanius, come to save the ships. They beg for Jupiter's help, and the father of the gods sends down a rainstorm that saves four of the ships.

One of the elder Trojan men, Nautes, offers Aeneas advice: he recommends that the older, weak, and tired men and women stay in Sicily. Anchises then comes and speaks to Aeneas in a dream, telling him to listen to Nautes. He also tells him to visit him at once in Italy, in the Elysian Fields, so Anchises can tell him about the future of the city he will found. Finally, Anchises assures Aeneas that his soul is in heaven, not hell.

Aeneas tells the Trojans of his dream, and everyone helps the elderly and weak to plot land for new homes and to set up laws. After several days of feasting and sacrificing, Aeneas and the remainder of his people set sail.

Meanwhile, Venus, very upset, speaks to Neptune about Juno's actions. Recalling the various incidents of Juno's ruthlessness, Venus begs the god of the sea for a safe journey for her son. Neptune promises a safe trip, but tells Venus that one life will be lost at sea in exchange.

The seas are calm, and Palinurus is at the helm of the ship. Although tired, he will not give up the helm because he fears another storm. Unfortunately, sleep overcomes him and he falls overboard. Palinurus' life is the payment to Neptune for the safety of the voyage.

Book VI The ships finally land at Cumae near Italy. The Trojans set up camp. Aeneas, following Helenus' orders, goes to Apollo's temple to meet Deiphobe, the sibyl. She first orders Aeneas to make sacrifices.

The sibyl tells the Trojan leader that although his sea battles are over, tougher land battles are to come. Specifically, she says the wars with the Greeks are not over and Juno will not relent. Aeneas asks the sibyl to show him the way to the underworld, so that he may see his father. She gives him advice about the journey and warns Aeneas of the dangers.

Aeneas gets the golden bough, the key to the underworld, and takes it to the sibyl. After Aeneas makes sacrifices, the earth opens up and he enters the underworld.

First, Aeneas sees Palinurus, the helmsman who fell asleep on the ship and fell overboard, and promises Palinurus he will give him a proper funeral upon his return to the real world. Aeneas then meets Charon, the ferryman, whose job is to transport unburied souls across the river Styx to Hades. Initially, Charon refuses to take Aeneas across the river, but when he sees the golden bough he lets the Trojan leader pass.

Aeneas encounters Dido in the underworld home of the suicides. He tries to offer an explanation for his quick departure from Carthage and begs her forgiveness, but Dido cannot even look at him.

Next, Aeneas stops to visit heroes and friends from the Trojan War. He also passes by Tartarus, where sinners are punished for their wicked deeds.

Finally, he reaches the Blessed Groves, or the Elysian Fields, where the good spend their afterlife. Here, Aeneas is reunited with his father. Anchises tells his son that the very old souls who have been in Hades a long time drink in the Lethe, the river of forgetfulness, and will become reincarnated on earth as the future of the Trojan people.

Anchises also foretells of the wars that Aeneas will fight and advises his son how to survive and even avoid some of the tribulations that await the Trojan people. Aeneas leaves Hades excited about the future of his people. When Aeneas returns to the Trojans in the real world, everyone boards the ships and sets sail.

Book VII The ships sail north past the island of Circe and settle at the mouth of the Tiber river in Latium. As we meet the characters in this book, we are thrown into a plot already unfolding. King Latinus rules the Latin kingdom. He wants his only daughter, Lavinia, to marry the prince Turnus, a Latin of the Rutulian tribe. However, the priest's omen says that Lavinia will marry a foreign prince.

Aeneas and his men have docked in Latium. Celaeno, the harpy, had earlier predicted that the Trojans would wander until hunger forced them to eat their tables. In Latium, they eat the grass cakes that they use as tables, so Aeneas determines that they have reached the final point on their journey. The feasting begins and the Trojans rejoice. As they begin setting up their new city, Aeneas sends some men to present the King with gifts and to assure him that they have come in peace.

Latinus asks the Trojans their purpose in coming to his kingdom. The messengers explain that Fate has decreed the Trojan nation to found a new homeland in Italy. They tell of the storms and other situations they have encountered during their long years of wanderings. Latinus, thinking about the prophecy that his daughter will marry a foreign prince, realizes that Aeneas may be part of the fate of Latium. He happily welcomes the people and offers Lavinia's hand to Aeneas.

Back at Mount Olympus, Juno is furious with this turn of events. Aeneas and the Trojans have survived every test put to them. She decides that if she cannot change the course of fate, she can still delay it by causing strife between the Trojans and the Latins.

She calls to Allecto (or Grief), one of the Furies, to fill Prince Turnus with hatred for Aeneas. Juno also sends the Fury to Amata, the Queen of Latium. Allecto throws a viper breathing poisoned ideas into the Queen's soul, so both Amata and Turnus now oppose Aeneas. Finally, the Fury goes to the Latin people and kindles in their hearts a desire to fight the newcomers.

The whole of the kingdom is now effectively turned against the Trojans. In despair, the King gives up rule of the kingdom. He refuses to declare war on the Trojans. At this, Juno bursts into the Temple of Janus, the god of war. The people of Latium take this as a sign for war and the battles begin.

Book VIII With the assistance of Juno, Turnus prepares for his attack. Aeneas is absent, trying to gain support against the angered Rutulian. In his sleep, Aeneas is visited by Tiberius, god of the fair waters, who instructs the Trojan prince on the proper strategies for winning what is rightfully Trojan. He tells Aeneas to go to Arcadia and join forces with Evander, King of Pallenteum (the future home of Rome). Aeneas awakes from his dream and follows Tiberius' orders. He and some men sail up the Tiber River to Arcadia and ally with Evander.

At a feast uniting the two forces, Evander gives a speech telling Aeneas the history of Arcadia and the importance of the bond between Arcadians and Trojans. Meanwhile, Venus, desperately worried about her son, asks her husband, Vulcan (god of fire), to forge armor and a shield for Aeneas.

The next day, Evander suggests that the Etruscans might also be willing to join forces with the Trojans. So Aeneas and his new troops go to the Etruscans for help as well.

Book IX Juno calls upon Turnus to attack the Trojans. As the Rutulian leads his forces, the Trojans prepare their defenses. Following the advice from Aeneas before his departure, the Trojans remain close to camp in an effort to hold out.

When Turnus' first attack fails, he turns his efforts to burning the Trojan fleet. But as the Latins prepare to set the ships afire, Neptune intervenes and transforms each ship into a sea nymph that swims away from its predator.

The Trojans keep their defenses up well during the first attack. Two brave messengers, Nises, a veteran, and Euryalus, a young soldier, volunteer to deliver a message to Aeneas through enemy lines, but they are caught by a Latin cavalry and killed. Turnus begins a second attack that leads to the deaths of several Trojans.

The Trojans, however, are encouraged by Mars, the god of war. Their courage increases and they kill a large group of Latins; Turnus, however, is not one of them. He kills a Trojan hero, Pandarus, and then jumps off a battlement into the river to escape.

Book X The next morning, Jupiter calls all the gods and goddesses together for a meeting. He orders everyone to stop interfering in the events of the Trojans. Venus begs Jupiter to pull Ascanius from the war for the safety of the Roman people. Juno argues her side, to keep Aeneas from founding the Roman nation, but Jupiter holds firm. No longer will anyone interfere.

The battles continue and the Latins still overpower the Trojans. Aeneas, unaware of the attacks, has sailed back to camp with the Etruscans. The Trojans, seeing Aeneas' ship coming into shore, feel a surge of power. Now the Latins are forced to fight the Trojans both on land and at sea.

During the heavy fighting, Turnus kills Pallas, one of the Trojans' bravest fighters. Aeneas, filled with wrath, hunts down Turnus for revenge. However, Juno begs Jupiter to let her save Turnus' life. Jupiter gives in to her wish, but says that Fate has doomed Turnus to die at the hand of Aeneas, and that cannot be changed. Juno, disguised as Aeneas, goes down to the battle and entices Turnus onto a ship. As soon as the Rutulian prince sets foot on the ship, the Queen of the gods sets it to sea, saving Turnus' life.

A break in the fighting occurs. Both sides mourn their losses. The Latins retreat without Turnus. Meanwhile, Evander calls upon Aeneas to kill Turnus.

In a meeting with the Latin leader Drances, Aeneas suggests that in order to spare lives, the war be simplified to a battle between Aeneas and Turnus. Drances and his men begin to see that Turnus alone should fight this battle. Turnus accuses Drances and his group of cowardice but agrees to battle Aeneas.

King Latinus emerges out of retirement, insisting that peace be made and that part of Latium be given to the Trojans. But Turnus hears of the Trojan's advance on the Latin stronghold of Laurentum and sends word out to the cavalry to prepare an attack. The Trojans approach the city and the fighting begins again.

Turnus' cavalry meets the Trojan forces and is quickly beaten. When Turnus gets news of the defeat, he rushes to defend the city walls. Aeneas and Turnus come face to face as Book X ends. Night falls; the battle is set for the following day.

Book XI The final battle of the story is also the final book of the *Aeneid*. The last three books have been leading up to the climax of the story: the duel between Aeneas and Turnus.

Turnus proposes that whoever wins the fight will marry Lavinia and have peace. The King and Queen beg the Rutulian prince not to fight, but Turnus feels that an end to the bloody war is imminent.

The following day, the Latins and the Trojans set up the field for the duel. Juno, watching from above, calls upon the nymph, Juturna (Turnus' sister). Unable to protect Turnus any longer, Juno asks the nymph to save her brother from his death. Juno also suggests to Juturna to try to end the peace pact and start up the war between the kingdoms again.

The Latins see that Aeneas is stronger than Turnus. Juturna goes down to the Latin men to increase their doubts in Turnus' ability to defeat Aeneas. A bad omen heightens their desperation; a soldier hurls a spear into the Trojan camp, and a Trojan falls. The pact is considered broken and battle again breaks out. Aeneas and Latinus attempt to prevent the fighting, but Aeneas is wounded in the process. Turnus takes advantage of Aeneas' wound and encourages the attacks on the Trojans.

Aeneas, his wound better, returns to the field. He tracks Turnus down and calls for him to battle him one-on-one. Juturna drives her brother away in a chariot to try to secure his safety. Aeneas chases the chariot, but Juturna keeps Turnus at a safe distance from the Trojan leader.

One of Turnus' soldiers hurls a spear at Aeneas. Enraged, the Trojan calls on Jupiter. He begs the King of the gods to explain the need for such slaughter. Here we see the human side of Aeneas. He is not the typical "macho hero" (found in Homer's works). Instead, he is pained by human loss and finds these bloody wars senseless.

The fighting is at full force. In a fury, both Aeneas and Turnus go on killing sprees on the battle line en route to their central fight. At the height of the fighting, Aeneas decides to capture the city, which has been left undefended. He and the Trojans take Latinus. Amata, thinking that Turnus must be dead if the Trojans have entered the city so easily, commits suicide. Turnus decides that it is time to meet Aeneas hand to hand.

The fighting between the two leaders begins. As they fight, Juturna and Venus both help their chosen warriors. Finally, Jupiter forbids any more intervention. Juno, however, does win in a small way. Because of her hatred for the name Trojan, Jupiter promises that the new civilization will abandon the Trojan name. Juno vows to curb her hatred if the name changes.

After a great deal of fighting, Aeneas mortally wounds Turnus. The Rutulian heroically accepts his fate and asks Aeneas to return him to his family for a proper funeral. Aeneas is prepared to honor the request when he notices that Turnus is wearing the sword-belt of Pallas, the brave Trojan warrior he had killed earlier. Aeneas changes his mind and delivers the final blow to Turnus.

Aeneas' triumph over Turnus symbolizes Rome's victory over Italy and all of her other enemies. The end of the story illustrates the rebirth of a people.

ANIMAL FARM

ABOUT THE AUTHOR

George Orwell (1903–1950) is the pen name of Eric Arthur Blair, an Englishman who primarily wrote political tracts concerning contemporary events. Born in Bengal, India, Blair attended Eton and later served in Burma with the Indian Imperial Police.

He then went on to Paris and England, where he lived in poverty. He did not have to experience such poverty, but did so to understand the condition of those having no choice. His experiences were recorded in his first book, *Down and Out in Paris and London*, which was published in 1933. His support of the independent left was firmly established with *The Road to Wigan Pier*, about the English unemployed, and *Homage to Catalonia*, which described his experiences during the Spanish Civil War.

Unlike many writers who simply commented about the problems of the world, George Orwell actively sought to change things. He served in the Spanish Civil War on the side of the Loyalists, emerging a strong socialist, but one wary of totalitarianism either of the left or the right. His two most important books are *Animal Farm* (1945) and *1984* (1949).

Animal Farm and *1984*, while both maintaining a sense of fantasy, were intended to depict the social and political evils of the world in the 1940s and also to stand as a warning for the future. In the aftermath of the Russian Revolution, fascist and communist dictatorships, two world wars, and the nuclear bombings of Hiroshima and Nagasaki, the Big Brother of *1984* seemed inevitable to George Orwell.

Despite his activism, his reputation as a writer did not begin to flourish until after his death. Orwell died of tuberculosis at the age of 47.

THE BIG PICTURE

Orwell's *Animal Farm* is considered to be one of the finest political satires in English literature. The story of the rise and decline of a group of revolutionary farm animals, it is sometimes humorous, sometimes disturbing, and at all times insightful.

Why you're reading this book:
- The story is a parable of life in a totalitarian regime.
- It closely parallels Soviet history.
- It is an excellent example of political satire.
- It uses a fictional, seemingly unbelievable story to make a political point about the real world.

Your teachers are looking for:
- The way the actions and beliefs of the animals correspond to human actions and beliefs.
- The manipulation of the simpler animals, particularly those who can't read, by the educated pigs and their dogs.
- How the struggles between Animal Farm and the surrounding communities compare with those between rival nations.
- Orwell's satire of things many people consider sacred, like the Ten Commandments or English jurisprudence.
- The allegorical portrayal of the pigs as dictators and their dogs as police forces.
- The parallel between the animals' revolu-

tion and the Russian Revolution: particularly how the animals' revolution has failed to really free them from the oppression of the humans.

- The way the commandments and laws change to fit the pigs' desires. This book shows us how easily subjugation can take place and how easily history can be rewritten.

Animal Farm carries the sub-title *A Fairy Story*, but was intended to be anything, it seems, but that. While reading, note the similarities to real historical events and people. If you can, take a few minutes to look up the Russian Revolution in the encyclopedia.

KEY CHARACTERS

Old Major: The benevolent pig who teaches the animals to sing "The Beasts of England" and to believe in a world where there is no cruelty and where man does not rule. He is the incarnation of Lenin.

Mr. Jones: The human who originally controls the farm. After the animals' revolution he leads raids against the farm in an attempt to recapture it. Napoleon is quick to use Mr. Jones as a symbol for all that is evil.

Napoleon: A pig and leader of the animals. He is a very cunning leader who shows no remorse when killing other animals or forcing them to work for his own insatiable greed. In the end, he even begins drinking, gambling, and walking on his hind legs like a human. He represents Stalin.

Snowball: A pig who holds an important place early in the revolution, having been wounded in the first of Mr. Jones's attempts to retake the farm. Snowball devises the plans, later stolen by Napoleon, for a windmill that will bring electricity to the farm. Napoleon banishes Snowball and turns him into a symbol for treason and an object of contempt. Snowball's situation is much like that of Trotsky during Stalin's regime.

Squealer: Another pig, Napoleon's right-hand "man." Squealer's duties on the farm involve the spreading of lies and rumors that discredit Snowball. He is also a great orator, capable of making everyone on the farm believe in Napoleon's benevolence and abilities as a leader.

Boxer: The strongest horse on the farm. Though rather stupid, Boxer truly believes in the animals' cause—he lives their motto, "I will work harder." When he gets old and can no longer work, the pigs sell him for glue. Boxer's death makes him a symbol for the hardworking laborers who have died under the yoke of oppression.

Benjamin: The cynical donkey. The oldest animal on the farm, Benjamin spends most of his time complaining and never laughs. His belief that "life would go on as it had always gone on—that is, badly" is a central theme of the novel.

Moses: A tame raven who acts as a religious leader to the animals. Through Moses, Orwell satirizes religious leaders who try to make hardship bearable by promising a wonderful afterlife. The animals are wary and distrustful of Moses and his stories, but the pigs find him useful in diverting the animals' minds from their sorry state of affairs.

ESSAY IDEAS

- Compare/contrast Squealer's actions with government propaganda. What are his methods? How realistic is his ability to change the animals' minds?
- Compare/contrast the Seven Commandments of Animalism to the laws of human

society, the Judeo-Christian Ten Commandments, or Marxist doctrines.

- What does *Animal Farm* have to say about oppression and the responsibilities of those who rule?
- Identify and explain the meanings of the animals' names. Why do you think Orwell chose them?
- Does Orwell offer any alternative to the exploitation found in Animal Farm? If so, identify and explain them. If not, why do you think Orwell chose to leave the animals with no alternative and what does this say about our human situation?
- What are the similarities/differences between the pigs' concept of Animalism and that of Communism?
- Why do the pigs enter into trade with humans? Is this inevitable? What does this say about developing nations and their problems in dealing with the world's economic order?

A SAMPLE ESSAY IN OUTLINE FORM

Propaganda as a means of political control in *Animal Farm*
- Techniques and examples of propaganda:
  - Changing the name of Manor Farm to Animal Farm.
  - Singing "The Beasts of England."
  - Squealer's role as the mouthpiece and explainer.
  - The pigs' privileged position.
  - Bestowing and removing the military award of "Animal Hero, First Class" (and "Second Class").
  - Sunday Meetings—for spreading information and giving orders.
  - Altering the Seven Commandments.
  - The distortion of Snowball's reputation.
  - Mottoes such as "Long live Napoleon" and "Four legs good, two legs bad."

Orwell uses events in the story to show how a passive population can be ruled by simple explanations and the quiet changing of the Laws of Animalism. Old Major's view of a community of animals working together is then easily manipulated into a tyranny ruled by the intelligent and the cunning. The way propaganda is used in *Animal Farm* is paralleled in history: Nazi Germany, Soviet Communism, and even to some extent our own government.

PLOT SUMMARY

Chapter I The book opens on the prerevolutionary farm with the farmer, Mr. Jones, going to bed drunk. When the humans are asleep, Old Major, a wise and benevolent pig, gathers the animals together to discuss the life of animals on a human's farm. "The life of an animal is misery and slavery: that is the plain truth," he tells the other animals. During his speech, the dogs and a few wild rats scuffle and Old Major intervenes. The question of wild animals versus tame animals must be decided and so it is put to vote. The wild animals are included with all animals.

Old Major continues, telling his audience that mankind can be overthrown. He tells them a few simple rules to keep in mind: "Whatever goes upon two legs is an enemy. Whatever goes upon four legs, or has wings, is a friend." Old Major warns them not to become like man or to adopt his vices, but, more importantly (and ironically), demands that "no animal must ever tyrannize over his own kind. Weak or strong, clever or simple, we are all brothers. No animal must ever kill any other animal. All animals are equal."

He then goes on to tell them of a dream he has had, a dream of a future time when mankind shall rule no longer. The dream reminds him of a song, "The Beasts of England," and he teaches the animals to sing it.

Orwell uses most of this chapter simply to create a scene and a feeling for the activity on the farm before the revolution. Only Old Major and Moses, the tame raven, appear. Old Major's speech forms the body of the soon-to-be-developed concept of Animalism.

Chapter II Old Major dies and the animals set about preparing for a revolution that they may never live to see. The task of organizing the revolution falls on the pigs, for they are more intelligent and clever. Three promising pigs, Snowball, Napoleon, and Squealer, begin turning Old Major's speech into the concept of Animalism. Already we learn that Napoleon is fierce, Snowball inventive, and Squealer is a great orator capable of "turning black into white."

The first of their tasks is to overcome the "stupidity and apathy" of the animals. They must answer such questions as "Why should we care what happens after we are dead?" or Mollie's questions concerning the wearing of ribbons and the availability of sugar. But hardest of all is the pigs' task of convincing the animals that Moses' tales of a heaven called "Sugarcandy Mountain" are lies.

Two horses, Boxer and Clover, prove to be useful to the pigs. Once they are convinced of the pigs' position, they show great faith and pass the pigs' words on to the other animals. The animals hold secret meetings and sing "The Beasts of England." Life on the farm seems to go on as usual until one day when the men forget to feed the animals. The animals break into the feed shed and help themselves to the food. Jones and his men, hearing the uproar, come out with their whips. The hungry animals, who can no longer stand the men's torture, turn on their masters. The men flee the farm, and the animals find that the rebellion has come at last. In a celebration of their victory, the animals destroy all the tools Mr. Jones and the men had used to control them.

In the morning they hold another meeting in which it becomes obvious that Snowball and Napoleon have assumed control. They change the name of the farm from Manor Farm to Animal Farm and write the Seven Commandments of Animalism on the barn wall:

1. Whatever goes upon two legs is an enemy.
2. Whatever goes upon four legs, or has wings, is a friend.
3. No animal shall wear clothes.
4. No animal shall sleep in a bed.
5. No animal shall drink alcohol.
6. No animal shall kill any other animal.
7. All animals are equal.

The first day of the rebellion is also the first day of the hay harvest. The animals pledge that they can harvest more efficiently than the men. But before they can begin, the cows need to be milked, a task that the pigs assume responsibility for. The animals want to know what is to be done with the milk, but Napoleon is cunning and diverts their attention: "Forward Comrades! The hay is waiting." When the animals return, the milk has disappeared—a hint to the reader that these are greedy pigs.

This chapter serves two purposes: first, to show the reader how easily Snowball and Napoleon assume the roles of leaders, and second, to show the reader the beginnings of deceit in the animals' new leaders.

Chapter III The harvest is a great success and the animals begin to enjoy some prosperity. Boxer, the strongest horse, shows great loyalty and adopts the motto "I will work harder." Life on the farm settles down, and everyone is relatively

happy. The animals develop a Sunday ritual involving a late breakfast and the raising of their flag. The flag, as Squealer explained, is green for the fields of England with a hoof and horn to represent the future of the Republic of Animals. Afterwards, all the animals meet in the barn in order to plan out the week and to put forward any resolutions. Of course, none of the animals are smart enough to come up with any resolutions of their own, so Snowball and Napoleon are left to debate on subjects of their choosing.

Snowball forms many committees to improve the animals, but most fail. Napoleon is not interested in Snowball's ideas, feeling that it is more important to educate the litter of pups. The animals discover that the pigs are hoarding all the apples and the milk. When confronted, Napoleon and even Snowball insist that it is best. They send Squealer to explain that the pigs are not privileged, that in truth the pigs hate milk but must drink it in order to do all their "brainwork" successfully. He adds the catch–phrase, "Surely there is no one here among you who wants to see Jones come back?" This settles the argument in the pigs' favor.

In this chapter, Orwell creates the early stages of tension between Snowball and Napoleon, and also illustrates the pigs' increasingly privileged position among the animals.

Chapter IV This chapter begins with a discussion of events occurring outside of the farm's immediate vicinity. The pigs send pigeons out in order to spread the news of the rebellion and its successes. Mr. Jones seeks sympathy from the other farmers, but he receives no support. Animal Farm's neighbors, Mr. Pilkington and Mr. Frederick, are frightened of the possibility of the revolution spreading, so they

tell mean lies about the animals being cannibals or having "their females in common." But the tune "The Beasts of England" catches on and the humans become more nervous.

Finally, Jones and some men from the neighboring farms launch an assault on the animals, which results in the Battle of the Cowshed. The attack is a failure and the battle ends. One sheep dies and the animals decide to create two decorations called "Animal Hero, First Class," which is bestowed upon Snowball and Boxer, and "Animal Hero, Second Class," which is bestowed upon the dead sheep. They also decide that they will fire a gun taken from Mr. Jones on the anniversaries of the rebellion and the Battle of the Cowshed.

Chapter IV is short and deals primarily with the battle. It shows that the animals are willing to give up their lives in order to protect their concept of Animalism, an ideal which will soon sour and become another tyranny.

Chapter V Mollie, the vain mare, leaves the farm and is seen pulling a cart for a man who feeds her sugar. Snowball and Napoleon have increasingly fierce debates, the biggest concerning Snowball's idea to build a windmill in order to produce electricity that would heat the animals' stalls and grind their corn. Napoleon, in an obvious show of contempt, urinates over Snowball's plans for the windmill and the whole farm becomes deeply divided between Snowball and Napoleon.

At the final meeting to decide on the windmill project, Snowball is chased off the farm by nine large dogs that had been trained by Napoleon. Napoleon is now the dictator and orders the cessation of the Sunday meetings, stating that all decisions will be made by the pigs alone. Four pigs try to stand up to Napoleon, but the dogs back them down; afterwards, Squealer is sent around to explain Napoleon's actions. Squealer's arguments are so good that Boxer adopts a new motto—"Napoleon is always right."

Weeks later, Napoleon announces that the windmill will be built, and Squealer is sent around again, this time to say that the plans had been Napoleon's all along and that Snowball had stolen them. Again, the animals are convinced. Orwell shows us, in the last paragraph of the chapter, just how convincing some well-chosen words can be—especially when there are three dogs growling as a warning against dissension.

Chapter VI The windmill project continues, and the animals find themselves working harder than ever now that Napoleon has declared Sunday a day of voluntary labor. Ironically one's rations will be cut in half if he doesn't 'volunteer.'

A few fields haven't been planted in time and the coming winter will be rough. The windmill project runs into many problems, particularly in the breaking of boulders and in the procurement of materials that can't be produced on the farm. Napoleon tells the animals that he has begun to make trade agreements with the surrounding farms in order to get the necessary materials. When some pigs try to object, they are again silenced by the dogs and Squealer is sent around to explain Napoleon's reason for dealing with two-legged 'enemies.'

Napoleon, breaking still another commandment, moves into the farmhouse; the animals discover that the commandment against sleeping in beds has been changed to no sleeping in beds with sheets. Napoleon has the sheets removed from the beds so that he is within the law. Orwell shows us how simply changing the wording of a law or bending a meaning can allow a shrewd leader to get away with anything.

Later, the windmill is blown down in a gale and Napoleon immediately claims that Snowball is at fault. He offers a reward for the death or capture of Snowball and promises to rebuild the windmill. Notice that the windmill becomes both a symbol for the traitorous acts against Animal Farm, and a kind of carrot which Napoleon can use to lead the animals into more drudgery.

Chapter VII This chapter opens on a bitter winter day. The animals are near starvation and the outside world is spreading rumors again. Napoleon begins to retreat from the community. When he goes out, he is in the company of dogs and remains aloof. Power begins to warp him. Napoleon forces the hens to give up their eggs, and for the first time there is some dissent as the hens fly up to the rafters and attempt to hide their clutches. Napoleon cuts off their rations, crushing their rebellion. Snowball is thought to be raiding the farm at night, and Squealer spreads lies that Snowball was actually a traitor during the first days of the revolution.

Later, Napoleon and his dogs publicly execute four pigs for siding with Snowball. Notice that they confess to crimes that Squealer has concocted—destroying the windmill and betraying Animal Farm—and that are particularly heinous in the eyes of the animals. In another strange Orwellian moment, the hens who led the rebellion actually come forward and confess their crimes. Suddenly, many animals come forward and confess to various crimes, for which they are executed. Afterwards, Boxer believes that executions were all due to some "fault in ourselves," and he declares that he will work harder than ever. Here Orwell shows how the animals blame themselves for failing to be "perfect" citizens. Yet, to Napoleon, they are in a way perfect because they allow themselves to be totally subjugated to him.

Clover, unable to express her emotions, believes that this bloodshed is not what the animals have worked for. In another of his dictatorial moods, Napoleon banishes the song "The Beasts of England" because, as Squealer explains, it has "no longer any purpose." There is a grim parallel here to the Russian Revolution and the power that enabled Stalin to rule with the weapons of murder and terror.

Chapter VIII The animals, thinking that there is a commandment outlawing the murder of animals, check the list on the wall and find that it now reads, "No animal shall kill any other animal without cause." Life continues on the farm and the animals are reassured by Squealer that things are better than in the days of Mr. Jones. Napoleon has become a hermit, coming out rarely and only with an entourage of dogs. He is now called "Our Leader, Comrade Napoleon," and has taken to claiming various immodest titles like "Terror of Mankind," or "Ducklings' Friend." Negotiations are still under way with the neighboring farms, though the rumors that the farm will be handed over to humans continue. There are many more confessions and executions.

A deal is struck with Mr. Frederick, but he pays with forged banknotes and Napoleon demands his death. Before anything can be done, Frederick's men attack the farm and destroy the windmill. In a frenzy the animals are able to repel his forces, but they are saddened at the loss of the windmill. Through Squealer's eloquence and Napoleon's speeches declaring victory at the Battle of the Windmill, the animals forget about the banknotes and feel that they really have won a victory.

Orwell, in one of his most comic satires of human actions, tells of the pigs' finding a case of whiskey. On the following morning, the pigs do not stir until late and when they do, Squealer announces that Napoleon is dying. Napoleon decrees that the drinking of alcohol is to be punished by death, but he recovers from his hangover and late that night Squealer is caught in the barn repainting a commandment to read, "No animal shall drink alcohol to excess." This is the first time that Squealer is caught redhanded rewriting history, but he is not punished.

Chapter IX Boxer has become ill. Rations are reduced, yet Squealer is still trusted and believed when he tells them that they are better off now than ever before. Thirty-one piglets are brought into the world and begin their education under Napoleon. New rules are laid down concerning pigs mixing with other animals. Pigs begin wearing ribbons on their tails and brewing beer, for which they require all of the barley harvest.

But, in the manner of good propaganda, Napoleon attempts to raise the animals' sense of dignity by a profusion of songs, speeches, and parades. He sets up a mandatory Spontaneous Demonstration to celebrate the events on the farm. However, many animals complain when they're not in the vicinity of the dogs or the pigs, and their outlook has in fact become bleak.

In the spring, the farm becomes a republic and Napoleon is elected President. Moses, the raven, appears again with more tales of "Sugarcandy Mountain." Now that the revolution is successful, one can see why Napoleon would allow Moses back, for he can promise the animals a better life after they are dead. The pigs, who hate the raven, allow him to stay and feed him, since Napoleon reasons that Moses' promise of a better world will make their suffering here seem worthwhile.

Boxer's illness gets worse and, under the pretense of sending him to a vet, the pigs sell him for glue and use the money to buy whiskey. Boxer's death symbolizes the sacrifice of the loyal laborer to the dictatorial power. The chapter ends, then, with the bleakest and direst outlook for the animals. Through the pigs' machinations, all of the good and fair tenets of Animalism have been cheapened and reduced to justifications for the pigs' cruelest actions.

Chapter X Much time has passed and only Clover, Benjamin, Moses, and the pigs remember the rebellion. The windmill is repaired. The farm is enlarged and modernized. The animals work just as hard as ever, but only the dogs and the pigs seem to get any richer. "The Beasts of England" has to be sung secretly and no one puts up a fight or resists the pigs. The animals still believe in Old Major's vision of an England without men.

Then one day, the pigs began to walk upright. They have become like humans and even wear clothes. Everything Old Major had warned against has happened.

Napoleon even carries a whip. Squealer has taught the sheep to bleat out, "Four legs good, two legs better!" and the Seven Commandments are reduced to one that reads: "All animals are equal but some are more equal than others."

One night, the animals witness humans in the farmhouse playing cards with the pigs. Napoleon makes a toast in which he reinstates the name Manor Farm and, in Orwell's finest ironic twist, the animals witness Mr. Pilkington and Napoleon cheating as they both lay down the ace of spades. The last line of this fairy story sums up its meaning completely: "The creatures outside looked from pig to man, man to pig, and from pig to man again; but already it was impossible to say which was which."

Thus, the animals' dream has failed, and we as readers are left to face up to our own governments, and to question if what is said can be believed, or if what is dreamed can be achieved.

BEOWULF

ABOUT THE AUTHOR

No one knows who wrote *Beowulf*, primarily because it wasn't really written in the way that literature is written now. It is an epic poem, meant to be spoken out loud by poets and bards. It is the oldest epic poem known in English. Because these epic poems were meant to be spoken aloud, very few of them were ever written down, and even when they were, very few of those manuscripts survived into modern times. *Beowulf* did.

Note: The manuscript for *Beowulf* was written around the year 700. This manuscript was written in Old English, a precursor to our language. It has been translated into modern English by many different scholars; therefore, there are many different translations. The one used to write this guide is set up as a poem, like the original, but there are also translations in prose. The plot summary in this guide is divided into sections, each of which covers 200 lines of the original poem. These divisions should be small enough to keep you from getting confused.

THE BIG PICTURE

The epic poem *Beowulf* is a sweeping story of heroes and monsters, good and evil. It is an ancient piece, steeped in the oral story-telling traditions of the Dark Ages. However, age does nothing to take away from the stature of Beowulf or the excitement of his adventures.

Why you're reading this book:
- It is the oldest known piece of literature in English.

- It describes the Dark Ages, a time of which we have few other firsthand records.
- Epic poetry is an important literary form, and this is its earliest English example.

Your teachers are looking for:
- The role of religion in the poem. The narrator is Christian, but the characters aren't. How does that affect the narrator's presentation of the story?
- The search for glory by nearly all the characters in the story.
- The ways the values expressed in this poem differ from our present-day values.
- The historical references in the poem (especially in advanced courses). Who are all those other people that keep appearing without explanation, and why are they mentioned?

This is not an easy poem to read. The figures of speech are very unusual to modern readers, and some of the references are obscure. Keep in mind, though, that this poem can be exciting if you try to visualize as you read. This is a violent, gory, scary poem, and if you try to see it that way in your head, you will come a lot closer to the experience of the poem's original audience than if you read it as just another dusty old story.

KEY CHARACTERS

Beowulf: The title character and hero. He is first the prince of the Geats and becomes their King. He is boastful and arrogant, but these are not portrayed as negative attributes since he can back up all his boasts. He is often referred to as the son of Edgetheow.

Hrothgar: The old, once great King of the Danes whose hall, Heorot, is attacked by Grendel. He is still regarded as a great man, but he feels he is past his prime since he can't get rid of Grendel single–handedly. He is often referred to as the son of Healfdene.

Grendel: The monster who attacks Heorot. He is an evil giant, a descendent of Cain, the first murderer. He attacks Heorot because he is insanely lonely and jealous of the friendships and happiness of the Danes. He is sometimes disturbingly evil, and other times very sympathetic, a sort of Dark Ages Frankenstein.

Grendel's Mother: Has no name of her own in the poem. She is a monster as well and gives Beowulf just as difficult a fight as her son does. She is even more sympathetic, since she is only after revenge, but she comes close to killing Beowulf.

The Dragon: The enemy that finally kills Beowulf. It guards a great treasure hoard, and when that hoard is disturbed, the dragon attacks the Geats. In the end it dies due to the efforts of Beowulf and Wiglaf.

Unferth: One of Hrothgar's soldiers/servants (called a thane) who challenges Beowulf. He is nearly as arrogant as Beowulf, but he cannot back up his attitude.

Wealhtheow: Hrothgar's wife, queen of the Danes. She is kind to Beowulf and is shrewd enough to try to turn that kindness into an alliance between her sons and the soon-to-be-great Beowulf.

Hygelac: Beowulf's uncle and the King of the Geats. He dies soon after Beowulf's return from Heorot, leaving his kingdom to Beowulf.

Wiglaf: The bravest of Beowulf's warriors and the one that helps him defeat the Dragon. Beowulf leaves him the kingdom of the Geats, since he has no son of his own. Wiglaf is very loyal to Beowulf.

ESSAY IDEAS

- How does the narrator judge the events and characters of the story? Do you agree with his judgments?
- Grendel and his mother are monsters, but in some ways they are portrayed sympathetically. Do you agree or disagree, and in what ways?
- Beowulf is presented as the ultimate hero of the time in which he lived. Do his ideals of heroism differ from ours? If so, how?
- This poem goes off on several tangents about other noble Danes and Geats. What significance do these stories have?
- What are the few women in this poem like? Compare them to the men.

A SAMPLE ESSAY IN OUTLINE FORM

Describe how heroism is defined in *Beowulf*. How does that definition compare to today's notion of heroism?

- Heroism in *Beowulf*:
  - Arrogance and boastfulness are valued, humility is not.
  - Both Beowulf and Unferth are arrogant.
  - Of the two, Beowulf is the "hero" because he can back his boasts up.
  - Displays of strength (might makes right) are very important.
  - Violence is seen as a valid—and perhaps the only—proof of heroism. For example, Beowulf can only become

a hero through his bloody confrontation with Grendel.
- A hero is one who helps his country.
- How today's heroism is different than *Beowulf*'s:
  - There is no longer one universally agreed-upon definition of what makes a hero—different people have different conceptions of heroism.
  - Intelligence is more valued.
  - Humility and grace are considered by many to be heroic.
- How today's heroism is similar to *Beowulf*'s:
  - Violence and physical strength are still seen by many as heroic traits (heroes in the movies, for example, oftenprove themselves through violence and displays of strength).
  - Nationalism is still considered heroic.

While it is possible that Beowulf could be considered a hero today, he probably would not be thought of as highly as he is in the story. Many people today demand more than just physical strength in a hero, and many would object to Beowulf's way of solving problems through violence.

PLOT SUMMARY

Lines 1–199 These lines set up the story. They talk about Denmark's great history and how great its kings have been. Once a child was found mysteriously in a boat and grew to be the great King Scyld Sceafing. He had a son named Beowulf (no relation to the hero of the story) who was sent from God to continue Scyld's rule. After Scyld's death and burial in a majestic funeral boat, his son ruled for many years and had four children.

One of these children is Hrothgar, who becomes King of the Danes. He is a great hero and a leader of men. His army builds a grand meeting hall called Heorot. The group is very loyal and happy. However, while they enjoy the company and the poetry that is sung in the hall, Grendel is listening.

Grendel is a descendent of Cain, the first murderer. That evil heritage has made him a monster. He begins a siege on Heorot, sneaking in at night and killing and eating warriors, because their friendship and happiness drive him mad with jealousy. His raids go on for twelve years. Hrothgar is too old to fight, but Grendel will not make peace any other way. News of the Danes' troubles spreads.

Lines 200–399 Beowulf, a great warrior of the Geats, learns about the Danes' problem and decides to help. He and his army sail to Denmark and are challenged on its shore by a guard. They win the guard's confidence and are led to Heorot. They offer their help and friendship to Hrothgar and his army.

When Hrothgar hears of this, he welcomes them happily, for he knows of the royal family of the Geats and of Beowulf's reputation. The Geats enter Heorot.

Lines 400–599 Beowulf formally offers his help. He tells of his strength and of his experience in fighting monsters. He tells the Danes that they have nothing to lose: if he fails, they need not bury him. He asks only that his armor be sent to his uncle Hygelac, the King of the Geats.

Hrothgar welcomes Beowulf and his bargain, but he warns Beowulf that other warriors have boasted that they could kill Grendel. Those warriors, he says, have ended up as bloody carcasses.

Hrothgar holds a banquet for the warrior. Unferth, one of Hrothgar's men, insults Beowulf by telling of a swim race that Beowulf once lost. Beowulf rises to the challenge, saying that his opponent won because he had no sea monsters to fight, and Beowulf did. Then he retaliates against Unferth. He implies that if a real warrior such as himself had been at Heorot, Grendel would have long been dead. Beowulf has won his first battle of the poem, the traditional war of words.

Lines 600–799 Hrothgar has great hope that Beowulf will win. His queen Wealhtheow serves the warriors beer and thanks God for Beowulf's arrival. He promises her success or his own death. Hrothgar and his army leave, and Beowulf and the Geats stay behind to wait for Grendel.

Beowulf takes off his armor to make the fight more fair. When the army goes to bed, Grendel arrives. Grendel picks up a soldier and bites him into little pieces. Beowulf watches quietly, seeing how Grendel attacks. When Grendel reaches for him, he finds his clawed hand met by Beowulf's. Grendel is surprised by Beowulf's great strength, and when Beowulf begins to hurt him, Grendel panics. They wrestle, damaging the hall with their efforts. The other Geats try to kill Grendel with their swords, but because of a magic spell, he is immune to their attacks.

Lines 800–999 Grendel's arm is severed in the fight and he runs away. Beowulf has won the battle. His trophy, Grendel's arm, is hung up in Heorot. The warriors follow Grendel's trail of blood, and it leads them to a bloody lake. Grendel has died, but the body is not found.

The victors celebrate by listening to the tale of two heroes, Sigemund and Heremod. Sigemund remained a hero all his life but Heremod succumbed to bloodlust and power and went mad at the end of his life.

Hrothgar returns and sees Grendel's arm. Even though Beowulf regrets that Grendel has escaped, Hrothgar gives him thanks and promises to love him as a son forever.

Even Unferth acknowledges Beowulf's success. Heorot is repaired and decorated.

Lines 1000–1199 There is a great banquet in Beowulf's honor, and Hrothgar gives him golden weapons, horses, and a great jeweled collar. He gives gold to all of Beowulf's company.

They hear a song about Finn, a King who was forced to share a hall with his conquerors and to die with them when his allies arrived to claim their revenge.

Lines 1200–1399 Wealhtheow asks for Beowulf's friendship on behalf of her sons, so that Geatland and Denmark might be allies in the future.

Many now sleep in Heorot as they had done before Grendel forced them to leave it at night. On this night Grendel's mother comes to avenge his death. She is discovered, but takes with her Aeschore, one of Hrothgar's most trusted knights, and Grendel's arm. Beowulf is not there, so she cannot take her revenge on him.

Beowulf and Hrothgar arrive. Hrothgar is both saddened and angered at the loss of his knight. Hrothgar describes Grendel's mother to Beowulf and asks for his help. Beowulf accepts the challenge.

Lines 1400–1599 A small band of warriors follows the trail of Grendel's mother through a wood to a dark, gray lake full of strange creatures. There they find Aeschere's head. Beowulf decides to go into the lake after her. He puts on his armor and Unferth lends him his good sword. Beowulf asks Hrothgar to take care of his men if he doesn't survive.

He dives in and swims down for a day before he reaches the bottom. There Grendel's mother grabs him but cannot claw through his armor. She drags him to her hall, which is magically dry and lighted. He tries to cut her with the sword, but, like Grendel, she is immune.

He tries to wrestle her as he did her son but loses the wrestling match, and only his armor saves him from her knife. He finds a sword made to kill giants and manages to kill her with it. He then searches her hall for the body of Grendel. He finds the dead body lying in a corner, and chops off its head for a trophy. The monster's blood melts the sword's blade, leaving only the handle.

Lines 1600–1799 Beowulf swims back to the surface, bringing only the giant sword's handle and Grendel's head. He and his band return to Heorot, where he tells his story. Hrothgar praises Beowulf again, but warns him of the dangers of blood-thirst and arrogance. There is another great banquet.

Lines 1800–1999 Beowulf returns Unferth's sword, and he and his band prepare for their journey home. Beowulf says good-bye and offers his help to Hrothgar any time it is needed. Hrothgar compliments Beowulf further and cries when Beowulf finally leaves to return home. Upon Beowulf's return to Geatland, King Hygelac asks Beowulf to tell him about his adventure.

Lines 2000–2199 Beowulf tells his story and talks about Hrothgar's daughter, Freawaru, and her fiancé, Ingeld, who are being married to end a feud. Beowulf predicts that this attempt at peace will be unsuccessful, and that Ingeld's people will eventually start the feud again.

Beowulf then tells all about Grendel and his mother. Beowulf and his King exchange gifts. For the first time the Geats praise his efforts. Beowulf is beginning to be acknowledged as a hero.

Lines 2200–2399 Hygelac dies and leaves the kingdom to Beowulf, who rules for half a century in peace. Then, one of his subjects stumbles upon a treasure guarded by a dragon. The dragon has been peaceful until now, but when the Geat takes a goblet, the dragon attacks Geatland.

Beowulf's own hall is destroyed by the dragon, and he realizes that he must kill it. He prepares for the battle. Beowulf believes he can win because of his past glories, but the narrator warns us that this will be Beowulf's last battle.

Lines 2400–2599 Beowulf takes eleven warriors to accompany him, plus the thief to guide them to the dragon's lair. This makes a company of thirteen, a very bad omen. Beowulf seems to know that something is wrong, and he dwells on his past and on his people's fate.

Beowulf boasts one last time to raise his company's spirits. He claims that he would like to battle the dragon unarmed, but that the dragon's fire makes a fair fight impossible. He carries a metal shield because he knows that a wooden one will not withstand a fire-breathing dragon.

He enters the cave alone, but the dragon keeps him away from the hoard. He tries to hit the dragon with his sword, but the dragon's hide is too tough. The dragon begins to burn him. The other warriors run away as Beowulf is being attacked.

Lines 2600–2799 This final battle is very exciting and very violent. Wiglaf, one of Beowulf's thanes, goes back to help his leader. The dragon attacks him but does not hurt him, and the distraction gives Beowulf time to gather his wits and attack the dragon with his sword. The sword breaks against the dragon's hide.

The dragon retaliates by biting Beowulf on the neck with his huge, poisonous fangs. As Beowulf bleeds all over the cave, Wiglaf finds the dragon's weak spot on its neck and hits it with his sword. Beowulf manages to stab the dragon with a sharp knife from his vest. The dragon falls as Beowulf collapses.

Wiglaf bathes his King's wounds, and Beowulf speaks to him. He asks Wiglaf to look at the dragon's huge hoard. Wiglaf takes only the most beautiful things back to his King. Beowulf asks him to take care of his people.

Lines 2800–2999 Beowulf asks for a high tomb, and gives his golden collar and his kingdom to Wiglaf. He then dies.

The runaway thanes return, and Wiglaf scolds them for their cowardice. He says they have failed to earn the trust Beowulf placed in them and that he will exile them as punishment.

A messenger is sent out to tell all the land of the death of their King. The messenger delivers not only the news, but a prophecy as well. He says that with the death of their King, they will face wars in the future, especially with the Swedes. He talks about the history of the two nations and of the bad feeling between them.

Lines 3000–End The messenger predicts that the Geats will lose. The army goes to view Beowulf's body, where they see the dead dragon and the golden hoard. The narrator tells us that the gold was accursed, and it was that curse that cost Beowulf his life.

Wiglaf says that these riches are not worth the life of their great leader. He then instructs them to build Beowulf's funeral pyre. It is covered in armor and finery, and while Beowulf burns, a woman begins to sing her sorrow. Finally, the warriors build Beowulf a high barrow as he had asked. They bury him with the dragon's hoard, praising him as the best King in all the world.

BRAVE NEW WORLD

ABOUT THE AUTHOR

Aldous Huxley (1894–1962) was born in Surrey, England. His public school education was interrupted by an affliction of the eyes that left him partially blind for several years. Huxley later regarded this break in his "proper" social and scientific education as a blessing in disguise. He eventually continued his education in English literature at Oxford University, reading his textbooks through a magnifying glass. A prolific writer of poetry, essays, and criticism, Huxley first gained public acclaim for his satirical novels. After several years of writing in Italy and the South of France, Aldous Huxley moved to Taos, New Mexico, where he wrote a number of works. He died in California. His final novel, *Island*, was published the year he died.

THE BIG PICTURE

Huxley's *Brave New World*, in which he describes a civilization devoid of individualism and emotion, is a disturbing view of a Utopia that may yet come to pass. The book's conflict between the so-called "savages" and the "civilized" is highly relevant to our society.

Why you're reading this book:
- Huxley's powerful use of dystopia:
  - He has created a future world of so-called "perfection."
  - By showing that this future world really isn't perfect, he forces us to examine the imperfections of our own world.
  - When you ask yourself, "What's wrong with the Brave New World?" your answer will be true of our world as well.
- The relationship between society and the individual in the novel.

Your teachers are looking for:
- The notion of a utopian society and its implications.
- Specific parallels between Huxley's "Brave New World" and the world of today.
- The roles of history, education, sex, and drugs in the new world and what they say about how this society is run.
- The elements that make up the so-called "perfect" society—its people, customs, and rules.

KEY CHARACTERS

Bernard Marx: A misfit in Utopian society, Bernard is too self-conscious and awkward an individual to fit in comfortably. While rebellious at heart, Bernard is capable of petty, and often pathetic, behavior.

Lenina Crowne: A good Utopian citizen. Lenina stands out only because of the situations in which she finds herself, especially those dealing with romance: her relationship with Henry Foster, her vacation with Bernard Marx, and her romantic dilemma over the savage. Lenina provides a constant example of the Utopian norm.

Fanny Crowne: Lenina's peer.

Henry Foster: An intelligent and eager young worker at the hatchery. He is an example of a proper Utopian man.

John: A character caught between the Utopian world and the savage world. The son of Utopians, he grew up in a pre-Utopian reservation. Rejected by both the savage community and his confused mother, John tragically seeks fulfillment in Utopian society. He finds only emptiness.

Linda: John's mother. Once a Utopian very much like Lenina Crowne, Linda is stranded in the savage reservation. Unable to let go of her Utopian sense of reality, Linda has become hated by her savage community. Obese and filthy, Linda can only find consolation in intoxication.

Helmholtz Watson: Bernard's friend and fellow misfit. Gifted with every imaginable social, physical, and intellectual grace, Watson feels separate from society because he finds it so unchallenging. While Watson's job requires him to write Utopian propaganda, his true interest lies in poetry.

Mustapha Mond: A World Controller, Mond is a designer of Utopian society. A man with access to pre-Utopian literature and ideas, Mond understands the necessity of sacrificing art for stability.

DHC: The Director of Hatcheries and Conditioning and John's unwitting natural father. The DHC, another Utopian team player, holds a grudge against Bernard.

ESSAY IDEAS

- How does a sense of individuality first develop in the more rebellious characters?
- Compare the advertising techniques of Huxley's world to today's typical TV fare?
- How does Utopian society guarantee stability?
- What aspects of the Brave New World do you think have already happened?

- Compare and contrast modern advertising techniques with Utopian conditioning techniques.
- Why do you think Huxley uses Ford as the mentor of Utopian society? What other potential candidates for this position can you think of?
- Is the savage doomed from the start by his background? Who does our society view as "savages"?
- Do you see any option for the individual within Utopian society?

A SAMPLE ESSAY IN OUTLINE FORM

Compare/contrast Huxley's "Brave New World" with our world today.
- Aspects the two worlds share:
  - Social norms and pressures.
  - Reliance on drugs.
    - Soma in *Brave New World*.
    - Prescription and illegal drugs in our world.
  - Attempts to "plan away" all of life's ills.
  - Constant bombardment from advertising.
- Differences:
  - The Brave New World seems more planned and more tightly controlled.
  - The Brave New World is more impersonal and automated.

Many would say that our world is not far from Huxley's creation, that the only difference is one of degrees. Huxley's novel succeeds in making us not only look at what might happen but also at what has already happened in our world.

PLOT SUMMARY

Chapter One The planetary motto of this new world is "Community, Identity,

Stability." To achieve this goal, individuals must not only perform the tasks that are necessary to society as a whole, they must also *want* to perform these tasks.

The Director of Hatcheries and Conditioning (DHC) leads a fascinated group of students through the Central London Hatchery and Conditioning Centre. Here, mass production techniques are used for human reproduction. In this "factory," human eggs are fertilized and "decanted." The babies are then conditioned according to their social class. Each human embryo in this factory is designed for a particular level of intelligence, depending upon its predestined social function. These social classes are designated Alpha, the highest, through Epsilon, the lowest. Biological manipulation of the embryos is followed by careful social training for the children. When children leave the factory, they are fully socialized into class and occupation; from sewer workers to directors of hatcheries or even predestinators, known as World Controllers. This world, Utopia, is built on theories of mass production popularized by the American automobile manufacturer Henry Ford.

The citizens of Utopia know no more about their world than is necessary. All history before the year 141 A.F. (After Ford) has been erased, as has all literature. The notion of a creator (God) has been replaced with that of a founder (Ford). In the conditioned minds of the Utopian citizens, the past is a bottomless and unhygienic hell. The citizens of Utopia are bred and conditioned to love what they must do for the good of a stable and happy society. In this world there is no totalitarian "Big Brother" ruling society with an iron fist. Rather, citizens are conditioned so that social conformity is natural, fun, and comfortable. Thus, those bred for menial labor are retarded and trained to loathe learning while those predestined for white collar

functions are fed a greater breadth of Utopian knowledge. Both castes are conditioned to respect the other social levels for their contributions while simultaneously retaining the belief that their caste is preferable. The result is the unified, and thus stable, population of workers and followers necessary for "Community, Identity, Stability."

Henry Foster takes over the tour at the request of the DHC. He throws out statistics and information with smug expertise. Henry is an enthusiastic member of Utopian society. He delays the tour momentarily to make a date with a nurse, Lenina Crowne. These upper-caste students think of the information given them in the DHC's lecture as absolute truth. They copy down the director's comments verbatim, regardless of their relevance.

Chapter Two The DHC explains to the students that immediately after the decanting process (literally the "uncorking" of newborn babies), the "conditioning," or citizen education process, begins. Nurses place babies from the lower, "Delta" caste in front of a display of books and flowers. As the curious babies crawl toward this display they are discouraged by shrieking sirens and electric shocks; books are dangerous time wasters and idea builders that impede the efficiency of the working classes. Delta babies are thus conditioned to loathe and fear them. Deltas are also trained to dislike flowers because an appreciation of nature does nothing for society. They are instead conditioned to enjoy those sports that require elaborate equipment. In this way, the vacationing Deltas consume both transport and supplies, thus supporting industry.

The students display their own conditioning when quizzed by the DHC about society before the Utopia. They blush and giggle at the mention of such concepts as "parents" and "birth," since the DHC reminds them, "Historical facts are unpleasant." The tour leads to the sleep teaching (hypnopaedia) centers. The director explains that while hypnopaedia cannot be used to teach factual information, it is a very useful technique for instilling ethical lessons in children. The students are led to the dormitory where sleeping Beta children are taught lessons in "Class Consciousness" and "Elementary Sex" through loudspeakers. These recorded messages tell the children which colors to like, which children to play with, etc. The touring students display their own conditioning in their sentimental responses to these messages.

Chapter Three It is playtime at the nursery. The naked children play games designed to encourage "correct" social attitudes. These activities include games that require extensive equipment, as well as activities called "erotic play," designed to have the children grow up without sexual guilt or repression. In the "Brave New World," everyone belongs to everyone else. In a stable world, there is no room for jealousy or repressed desire. The director lectures the students about the shocking world "before Ford": the world in which erotic play was considered abnormal, the world in which games were played without extensive apparatus. The students react with disgust to this shocking history.

The students are in for a rare treat: the Resident Controller of Western Europe, Mustapha Mond, happens to be touring the same facility. As a World Controller, Mustapha Mond is privileged with a knowledge of world history before Utopia. Both his demeanor and the selective details of his lecture attest to his elite position of Controller.

Mond describes the horrors of the pre-Ford world: the cramped and unsanitary nightmare of family life, the animalistic domination of protective mothers over "their" babies, the unnecessary sexual repression, and the resulting confusion of closed relationships.

This chapter ends with a montage of conversations between various characters mixed with Mustapha Mond's lecture on history. Through the conversations, we learn that Lenina Crowne and Henry Foster are preparing for their evening date. Lenina's friend, Fanny Crowne, explains her upcoming Mock Pregnancy, a process regularly prescribed by doctors for women's health and well-being.

Fanny voices her concern over Lenina's long-standing relationship with Henry Foster; the two have been seeing each other exclusively for almost two months. Monogamy, the dangerous channeling of emotion and time into a single object of desire, is forbidden by the state. Fanny, a product of conditioning, knows that monogamy is not only illegal, but also antisocial, and thus morally reprehensible. Fanny is further appalled when Lenina mentions that she has been invited to go on holiday to a savage reservation with the strange-looking and rebelliously intelligent Bernard Marx.

In the final pages of this chapter, the snippets of conversation and lecture, shuffled now with passages of the hypnopaedic lectures given to children, become increasingly rapid-fire. Mond explains that in the interest of smooth societal sailing all books published before the year 151 A.F. have been banned, while human worries such as aging, death, and sexual desire have been planned away. With birth centers, lifelong social conditioning, and chemicals, New World citizens have been successfully freed of worry. They now love what they must do.

Chapter Four Bernard and Lenina meet as planned in the conditioning building.

When Lenina begins to discuss their relationship in the crowded building, Bernard demonstrates his embarrassingly "rebellious" nature by suggesting that they speak in private. Lenina finds this request ridiculous. Insult is added to injury when she mentions her upcoming date with Henry Foster. Bernard can take no more and leaves.

Lenina is late for her date anyway. Moments later she is taking a panoramic tour of London in Henry's helicopter. Meanwhile, Bernard Marx is angry. He barks at the lower caste workers to ready his helicopter. Bernard demonstrates well Mond's lecture about desire and discomfort; in eliminating desire to prevent its painful antisocial effects, world planning has also eliminated the potential for great satisfaction. Bernard flies to the emotional engineering building to await a visit with his friend Helmholtz Watson.

Watson, a talented writer of hypnopaedic lessons for the state, also appears dissatisfied with Utopian society. While Bernard first felt his individuality because of his physical inadequacies, Watson felt his individualism through his lack of interest in the limited socially correct options offered by Utopian society. As a result of their differences from society, both men have discovered themselves to be individuals. This simple discovery is not yet articulated between the two, but it will prove to be the root of their discomfort, and thus their rebellion.

Chapter Five The closing of the golf course for the evening sends the lower classes home by the monorail. The description of their departure is reminiscent of the train-like motion of moving ants; as social insects, ants are an excellent example of central social planning. Lenina and Henry are upper caste, and thus leave in Henry's helicopter. As they fly, they take note of the smoke from a crematorium. As Henry explains, the crematorium includes a phosphorus recovery process. Thus even dead individuals can be useful to society. As conditioned, Henry reminds Lenina that members of every caste are chemically equal. The couple enjoy dinner and take several grams of soma with their coffee. High on this ecstatic drug, they eagerly look forward to the ensuing evening of dancing and entertainment.

Part two of this chapter describes Bernard's mandatory biweekly visit to the Fordson Community Singery. This event involves a communion of soma. This is followed by group "prayer"—for the annihilation of the individual for the betterment of the societal body. The event climaxes in an orgy. As usual, Bernard is too self-conscious to enjoy this communal unconsciousness. Instead of concentrating on the coming of the spirit of Ford, Bernard obsesses over the disturbing uni-brow of his orgy-mate.

Chapter Six Lenina has second thoughts about taking a holiday to a savage reservation with someone as odd as Bernard Marx. After all, he seems to hate crowds, opting sinfully for solitude and contemplation instead. What's worse, Bernard does not enjoy the sports encouraged by society, and he refuses to ease his anguish with soma. Lenina cannot understand Bernard's desire to experience emotions beyond the comfortable range of those encouraged by his conditioning. Lenina considers going to the North Pole with a more sociable partner.

Bernard needs permission from the DHC before he can go on his vacation. While reviewing his papers, the DHC notices that Bernard intends to visit the savage reservation. Bernard is shocked as the DHC lapses into reminiscence (an antisocial indulgence) about his own vacation to that reservation as a youth; during this traumatic vacation the girl he was "having" at the time was lost and never found. This event was clearly one of embarrassing emotional anguish for the DHC. Humiliated by his public slip into sentimentality, the DHC turns on Bernard in anger. He reprimands Bernard for his antisocial behavior. As he signs Bernard's vacation papers, the DHC threatens to send him to Iceland if he doesn't change his antisocietal ways.

The savage reservation is an enclosed compound of real estate without redeeming economic value. It is inhabited by a group of pre-Fordian "primitives" whom the Controllers did not feel were worth converting to the "New World" order. While the reservation Warden lectures Bernard and Lenina on the anthropological wonders of the reservation, Bernard suddenly remembers that he left the eau de cologne tap running in his hotel room; it will cost him a small fortune. Excusing himself from the tour, Bernard calls back to Watson in London to rectify the problem. Watson gives Bernard the bad news over the phone: the DHC has made good on his threat to assign Bernard to Iceland immediately after his vacation. Quickly swallowing several grams of soma, Bernard resigns himself to intoxicated pleasure for the moment. The future looks bleak.

Chapter Seven Although Lenina has consistently assured Bernard that she will not find the reservation appalling, she is immediately repelled to the point of nausea. She dislikes the way the physical setting makes her feel small and insignificant, and the abundance of dirt and disease offends her sensibilities.

The couple watches a snake ritual followed by a spectacle of frenzied self-flagellation. In this religious ceremony various icons of the primitive past are combined; snakes, feathers, the coyote spirit, and a crucifix all figure into the complex mythology of the rite. Even the soothing, orgy-like rhythm of the primitive drums cannot completely drown out Lenina's horror. She wails for her lost soma.

Where Lenina is repulsed, Bernard is fascinated. He is amazed by the novel appearance of aged people, the dedication of the self-flagellants, and the amazing sight of mothers nursing their babies. In the midst of this ceremony a blond savage named John introduces himself to Lenina and Bernard. From his appearance and language it is immediately apparent that John is different. John regrets being forbidden the honor of participating in the snake ritual because of his coloring and origins; his parents came from Utopia. He doesn't know what has happened to his father, but the fate of his mother (Linda) is obvious: fat, dirty, and aging, Linda embraces the disgusted Lenina with the enthusiasm of a woman saved from a shipwreck.

Linda is barely coherent as she tells her story. Stranded in the reservation after a vacation similar to Bernard and Lenina's, Linda found herself completely unsuited to the nightmare of savage life. She was ridiculed for her Utopian obsessions with new clothes and cleanliness. Her conditioned promiscuity further made her an enemy of the savage wives, whose husbands she openly seduced. Finding herself pregnant and alone, Linda turned long ago to mescal tequila to relieve the nightmare.

Chapter Eight Fascinated, Bernard listens to John's account of Linda's Utopian nursery rhymes and her inability to fit into savage life. John recalls his mother's lover Pepe and the mescal he would bring. He remembers the brutal whipping his mother received at the hands of the jealous reservation wives, and the way Linda translated her own anguish into abuse of her son. As a well-conditioned Utopian, Linda was totally unprepared for motherhood. She blames her inability to return to Utopia on John's humiliating existence.

John has constructed a vision of Utopian life based on a combination of his mother's descriptions and passages memorized from the tattered book of Shakespeare which Pepe had given his mother. In the savage world, John has been able to feel the depth of emotion caused by the separation of desire and fulfillment. Although he has experienced exhilaration, most of his experiences have been ones of failure and pain. As he will clearly never find a true community in the savage world, John hopes for fulfillment in Utopia. A misfit himself, Bernard feels a bond with John, and invites him to join him in Utopia.

Chapter Nine The reservation is all too much for Lenina. She swallows a large dose of soma, putting herself effectively out of the picture. As she travels through her "lunar eternity," she is unaware that John has fallen in love with her. He kneels before her dreaming body in adoration and worship. Bernard, on the other hand, is more alert than ever. He formulates his plan for bringing John and Linda back to Utopia. Bernard realizes that Linda is the woman the DHC had lost on his vacation long ago. By bringing John and Linda back to Utopia, Bernard hopes to humiliate the DHC, and thus save himself from Iceland. Bernard calls Mustapha Mond in London and informs him of his discovery of two Utopian savages. Interested in the scientific value of such rare specimens, Mond gives Bernard permission to bring the savages back to London with him.

Chapter Ten It is business as usual in the decanting factory. Speaking to the assembled workers about the dangers of antisocial behavior, the DHC eagerly awaits

Bernard's return. Bernard is to be made a public example. The DHC confronts Bernard immediately upon his return to work. Bernard takes advantage of the situation to call his plan into action; on cue, Linda bounces forth. To the amazement of the assembly, this savage creature announces that "Tomkin," the DHC, was her lover. John appears and claims the DHC as his natural father. The assembly bombards the DHC with mocking laughter. The director is frozen in humiliation.

Chapter Eleven The DHC resigns from his post in utter disgrace. The story of the events in the decanting room spreads quickly. Linda and the Director have become a running joke, and John has become a sought-after celebrity. Riding on the coattails of this fame, Bernard declares himself John's guardian. Bernard becomes a popular socialite; suddenly successful, he quickly forgets his hatred of Utopian society. Watson is openly disappointed with his friend's shallow character. Linda's return to Utopia means a return to her beloved soma, of which she takes increasingly larger doses despite John's strong objections. His maternal allegiance, novel in the New World, causes him great anguish. On a tour of a Utopian school, John is horrified to find the students laughing at a documentary film about primitive religious rites similar to those in which he aspired to participate.

In his written report to Mustapha Mond, Bernard presumes to lecture the Controller on Utopia's shortcomings. A man of quiet power, Mond clearly intends to teach Mr. Marx a lesson, but only when he gets around to it.

Lenina finds John's savage properties attractive. She tells Fanny that although she suspects John's romantic interest, he has made no moves. When Bernard has to cancel his appointment for the feelies with John, Lenina jumps at the chance to take his place. Lenina and John have learned the rules for romance in different worlds; we expect a comedy of errors. The feelie movie lacks the depth of emotion which John expects from "good art." Lenina, surprised and a bit disappointed by John's lack of enthusiasm, looks forward nonetheless to an evening of casual Utopian lovemaking with her savage. John, however, is skittish. He wishes Lenina a hasty good night and retreats to his Shakespeare. Confused and dejected, Lenina drowns her troubles in a large dose of soma.

Chapter Twelve John is losing interest in Utopia. He has grown especially tired of his role as a vehicle for Bernard's socialite aspirations. On the evening when Bernard has assembled a particularly influential group for dinner and savage viewing, John refuses to come down from his room. Arriving alone, Bernard is scolded by the dinner party. Lenina is present at the dinner and takes John's absence personally. Suddenly realizing the parasitic nature of his recent social success, Bernard becomes horribly depressed and takes soma.

John finds that he likes the depressed Bernard. Bernard, however, is petty and resentful and plots secret harm to the savage. Bernard also jealously resents Watson's magnanimity in forgiving his own former star-struck behavior. Bernard introduces Watson to John and the two find an instant connection. To Bernard's annoyance, they recite poetry to each other. Despite his enlightened aspirations, Watson is still limited by his conditioning, and finds the romantic love between John's Romeo and Juliet characters humorous and incomprehensible.

Chapter Thirteen Lenina runs into Henry Foster at work and coldly declines his requests for a date. He tells her that what she really needs is a good pregnancy substitute. Lenina is troubled by her unfulfilled desire for John, and she expresses this to Fanny after work. Fanny tells her to swallow some soma and "just do it." Lenina takes this advice and hurries to find John. Thus confronted, John poetically professes his love. Lenina is offended at his references to marriage but is thrilled that he at least wants her. While John speaks of love, Lenina hears only lust. In a flurry of zippers, she removes all of her clothing. John is disgusted to the point of violent anger by her baseness and attacks her. The passionate scene is interrupted by a phone call from the hospital; John's mother is dying. John rushes off to the hospital. Lenina, frazzled and confused, slips away.

Chapter Fourteen John finds his soma-entranced mother on her deathbed in the hospital. The nurse finds John's melodramatic attitude inappropriate, as Utopians have been conditioned to find death a positive experience for society. John is infuriated as his final moments with his dying mother are interrupted by a school field trip. The nurse fears that the savage's mourning might ruin the children's death conditioning. She tries to undo the damage by offering eclairs.

Chapter Fifteen John is distraught as he leaves the hospital. He encounters a mob of lower caste twins lining up for their deadening communion of soma and is moved to action. John grabs the lock boxes of soma and lectures the workers on freedom. He begs them to give up their servitude and their soma. The workers find no inspiration in John's words, only annoyance and insult. Bernard and Watson have been called to the scene. Watson sees his chance for freedom and joins John in fighting off the rioting workers. Bernard, supportive of the two men's general stance, is too afraid of the repercussions to participate. The riot police arrive and defuse the situation with fire hoses emitting vaporized Soma. A synthesized feel-good voice tells everyone to relax and disperse.

Chapter Sixteen John, Bernard, and Watson are summoned to Mustapha Mond. John takes an immediate stand and rails against Utopia before the controller. His display makes Bernard rather nervous. To everyone's surprise, Mond quotes Shakespeare. Mond has "God in the safe and Ford on the shelves"; as he makes the rules, he doesn't have to follow them. He calmly explains to John the necessity of sacrificing art for stability and happiness; to this end the masses must be kept busy with work and entertainment. Bernard goes berserk with fear. He blames his companions for his part in the insurrection and pathetically begs for mercy. Mond calmly has Bernard restrained and removed. Mond informs Watson that he is to be put into exile with other freethinkers. The sentence is agreeable to Watson, and Mond himself is almost envious. Like Watson, Mond once ran into trouble with the state. His position as Controller, subordinating his own happiness for that of the masses, is the price he pays.

Chapter Seventeen John is left alone with Mond to discuss the engineering of Utopia. Mond explains that Utopians, safely protected from aging and poverty, have nothing to fear, and thus no use for God. A properly conditioned worker wants only what he must have. Heroic actions by freethinking individuals, he says, are the results of poor government. Religion has been replaced by Soma, Shakespeare by

the feelies, and contemplation by drone-like activity, all in the interest of stability. John feels that such a sacrifice is too great. In a dramatic proclamation to Mond, John chooses freedom, poetry, and true danger over Utopia. Mond informs him that he is also choosing pain, poverty, disease, torment and unhappiness. John claims it all. He will get it.

Chapter Eighteen Bernard and Watson say good-bye to John, who is in the bathroom purifying himself by vomiting. His nausea comes from having swallowed civilization.

While the others have been exiled to islands, John is forced to stay in Utopia to continue the experiment. He retreats to an abandoned lighthouse to live a hermetic life of denial and prayer. His first night is spent in penance and self-flagellation. John is determined to make the rest of his life a purge. His hermitage is accidentally discovered by vacationing motorists, and soon he is swarmed over by the press.

John is tormented with lustful memories of Lenina, and punishes himself with nettles and the whip. A stealthy cameraman makes a Feelie of John's fanatic antics. The film is a huge success; soon hundreds of tourists flock to the lighthouse to watch the savage show. When Lenina herself arrives, John whips her ruthlessly. Fascinated by this spectacle of pain, the crowd starts into an orgy. John is seduced by the sensuous event and takes Soma. He wakes in the morning disgusted with his moral weakness—his failure in the face of the Utopian enemy. Seeing no other way out but death, John hangs himself in the lighthouse.

THE CANTERBURY TALES

ABOUT THE AUTHOR

Geoffrey Chaucer (ca.1340–1400) is considered by many to be the father of English poetry. His family lived in the parish of St. Martin's-in-the-Vintry in London, an upper middle class neighborhood.

Much of Chaucer's life was spent in the service of the aristocracy; he began his career as a page for the Countess of Ulster. As a page in such an eminent family, he waited on some of the highest nobles in England, including John de Gaunt, the Duke of Lancaster. He would later become one of Chaucer's most faithful patrons.

In 1367, Chaucer was promoted to the position of courtier to the King. That year he also chose to marry Philippa de Roet, one of the Queen's waiting women. He continued to rise in prominence through the year 1386, when he was made Knight of the Shire.

Chaucer received a stipend until his death. He left the employ of the Custom House for political reasons in 1386. He outlined *The Canterbury Tales* around 1386, and wrote the book until his death.

Chaucer is also known for the works *Troilus and Criseyde* and *The Legend of Good Women*.

THE BIG PICTURE

The Canterbury Tales is first and foremost an extremely funny piece of writing. All the characters' tales are witty and satirical, some bawdy, and some outright crass. There is another level to the *Tales*, however: they very accurately reflect society in Chaucer's day, with all of its faults and foibles.

Why you're reading this book:
- It is the most important work in the creation of the English vernacular language, just as Dante's works are for the vernacular Italian.
- It is a precursor to the novel.
- It accurately portrays English society in the fourteenth century.
- Its humor and insights are easily applied to modern culture.

Your teachers are looking for:
- How the characters reflect English society.
- The way the pilgrims interact with each other.
- The subject matter each pilgrim chooses for his or her tale.
- The way foreign cultures are portrayed.
- The conflict between the ideals of Love and Marriage.
- The conflicting ideals and points of view illustrated in the different tales.
- Elements of satire:
  - With regard to the Church: what is "appropriate" conduct for the various classes of clergymen.
  - With regard to manners: what is sin and what is merely poor manners, and whether these rules apply to all classes.
  - The sense of realism via Chaucer's attention to detail.

KEY CHARACTERS

The Knight: A "most distinguished man," he has fought in many famous battles, yet he is as "modest as a maid." He rides a fine horse but his armor is a bit stained as he is just home from war.

The Squire: The Knight's 20-year-old son who is "fresh as the month of May."

The Yeoman: A landowner, of a class below the gentry, he still dresses very well in the costume of a "proper forester."

The Prioress: A nun known as Madame Eglantyne who is rather fat but strains "to counterfeit a kind of courtly grace."

The Monk: A man who does not believe in the old-fashioned idea of monks cloistering themselves in a cell. Rather he is a "modern" monk, in that he likes to hunt, and to dress and eat well.

The Friar: He uses his social graces to get money.

The Merchant: A solemn man who brags a bit about his profits.

The Clerk: A thin man with an even thinner horse. He loves reading above all else.

The Man of Law: An honorable man who has studied hard and earnestly to get his position.

The Franklin: He has an abundance of the finer things of fourteenth century living and is, therefore, "a model among landed gentry."

The Cook: His taste buds are so refined that he can "distinguish London ale by flavour."

The Shipman: Though he is from Dartmouth and rides a farm horse, he is one of the best skippers of the time.

The Physician/Doctor: He seems to profit from prescribing all sorts of remedies, and keeps the gold he makes next to his heart.

The Wife of Bath: A very well-dressed woman who has been widowed five times; gap toothed, with large hips.

The Parson: A devout and patient man.

The Reeve: An intermediary between a lord and his serfs, he is so shrewd that the serfs are afraid of him.

The Miller: A big, brawny man with a red beard and a wart on the tip of his nose.

The Manciple: The steward and buyer of supplies for a college; though illiterate he can still negotiate a better deal than the scholars.

The Summoner: A man who is paid to summon sinners to trial before an ecclesiastical court. "Children were afraid when he appeared."

The Pardoner: He has authority from the church to sell pardons but he often tricks country people with his "holy relics."

The Host: A personable man fit to lead the expedition. He has a very jolly disposition.

ESSAY IDEAS

- Choose three tales and describe how they are "personalized" to the teller.
- Discuss the conflict of values between love and marriage. Are they compatible elements of a relationship? Why or why not?
- Compare and contrast the various members of the clergy who are traveling with the group. How does Chaucer criticize them without being sacrilegious?
- Choose one tale to be the winner of the contest. Defend your opinion.
- Consider the dilemmas of Arcite and Palamon in the Knight's Tale and Aurelius and Arveragus in the Franklin's Tale. Whose dilemma is the most difficult? Compare and contrast the two stories.
- How many times do people have sex in *The Canterbury Tales*? Is each encounter because of a promise broken or a promise kept, or both?

A SAMPLE ESSAY IN OUTLINE FORM

The incompatibility of love and marriage in *The Canterbury Tales*

- The ideal of Love—especially men's love for women—is portrayed as an element unto itself, not as a part of everyday life:
  - Consider Absalon in the Reeve's Tale.
  - Consider Aurelius in the Franklin's Tale.
  - Consider Damien in the Merchant's Tale.
- Men and women are married not for love, but for convenience or by arrangement:
  - January chooses to marry May in the Merchant's Tale.
  - Cecilia is forced to marry Valerian in the Second Nun's Tale.
  - Constance is sent to Syria to marry an infidel in order to cement an alliance for her father in the Man of Law's Tale.
- It is possible to find love within marriage, but only after some sort of suffering:
  - Palamon and Emily are supposedly happy after he has spent most of his life longing for her.
  - Constance and King Alla love each other but most of their marriage is spent apart, clouded by misunderstanding.

PLOT SUMMARY

PROLOGUE

In the Prologue, Chaucer describes each of the pilgrims in detail. Chaucer characterizes his tale-tellers so that the reader can understand how the tale suits the individual. Toward the end of the first section, the host offers up his plan to make the journey pass quickly. Each pilgrim is to tell two tales on the way to Canterbury and two on the return. The individual with the best tale will get a free dinner at the inn when the group arrives back in Southwark. At this point Chaucer comes forward as the "author," saying that he will attempt to record the pilgrimage "stage by stage." In this way, the author himself becomes a character in the book.

The host rouses them early the next morning. When they draw lots to see who will tell the first tale, the Knight wins.

THE KNIGHT'S TALE

Part I It is long ago; a great duke, Theseus, is Lord of Athens. In one of his more famous adventures, he conquers Scythia, land of the Amazons. He kidnaps the Amazon queen, Hippolyta, and her younger sister, Emily, with the intention of bringing Hippolyta to Athens as his wife.

On the journey home, Duke Theseus' party encounters a group of wailing women on the road. The women tell the duke that their husbands have been slain at Thebes and that the ruler, Creon, plans to dishonor the men's bodies. Enraged, Theseus takes his war party to Thebes to vanquish Creon. After the battle, a scavenger finds the bodies of two princes of the House of Creon, Arcite and Palamon. The princes are wounded but not quite dead. Theseus orders the two young men be taken to Athens and imprisoned for life.

One morning in Athens, a few years later, Prince Palamon looks out the window and catches a glimpse of the fair Emily. He is so taken by her beauty that he cries out and wakens Arcite. Arcite hurries to the window and he too is struck with love. Palamon is angry and accuses Arcite of being a traitor for loving a woman he loved first. Thus begins the feud between Arcite and Palamon.

Some time later, a duke, Perotheus, arrives in Athens. Learning of the captive princes, he asks for Arcite's release. Theseus agrees, but only on the condition that Arcite never return to Athens, or he will be beheaded. Jealousy consumes Palamon because Arcite now has the freedom to raise an army in Thebes and return to win Emily's hand. Despite his freedom, Arcite envies Palamon his prison cell, from which he can see the lovely Emily walking in her garden.

Part II Arcite returns to Thebes and grieves for two years. His suffering changes his appearance so much that he changes his name to Philostrate and returns to Athens. There, he is taken in as a page in Emily's household. A few years pass and Arcite is accepted and liked by Theseus. In the seventh year after Arcite's departure, Palamon escapes from prison.

One day soon thereafter, Palamon, hidden in a grove near the castle, overhears Arcite sighing over his frustrated love for Emily. Palamon jumps from the bushes and confronts Arcite. They agree to duel the next morning.

In the morning, however, their fight is interrupted by the royal hunting party. Theseus calls for them to halt and explain themselves. Each man tells of his desperate love for Emily. Theseus condemns them both. Both Emily and the Queen plead their cases. Theseus relents and agrees that both shall go free on one condition: within one year, they must return to Athens, each with an army of knights. A full-scale joust will decide who will take Emily's hand.

Part III As the day of the joust approaches, Theseus builds an enormous stadium with three great shrines, one dedicated to the Goddess Diana, one to Mars, and one to Venus. At dawn on the day of the fight, Palamon rises and goes to pray at the shrine of Venus. Her statue shakes after his offering, a sign he takes to mean that his request for Emily's love has been granted. Emily throws herself at the mercy of Diana, begging her to destroy the love of the two knights, or if not, to give her to the one who loves her the most. Lastly, Arcite asks Mars for victory and Mars grants the request. Immediately, the gods in heaven get into an argument over the outcome of the joust and old Saturn has to intervene. He resolves the conflict by giving Palamon his love and Arcite the victory.

Part IV At the beginning of the contest, Theseus announces that the battle will be fought only until one of the knights is severely wounded. During the battle, Palamon receives a terrible wound and is carried from the field. Arcite begins to gallop his horse around the arena in celebration, only to be thrown to the ground and killed. Before he dies, he tells Emily to love Palamon in his place.

After Arcite's death, Theseus sends for Palamon in Thebes. He declares that he shall wed Palamon and Emily so that Athens and Thebes will be in peace.

THE MILLER'S TALE

In Oxford, there lives a rich old carpenter named John. He takes in a lodger named Nicholas, a young ladies' man. Nicholas falls in love with Allison, the carpenter's 18-year-old wife. She protests briefly when he professes his love, but then agrees to go to bed with him as soon as they are alone for a night.

Meanwhile, Allison goes about her daily life as usual, including going to church. Absalon, a clerk of the church, is quite smitten with Allison, even refusing to take collection from her. Absalon is a rather silly, effeminate man who likes to sing, dance, and go to bars, but is "a little squeamish in the matter of farting." He woos Allison constantly, but she ignores him because she is only interested in spending the night with Nicholas.

Nicholas devises a plan for their meeting. He locks himself in his room for several days. When the carpenter finally checks on him, Nicholas acts as if he's been in a trance, seeing the future. He tells John a flood is coming; in order to survive, they must hang floatable tubs from the ceiling of the mill, each tub to hold one person and a day's supply of food and water.

The carpenter believes Nicholas and spends the day following his instructions. When night falls, he goes quickly to sleep. Allison and Nicholas sneak down to the bedroom to enjoy each other. Absalon walks under the window, however, loudly professing his love and begging for a kiss. Allison tells him to "go to hell" and sticks her bottom out the window to spite him. It is so dark that Absalon doesn't realize at first what he's kissing. Then he gets very upset and leaves. Angry, he returns with a hot poker. This time when he begs for a kiss, Nicholas sticks his bottom out the window and farts loudly. Shocked, Absalon hits him in the behind with the poker. Nicholas screams and John, thinking the flood has come, cuts the ropes of his tub. John crashes to the floor and breaks his arm. The uproar brings neighbors running and John tries to explain about the flood. Nicholas and Allison, however, convince the whole town that John is crazy.

THE REEVE'S TALE

Near Cambridge lives a Miller notorious for stealing corn. One day, he steals a great deal of corn meal from a nearby college. Two outraged students, John and Alan,

come to the mill to watch him. The arrogant Miller decides to steal even more grain from them, to prove that scholars are not always as clever as they are smart. To distract their attention from his activities, he sets the students' horses loose.

When John and Alan finally catch their horses, it is late and they ask the Miller for a place to stay the night. He consents, although the students will have to share the family's one bedroom with them. They all drink quite a bit before bed and the Miller and his wife begin to snore loudly. Alan pokes John and tells him he intends to have the Miller's oldest daughter, Molly. She is sleeping, so he surprises her before she has a chance to cry out. John, feeling jealous, moves the baby's cradle to the side of his bed to try to trick the Miller's wife. It works. Returning from the bathroom during the night, she finds the cradle in the dark and gets into the closest bed. John initiates lovemaking with her almost immediately, and she complies, thinking he is her husband.

Just before dawn, Alan leaves Molly to get back into bed with John. The misplaced cradle tricks him as well, and he inadvertently gets in bed with the Miller. Unable to control himself, he boasts aloud how he has had intercourse three times with Molly that night. This, of course, wakes the Miller, who screams that Alan is a liar. The Miller's wife wakes, and thinking she is in bed with her husband, mistakes the Miller for one of the students and clubs him. John and Alan escape with their grain, making a complete fool of the dishonest Miller.

THE MAN OF LAW'S TALE

Part I Some Syrian merchants journey to Rome to trade and see the city. During the month that they are there, they hear tales of the beautiful and pious Constance, the Emperor's daughter. On returning to Syria, they repeat these tales to the Sultan. He becomes so taken with the idea of marrying Constance that he decides to convert to Christianity.

The Sultan's eagerness to convert himself and all his followers, plus a significant sum of gold, prove very persuasive, and the Sultan's quest is successful. Although Constance is sad to leave Rome, she reminds herself that "all husbands are good husbands."

Meanwhile, the Sultan's mother and certain high officials conspire to keep the marriage from happening.

Part II During the ceremony, assassins burst in and kill everyone except Constance. She is put in a rudderless but well-supplied boat and is told to find her own way to Italy. The boat eventually beaches in Northumberland, near a castle. A constable finds Constance and takes her in. During her stay with the constable and his wife, Hermengilda, Constance converts them to Christianity.

Satan, seeing how good and noble Constance is, plots to destroy her. One night, when the King, Alla, and the constable are away, he sends an evil knight. The knight kills Hermengilda and lays the bloody knife next to Constance. The constable and the King are horrified to see Constance with the knife and bring her to trial. The evil knight accuses her of the murder. The King asks him to swear it on a holy book. When the knight attempts to speak he is struck by God. This vision overwhelms King Alla so much that he converts to Christianity as well.

Soon after, King Alla and Constance fall in love and get married. Donegild, the King's mother, is the only person displeased by their union. While the King is away in Scotland, Constance bears a son

and names the child Maurice. Donegild forges a letter to Alla saying that Constance's child is a deformed creature from hell. The King, now a Christian, replies that he will accept the child no matter what. Angrily, Donegild forges a second letter, one to Constance from the King, saying the child must be destroyed. Constance escapes in a ship.

Part III The King returns and discover's his wife's absence and his mother's treachery. Donegild is put to death. Eventually, the Roman Emperor learns of the assassinations in Syria and sends an army to kill the conspirators. On the return voyage, the Roman ships encounter Constance's ship. Failing to recognize her, they find her an obscure place to live in the household of a senator and his wife.

Some time later, King Alla comes to Rome to do penance. At one point he sees his son, Maurice, and recognizes his similarity to Constance. He asks the senator about the boy and goes to his house to see the woman who is Maurice's mother.

Alla and Constance are joyfully reunited and present their marriage and their son to the Emperor. They return to Northumberland to live happily until Alla dies. Constance and Maurice then return to Rome where Maurice later becomes Emperor.

THE WIFE OF BATH'S TALE

In the time of King Arthur, a lusty young knight on his way to court sees a maiden walking alone and rapes her. Her kin and her village make so many petitions to the King to recognize the crime that, in time, the knight is condemned to death. The Queen intervenes on the knight's behalf. The King decides that the knight's punishment should be up to the Queen.

The Queen calls the knight to her and tells him that he will live if he can answer the question, "What is it that women most desire?" She gives him a year and a day to return the answer to her. The knight searches the countryside, speaking to all sorts of women, but each one gives him a different answer. When his year is nearly over, he begins his return to the castle.

On the way, he is distracted by a group of maidens dancing. As he approaches, they vanish and an ugly old woman appears. The woman asks him about his quest. She tells him she has the answer he seeks but will share it only if he agrees to do something in return for her. He agrees to do whatever she should ask of him.

Back at the castle when the Queen repeats her question, the knight replies, "A woman wants the selfsame sovereignty over her husband as over her lover." No woman in the court can disagree, so the Queen grants the knight his freedom. Before the court disperses, the old woman approaches the Queen. She explains the terms of her agreement with the knight and asks that they be united in marriage. For the sake of his honor, the knight can do nothing but comply.

On their wedding night, the knight is reluctant to touch his new wife. He tells her how repulsive she is. She explains to him that her virtues are not related to her appearance. She commands him to kiss her, saying that if he does, all will be well. He does and when he looks at her, she has become young and beautiful.

THE FRIAR'S TALE

A summoner who works for the archdeacon of the district makes a good living by spying on people and blackmailing them. One day on his way to a village he encounters a brightly dressed yeoman.

As they start talking, they realize they both do about the same type of work. They discuss working together and swear to be brothers. When the Summoner asks the yeoman's name, he replies, "Brother would you have me tell...I am a fiend; my dwelling is in hell."

On the road they see a farmer whose cart has gotten stuck in the mud. He swears at his horses and invokes the devil to take them away. The Summoner urges the yeoman to take what's been offered. The yeoman cautions him to wait. In his next breath the farmer is blessing the horses in God's name.

The Summoner goes to the house of an old woman and demands money from her or he will report her to the archdeacon. He threatens to take her new frying pan. She swears that the Devil should take him and the frying pan away if he doesn't repent and leave her alone. The yeoman asks her if she is sincere and she says yes. He takes the Summoner off to hell, where, according to the Friar, there is a special place for summoners.

THE SUMMONER'S TALE

Naturally, the Summoner is furious with the Friar for telling such a tale, and sets out to prove that it is friars who are truly in league with the Devil.

In Yorkshire there lives a friar who requests money and gifts for prayers. His corruption lies in his taking the gifts but not saying the prayers. One evening he goes to visit a sick old man named Thomas. Thomas scolds the Friar for not coming sooner. The Friar protests that he has been spending all his time praying for Thomas.

When Thomas' wife comes in, the Friar gives her a lusty kiss. She asks if he can do anything to mellow Thomas' grumpy disposition. She also asks him if he knows her baby died. The Friar replies that, yes, he saw the child in a vision. When she offers dinner, the Friar lists several rich dishes he'd like but then says that studying the Bible is his nourishment.

While eating gluttonously, the Friar lectures Thomas on trying to lead an austere life. He advises Thomas to give him money. Thomas says that he has donated money in the past and it has not done any good. The Friar responds that Thomas spread out his giving to too many convents.

Seeing that Thomas is quite irritated, the Friar changes tactics. He suggests that if Thomas will give him gold, it will help him get rid of his anger. Thomas agrees to give a gift to the Friar if he promises to divide it evenly among all in the convent. Thomas directs him to the "gift," supposedly hidden beneath his buttocks. When the Friar reaches for it, Thomas farts loudly.

The indignant Friar runs to his patron's manor house to complain. Instead of being upset, everyone in the manor tries to figure out how to divide a fart twelve ways. Finally, the lord's valet suggests using a great wheel with twelve spokes. This solution pleases all but the Friar, and the valet is rewarded with a new shirt.

THE CLERK'S TALE

In Italy rules a Lord Walter who pleases his subjects in every way except in his failure to take a wife. One day, some of his advisers come to him and offer to find a suitable woman. He refuses, preferring to make his own choice. They settle on a date for a wedding, provided that Walter finds a bride.

On the day of the wedding, Walter goes to the hut of a peasant and asks for the hand of his daughter, the fair and virtuous Griselda. Before the wedding, he tells Griselda to be ready to obey him in everything, no matter what. She agrees and they are married amid much festivity. The people soon come to love Griselda for her gentle virtue. She later gives birth to a daughter.

To test her loyalty, Walter takes the baby girl away from her and lets her think the child will be killed. Griselda stays true to her promise, however, and does not fight him or treat him differently.

Griselda gives birth to a son four years later. Still not sure of her, Walter takes away the boy as well. Griselda again accepts his tyranny lovingly and without complaint. For the final test, Walter tells Griselda that he has chosen to remarry and gives her a forged church document allowing him to do so. At this time, he sends for the two children, now ages 12 and 7, who have not been killed but have been raised by another part of the family. Griselda is sad to leave Walter but does not break her oath. She merely asks for a smock to cover herself for her return to her father's hut.

When the children arrive, Lord Walter sends for Griselda. She has no idea that the beautiful girl is her daughter. Finally, Walter can no longer bear his own cruelty. He confesses everything and reconciles Griselda to her children.

THE MERCHANT'S TALE

A 60-year-old knight in Lombardy named January becomes obsessed with the idea of getting married. He spends much time idealizing the state of marriage, finally calling his friends together to ask their opinions. His friend Placebo tells him to do what he thinks is best. Justinus, another friend, expresses doubt that January should marry, especially considering that he will only be able to please a wife sexually for a few more years.

January eventually chooses a beautiful young girl named May. Everyone has a good time at the wedding feast except a servant named Damian who is stricken with love for May. A few days later, Damian sends a letter to May professing his love. She begins to care for him in return.

Quite suddenly, January goes blind. He becomes very possessive of May and insists that she stay by him always. One day, she signals to Damian to go to the walled garden. When she and January arrive, May motions for Damian to climb into a pear tree. The King and Queen of Fairyland, Pluto and Prosperina, see this and take interest. Pluto declares that he is going to restore January's sight and Prosperina counters by preparing a believable excuse for May. As they are walking around the garden, May asks January's permission to climb the tree to get a pear.

She climbs the tree to Damian and the two begin to fondle each other. At that moment, the fairy King restores January's sight. Seeing his wife in Damian's arms, he cries out. May reassures him that his eyes, only just beginning to work again, are playing a trick on him. January decides to believe her. She jumps down and he leads her home.

THE FRANKLIN'S TALE

In Brittany lives a knight named Arveragus, who after a great deal of effort wins the lovely Dorigen to be his bride. He swears his faithfulness to her but has to go to Britain to "seek higher deeds of arms and reputation." Dorigen mourns his absence and begins to go on long walks along the castle ramparts watching for his ship. She wonders at the rocky coastline and how a benevolent God could have allowed so many sailors to die on those rocks.

One sunny morning, her friends take her on a picnic. Aurelius, a young squire who has been in love with Dorigen for some time, approaches her. She tells him that she is a faithful wife, but jokes that if he could remove all the rocks from the coast of Brittany, she would "love him more than any man on earth." Dorigen forgets the incident when Averagus returns home "in health and power the very flower of chivalry."

Aurelius spends the following two years devastated by his unrequited love. His brother suggests that he consult a student of magic in France. Aurelius, revived by this hope, travels to France and offers the student 1,000 pounds for his services.

Through illusion, the student makes the coast look as though the rocks have disappeared. Aurelius shows the accomplishment to Dorigen and demands that she stay true to her oath. Averagus and Dorigen unhappily decide to do the honorable thing, and so Dorigen gives herself to Aurelius. Aurelius, however, sees her unhappiness and releases her from her promise.

THE PHYSICIAN'S TALE

The honorable knight Virginius has a beautiful and virtuous 14-year-old daughter named Virginia. One day she and her mother are walking in town when she catches the eye of an old judge. He begins to plot a way to have the girl. He calls on a rather treacherous man named Claudius to help him.

Claudius brings Virginius before the judge on the charge that Virginius has stolen one of his slaves from his house. Claudius demands the return of his "slave"—Virginia. Before Virginius can defend himself or his daughter, the judge finds in favor of Claudius.

Virginius returns home. He tells Virginia that she must die or be shamed. The pious

Virginia thanks God that she might die a maiden and begs her father to do what he thinks best. She faints and Virginius cuts off her head, which he presents to the judge. The judge, infuriated, orders Virginius to be hanged. However, a mob of a thousand men, having suspicions of the judge's treachery, seize him and throw him in prison. They intend to hang Claudius but Virginius asks that they spare his life and banish him instead.

THE PARDONER'S TALE

As three rowdy men sit in an inn in Flanders drinking, they hear a funeral bell toll. A servant in the tavern tells them that the funeral is for a friend of theirs who was killed by a thief named Death. The three men, in a drunken rage, swear to track down Death and kill him.

Before they've traveled far, they encounter an old man. The men ask if he has seen Death nearby. The old man directs them up the road and says he last saw Death up there, under a tree.

Under the tree, the three men do not find Death, but eight bushels of gold. They decide to wait until nightfall to steal the gold and draw lots to see who will go back to town for supplies. The youngest loses and heads into town. Looking to get all the gold for himself, he buys a large quantity of wine and some poison. He puts poison in two of the three bottles of wine. While he is gone, the other men plot to kill him. When he returns, they stab him. However, they die when they drink the poisoned wine.

THE SHIPMAN'S TALE

In a large house in St. Denys lives a merchant and his beautiful wife. The couple often have house guests, one of the more frequent visitors being a young monk called Sir John. At the monk's suggestion, the merchant regards him as a brother, and they get along quite well.

On one particular visit, Sir John encounters the merchant's wife in the garden, looking pale and unhappy. She tells the monk that her husband mistreats her. He won't give her any money to buy things for herself, she complains, and she needs at least one hundred francs to keep up appearances. She asks Sir John to lend her the money. He agrees to bring it to her as soon as the merchant leaves on business. He kisses her passionately. That night, the monk asks the merchant to lend him 100 francs. The merchant readily agrees. The next day, the monk brings the money to the wife and, to thank him, she agrees to spend the night with him.

On his return trip, the merchant stops in to see Sir John and casually mentions the money. Sir John replies, a bit indignantly, that he has already given the sum to the merchant's wife. When the merchant asks his wife about the matter, she admits that Sir John gave her a sum of money, but she has spent it all on pretty clothes. Because his trip was good, the merchant forgives her but tells her not to spend so much again.

THE PRIORESS' TALE

Somewhere in Asia stands a Christian town with one Jewish neighborhood. Since the Christian school is on the far side of that part of town, the Christian children have to walk through it twice a day.

One little boy begins to pick up a song the older students are learning. He practices the tune every day even though he doesn't understand the Latin. Finally, he asks another boy to explain the song to him. *O Alma Redemptoris*, answers the older boy, "is a salute to the Blessed Lady." The little boy vows to memorize the song so he can sing it on Christmas Day.

Satan takes offense at this little Christian boy singing the praises of the Virgin Mary twice a day, and sends resentment and malice to the Jews. They hire a murderer who grabs the boy and slits his throat.

Naturally, the boy's widowed mother becomes quite concerned when her son doesn't come home that evening. The people she asks say he was last seen in the Jewish neighborhood. Jesus sends a message to her to look in a certain alleyway in a pit. As she nears his body, the boy begins to sing. The Provost comes and orders all the Jews to be chained and locked up.

They carry the boy's body to the church where an abbot asks him how he was able to sing. The child replies that the Virgin Mary bade him sing the song until he was buried. She had placed a special grain on his tongue to help him keep singing. A monk takes the grain from the boy's mouth, and he dies peacefully. The town builds a marble tomb to commemorate the little boy.

CHAUCER'S TALE OF MELIBEE

The house of a man named Melibee is robbed while he and his wife, Dame Prudence, are away. The robbers leave their daughter, Sophia, with grave injuries. The majority of the tale is devoted to whether the couple should take violent revenge or not. All manner of authorities are consulted on the matter, including doctors, lawyers, and clergymen. The burglars are found, but to everyone's pleasure, a peaceful arrangement is made.

THE MONK'S TALE

The Monk chooses to tell many familiar tales of great griefs rather than a longer tale of his own. The histories he relates are those of: Lucifer, Adam, Samson, Hercules, Belshazzar, Zenobia, King Peter of Cyprus, Bernabo Visconti of Lombardy, Count Ugolino of Pisa, Nero, Holofernes, King Antiochus the Illustrius, Alexander, Julius Caesar, and Croesus.

THE NUN'S PRIEST'S TALE

This tale is about a poor widow and her two daughters living long ago. They keep a few animals, including a rooster named Chanticleer who is known throughout the land for his fine crowing. Lady Pertelote is his favorite companion hen.

One night, Chanticleer has a nightmare in which a predatory beast is stalking him in the yard. Lady Pertelote tells him not to be such a coward. She advises him to take a laxative to free himself "from vapours." Chanticleer disagrees with her, citing several examples where people's lives were saved because they followed the warnings in their dreams.

One day in May, a coal-tipped fox lies hidden in the cabbage patch. Chanticleer, idly watching a butterfly land in the cabbage patch, suddenly glimpses the fox. He begins to run and cry out. The fox tells him not to fear, that he's only come to hear Chanticleer's famous crowing. Chanticleer, flattered, closes his eyes and begins to sing. Instantly, the fox grabs him in his mouth. The hens cry out, and the widow, her daughters, and all the animals go chasing after the fox. Chanticleer advises the fox to turn around and say, "Turn back you saucy bumpkins all!" As soon as the fox opens his mouth to speak, Chanticleer flies away to safety.

THE SECOND NUN'S TALE

In Rome, a Christian woman named Cecilia lives a very chaste life. When she marries a man named Valerian, she prays all through the ceremony that she will keep her virginity. That night, she tells her new husband that he must not touch her or he will be killed by her guardian angel. Valerian asks her if he can see the angel. She says yes, but only if he seeks out a holy man named Urban and is baptized by him.

After being baptized, Valerian sees Cecilia with the angel. The angel offers him a wish. Valerian wishes that his dear brother, Tiburce, will see the light and become a Christian as well. Cecilia helps to convert Tiburce and he is baptized as well.

Later on, the Romans seek out the brothers to force them to renounce their Christianity. Valerian and Tiburce refuse and are sentenced to death. However, their testimony is so convincing that during the trial several of the Roman officers convert. The prefect Almachius sends for Cecilia to have her condemned as well.

First he orders her to be killed in a boiling bath, but the water does not scald her. An executioner tries three times to cut off her head, but she lives for three days after his attempts, during which time she continues to teach and convert people. When she dies, her house becomes the Cathedral of St. Cecilia.

THE YEOMAN'S CANON TALE

The Yeoman's tale is about a canon who also practices alchemy. This canon uses the trappings of alchemy to swindle people. He goes to the house of a pleasant priest in London and borrows money from him, promising to return it in three days. He pays it back promptly and tells the priest that since he was so charitable, he wants to do him a favor in return.

The canon arranges a demonstration to show the priest how he can turn quicksilver (mercury) into real silver. The canon also demonstrates how he can turn chalk and a hollow stick into silver. These "demonstrations" are all faked but the priest believes they are real. The canon sells his "secrets" to the priest for forty pounds. The priest realizes he's been tricked when he tries to do the conversions himself.

THE MANCIPLE'S TALE

When Phoebus lives on earth, he is known all around for his skills with the bow and arrow and with musical instruments. He has a mortal wife whom he guards a bit jealously although he loves her very much. He also has a pet white crow that he has taught to speak beautifully.

Once when Phoebus is away, his wife commits adultery. The crow witnesses their lovemaking. When Phoebus returns, the crow reports what he saw. Phoebus kills his wife in a rage and then blames the crow for telling the news in the first place. He takes away the crow's melodious speaking voice and replaces it with a squawk. He also pulls out all the crow's white feathers and replaces them with black ones. This is why, says the Manciple, all crows are black.

THE PARSON'S TALE

The Parson's Tale is a sermon on the nature of sin. The Parson says that God does not want any man to be damned and lose his soul; therefore, "There are many ways into the celestial city." One of the noblest ways to heaven is through true penitence. Linked to the idea of penitence is that of contrition, which the Parson defines as the heart's sorrow for sin.

In the second half of his sermon, the Parson goes on to describe the seven deadly sins and their remedies. The first deadly sin is Pride; humility is its cure. The second deadly sin is Envy, which can be purged by Love of God, neighbor, and enemy. Anger, the third deadly sin, can be remedied by patience. Fortitude will dispel the fourth deadly sin, Sloth. Avarice is the fifth deadly sin; its cure is mercy. The sixth deadly sin, Gluttony, can be cured through a combination of abstinence, temperance, and sobriety. Chastity and continence can overcome the seventh deadly sin, Lechery.

CHAUCER'S RETRACTIONS

Unfortunately, *The Canterbury Tales* was never finished. Chaucer instead tacked on his obscure retraction asking forgiveness for the things he had written that "tended towards sin." More importantly, he begs "those that listen to this little treatise, or read it, that if there be anything in it that pleases them, they thank Our Lord Jesus Christ for it, from whom proceeds all understanding and goodness."

DEATH OF A SALESMAN

ABOUT THE AUTHOR

Arthur Miller (1915–) was born in Manhattan, one of three children. His elder brother became a businessman, and his sister was an actress. The Miller family was the very picture of middle-class Jewish society. Miller attended grammar school in Harlem, then went to high school in Brooklyn. After graduating from high school, Miller worked in a warehouse until he convinced the University of Michigan to admit him despite a less-than-exemplary high school record.

In college, Miller began to write plays that drew attention. He went on to work for the Federal Theater Project. Miller's first professional play opened on Broadway in 1944 and closed four days later. Although the play failed, Miller attracted critical attention as a promising and talented playwright. Miller's second play, *All My Sons*, opened on Broadway in 1947. It was financially successful, and was voted Best Play of the Season by the Drama Critics' Circle.

In 1956, Miller was called to appear before the House Un-American Activities Committee, and was convicted for contempt of Congress because of his alleged involvement with the Communist Party. This conviction was overturned in 1958 by the Supreme Court.

Miller has been married three times. His first wife was Mary Slattery, whom he divorced in 1956, the same year he married his second wife, Marilyn Monroe. Miller and Monroe were divorced in 1960. In 1962 he married Inge Morath, an Austrian-born photographer.

Miller's importance to American theater ranks with the work of great playwrights such as Eugene O'Neill and Tennessee Williams. He is the author of nine plays, including *Death of a Salesman, The Crucible, A View From the Bridge,* and *After the Fall*, as well as numerous short stories and essays. *Death of a Salesman* won the Pulitzer Prize for Drama in 1949.

THE BIG PICTURE

Death of a Salesman tells the bleak story of Willy Loman, a common salesman who falls apart when his illusions about the "American Dream"—and about himself— are shattered. Miller himself has referred to this play as a "tragedy of the common man."

Why you're reading this book:
- This play is a landmark in American theater:
  - Using minimalist stage settings, it focuses intensely on the minds of its characters.
  - By making Willy's mental flashbacks part of the action, it lets the audience become part of his thoughts.
- It strikingly illustrates the discontentment of the modern-day common American.
- It shows the "American Dream" of prosperity and opportunity as an empty, even destructive, illusion.
- It questions the common notion of "success" in American society.

Your teachers are looking for:
- Miller's treatment of the common man as a hero or a villain.
- The play's parallels with classic tragedy.

- Miller's use of theatrical conventions—dream sequences, flashbacks—to enhance the play.
- How the illusion of being "well liked" has replaced hard work and honesty as a way to achieve success.

KEY CHARACTERS

Willy Loman: Traveling salesman who has worked the New England area for some forty years. He aspires to a level of success that he cannot reach. He has seen almost all his hopes and dreams for his family and himself destroyed, mostly by his own doing. Willy clings to the past and often loses himself in recollections of an earlier time.

Linda: Willy's wife. Has stayed at home caring for the family while Willy is on the road. Her love for her husband remains undiminished.

Biff: Willy's eldest son. A former high school football hero, Biff began to question the values of his upbringing after finding his father in a compromising position in a hotel room in Boston.

Happy: Willy's youngest son. Currently an assistant to the assistant buyer at an unnamed firm. Still holds on to the empty dreams of his youth. Although promiscuous, he is lonely.

Bernard: Childhood friend of Biff and Happy, and son of Charley. Bernard, the unliked "worm" in high school, has grown up to become a lawyer who argues cases before the U.S. Supreme Court.

The Woman: A secretary in Boston with whom Willy commits adultery.

Charley: Willy's next door neighbor, Bernard's father, and an entrepreneur. He attempts to help Willy in any way possible, giving him money and offering him jobs. In return, Willy acts offended and insults Charley.

Uncle Ben: Willy's older brother who left the family to seek his fortune in Africa, thinking it was Alaska. Ben walked into a jungle in Africa, and walked out a few years later with a fortune. Willy holds Ben up as an example of success.

Howard Wagner: Willy's boss, the son of Willy's original boss. Places Willy on a commission-only pay basis, then fires him.

ESSAY IDEAS

- Discuss Linda's assertion that "attention must be paid" to Willy.
- What does the flute music in the play symbolize?
- How does Biff's habitual stealing reflect his upbringing?
- How does Willy regard Uncle Ben?
- Why is a sixty-three-year-old man (Willy) referred to by everyone except Ben with a diminutive (Willy, instead of William or Bill)?
- How does Miller's use of flashbacks emphasize the theme of illusion?

A SAMPLE ESSAY IN OUTLINE FORM

Illusion in *Death of a Salesman*
- Willy's view of life is based on illusions:
  - Success is based on material wealth and being "well liked," not on production.
  - Selling is based on personal image, not the quality of goods.
  - Dave Singleman, Willy's ideal of success:
    - Made his living on a smile and the telephone.
    - Died the "death of a salesman," with buyers coming to the funeral from a four-state radius.

- Ben's "success" is an illusion that Willy has created.
- Shattered illusions:
  - Willy's instructions to the boys that stealing sand from the construction site is OK—that it's "not really stealing."
  - Willy's lying to Linda about commission earnings.
  - The discord between the past and present—Willy's old ideals don't apply to the present reality.
  - The illusion of Ben's productivity.
  - That Bernard will never get anywhere because he isn't "well liked"—he achieves success through honest hard work and patience.
  - The destruction of Biff's image as a golden boy destined for greatness caused by his failing math.
  - Weaknesses in Happy's cheerful façade:
    - Exaggerates position.
    - Still lonely though promiscuous.
  - Biff's discovery of Willy and "The Woman" in Boston.

PLOT SUMMARY

Act I The lights rise on the set, a minimalist representation of the Loman house and the surrounding urban environment. Willy comes home with his sample cases. He tells Linda that he aborted his trip to New England because he had trouble driving. We find out that Biff and Happy, the Lomans' grown sons, are home for a visit. Willy and Linda discuss Willy's job, and Linda suggests that Willy ask Howard (his boss) if he can work in New York. Linda comments on the presence of their sons, and criticizes Willy for losing his temper at Biff. Willy defends himself by saying he only asked if Biff was making any money. Linda defends Biff, saying he's finding himself. Willy scoffs at this, then condemns

Biff as lazy. Nine lines later, Willy contradicts himself, claiming that whatever other faults Biff may have, he is not lazy.

The scene shifts from Willy and Linda to the boys in their bedroom. They discuss Willy's condition. Happy mentions that Willy has been destroying cars and talking to himself, often seeming to be talking to Biff. Happy suggests that Biff apply to work for Bill Oliver, a former employer who has become very successful. Biff recalls that he quit his job over the disappearance of a carton of basketballs and wonders if Bill Oliver still thinks he stole them. They discuss plans for a business, "The Loman Brothers," either in farming or sports equipment. The discussion then turns to their dates. Happy mentions that his date is engaged to be married in five weeks.

Biff suggests that Happy go to see Bill Oliver about a loan to back their sporting equipment idea. They hear Willy talking to himself downstairs, and Biff mentions that he doesn't think his situation is the only thing bothering his father.

Willy, alone in the kitchen, experiences a flashback as he speaks to a younger Biff about Biff's simonizing cars. Willy warns Biff to be careful with the girls who have taken to following Biff around. The talk turns to sports, and Biff mentions that he has "acquired" a football from the school. Willy is upset, until Biff tells him that he is planning to return the ball. Willy rationalizes the action, convincing himself that the coach will appreciate Biff's initiative. Biff's friend and next door neighbor Bernard enters, telling Biff that he has to come study for his math Regents test. Biff promises to go over later, and Bernard exits. The Lomans conclude that Bernard, like his father Charley, is "liked, but not well liked."

Still in the flashback, Linda enters and questions Willy about the productiveness of his trip to New England. First he tells her that he's sold about 1300 gross, but later admits that the whole trip was worth just 200 gross. Willy and Linda discuss their finances, then their relationship. Willy mentions that he gets lonely on the road. The Woman is seen in the background, talking to Willy. We learn that he has been carrying on an adulterous affair in Boston. Willy's wandering mind then shifts back to Linda, and the two discuss young Biff's situation.

Charley, Bernard's father, enters, breaking the flashback. Charley and Willy play cards. They discuss the situation of the Loman family. Every time Charley tries to help Willy, Willy takes it as an insult. Charley offers advice about Biff, a compliment on the ceiling construction Willy has just finished, and a job. At each offering, Willy snaps at Charley. Willy sees an apparition of his brother Ben and speaks to it. Charley, who doesn't see the image, is confused. Willy laments his decision not to follow Ben to Alaska, claiming that all his problems would have been solved by the opportunities there. Charley leaves, and Willy has a flashback involving Ben and his family. We learn that Ben left for what he thought was Alaska after their father had abandoned them on the trail in South Dakota. Images of Biff and Happy as teenagers appear. Willy tries to justify his life to Ben by demonstrating the quality of his boys through their fighting and other "masculine" activities.

The recollection is interrupted as Linda enters the kitchen. Willy leaves the kitchen and Biff replaces him. He and Linda talk about his wanderings and his relationship with his father. Biff expresses a love for his mother that is greater than his feelings for his father. Linda claims that he cannot merely love her without loving his father.

Happy joins them, and they discuss Willy's situation at his firm. Linda reveals that Willy has been working on straight commission for some time, and she expresses her regret that her sons have little respect for their father. Biff then brings up the fact that Willy threw him out of the house because he (Willy) is a fake who doesn't like people around who know he is a fake.

Linda then reveals that she believes that Willy is trying to kill himself. She tells her sons that a woman had told the car insurance company that Willy's recent car accidents were not accidents at all, but purposeful incidents. Then she tells them that she has found a piece of rubber hose in the basement, with an attachment at the end, and a similar attachment on the gas nozzle under the water heater. She is afraid to remove it for fear of confronting Willy with her knowledge of his activities.

Willy reenters the room, and he and Biff have a brief argument about Biff's accomplishments. Happy brings up their plan to apply to Bill Oliver for backing for a sports equipment line, and Willy becomes extremely excited. The evening ends in optimism, with the boys going to bed to prepare for the big day, and Willy enthusiastically giving advice to his sons.

Before going to sleep, however, Biff goes to the basement to verify that Willy's rubber hose is there.

Act II The morning begins with Willy and Linda discussing their finances. The discussion turns to the subject of the mortgage on the house, and their accomplishment of weathering a twenty-five year mortgage. Willy decides to go to his boss, Howard, and request a reassignment to New York.

Willy arrives at the office and waits to see Howard. Howard shows him his latest purchase, a device that records sound on a wire. He plays back recordings of his family. Howard then effectively fires Willy, telling him to take some time off. Willy relates to Howard the story of how he came to be a salesman.

He tells Howard of a man named Dave Singleman, a salesman who died at age eighty–four. Willy describes the way in which Dave's personality and personal relationships formed the foundation of his business, how he died the "death of a salesman," on the road, and how he was so loved that hundreds of people came to his funeral. Howard is unmoved by this story and dismisses Willy.

Willy sees a vision of Ben, who tells him to move out to the wilderness, to seek his fortune in Alaska. Then Willy calls for Linda, and a vision of Linda appears. Linda defends Willy's chosen career in front of Ben, claiming that Willy is building something with the firm. Ben asks where this something is, how tangible it is.

A vision of Biff and Happy in high school garb appears on the scene. Willy decries the value Ben places on cold hard capital, claiming that investment in interpersonal relationships is more vital. Ben exits, and the vision transforms into a recollection of Biff's Ebbets Field football game. Bernard enters, asking to help carry some equipment. Charley enters, and Willy tells him there is no room in the car for him to go to the game. Charley replies that he just wanted to play cards. The two men argue over the value of Biff's supposed athletic future.

The vision fades and Willy is back in the present, approaching the door to Charley's office. Bernard is inside, now grown. He greets Willy and tells him that his train to Washington leaves shortly. Willy tells Bernard about Biff's plans for a sports equipment business, then asks Bernard what the secret of his success is. Willy wonders why nothing good ever happened to Biff after the age of seventeen. Bernard replies that Biff never trained himself to do anything. Bernard brings up the subject of

the end of Biff's senior year, when he flunked math. He asks Willy if Biff went to Boston after their grades were released. Willy admits that Biff went to Boston, but sees no relevance in the trip. Bernard tells him that when Biff returned, he burned his decorated sneakers in the furnace, and he and Bernard had a fist fight, after which Bernard felt that Biff had given up on life.

Charley enters and tells Willy that Bernard is a lawyer, scheduled to argue a case before the U.S. Supreme Court. Bernard leaves to catch his train. Charley and Willy discuss Willy's situation. Charley offers Willy a job, and Willy turns him down, claiming that he has a job. Charley gives Willy money to finish paying off his life insurance and tells Willy to take care of himself, because nobody is worth anything dead.

The scene shifts to Happy in a restaurant, reserving a table for dinner that night. He chats with Stanley, the waiter, and spots a woman entering the restaurant. He sends Stanley over to the table with a bottle of champagne. Biff enters, and Happy introduces him to the woman, Miss Forsythe, as the quarterback of a professional football team. He tries to pass himself off as a West Point graduate. Happy sends the woman to call a friend.

Biff tells Happy about his day at Oliver's office. He tells him that he spent six hours waiting for Oliver, who didn't remember him. Biff then admits that he went into Oliver's office and stole his fountain pen.

Willy enters, and after ordering drinks, the Loman men launch into a discussion of the day's activities. Biff wonders how his position as a shipping clerk for Bill Oliver was transformed in the family memory into a selling position. At this point, Willy tells his sons that he's been fired. Happy makes up a more flattering version of Biff's appointment with Oliver, and Biff follows along for a while. Biff finally tries to tell Willy the truth about the afternoon, but a flashback takes Willy away from the conversation.

A young Bernard tells Linda that Biff has flunked math for the year, and he is nowhere to be found. They decide that he must have gone to Grand Central Station to catch a train for Boston.

The scene switches back to the present. Biff admits the theft of the fountain pen to Willy.

Willy's flashback continues. He and The Woman are in the Standish Arms Hotel when Biff comes to see him. Willy ignores Biff, who is paging him from the hotel desk. Reality intrudes again, and Biff makes up a story about an upcoming lunch appointment with Bill Oliver to try to save Willy's feelings. Biff then admits he has no appointment, and that it was difficult to drag himself back to see Oliver. Happy interrupts, telling them to be conscious of the surrounding restaurant. Miss Forsythe returns with her friend Letta. Images of the restaurant continue to mix with images of the hotel room flashback.

In the restaurant, Biff is critical of the way Happy treats Willy, pretending there is nothing wrong and hiding the truth. He pulls out the length of rubber hose and puts it in front of Happy. Biff and Happy leave with the girls, abandoning Willy.

Willy's flashback once again takes the stage. Biff eventually comes up to the hotel room in Boston. Biff and Willy discuss the math situation, while The Woman hides in the bathroom. The Woman eventually comes out, and Biff sees her in a state of undress, wearing the nylon pantyhose meant for his mother. He figures out the rest of the scenario.

Willy comes back to reality, and is helped home by some of the restaurant's waiters.

The boys return home to an angry Linda, who has seen what their actions have done to Willy. Biff asks to see Willy, and Linda tells him he cannot, almost throwing him out of the house. She tells him that Willy is planting a garden, talking to an image of Ben. He is discussing his plans, and Ben voices objections to them.

Biff goes to talk to Willy and tries to explain that he has failed with Oliver. They go into the kitchen. Biff tells Willy he's leaving and tells him not to worry. Willy will not accept this and refuses to shake Biff's hand.

Willy says that Biff has thrown out his entire life for spite, and that Willy should not carry the blame. Happy comes down from the bedroom and stands on the steps. Biff then pulls out the gas hose and confronts Willy with it. Linda is shocked. Willy acts nervous, and denies ever having seen the hose before. Biff then makes Happy admit that he is only one of two assistants to the assistant buyer, and Biff admits that the reason he had no address in Kansas City for three months is that he was convicted of stealing a suit. Biff goes all out, admitting all of his shortcomings, and tells his family that he's leaving in the morning. In the midst of all this, Happy continues to try to play to Willy's expectations.

The boys go upstairs to bed, and Willy stays behind. Linda goes upstairs and becomes nervous when Willy doesn't follow.

We hear the sound of a car ignition followed by the car pulling away from the house at full speed, then a screech and a crash.

Requiem The scene is the cemetery at Willy's funeral. Linda, Charley, Happy, Bernard, and Biff are present. Biff has come to grips with himself, saying that he now knows who and what he is and can begin to deal with it. Charley explains that Willy's fate was not his fault. The life of a salesman is nothing but a dream, an illusion; when the illusion fails to charm the buyer, there's nothing left. Happy still clings to Willy's illusions. He is determined to "fight the good fight" in his father's memory.

Linda says good-bye to her husband. She is at first unable to cry, but the tears come when she mentions the fact that their mortgage has been paid off on the very day of Willy's funeral. The Lomans have finished paying off the last of their debts. She closes the play with the words, "We're free."

THE DIVINE COMEDY—INFERNO

ABOUT THE AUTHOR

Dante Alighieri (1265–1321) was born in Florence, Italy, shortly before the Renaissance, Florence's period of rebirth of literature and art. He was to become Italy's greatest poet.

When he was nine years old, Dante met a woman named Beatrice. His love for her never died, and it influenced the course of his life. In 1292 he married Gemma Donati. They had two sons and one or two daughters.

Dante played a part in the violent political and military conflicts that engulfed Italy during his lifetime. He rose to high office in Florence and was sent as an ambassador to the Pope at Rome, in 1301. The victory of the more extreme party in Florence, the Black Guelfs, resulted in the banishment of the leaders of the opposite party, the White Guelfs. Dante was among those sent into exile in 1302. He settled in Ravenna, where he stayed until his death.

Dante's major work, *The Divine Comedy*, has led to more published literary criticism than any other work, with the exception of the Bible and Shakespeare's works. It has been translated into more than 300 foreign languages. The poem is a narrative of an imaginary journey through Hell (Inferno), Purgatory (Purgatorio), and Heaven (Paradiso). This masterpiece, with its multi-layered religious, political, and autobiographical meaning, is one of the richest examples of Western literature.

THE BIG PICTURE

Dante's *Inferno*, the first part of *The Divine Comedy*, describes the poet's journey through Hell under the guidance of the Roman poet Virgil. As he travels through the Inferno, Dante sees all the different kinds of sinners and how they are punished in the afterlife. Each sin has a fitting punishment, described in vivid, graphic detail.

Why you're reading this book:
- It is a beautifully and ingeniously constructed allegory.
- It epitomizes the mode of thought of the Middle Ages and early Renaissance.
- It is a colorful and sensual poem, full of rich, almost three-dimensional, imagery.
- It is powerful both as a personal and political work.

Your teachers are looking for:
- Timeless themes of:
  - Good versus evil.
  - Man's responsibilities.
  - Free will.
  - Predestination.
- Allegorical representations—Dante's use of a single person or thing to represent a whole idea:
  - Virgil as Human Reason.
  - Dante as the Noble Soul, or mankind.

KEY CHARACTERS

Dante: The poet who decides that he has strayed from the straight and narrow path. Virgil presents himself as his willing guide through Hell and Purgatory.

Virgil: Dante's guide on his journey through Hell and Purgatory. Like Dante, he is a poet. Allegorically, he represents Human Reason. As a Virtuous Pagan, he is forever damned to Limbo. He is not tortured; his only pain is that he has no hope.

ESSAY IDEAS

- Based on this work, would you guess that Dante is a religious man? Why or why not? Is Dante a "fan" of God, so to speak?
- Does Dante portray Catholicism as a tolerant, sympathetic religion? How does he address this issue?
- How does the use of allegory enrich this story? Some critics have argued that the work could stand on its own without the added element of the allegory. Do you agree? Would it be as powerful?
- Pick three or four of the allegorical characters and explain their significance in *The Inferno*.
- Why did Dante choose this order for Hell? Why are some sins punished worse than others? Are there political reasons?
- Why did Dante choose Virgil to act as his guide? What is Beatrice's role?

A SAMPLE ESSAY IN OUTLINE FORM

Allegory in *The Inferno*.
- Allegory adds to the brilliance and depth of the poem.
- Dante uses allegory to make political, social, and religious points.
- Some of the poem's most effective allegorical representations:
  - Dante as Mankind.
  - Virgil as Human Reason.
  - The Leopard of Malice and Fraud.
  - The Lion of Violence and Ambition.
  - The She-Wolf of Incontinence.
  - The Mount of Joy.
  - The Virgin Mary as Compassion.

Dante uses allegory to add an important dimension of meaning to a wonderfully constructed poem. Illustrating big ideas (i.e. Ambition, Malice, and Joy) through individual characters or symbols in the poem, Dante can make his points in an active, dramatic way rather than simply telling them to the reader.

Canto I: The Dark Wood of Error

Midway through his life, Dante feels he has strayed from the True Way into the Dark Wood of Error. He sees the sunrise over the hill, the Mount of Joy. It is Easter, time of resurrection. Dante sets out to climb the Mount of Joy, but he is blocked by the Three Beasts of Worldliness: The Leopard of Malice and Fraud, The Lion of Violence and Ambition, and The She-Wolf of Incontinence. Suddenly Virgil appears as the symbol for Human Reason. He has been sent to lead Dante from error. He tells Dante not to try to bypass the beasts, as the journey will be harder and longer. Virgil offers to guide Dante as far as Human Reason can go. Dante must go through Hell, the Recognition of Sin, up through Purgatory, the Renunciation of Sin, and finally to heaven. Dante consents and they go.

Canto II: The Descent

It is evening of the first day of the journey, Friday. Dante is tired and feels unworthy of the things Virgil describes. He is tempted to give up his first test. Virgil explains how Beatrice descended to him in Limbo and spoke of her worry about Dante. Beatrice was sent with the prayers of the Virgin Mary (Compassion), Saint Lucia (Divine Light), and Rachel (The Contemplative Life). Virgil rebukes Dante for hesitating when such great powers are concerned for him and Virgil himself has promised to lead him safely. Dante sees that such forces cannot fail him and he grows excited again.

Canto III: The Vestibule of Hell; The Opportunists

Virgil and Dante pass the Gate of Hell. The first souls in torment that Dante sees are the Opportunists, those who in life were only out for themselves. Mixed with them are those who took no sides in the Rebellion of the Angels. They are neither in Hell nor out of it. Unclassified, they race around forever through the dirty air; they are pursued by wasps who produce a constant flow of blood that is eaten by maggots. These people are punished as they sinned; they took no sides, therefore they are given no place. Since their own guilty consciences pursue them, they are pursued by wasps and hornets. Their actions were morally filthy, so they run eternally through the filth of maggots. Dante and Virgil move on to Acheron, the first of the rivers of Hell, where Charon ferries the newly arrived souls to punishment. Charon knows Dante is a living man and refuses him passage. Virgil forces Charon to serve them. Dante faints from fear and doesn't reawaken until he is on the other side.

Canto IV: Circle One—Limbo; The Virtuous Pagans

Dante wakes to find himself on the brink of Hell, which is a funnel-shaped cave below the northern hemisphere with its bottom point at the earth's center. Around the cave runs a series of ledges which Dante calls the Circles. Each Circle is assigned to punish one type of sin. The poets start to cross the First Circle, where they find the Virtuous Pagans who, because they were born without religion, can't come into the Light of God. Dante sees a great light and hears a voice welcoming Virgil back. This First Circle is Virgil's eternal place in Hell. Some of the great poets appear: Homer, Horace, Ovid, and Lucan. The group enters the Citadel of Human Reason and sees the Master Souls of Pagan Antiquity gathered, illuminated by the radiance of Human Reason, the highest state man can achieve without God. It dazzles Dante, yet he knows it is nothing compared to the glory of God.

Canto V: Circle Two—The Carnal

The poets enter the Second Circle, the Hell of the Violent and the Bestial. Minos, the semi-bestial judge who assigns each soul its eternal torment, blocks the way. Virgil silences him and they move on. They are on a ledge swept by a whirlwind, where the souls of the Carnal spin. The Carnal are those who abandoned reason in favor of their appetites; as punishment, they are swept forever in the wind of Hell. Dante recognizes Paolo and Francesca, two Italian lovers who had been caught and killed in the act of adultery. He asks them to tell their story. They pause from their flight to come to him. Francesca tells their story while Paolo cries. Overwhelmed, Dante faints again.

Canto VI: Circle Three—The Gluttons

In the Third Circle, a shower of stinking snow and rain forms a vile slush. Everything suggests garbage. The souls lie in the icy goop, and Cerberus, the three-headed dog of Hell, stands guard over them. As the souls climb out, Cerberus tears at them with his claws and teeth. These are Gluttons, those who made no other use of their lives than to wallow in food. As punishment, Cerberus slobbers over them as they slobbered over their food. On the edge of the next Circle, the poets encounter the monster Plutus

Canto VII: Circle Four—The Hoarders and The Wasters

Circle Five—The Wrathful and The Sullen

The poets enter the Fourth Circle and see a war in progress. The sinners are divided into two mobs, each soul pushing a boulder-like weight. The mobs meet, crashing their weights against each another, after which they separate, pushing the weights apart, and begin again. One mob is made up of the Hoarders, the other of the Wasters. In life, they lacked moderation, thinking of nothing but money. In death, their souls are encumbered by dead weights.

The poets come to a Black Spring that forms the Marsh of Styx, which is the Fifth Circle, the last station of Upper Hell. Across the marsh they see the souls of the Wrathful attacking one another in slime. The Sullen lie below the mud. In life they refused to welcome sunlight, so in death they are buried forever.

Canto VIII: Circle Five—Styx, The Wrathful, and Phlegyas
Circle Six—Dis and The Fallen Angels

The poets see the flames of the red tower of Dis, capital city of Hell, in the distance. Suddenly, Phlegyas, Boatman of Styx, races towards them across the river. He is greatly angered when he learns that his passengers will be allowed to return to the world above; however, he must bring them across the river.

While the boat is journeying across the water, a shiny form rises up and tries to grab Dante. The form—Filippo Argenti, a political enemy of Dante's—is quickly dragged off by other sinners.

Dante and Virgil come to the Iron Gate, where the Rebellious Angels refuse to let the poets pass. Even Virgil is powerless, for Human Reason cannot cope with evil. Only Divine Aid can bring hope. Virgil sends a prayer for help and waits for a Heavenly Messenger to appear.

Canto IX: Circle Six—The Heretics

The poets wait in dread. Three Infernal Furies, symbols of Eternal Remorse, appear on a nearby tower. They threaten the Poets and call for Medusa to change them to stone. Virgil tells Dante to turn and shut his eyes, and puts his hands over Dante's eyes to protect him. The poets then enter the Sixth Circle, where they see many tombs with their lids lying beside them, each in flames. These tombs belong to the Heretics, those who denied immortality, and their cries sound endlessly. In life the Heretics taught that the soul dies with the body, so their punishment is an eternal grave in a fiery morgue.

Canto X: Circle Six—The Heretics

Traveling further into the Sixth Circle, the poets meet two heretics. First, Farinata Degli Uberti, a great war chief of the Tuscan Ghibellines. Farinata recognizes Dante's voice as a Tuscan's and identifies him as an enemy. Their talk is interrupted by Cavalcante Dei Cavalcanti, the father of a contemporary poet, Guido. Cavalcanti asks Dante why Guido is not with him, if it is genius that leads Dante on his journey. Dante replies that he comes only with aid of powers Guido hasn't sought.

Farinata continues where he left off, defending his part in Florentine politics. He explains how the damned can foresee the future, but have no sense of the present. Dante leaves, telling Cavalcanti that his son Guido is still alive.

Canto XI: Circle Six—The Heretics

The poets reach the inner edge of the Sixth Circle and run for shelter because the air is so rank. Virgil outlines the divisions of Lower Hell, based on The Ethics and the Physics by Aristotle. It is about two hours before sunrise on Holy Saturday.

Canto XII: Circle Seven—The Violent
Round One—The Violent Against Neighbors

The poets have to evade the Minotaur, the half-man, half-bull creature that oversees Circle Seven. Virgil tricks him and they hurry by. They see the River of Blood, which marks the First Round of the Seventh Circle. Here, the Violent Against Their Neighbors—those who shed the blood of their fellow men—are punished by being eternally immersed in boiling blood. Centaurs patrol the banks, ready to shoot any sinner who raises himself out of the boiling blood beyond his permitted limit. Alexander the Great is here, up to his lashes in blood. One of the sinners, Chiron, assigns Nessus, a Centaur, to guide the poets across the boiling blood.

Canto XIII: Circle Seven, Round Two—The Violent Against Themselves

Nessus carries the poets across the river to the Second Round of the Seventh Circle, The Wood of the Suicides. These souls are encased in thorny trees; thus, those who destroyed their own bodies by committing suicide are denied a human form in the afterlife. The Harpies, half-man, half-beast creatures, eat the leaves of the trees, and the trees bleed. As long as the blood flows, the souls of the trees are able to speak. Since the point of their lives was self-destruction, in death they are allowed to speak only through that which destroys them; their voices can be heard only through their own bloodshed.

Canto XIV: Circle Seven, Round Three—The Violent Against God, Nature, and Art

The poets move on to the next round, a Plain of Burning Sand onto which an eternal Rain of Fire falls. This burning plain symbolizes sterility; the rain, which should bring life and fertility, is a deadening fire. Three classes of sinners must brave this fire: The Blasphemers, or The Violent against God; The Sodomites, or The Violent against Nature; and The Usurers, or The Violent against Art (which is the Grandchild of God).

The poets continue along the edge of the Wood of the Suicides and come to a red rill that flows boiling from the Wood and through the burning plain. Virgil explains the origin of the rivers of Hell. The rivers flow from the Old Man of Crete's tears. Each tear is symbolic of original sin.

Canto XV: Circle Seven, Round Three—The Violent Against Nature

Protected by the boiling rill, the poets walk along its banks across the burning plain. The Eighth Circle is before them. As they pass a band of Sodomites, one of them stops Dante. Dante barely recognizes him as Ser Brunetto Latino, a writer who had great influence on Dante's development. Brunetto prophesies Dante's sufferings at the hands of the Florentines and runs off across the plain.

Canto XVI: Circle Seven, Round Three—The Violent Against Nature and Art

Three Florentines whose policies Dante admired come running toward him to ask for news of Florence. Dante cannot stay, however, and the poets press on to the top of the falls. At Virgil's request, Dante removes the cord from his waist and Virgil drops it into the falls. From the teeming pool comes a distorted shape

Canto XVII: Circle Seven, Round Three—The Violent Against Art

The grotesque shape is Geryon, the Monster of Fraud. Virgil announces that they must fly from the cliff on the back of this monster. Dante examines the Usurers, the Violent against Art. They sit along the edge of the burning plain. Each has a purse with a coat of arms. Their eyes, gushing with tears, are forever fixed on these purses. Dante recognizes the coats of arms as those of well-known Florentine families. He rejoins Virgil and they fly from the great cliff. They are carried from the Hell of the Violent and the Bestial into the Hell of the Fraudulent and Malicious.

Canto XVIII: Circle Eight (Malebolge)—The Fraudulent and Malicious
Bolgia One—The Panderers and Seducers
Bolgia Two—The Flatterers

The poets are in the Eighth Circle, called Malebolge, The Evil Ditches. The Panderers and Seducers form two lines, driven at an endless fast walk by demons who hurry them along with lashes. In life these sinners goaded others to serve their own purposes. The demons who drive them symbolize the sinners' own vicious natures. The Flatterers are sunken in excrement as a punishment for their false flatteries when they were alive.

Canto XIX: Circle Eight, Bolgia Three—The Simoniacs

Dante next sees the Simoniacs, sellers of ecclesiastic favors and offices. As the Simoniacs mocked holy office, they are turned upside down in a mockery of the baptismal ceremony; because they made a mockery of the holy water of baptism, their punishment is a baptism by fire. Virgil brings Dante up to the Fourth Bolgia.

Canto XX: Circle Eight, Bolgia Four—The Fortune Tellers and Diviners

Dante stands in the middle of the bridge over the Fourth Bolgia looking down at the souls of the Fortune Tellers and Diviners. Their heads are turned backwards on their bodies, and they must walk backwards for eternity. Thus, the sin of these souls is now reversed on them: those who claimed to see the future cannot even see in front of themselves.

Canto XXI: Circle Eight, Bolgia Five—The Grafters

The poets reach the Fifth Bolgia, where the souls of the Grafters—those who have swindled in public office—dwell. The Grafters are caught in sticky, boiling tar and guarded by Demons, who tear them apart if they are caught above the pitch. The sticky pitch is symbolic of the sticky fingers of the Grafters. It also hides them from sight just as their dealings were hidden. Malacoda, the Grafters' leader, assures Virgil a safe trip. Virgil and Dante discover that the Bridge across the Sixth Bolgia is shattered, but some demons escort them to another one further down.

Canto XXII: Circle Eight, Bolgia Five—The Grafters

The Grafters disappear as soon as they see demons. One Grafter ducks too late and the demons seize him, about to claw him. The Grafter dives into the pitch. Two demons fly after him, but they are too late. The poets escape amid the confusion.

Canto XXIII: Circle Eight, Bolgia Six—The Hypocrites

The poets arrive in the Sixth Bolgia. Here the Hypocrites, weighed down by leaden robes, walk eternally around a narrow track. The robes are beautiful on the outside, but underneath the sinners must carry the terrible weight of their deceit eternally. The poets come upon Caiaphas, the High Priest of the Jews who advised the Pharisees to crucify Jesus. He is punished by being crucified on the floor of Hell by three stakes, positioned so that every passing sinner walks upon him. Virgil discovers that Malacoda lied to him about the bridges over the Sixth Bolgia—there is no passable bridge.

Canto XXIV: Circle Eight, Bolgia Seven—The Thieves

The poets climb the bank, cross the bridge of the Seventh Bolgia, and descend to observe the Thieves. The pit is full of reptiles who wrap themselves around the sinners, tying each sinner's hands behind his back. Because thievery is reptilian in its secrecy, it is punished by reptiles; the thieves' hands, the means by which they committed their crimes, are bound.

Canto XXV: Circle Eight, Bolgia Seven— The Thieves

Dante meets five noble thieves of Florence. All but one of the thieves transform before Dante's eyes. Agnello appears in human form and is merged with Cianfa, who has the form of a six-legged lizard. Eternal, painful transformation is the fate of the Thieves. Since they took others' belongings and made them their own, in Hell their own bodies are taken from them, leaving them to steal back a human form from another sinner.

Canto XXVI: Circle Eight, Bolgia Eight— The Evil Counselors

Dante turns to the Evil Counselors of the next Bolgia—those who have given fraudulent advice—who are hidden from view inside flames. Since they worked through hidden ways, they are hidden in great flames; as they sinned by speaking, the flames are a fiery imitation of tongues. The poets see a doubleheaded flame and discover Ulysses and Diomede punished together within it. They are being punished in the flame together because they warred against each other in their mortal life. Ulysses narrates the tale of his last voyage and death

Canto XXVIII: Circle Eight, Bolgia Nine—The Sowers of Discord

The poets come to the edge of the ninth Bolgia and look down at a group of grossly disfigured souls. They are the Sowers of Discord. Their sin was to destroy things that God meant to be united. They are hacked and torn for eternity by a demon with a sword. After each mutilation, the souls drag their broken bodies around the pit and return to the demon. During the circuit, their wounds heal in time to be ripped open again. These sinners are divided into three classes: The Sowers of Religious Discord, the Sowers of Political Discord, and lastly, Bertrand De Born, Sower of Discord Between Kinsmen. He separated father from son, so he now carries his head separated from his body; holding it with one hand by the hair.

Canto XXIX: Circle Eight, Bolgia Ten— The Falsifiers (Class I, Alchemists)

The Falsifiers are punished with many kinds of torment: darkness, stench, thirst, filth, disease, and shrieking. Some tear others to pieces. In life they corrupted society with their deceptions; in death they are in turn corrupted. Their senses are now an affliction, since in life they deceived the senses of others.

Canto XXX: Circle Eight, Bolgia Ten— The Falsifiers (The Remaining Three Classes: Evil Impersonators, Counterfeiters, False Witnesses)

The poets see two Evil Impersonators, or Falsifiers of Persons, racing around the pit. In life they preyed on the appearance of others. In death, they run without a break, seizing upon the apparition of those souls, while they in turn are preyed upon by the same souls they pursue. Next, the poets encounter Master Adam, a sinner of the third class, a Falsifier of Money or Counterfeiter.

Canto XXXI: Circle Eight, The Central Pit of Malebolge—The Giants

The poets approach the Central Pit, where Cocytus, the Ninth and final circle of Hell, lies. Dante sees a city of great towers, which are really Giants and Titans who stand guard inside the pit with the upper halves of their bodies rising above the rim. Virgil identifies Nimrod, who built the

Tower of Babel; Ephialtes, who warred against the Gods; and Tityos and Typhon, who insulted Jupiter. These sinners are returned to the darkness of their origins, as guardians of the earth's last depth.

Canto XXXII: Circle Nine, Cocytus—Compound Fraud
Round One—Caina, The Treacherous to Kin
Round Two—Antenora, The Treacherous to Country

Dante is on a huge frozen lake at the bottom of the Central Pit. This is Cocytus, the Ninth Circle, the last great water of Hell. Here, stuck in the ice, are sinners guilty of Treachery Against Those to Whom They Were Bound by Special Ties. The center of the ice expresses their natures. The first round is Caina, named for Cain. The second round is Antenora, named for the Trojan who betrayed his city to the Greeks. The poets discover two heads frozen together in one hole, one of them gnawing the nape of the other's neck.

Canto XXXIII: Circle Nine, Cocytus, Compound Fraud
Round Two, Antenora—The Treacherous to Country
Round Three, Ptolomea—The Treacherous to Guests and Hosts

The sinner who is gnawing his companion's head is Count Ugolino, and his victim is Archbishop Ruggieri. Both are in Antenora being punished for treason. In life they had plotted together, but Ruggieri betrayed Ugolino and caused him and his four sons to die of starvation. The killer is now the food of his victim. The poets now enter Ptolomea, named for the Maccabee who murdered his father-in-law at a banquet. Here are punished those who were Treacherous Against the Ties of Hospitality.

Canto XXXIV: Circle Nine, Cocytus, Compound Fraud
Round Four, Judecca—The Treacherous to Their Masters
The Center—Satan

The poets see Satan in the distance. All around him in the ice are the sinners of the last round, Judecca, named for Judas Iscariot. These sinners were Treacherous to Their Masters. They are completely sealed in the ice, twisted and distorted into every position. It is impossible to speak to them, so the poets move on to Satan. He is in the ice at the center to which all the rivers flow. In a parody of the Trinity, he has three faces, and in each mouth he holds a sinner whom he rips eternally with his teeth. Judas is in the central mouth; Brutus and Cassius are in the mouths on either side.

Having seen all of the Inferno, the poets climb through the center, pulling hand over hand up Satan's hairy body. They emerge from Hell. A long climb from the earth's center to the Mount of Purgatory awaits them, and they push on until they emerge to see the stars of Heaven, just before dawn on Easter Sunday.

THE GRAPES OF WRATH

ABOUT THE AUTHOR

John Steinbeck (1902–1968) was born in Salinas, California, a small town located a few miles from the Pacific coastline. Salinas is very near to the fertile agricultural land of the Salinas Valley, the setting of many of Steinbeck's stories.

Steinbeck studied Marine Biology at Stanford University but left before getting his degree. Steinbeck tried a free-lance writing career in New York, but he was highly unsuccessful. He returned to California, where he continued his literary attempts. His first success came in 1935, with the short novel *Tortilla Flat*. This was soon followed by other very well-received works, among them *Of Mice and Men*.

These early writings paved the way for what is generally acknowledged as Steinbeck's greatest novel: *The Grapes of Wrath*. In it, as in much of his other fiction, he writes of the hard and often disturbing life of the California migrant workers of the Depression. Steinbeck writes of a bitter reality that is at once grave and beautiful.

In 1962, Steinbeck was awarded a Nobel Prize. He died in his New York home in 1968.

THE BIG PICTURE

The Grapes of Wrath tells the story of the Joads, a family of poor farmers from Oklahoma who are forced to migrate to California in search of work. As they try desperately to survive, the Joads run into hardship after hardship at the hands of an unjust system run by those in positions of wealth and authority. But despite its bleak story, the novel also celebrates the strength of the human spirit in the face of adversity.

Why you're reading this book:
- *The Grapes of Wrath* is considered to be one of the finest works by one of America's greatest authors, John Steinbeck.
- It can be read on three levels:
  - As the story of the Joad family and their personal experiences.
  - As an overall history of all migrant farmers and their experience during that time in history.
  - As a depiction of American society at the time of the Depression—class conflict, who was in power, who was exploited.
- Steinbeck paints a very human, very moving picture of his characters. They are realistic and sympathetic.

Your teachers are looking for:
- The importance of symbols in the general chapters that create the setting and background for the Joads' story:
  - The turtle in Chapter III.
  - The grapes in Chapter XXV.
- The importance of family.
- The interplay between Steinbeck's realism and symbolism.
- The relationships and roles of the characters and how they change throughout the story.
- The "theology" of Jim Casy and its significance.
- The Californians' attitude toward the migrants
- The way the novel's plot alternates between the Joads' story and the general history of the migrant farmers.

KEY CHARACTERS

Tom Joad: The Joads' second son, he has just been released from prison, where he served four years for manslaughter. He is good at heart but quick to anger.

Ma Joad: The leader of the Joad family, strong and tough. She is the calming force that keeps the family together through the journey West.

Jim Casy: A former preacher who joins the Joad family on their trip. He believes in the goodness of man and his actions.

Pa Joad: The head of the Joads, he has the final say in family matters. Despite his strength and fairness, he cannot hold the Joads together.

Rose of Sharon: The Joads' eldest daughter, pregnant throughout the novel. Although she whines and complains a lot, at the end of the novel she makes a truly heroic gesture.

Al Joad: The irresponsible, woman-chasing youngest son. He idolizes Tom.

Noah Joad: The oldest of the Joad boys, slightly retarded due to injuries that he suffered during birth.

Grampa and Granma Joad: Very loving of each other and their family, both die on the trip out West.

Uncle John: Quietly industrious, he lost his wife when the two were young and has never quite recovered.

Mr. and Mrs. Wilson: A couple who travel with the Joads before stopping at the California border.

Mr. and Mrs. Wainwright: A couple who live with the Joads in a boxcar in California. Their daughter, Agnes, gets engaged to Al.

Muley Graves: The Joads' old Oklahoma neighbor who will not leave his land.

Winfield and Ruthie: The youngest Joad daughters, ages ten and twelve.

ESSAY IDEAS

- Who is the strongest member of the Joad family? Why?
- Would you consider Jim Casy a Christ figure? If so, what is his "religion"? His message? Who are his disciples?
- Discuss the symbolism Steinbeck uses in the general chapters. Is it effective? Why? How does it add to the story?
- How do you think a wealthy landowner would write this story?
- Discuss the notion of family. What does it mean to Jim Casy? To Ma? To Al?
- What is the role of authority in *The Grapes of Wrath*? What is Steinbeck's opinion of those in authority?
- Discuss the deaths of Grampa, Granma, and Rose of Sharon's baby. What does each one show about the Joad family?
- What do you think Steinbeck's message is in *The Grapes of Wrath*? Is he making a political statement or telling one family's story, or both?

A SAMPLE ESSAY IN OUTLINE FORM

Discuss Jim Casy as a Christ figure. What characteristics and events make him one?
- Casy is at first contemplative, figuring out the "message."
  - Christ spent the first part of his life trying to decide his course.
- Casy develops his own "religion" of the good of humanity.
- Casy is willing to sacrifice himself for others:
  - Gives himself up to police in the camp for Tom's sake.
- Challenges authority with his message and pays severely for it.
- Both Christ and Casy die trying to gather people together in their belief.
- Casy leaves behind a "disciple" (Tom) who will try and continue his work.

Both Jim Casy and Christ tried to challenge the status quo, and both died for their efforts. However, they both left the groundwork for progress even after their deaths.

PLOT SUMMARY

Note: *The Grapes of Wrath* has two different types of chapters: those dealing with the Joads and those describing their surroundings or situation (called "general" chapters). General chapters are easily recognized by their exclusion of details like names and faces.

Chapter I The story opens in the drought-stricken land of Oklahoma. There has been only a little rain since May—it is now late in the summer and the crops are ruined. The once fertile farm land has turned into a dustbowl. The men just stand and look helplessly at the dusty wasteland. The women and children can only watch the men and hope that they will somehow find a way to weather the drought.

Chapter II Having established the setting, Steinbeck takes us to a truckers' stop alongside a highway. A man sits on the running board of one of the trucks, hoping to hitch a ride. He is wearing a new suit, cheaply made. The driver comes out of the restaurant. At first he refuses to give the man a lift, pointing to the "No Riders" sign on his truck. The man replies that some drivers would help him "even if some rich bastard" makes rules against taking hitchhikers. After a minute, the driver relents and gives the man a ride.

On the road, the driver starts questioning the man, and we learn that his name is Tom Joad. Joad has just gotten out of prison, where he served four years for killing another man in a fight. He is return-

ing to his family's farm, a small plot of only forty acres. The driver is surprised that a tenant farmer on such a small piece of land has not yet been evicted by his landowner.

Chapter III A turtle is trying to cross the highway. A woman driving by swerves to avoid it, but a young man in a truck hits the edge of its shell, flipping it over. The turtle frantically struggles before finally managing to right itself.

Chapter IV The driver leaves Tom off at the road to his family's farm. Watching the trucker drive off, he notices a turtle in the road. He picks it up, planning to give it to one of the kids in the Joad family.

Walking along the road to the farm, he sees a man sitting under a tree who recognizes him. The man is Jim Casy, a preacher who baptized Tom. He is no longer a preacher, however—after an affair with a member of his congregation, he lost faith in religion and decided that a man did not need to preach to lead a righteous life. He believes that his actions are all that truly matter.

Casy asks Tom why he has been away for so long. Tom tells him of the fight that landed him in prison—a man had slashed Tom with a knife so Tom killed him with a shovel. Life in prison, says Tom, was not bad; at least they got food and a bath every night. One former prisoner who was starving out in the free world committed a crime just to get back in.

Tom starts to leave. Casy asks if he can come with him to the farm to see Tom's father. Tom agrees, and the two continue down the road. When they reach the house, however, there is no one there.

Chapter V Steinbeck uses this chapter to give the reader a general picture of the situation in Oklahoma at this time. When a landowner evicted a tenant farmer, the farmer often would beg for another chance, another year to get better crops. But the landowner, ordered by the bank to kick the farmer and his family off of the land, couldn't compromise. A big tractor sent by the bank would then come and plow a straight line across the land, knocking down anything in its path—crops, wells, homes.

A tractor driver tells a tenant that his farm is scheduled to be plowed through that afternoon. The farmer recognizes the driver as a local and asks why he would plow through the land of his own neighbor. The driver can only reply that he is as poor as the tenant and needs the money. The farmer becomes enraged, but his anger has no direction. Tractor drivers are ordered by landowners who are ordered by banks who are ordered by someone else again; there is no one to blame.

Chapter VI The Joads' house has been smashed in on one side, the well is dry, and there are no signs of neighbors. Everyone, it seems, has been evicted from their land.

Tom Joad and Jim Casy spot a man walking toward them, but they cannot recognize him through the dust. He eventually gets close enough, and Tom identifies him as the Joads' neighbor Muley Graves.

Graves tells Tom that his father, Old Tom Joad, has moved in with his brother John. The Joad family is picking cotton, trying to save enough money for a car to drive to California. Tom asks if they can stay at Muley's house, but Muley tells him that his house has been destroyed as well; he just cannot bear to leave the land.

Tom asks Muley if he has any food, and the old man produces two rabbits. Even though Graves has little, he is willing to share. The three men cook and eat the rabbit. Their dinner is interrupted by cars approaching. Muley tells Tom and Casy that they have to hide or they will get in

trouble for trespassing—particularly Tom, who is on parole.

Muley takes them to a small cave. The three spend the night there, Tom outside on the ground, Casy lying awake thinking, and Graves asleep inside.

Chapter VII Steinbeck takes the reader to the used car lots. The lots are full of old, run-down cars and sneaky salesman who are willing to do anything to sell them. Their best clients are the tenant farmers, who know nothing about cars and are desperate for a way out of the Oklahoma dust-bowl.

Chapter VIII The sun has not come up, but Muley wakes up Tom and Casy, who decide to make their way to Uncle John's. Muley, however, does not go—he wants to remain with his land. On the way to Uncle John's, Tom tells Casy that John's wife died early in their marriage from complications during her pregnancy. Since then, Uncle John has been a pretty odd character.

When they reach Uncle John's house, they find that the family is moving out: all their furniture is out on the front lawn. Pa is there, bent down over a car, and Tom approaches him. At first his father does not recognize him; when he finally does, he asks Tom if he has broken out of prison. Tom assures him that he was paroled.

Old Tom tells his son that the family is moving to California, and that Ma has been distraught because she was afraid that she would never see Tom again. He brings Tom and Casy to Ma. She also asks Tom whether he escaped or was paroled, then joyfully welcomes him back.

Granma and Grampa enter in an excited bustle, followed by Noah, who is moving at a slower pace. Noah is slightly retarded, the result of Pa Joad trying to deliver him at birth without the help of a midwife. The family sits down to breakfast, and everyone turns to Casy for the prayer. Casy tries to explain that he is no longer a preacher, but Granma insists. He settles for a long speech on the holiness of mankind.

Pa and Tom go out after breakfast to look at the car, which Tom's brother Al—who is out chasing ladies—worked to buy. Tom asks about his sisters, Rose of Sharon, Ruthie, and Winfield. Pa tells him that Ruthie and Winfield (who are twelve and ten) are out with Uncle John, while Rose of Sharon is married and pregnant.

Al returns home. He idolizes his older brother Tom, and tries to imitate his every move.

Chapter IX Hundreds of families across Oklahoma are preparing to leave for California. They must sell almost all of their possessions. Buyers, realizing that the tenant farmers are desperate for money, only buy at the absolute lowest prices. Once possessions are sold and the truck loaded, the families begin their trek West.

Chapter X Ma talks with Tom about their impending trip to California. She has read handbills that depict it as a land of plenty, but she is not sure she believes them. Tom tells her that he heard in prison that the conditions out West were not much better than in Oklahoma.

Grampa awakes, talking of the grapes he will soon be able to eat when the family reaches California. Casy enters and asks Ma if he will be allowed to travel with the family—all he wants is to be with people. Ma says that the question will have to be decided by the men.

Pa returns from trying to sell the family's possessions, with only eighteen dollars to show for his efforts. With all the family present, the men sit down for the family "government." They decide that Casy will come along with the family, and

that preparations will run through the night so that the family can leave at dawn.

Before they go, Muley Graves visits them to say good-bye. Grampa then decides that he will stay on the land, like Muley. The family quickly huddles; while Grampa of course cannot remain in Oklahoma, the Joads are afraid he might get hurt if they force him to get on the truck. They decide to slip Grampa sleeping medicine in his coffee. He falls asleep and is loaded on the truck. Giving Muley their chickens, the family sets out.

Chapters XI–XII The farmland around Oklahoma, once populated by humans, now seems populated only by agricultural machines. Abandoned houses fall to the ravages of time and nature.

On Highway 66, the former inhabitants of the land make their way to California. Thousands of cars pass through, escaping from the abject poverty and hopelessness of the dustbowl. Along the way, cars often break down and spare parts are needed. Garage owners try to cheat the former tenants by overcharging for bad parts. Sometimes a man has to walk for miles to find an honest salesman.

Chapter XIII The Joad family is now traveling that road, on their way to California. Al asks Ma if she is afraid of what they'll find. Ma answers that she is only afraid of the waiting.

Granma asks if they can stop and go to the bathroom, and the family decides to pull over and have lunch as well. When they stop, the Joads realize that they forgot to pack water with everything else. They resolve to stop at the next gas station.

The station manager tells them that hundreds of families like the Joads have passed by, and he is planning to move West himself. While everyone is getting water, the family dog runs out in the road and is killed by a car. Everyone, particularly Rose of Sharon, is upset, but they must press on.

They drive until a little after nightfall. Pulling over to the side of the road to make camp, they meet two other migrants, Mr. and Mrs. Wilson from Kansas. Grampa is looking very ill and is suddenly unable to speak. The Wilsons offer their tent for him to lie down in. Soon after he lies down, Grampa has a heart attack. Despite Casy's best efforts (with Granma screaming at him to "Pray, goddamn you!"), he dies.

The family meets and decide that they will bury Grampa, even though it is against the law. The Joads wrap him up in a quilt and bury him with a note of explanation written on a page of their Bible. At the urging of the family, Casy makes a small speech, but he only speaks of the power of those still alive.

The two families eat dinner together, and we learn the Wilsons' story. They have been driving for weeks, but their car keeps breaking down and Mr. Wilson does not know how to fix it. After looking the car over, Al and Tom suggest that the two families travel together; the Wilsons can help carry some of the load, and Al and Tom can help take care of their car. The families agree to make the trip together.

Chapter XIV Steinbeck takes the reader out West, where there is the beginning of a migrant community. Hundreds of people, driven from their farms, have begun to form loose camps on the sides of roads. The people of the West regard this development with a mixture of confusion, fear, and resentment.

Chapter XV Dotting the roadside of Highway 66 are truck stops similar to the one described in Chapter II. At one of them, a waitress named Mae is serving some truck drivers. A poor migrant comes into the restaurant. He has only a few cents and a whole family to feed. Mae gives him a loaf of bread and some candy for his kids at almost no cost. The truckers leave, and Mae discovers that they have left extra money with their meals to cover her charity towards the family.

Chapter XVI Steinbeck returns to the Joads and the Wilsons, who are slowly making their way to California. The Wilsons' car, driven by Al, leads the way.

In the Wilsons' car, Rose of Sharon is telling Al and Ma about her husband Connie's dreams. When they reach the West, they want to leave the family and move into their own place. Her reverie is interrupted when the car begins making loud noises. The two cars pull over, and it is determined that the car has broken down again. Casy and Tom offer to stay with the car for the few days it needs to be fixed, then catch up with the rest of the family. Everyone agrees except for Ma. She takes the tire jack out of the car and threatens everyone with it, saying that she will not leave and break up the family. Everyone wisely decides it would be better to stay together.

While Casy and Tom work on the car, the rest of the family travels down the road in search of a place to stay. Casy confides in Tom that he is concerned about California—with so many people migrating there, will there be jobs for everyone? Tom only says that he is going to take things one day at a time.

Al returns, and the three men go in search of parts for the car. Luckily, they find a car lot run by a man who hates the owner, and he lets them get all the parts they need for only a quarter.

The family has camped out at a lot where it costs fifty cents per car, an expense that the Joads can ill afford. Tom tries to get the owner to give the family a break, but he will not hear of it. Tom is forced to look elsewhere for a place to stay.

An old man asks Pa where the family is going. Pa replies that they are going to California to look for work. The old man laughs harshly, saying that he is returning from the West and there are no jobs. He lost his wife and two children to starvation. Pa asks him about the handbills promising wealth and work. The man explains that landowners, to make sure they would get enough workers, had printed far more handbills than they needed. As a result, there are far too many workers, and wages and working conditions are very bad. The man then walks off into the night.

Chapter XVII In this chapter, Steinbeck interrupts the Joads' story to give a general narrative of how the migrant workers lived. The daily cycle of migrant families always remained the same. Early in the morning, they would start out on the road to the West, alone. Then, at night, all the families would come together in roadside camps, creating one big family. They would talk and laugh, share their stories. It was always early to bed; the traveling would begin again early in the morning.

Chapter XVIII The Joads finally reach the California border. They stop by a river to rest before attempting to cross the desert. A man and his son stop by the river, going the other way on the highway. The man says that he is going back home to Oklahoma; there isn't enough work in California and he would rather be poor at home. Pa presses him for more information, and he tells him that the fear of migrants has created a new slang word: "Okies." Okie at one time just meant that you were from Oklahoma; to those out West, it means "dirty son-of-a-bitch." Despite this, the Joads decide to try to reach the farmland that night.

Tom walks down the river with Noah, who tells him that he has decided to stay there. Tom tries to persuade his brother to stay with his family, but Noah only replies that he does not want to leave the river—he knows he is different from the other Joad children and wants to remain on his own. Our last view of Noah is of him slowly ambling down the river bank away from the Joad camp.

Back at the camp, Ma is tending to Granma, whose health is failing rapidly. A woman comes in and insists on holding a prayer meeting for the dying woman. Then a cop enters the camp and tells Ma that he wants the family back on the road by the morning; he doesn't want some "Okie" camp in this decent area.

Later in the evening, Tom explains the meaning of the word to her, and tells her of Noah's leaving. Low on food, money, and morale, the Joads prepare to get back on the road.

The Wilsons, however, cannot come. Mrs. Wilson is dying of cancer. The Joads, despite their own meager resources, leave some pork and two dollars with the couple. They load the truck with water for the desert trip and start back out on the road.

Ma, lying next to Granma, begins acting strangely during the trip. At a border patrol station, when an officer demands to search the truck, she says that they have a very sick old woman in the car and must hurry on. However, when they reach the next town, she says to continue driving and that Granma does not need a doctor.

When the family gets through the desert to the lush green of the California countryside, we find out the reason for Ma's behavior: Granma had died during the trip, and Ma wanted to be sure that the woman could rest in peace in beautiful country.

Chapter XIX This chapter once again places the Joads' story against a larger background, describing the history behind the migrant workers' situation. The land the Joads have entered, California, was once the property of Mexico. American settlers, lean and hungry, came and took it away. At first they only took a little of the land as "squatters," but gradually they took over.

California landowners see a parallel in the Okies. They are lean and hungry as the landowners themselves once were, before time and wealth softened their drive. The Okies represent the threat of change, and the landowners hate them for it. They offer the Okies only the lowest wages and use the money they save for guards to keep the Okies in line. Okies still pour into California, however, hoping to find some way to feed their families.

Chapter XX The Joads have to leave Granma's body at the coroner's office; they have neither the money nor the time to prepare her for burial. They continue on to find a spot to rest for the night. The camping space they find is filthy. A man explains the conditions to them: there is little work, at low wages. The police in the area expect the Okies to be "bull-simple"—if they show any signs of organization, the police will drive them off the land.

Casy sits off by himself. Tom approaches him and asks him what he's thinking of. Casy replies that he is thinking both of a way to repay the Joads for their hospitality and friendship and of a way to help the rest of the migrants.

Rose of Sharon and Connie are arguing. Rose tells Connie that she is very sick, and Connie says that they should have stayed in Oklahoma. Rose brings up their dream of owning a house; Connie answers her by getting up and walking away, out of the camp and down the road.

Ma makes stew for the family, the first meal with meat in it that they have had for a while. A group of hungry children gather around, and while the stew is not even enough for her family, Ma leaves a little in the pot for the kids.

Al has met a man named Floyd, who tells him and Tom that he has heard of possible work to the North. As they are talking, a man driving an expensive car comes into the camp and offers work. When Floyd asks him how much he is paying, the man will not answer and instead calls for a deputy. The deputy accuses Floyd of breaking into a car lot and arrests him. Tom speaks up for him, and the deputy threatens to arrest him too.

Floyd runs from the deputy. The deputy fires at him but misses, hitting a woman in the hand. When the deputy tries to give chase, Tom trips him up. Before the deputy can turn on Tom, Casy kicks him in the head and sends Tom away to hide. Casy then takes all the blame and lets the confused deputy arrest him.

When the chaos subsides, the Joad family decides that they must leave. Tom comes out of hiding and they pack up the truck. Uncle John, stinking drunk, has to be carried to the car. Out on the road, the Joads do not fare any better: a blockade keeps them out of the next town. Ma warns Tom to keep his cool, as he has already jeopardized his parole. She tells him that despite all the setbacks, they will make it: "...we're the people—we go on."

Chapter XXI All through the vast lands of California, the migrants looked for work and food. Wages continued to drop as competition for jobs increased. Native Californian workers began to hate and fear the Okies as much as the landowners did.

Chapter XXII The family finds a government-sponsored camp. It is cleaner than the last one, and the people govern themselves with little police intervention. The first morning, Tom finds a family that has been working on a farm, the Wallaces. They invite him to come along and work that day.

The rest of the family is not having as much luck. The other men cannot find work, and Rose of Sharon is bothered by a deranged woman who keeps babbling on about the evil of the people in the camp. Ma finally chases the woman away with a piece of wood.

The women's committee shows Ma and Rose of Sharon around the camp. There are working toilets (first discovered by Ruthie and Winfield, who were so surprised that the toilet flushed that they thought they had broken it), a market, and generally hospitable neighbors.

At work, however, Tom has found out that the police, spurred on by the landowners, are going to try to break up the camp. They are going to create a disturbance at the camp dance Saturday night, then use the disturbance as an excuse to make everyone leave.

Chapter XXIII In migrant camps, the constant fight to avoid starvation is broken up by nights of song and drink, when people can take comfort in each other and in alcohol. People bring along all sorts of instruments and noisemakers, and an impromptu orchestra is born.

Chapter XXIV Saturday comes, and the camp prepares for the dance. All the men are on the lookout for any disturbance—the camp will stop any fight or argument before the police can use it as an excuse to come in.

The possible "disturbance" is soon spotted when three men who claim to be invited by a camp member enter the dance. The camp's governor, Ezra Houston, instructs his men to stop any trouble the three men might try to make without hurting them. When one of the men tries to pick a fight,

all three are quickly and quietly detained.

Ezra's men are not quick enough, and the police come to the gate of the camp. But there is no disturbance for them to check out, only music. Houston has the three men put over the back fence and the dance continues. Rose of Sharon does not dance. Connie has left her and she is feeling sick, so she just sits and listens to the music.

Chapter XXV Spring has come, but while the land is beautiful, there are hard times for many. It is becoming increasingly difficult for smaller landowners to survive. They have to pay their workers almost nothing in order just to break even. Soon, they will have to sell out to the larger companies, much as the Okies themselves had to do.

Chapter XXVI Ma calls a meeting of the family. They have only enough food for the next few days, and work is scarce. While the government camp is the best they've seen, Ma says they have to leave to survive. They say their good-byes and head out on the road again.

While fixing a flat tire, they find out from a passerby that there is work only a little way up the road. The Joads are filled with excitement and anticipation, hoping that their luck has turned at last.

They find themselves at another worker's camp, in a peach orchard. Outside the camp are screaming migrants protesting the conditions inside. Wages are very low, and the manager will only accept the best peaches. As a family, the Joads only earn a dollar. That is not enough for Ma to feed the family, since the store at the camp is very overpriced.

Outside the fence encircling the camp are tents in which the protesters live. Tom sneaks out to visit them that night, and finds that it is Jim Casy who is organizing the people. The two talk about Jim's experience in the prison and the strike that Jim is leading.

Suddenly, a group of men surprises them. One of them hits Jim over the head and kills him. Enraged, Tom kills a policeman with a pickaxe and runs off into the night.

The next day, Tom finds Ma and tells her what has happened. He says that he will have to run away and hide so that the family will not get into trouble. Ma will not hear of it, however—the family must remain together. At night, the family drives out of the camp with Tom hidden in a pile of mattresses.

Later, on the road, Tom sees a sign for a camp for cotton pickers. He decides to go into hiding nearby, and the family drives to the camp.

Chapter XXVII Landowners have now begun advertising for cotton pickers. The job does not pay much, and the workers sometimes have to contend with rigged scales that cheat them out of their wages. But they do get food at the end of the day.

Chapter XXVIII Because they are one of the first to apply to the camp, the Joads get a boxcar to live in. They live with another family, the Wainwrights.

Trouble continues to follow them, however. Ruthie, while in a fight with a bigger girl, had threatened that her older brother who had killed two people would come and get her. When Ma hears this, she realizes that Tom must leave quickly or risk being found out.

She finds him hiding by a creek near the camp and says that they must say good-bye. Tom says that he is going to try to continue Casy's work, to try to organize the people. Ma reminds him that Casy was killed for his efforts, but Tom will not be swayed. Ma gives him some money and Tom leaves.

A farmer stops Ma on the way back to the boxcar and tells her that he needs cotton pickers the next day. Upon returning home, Ma finds a broken Pa, who is convinced that their lives are just about over. She tries her best to bolster his spirits. This is an important changing of roles: until now, Pa was still the acknowledged "head" of the family. Now Ma must try to lead on her own.

Al comes home with the news that he and the Wainwrights' daughter, Agnes, are getting married. This is a relief to everyone, as the two have been spending many late nights out together.

The Joads and the Wainwrights go to the job in the morning, but it is a dud—the farm is small and all the cotton is picked early in the day. When they return home, a heavy rain has begun to fall and Rose of Sharon is becoming increasingly ill.

Chapter XXIX A steady rain begins to drown out all hope in the migrant camps, washing away tents and cars and people. Men start to steal for food, while families crowd into barns above the flood line. The women watch their men, as they did back in Oklahoma, to see if the men will despair. But the setbacks only serve to fuel the men's anger, and life continues on.

Chapter XXX After a couple of days of rain, Rose of Sharon goes into labor. There is increasing danger that the boxcar will flood. Pa summons up one last bit of strength. and rallies the men to build a dam to protect the family's boxcar. Working through the night, the men are successful until a large tree hits the dam, punching a hole in it and letting the waters through. Pa returns to the boxcar to find that Rose of Sharon's baby is stillborn. They decide to bury it; they put it in a box and give it to Uncle John to take care of. Uncle John does not bury it, however; he merely lets it float away on the flood waters.

Despite efforts to build a platform in the boxcar, the Joads are flooded out in only a few days. They seek shelter in an abandoned barn, and are lucky enough to find some dry hay to lie down on.

Also in the barn are a boy and his father, who has been unable to eat anything solid for days and is slowly dying. Ma looks at Rose of Sharon, and the two women communicate without words: the man needs milk, and Rose of Sharon's breasts are filled with the milk intended for her stillborn baby. Ma takes everyone else out of the barn. Rose of Sharon, wrapped in a dry blanket, lies down by the man and pulls his head to her breasts.

GREAT EXPECTATIONS

ABOUT THE AUTHOR

Charles Dickens (1812–1870), the second of eight children, was born in the small town of Portsmouth, England. In 1823, his family moved to London. Soon after, Dickens' father, John, was sent to debtors' prison. Mrs. Dickens sent Charles, age 12, to work in the Warren's Blacking Warehouse. The early struggles of Dickens' life were to have great impact on his later writing. His experience in the factory, for example, is chronicled in *David Copperfield*.

Dickens eventually finished school at the Wellington House Academy and went on to work, first as an attorney's clerk and later as a law reporter. His industry and imagination eventually earned him a position as a reporter for the *Morning Chronicle* and sufficient readership to begin publishing *Sketches by Boz* and *Pickwick Papers* in serial form.

During this period of success, Dickens married Catherine Hogarth. Unfortunately, domestic harmony did not follow as Dickens, soured by a previous four-year courtship, had a rather odd perspective on "love." The marriage was for the most part unhappy.

Nonetheless, Dickens continued to write, publishing *Oliver Twist* in 1837, *Nicholas Nickleby* in 1838, *The Old Curiosity Shop* in 1840, *Barnaby Rudge* in 1841, *A Christmas Carol* and *Martin Chuzzlewit* in 1843, *Dombey and Son* in 1846, and *David Copperfield* in 1850. Through these novels, he became known for his sharp wit tempered by broad comedy, and for his social criticism.

Never resting on his laurels, Dickens went on to publish *Bleak House* in 1853, *Hard Times* in 1854, and *Little Dorrit* in 1857. By this time, however, Dickens' marriage had begun to fall apart, aided by his illicit relationship with an 18-year-old actress. He moved to Rochester and settled into his dream house, Gad's Hill Place. There he produced *A Tale of Two Cities* in 1859, *Great Expectations* in 1861, and *Our Mutual Friend* in 1865.

During 1867 and 1868, Dickens conducted an extremely successful reading tour in the United States, but returned on the brink of exhaustion. His health declined rapidly and he died in 1870, leaving his final work, *The Mystery of Edwin Drood*, unfinished.

THE BIG PICTURE

Great Expectations is the story of the life and ambitions of Pip, an orphan. He rises up to a life of wealth (thanks to an anonymous benefactor), but finds that ambition and success aren't always what they seem.

Why you're reading this book:
- It is considered to be one of the classic works of one of the finest writers in English literature, Charles Dickens.
- It is very accurate in its portrayal of Victorian life.
- Dickens' use of exaggerated characters is both entertaining and highly satirical.
- Its plot is finely woven and intricate.
- The book's central themes—good versus evil, ambition versus real values—are as relevant to day as in Dickens' time.

Your teachers are looking for:
- How this book relates to other books by Dickens.

- Dickens' use of foreshadowing.
- Your own views of Pip's "great expectations." Are they realistic? Are they worthy?
  - How the novel portrays women.
  - How Pip's values change throughout the novel.
  - What Dickens is saying about social status and social graces.

KEY CHARACTERS

Pip: The narrator and main character, he is an orphan whose "great expectations" are the focus of this book.

Miss Havisham: A strange and eccentric old lady who was deserted at the altar. She has remained in her house ever since.

Estella Havisham: The adopted daughter of Havisham, she is brought up to be cruel and cold. Pip loves her.

Magwitch: The convict who turns out to be Pip's benefactor and Estella's father. Despite his criminal traits, he turns out to be a sympathetic character.

Joe Gargery: Pip's adoptive father. He is coarse, a country blacksmith. Despite Joe's quiet dignity, Pip is ashamed of him.

Mrs. Joe: Pip's adoptive mother, in truth his sister. She is quick to swing her cane for discipline purposes. The quintessential heavy-handed matriarch.

Herbert Pocket: Pip's best friend in London. His father acts as Pip's tutor.

Mr. Jaggers: A reputable London defense lawyer, he oversees Pip's welfare.

Wemmick: Jaggers' assistant. He invites Pip to his home and helps Pip on many occasions.

Compeyson: Another convict. He is the man that deserted Miss Havisham, and is a lifelong enemy of Magwitch.

Biddy: Pip's common orphan friend that he leaves behind when he moves to London.

Bentley Drummle: A rather pompous young man who ends up marrying Estella. He lives at the Pockets' at the same time as Pip.

ESSAY IDEAS

- Discuss Pip's "expectations." Do you feel they are worthwhile? Realistic? How do they change throughout the book?
- Compare/contrast Joe and Magwitch. How are they alike? How do they represent good? Evil?
- Discuss Dickens' use of foreshadowing. What "clues" does he place throughout the story?
- Do you like Dickens' revised or original ending better? Why?
- Compare/contrast Biddy and Estella.
- Do you think of Pip as being good, evil, or a combination of both? Defend your answer.
- What do you think Dickens is trying to say about ambition?

A SAMPLE ESSAY IN OUTLINE FORM

Compare Joe and Pip. How are they alike? Who is happier?
- Similarities:
  - Background and home (Joe is Pip's guardian).
  - Fondness for friends, particularly Biddy.
  - Pip at first sees Joe as a role model.
- Pip changes:
  - Pride and "great expecations" take over.
  - Rejects Joe and Biddy—becomes ashamed of them.
- Joe remains the same:
  - Leads a simple but happy life.
  - Marries Biddy after Mrs. Joe's death.

Pip and Joe are friends and equals at the beginning of the story. However, Pip's ambition changes him and he turns away from his friends and his past. This does not gain him happiness, however, and at the end we realize that Joe's simple life, uncomplicated by "great expectations," has served him better.

PLOT SUMMARY

Chapter One   The novel opens on Christmas Eve, as our seven-year-old narrator Pip is visiting the graves of his parents. Suddenly, a terrifying man with a chain around his leg jumps out of the marshes—an escaped convict from the local prison. After finding no food on Pip, he demands that the boy get "wittles" and a file for him the next morning or he will kill him. He threatens Pip that he also has a companion who will do Pip great harm if he does not obey. Pip promises that he will return and runs home.

Chapters Two–Three   Pip returns home to his sister and her husband (Mrs. Joe and Joe). Joe is kind to Pip, but Mrs. Joe is a quick-tempered woman, often using the "Tickler," a piece of cane "worn smooth by collision with [Pip's] tickled frame." She does not hesitate to use the Tickler on her husband as well.

Pip keeps part of his dinner for the convict. Later that night, he hears guns going off outside—a sign that another convict has escaped. At dawn, he sneaks into the kitchen and steals more food, including a pork pie, as well as Joe's file. Pip then heads out to the marshes, wittles and file in tow.

In the foggy marshes, Pip approaches a man sitting with his back to him. When he taps the man on the shoulder, he is terrified to find that the man is not the original

convict. Pip runs away, thinking that this must be the convict's companion. Upon meeting the original convict, Pip tells him of the other man in the marshes. The convict becomes very angry, demanding to know where Pip saw the man. When Pip tells him that the other man had a bruised face, the convict loses all control and starts frantically filing away at the chain on his leg. Pip takes this opportunity to run away, unnoticed.

Chapter Four   Pip returns home to a brusque Mrs. Joe, who sends him and Joe out to church to represent the family at mass—she is too busy preparing the house for Christmas dinner. Neither Pip nor Joe enjoys the service, Joe because his clothes are uncomfortable and Pip because his conscience is itching.

Back at home, dinner is served and a number of guests—Mr. Wopsle, Mr. and Mrs. Hubble, and Uncle Pumblechook—are in attendance. Pip sits in fear of his theft being discovered, a fear that is well-founded as Mrs. Joe soon goes to get the pork pie. Pip moves to run away, but is met at the door by a group of soldiers with handcuffs, who he is sure have come for him.

Chapters Five–Six   Pip's overactive conscience is playing tricks on him, however; the soldiers have only come to get the handcuffs repaired by Joe, who is a blacksmith. Joe fixes the shackles; the men, including Pip, go out to the marshes to try to find the two escapees.

They find the convicts fighting in the marshes and promptly separate and chain them. Before the soldiers drag the prisoners off, Pip's convict announces that he himself stole the wittles, thereby getting Pip off the hook. Joe replies that he was welcome to the food: "We wouldn't have you starved to death." The convicts are taken away on a prison-ship.

Pip, despite his guilty feelings, cannot bring himself to tell Joe the truth about the food. The two return home, and Pip is sent to bed by Mrs. Joe.

Chapter Seven Pip's education consists of an apprenticeship with Joe and night classes, where the teacher consistently sleeps through the session. However, Pip's education is better than that of the illiterate Joe. One day, Pip shows Joe a letter that he wrote. Although it is poorly written, Joe is impressed: all he can make out are J's and O's. Despite Joe's lack of "book learning," Pip still looks up to him tremendously.

Mrs. Joe and Uncle Pumblechook return from a business trip with news for Pip: he is to go and play at Miss Havisham's house. Pip spends the night at Uncle Pumblechook's, preparing for his visit.

Chapter Eight The visit to Miss Havisham's is very strange indeed. Pumblechook and Pip are met at the gate to the house by a rude young girl. She lets only Pip in and brings him to see Miss Havisham. Miss Havisham is sitting in a darkened room, alone with her broken heart. She demands that Pip play for her amusement. Estella, the little girl at the gate, enters the room and the two play cards. Estella beats him easily and makes fun of his coarse appearance. At the end of the day, Miss Havisham orders Pip to return in six days. He is led out by Estella like "a dog in disgrace."

Chapters Nine–Ten When Pip returns home, he is immediately questioned by Mrs. Joe. Thinking the adults will not understand the truth about his visit, he tells an impressive tale of velvet couches and fighting dogs. Mrs. Joe and Pumblechook are quick to buy his lies. But when

Joe enters, Pip begins to feel guilty. He gets Joe alone and confesses that his stories were not true. Joe is not angry and merely tells Pip not to do it again.

The next day, Pip decides to try to make himself less common and enlists the help of another orphan, Biddy, in his effort. His thoughts on the subject are interrupted by a very strange occurrence at a tavern with Joe. There, Pip meets a stranger. He soon finds that the stranger is stirring his drink with Joe's file! The man gives Pip a shilling wrapped in two one-pound notes as he is leaving.

Chapters Eleven–Thirteen Pip again visits Miss Havisham's. He plays with Estella and some of her cousins in a strange, dusty room. The room has in it the cobwebbed remains of Miss Havisham's wedding cake.

This time, due to Pip's tussle with one of her sickly cousins, Estella is far more impressed with him. She even allows Pip to kiss her cheek. Pip, however, gains no pleasure from it, feeling "that the kiss was given to the coarse common boy as a piece of money might have been, and was worth nothing."

Pip's visits to Miss Havisham's continue regularly. Although the old lady asks about Pip, she makes no move to offer him assistance or advice of any sort. This lack of help does not keep Pumblechook and Mrs. Joe from babbling on about Miss Havisham's possible interest in Pip's future.

After several months, Miss Havisham instructs Pip to bring Joe with him on his next visit. She then officially names Pip apprentice to Joe and pays the boy a large sum of money. The pair return and Joe, Pip, Mrs. Joe, and Pumblechook celebrate in the tavern. Pip, however, is unhappy: "I was truly wretched, and had a strong conviction on me that I should never like Joe's trade."

Chapters Fourteen–Fifteen Pip is very ill at ease at home and in his apprenticeship, and his thoughts often return to Miss Havisham's—to Estella, in particular. He asks Joe for a holiday to visit the old woman, and Joe, after some protest, agrees.

On his visit, however, he is greeted at the door not by Estella but by Sarah Pocket, a cousin. Estella is away, overseas. Miss Havisham almost taunts Pip with the news, telling him that "she is far out of reach; prettier than ever; admired by all who see her. Do you feel that you have lost her?" She does invite Pip back for his birthday.

Upon returning home, Pip finds that Mrs. Joe has been knocked senseless during a break-in. Everyone assumes that it was an escapee from the prison, and Pip learns that a filed-away leg chain was found beside her.

Chapters Sixteen–Seventeen Life continues on, with at least one very important change: Mrs. Joe has been injured in the head and is no longer so quick to anger, which brings a bit of a peace over the household. Orlick, an assistant of Joe's, is suspected to have been the one who injured her, but nothing is ever proven.

Pip continues to visit with Miss Havisham. He begins to grow closer to Biddy, who has grown into a wholesome young woman. One day while the two are out walking, he tells her that he wants to become a gentleman so that he might win Estella. Biddy, who is secretly in love with Pip, takes the news quietly, commenting only that if Pip must become a gentleman to gain Estella, "I should think—but you know best—she was not worth gaining over." Pip agrees, but can do nothing to change his feelings. On their way home, the two are interrupted by Orlick, who offers to accompany them. Biddy asks Pip to keep Orlick away from them because

she is scared of him.

Chapters Eighteen–Nineteen Four unhappy years pass for Pip. However, his luck finally changes. One night at the tavern he meets a man named Jaggers, who informs him that because of an unnamed benefactor, he has become a "gentleman of great expectations." To meet these expectations, however, Pip must leave Joe and Biddy for London, where he will be tutored by Matthew Pocket. The final condition is that Pip must always keep his name.

Pip is happy but subdued, as he must leave his friends. Joe and Biddy keep a stiff upper lip, saying that they are happy for his good fortune. Biddy, however, takes issue when Pip says he intends to help Joe with his manners. Pip responds by accusing her of being jealous of his success.

Before leaving, he is showered with all compliments by everyone from Pumblechook to the tailor that outfits him with new clothes. Pip enjoys the attention. When it is time for him to leave, he does so quickly, without a proper good-bye to Joe or Biddy.

Chapter Twenty Pip travels to London to meet with Mr. Jaggers in his office. Jaggers' office is ill-kept and rather dingy, belying his stature as a highly sought-after defense attorney. Jaggers is out when Pip arrives, so he takes the opportunity to explore the area. At Newgate Prison, he encounters a "partially drunk minister of justice" who gives him a tour of the prison grounds.

Pip returns to Jaggers' office. Along the way, he finds the lawyer talking with some of his clients, all of whom are depending on Jaggers to get them acquitted. Jaggers is aloof, paying attention only to those who have paid his assistant, Wemmick.

In Jaggers' office, Pip finds out that he will receive many benefits from the lawyer:

a healthy allowance, tutoring, and credit lines with many of the local merchants. Pip then walks to the Barnard Inn with Wemmick. He is to stay there with his tutor's son, Herbert Pocket.

Chapters Twenty-one–Twenty-three At the inn, Pip finds much to his surprise that Herbert is a cousin of Estella's—the same cousin he had beaten up several years before during a visit to Miss Havisham's! Herbert and Pip click immediately; Herbert nicknames Pip "Handel," after "a charming piece of music by Handel called 'The Harmonious Blacksmith'."

Herbert tells Pip the story of the strange Miss Havisham. A wealthy heiress, she had been wooed by a gentleman who took much of her money then left her standing at the altar. From that point on, Miss Havisham kept herself locked up in her house. Estella, whom she adopted, is a product of Havisham's hatred for men.

We find out more about Herbert as well. The young Pocket is a dreamer, harboring even "greater expectations" than Pip while working unpaid in a counting-house. The next night the pair go to the Pockets', where Pip will be staying.

The Pocket household is chaotic and unruly, largely the result of Mrs. Pocket. Any order in the boarding house is maintained by the servants. Pip's neighbors in the house are Bentley Drummle and Startop. Dinner is highly eventful: Mrs. Pocket can't seem to corral all of her rambunctious kids, and Mr. Pocket tries "with one very strong effort to lift himself up by the hair."

Chapters Twenty-four–Twenty-six Mr. Pocket does turn out to be a helpful tutor, not only educating Pip with books, but also about London. Pip decides, with Jaggers' permission, to stay with Herbert at the Inn.

Pip begins to learn more of Jaggers, a hard man who keeps mementos from clients of his that have been hanged. He also learns more about Wemmick. He visits Wemmick's house at Walworth, a tiny psuedo-castle. There he meets Wemmick's father, the "Aged." Wemmick's doting behavior towards his father is far different from his brusque and businesslike manner when he is at work.

Pip visits Jaggers' house as well, bringing Herbert, Startop, and Drummle for dinner. Jaggers never locks his doors, daring any man to come rob him (none do), and keeps Molly, "a wild beast tamed," as a servant. At dinner, Drummle behaves terribly, nearly throwing a glass at the cheery Startop. Jaggers takes a liking to him, however, nicknaming him the "Spider." Despite his affection for Drummle, he warns Pip to stay away from him.

Chapters Twenty-seven–Twenty-eight Pip receives a letter from Biddy telling him that Joe will be visiting him soon. Here we see how much Pip has changed; he is ashamed of Joe and afraid that Drummle will see the uneducated blacksmith. When Pip brings Joe to Drummle's, both are tense and Joe leaves without taking dinner. He does give Pip an important piece of news: Estella is back at Miss Havisham's and wants to see him.

Pip travels by coach back to his hometown the next day. While riding, he realizes that among the passengers are two prisoners—one of whom is the original convict that he gave food and a file to. He overhears the convict telling his companion that he had sent a man to try to find out "that boy that fed him." Pip, who had originally planned to stay at Joe's while visiting Estella, decides to stay at an inn outside town.

Chapter Twenty-nine Going to Miss Havisham's, Pip is greeted by none other

than Orlick, who left Joe's employ at the
same time Pip did. The two have an unpleasant exchange.

While the house and Miss Havisham are
the same, Estella is completely changed,
now a beautiful woman. She is still arrogant, however, walking with an "air of com-
pleteness and superiority." Her high stature
again makes Pip ashamed of his lowly
friend Joe.

Pip visits further with Miss Havisham
and finds out that Jaggers will be coming
to the house that evening for dinner.
Before he arrives, Miss Havisham grabs Pip
and says of Estella, "If she favours you,
love her. If she wounds you, love her." Pip
takes this plea to heart and spends the
night saying over and over into his pillow,
"I love her!"

Chapters Thirty–Thirty-one Pip returns
to London and Herbert the next day. He
tells the young Pocket of his love for
Estella, to which Herbert replies, "This
may lead to miserable things," a remarkably clairvoyant response. The two find a
playbill from a production of *Hamlet* that
Joe left during his visit. The production,
slated for that night, stars Mr. Wopsle, an
acquaintance of Pip's from back home. Pip
and Herbert decide to attend. The play,
while marred by "several curious little circumstances" and a loudly active audience,
is enjoyable.

Chapters Thirty-two–Thirty-three A letter from Estella arrives, simply informing
Pip that he is to meet her at the coach in
London in two days. Pip cannot eat or
sleep until the day arrives, and shows up
hours early for the coach. He is rescued
from a long wait when he bumps into Wemmick, who takes him on a tour of Newgate
prison.

After a few hours' wait, Pip meets Estella
at the coach. He rides on with her to Rich-

mond, where she is to be staying with an
influential lady. During their short time
together, she is alternately kind and cold.
Pip returns to London "with a worse heart-
ache" than before.

Chapters Thirty-four–Thirty-five Pip begins to feel the contrast between his new
life and his life with Joe and Biddy. Estella
and her expectations of Pip take precedence: "Many a time of the evening, when I
sat alone looking at the fire, I thought,
after all, there was no fire like the forge
fire... Yet Estella was so inseparable from
all my restlessness...." Pip's life at London
has become dissolute, and he is debt-rid-
den.

A letter from home informs Pip that Mrs.
Joe has died. The news sends him into
depression, and memories of his childhood
pervade his everyday thoughts. The funeral gives Pip a chance to talk with Biddy
again, and he promises that he will visit
her and Joe more often. Biddy indicates
that she does not trust Pip to keep his
vow. Despite himself, Pip realizes that she
is probably correct.

Chapters Thirty-six–Thirty-seven Herbert and Pip continue to fall further into
debt. Pip, however, is bailed out when Jaggers gives him five hundred pounds (his
yearly allowance) on his twenty-first birthday. Pip asks Jaggers if he will find out the
identity of his anonymous benefactor
soon, but Jaggers will give him no hints.

Pip asks Wemmick if there is any way
for him to help Herbert with his finances.
Wemmick helps him by finding a merchant,
Clarriker, who employs Herbert without
disclosing Pip's involvement. Upon seeing
Herbert's great joy at finally getting gainful
employment, Pip narrates: "I did really cry
in good earnest when I went to bed, to
think that my expectations had done some
good to somebody."

Chapter Thirty-eight Referring to the house where Estella is staying, Pip narrates, "If that staid old house near the green at Richmond should ever come to be haunted when I am dead, it will be haunted, surely, by my ghost." He continues to visit Estella constantly, gaining no pleasure from their relationship but refusing to give her up.

The two visit Miss Havisham. Havisham still obviously hates men and intends to use Estella as her revenge against them, but the two women are growing apart. For the first time ever, Pip hears them argue. Pip and Estella also get into a fight over Drummle's advances toward Estella.

Chapter Thirty-nine Pip is now twenty-three. One evening after his birthday, he is visited in London by a strange man, "Substantially dressed, but roughly, like a voyager by the sea." Pip soon discovers that the man is the convict that he helped in the marshes so many Christmas Eves ago. Furthermore, he finds out that this man is his anonymous benefactor. In a rush, Pip realizes that all his great expectations have been but a mirage: "Miss Havisham's intentions to me, all a mere dream; Estella, not designed for me." But the harshest realization for Pip is that he deserted Joe for his ill-founded ambitions.

Chapters Forty–Forty-two Pip's benefactor, named Magwitch, stays at the inn, and Pip is presented with another problem: he is harboring a criminal. His fear is further intensified when he finds out from the watchman that another stranger had seen Magwitch enter the night before. The pair agree that Magwitch will pose as Pip's uncle, taking the name of Provis. Herbert is told of Pip's strange benefactor and meets Magwitch. The two younger men ask Magwitch for more information of his past, and the convict happily obliges.

Magwitch was a small-time crook until he met up with a hard-core villain named Compeyson, who worked many different scams. For one such crime, both Magwitch and Compeyson were found guilty. However, Magwitch had done most of the dirty work; Compeyson received a far lighter sentence. Both escaped, and Compeyson was the second convict that Pip came upon near his home as a child.

Magwitch also tells of meeting Compeyson and one of his partners, Arthur. The two had taken a large sum of money from a rich lady a few years back, but squandered it. Herbert, who has been listening to Magwitch, writes Pip a note: Arthur, the young man that Magwitch had met while working with Compeyson, was a Havisham; Compeyson was the notorious gentleman that stole Miss Havisham's money and left her at the altar. Magwitch does not know whether Compeyson is still alive.

These chapters illustrate Magwitch's strength of character despite his criminal background. He has been Pip's benefactor because of his gratitude for the little boy that stole "wittles" for him. Pip, however, is ashamed of the man, much as he is ashamed of Joe.

Chapters Forty-three–Forty-six Convinced that his repulsion towards Magwitch lies in his feelings for Estella, Pip goes to Miss Havisham's to visit her. There he finds an unrepentant Miss Havisham, who admits to letting Pip think that she was his benefactor. Pip also learns that Estella is to marry the unsavory Drummle. He professes his undying love for her and leaves.

Back at the inn, the watchman gives Pip a note from Wemmick telling him not to return home. Pip immediately goes to Wemmick's "castle."

He finds out that his room is under watch and guesses that Compeyson, who is alive and well in London, is responsible.

Magwitch is moved to the house of a young lady that Herbert is courting, where he will remain until things settle down.

Pip visits Magwitch/Provis, who is now using the name Campbell. He and Herbert come up with a plan to get Pip's benefactor out of England: they will row a boat daily on the river close to the boarding-house. Says Herbert, "You fall into the habit, and then who notices or minds?" Once their routine has been established, they will sneak Magwitch out to a ship.

Chapter Forty-seven The world begins to close in on Pip in more ways than one. He is falling deeper into debt, and is "pressed for money by more than one creditor."

Pip and Herbert go to see the hapless actor Mr. Wopsle in a Christmas show. A highly agitated Wopsle meets them after the play ends, saying that he is sure he saw one of the convicts from Pip's youth sitting behind him. Pip and Herbert realize it was Compeyson.

Chapter Forty-eight One night, while going to visit Magwitch, Pip meets up with Jaggers, who invites him over for dinner. Pip notices that Molly, Jaggers' servant, has "Estella's hands, and her eyes were Estella's eyes." Later, he asks Wemmick to tell him of Molly's past.

It turns out that Molly had come into Jaggers' care after the lawyer had represented her in a murder case. Molly was said to have killed another woman over jealousy, and Jaggers, through some slick legal maneuvering, had gotten her acquitted. Molly, Wemmick said, had a daughter that she was rumored to have killed.

Chapter Forty-nine Pip goes again to visit Miss Havisham, who has changed greatly. She begs for Pip's forgiveness for all the hurt she has caused him. She gives him a note for nine hundred pounds (to ease Herbert's financial woes) and begs him to write under her name, "I forgive her." Pip learns nothing more from her about Estella, except that she was brought to Miss Havisham by Jaggers.

He looks around the old place, trying to digest everything that Havisham has said. Upon returning to her, he finds that her dress is on fire—she has sat too close to the fireplace. Pip saves her life (and burns himself) by grabbing her and rolling on the floor. Miss Havisham is badly injured, however, and remains in a delirium until Pip leaves the next day, pleading over and over, "Take the pencil and write under my name, 'I forgive her!'"

Chapters Fifty–Fifty-one The mystery of Estella's birth is finally solved. When Pip returns to London, he learns that Magwitch was once married to a woman who was tried for murder, and that this woman was Molly. Magwitch had a baby girl by Molly, and this baby was Estella. Before they parted ways, Molly threatened Magwitch that she would kill the girl, and Magwitch assumed the threat was carried out. Magwitch's great hatred of Com-peyson arises partly from Compeyson's continually reminding him of that threat.

Pip confronts Jaggers with his discoveries, and the lawyer fills in the final pieces of the puzzle. Estella came into his care after Molly's trial. He sent her to Miss Havisham's in hopes "that here was one pretty little child out of the heap that could be saved." Jaggers asks that Pip not confront Estella with his knowledge, as it can only do her harm.

This final unraveling of a mystery is typically Dickensian. He is a master of placing small clues throughout the novel that eventually weave together to form a solution. For further examples of this, see *A Tale of Two Cities*.

Chapters Fifty-two–Fifty-three Pip receives two letters. The first is from Wemmick, who advises him to get Magwitch out by boat soon. The other, unsigned, tells him to go to the sluice-house if he wants "information regarding your Uncle Provis." Because Pip has not recovered from the burns he received saving Miss Havisham, he arranges for Startop to help Herbert with Magwitch's escape.

Pip goes to the sluice-house that night. It appears that no one is there, but when he enters the shed, "the next thing that I comprehended was that I had been caught in a strong running noose, thrown over by behind." He has been trapped by none other than his old enemy Orlick, who is now working with Compeyson. Orlick says that he is going to kill Pip and starts to come at him with a hammer. Before he can touch Pip, however, a group of men surprises him and he runs away. Pip and Herbert return to London to try to liberate Magwitch.

Chapter Fifty-four Pip and Herbert succeed in getting the old convict safely out of the boarding-house that night. Herbert and Startop row until they are too tired to continue. The group banks the ship and stays at a deserted inn along the river.

In the morning, they make for the steamer *Hamburg* that is to take Magwitch to safety. When they are only a short way from the ship, another boat comes up alongside, carrying a hooded man—Compeyson. The other boat, a police galley, demands that Pip stop, and rams into their boat. A struggle ensues, and a steamer rams into both of the smaller boats, spilling convicts and crew into the water.

Pip, Magwitch, Herbert, and Startop are hauled into the police galley; Compeyson is nowhere to be found. They are taken back to the inn, where Pip is allowed to get dry clothes for Magwitch. The police also confiscate Magwitch's possessions—Pip will no longer be benefitting from Magwitch's assistance as a benefactor.

All of Pip's original ill feelings toward Magwitch have vanished. He says, "I only saw in him a much better man than I had been to Joe."

Chapter Fifty-five Magwitch is imprisoned and his future looks bleak, as he is obviously guilty of many different crimes. Pip visits him often. Meanwhile, Herbert offers Pip a share in a business venture in Cairo. Pip asks him if he can take a little while before making a decision, to which Herbert replies that he can take as long as he wants.

Wemmick asks Pip if he will accompany him on a "walk" Monday morning. Pip agrees. Wemmick meets him early, with a fishing rod in tow, explaining that "I like to walk with one." His strange behavior continues; they come upon a church, and he suggests they go in. Inside are the Aged and Miss Skiffins, Wemmick's girlfriend, prepared for the marriage of Wemmick and Skiffins. The two are married and the group enjoy a hearty breakfast together.

Chapter Fifty-six Magwitch's health and legal chances deteriorate. He is found guilty and sentenced to death. His natural death is approaching rapidly, however. Pip hopes that his benefactor dies before realizing that the state has confiscated all of his property, leaving Pip penniless.

A little more than a week after the trial, Magwitch lies on his deathbed. Pip tells him that Estella, the child he had long ago, is alive. Magwitch brings Pip's hand to his lips and dies.

Chapters Fifty-seven–Fifty-eight All alone and hounded by creditors, Pip falls very ill. He awakens one day to the sound of familiar voices—Joe has come to nurse him back to health. He finds out that Miss Havisham has died, and that Biddy and Joe have grown much closer; she has even taught the blacksmith to write.

When Pip's health returns, Joe leaves without a good-bye, only a note: "Not wishing to intrude I have departed fur you are well and will do better without—Jo." He also leaves a receipt for the payment of Pip's debt.

Pip recovers for three more days, then goes back to his hometown to visit Joe and Biddy. He is worried when he finds that Joe is not in his forge, until he discovers that he has arrived on Joe's wedding day; he is getting married to Biddy. Pip congratulates them and takes his leave.

He returns to London and pays off as much of his debt as possible. He joins Herbert in his business, and eventually becomes a partner. Some years later, Herbert finds out that his original job was gotten through Pip, which brings the two men even closer.

Chapter Fifty-nine After a number of years, Joe and Biddy have a son, telling Pip, "We giv' him the name of Pip for your sake, dear old chap, and we hoped he might grow a little bit like you." Pip remains a bachelor, and despite telling Biddy that his thoughts for Estella have "all gone by," he still thinks often of his lost love.

Pip sees Estella one last time, at the lot where Miss Havisham's house used to stand. She has led a terrible life since the two parted, separating from the cruel Drummle soon after their marriage. They proclaim their friendship for each other and go their separate ways. Pip never sees her again.

It is noteworthy that this was not Dickens' original ending. The original is far more abrupt, with Pip only briefly seeing Estella and her child (from her second lover, a doctor) as they pass by in their coach. Edward Bulwer Lytton, a friend of Dickens' who was also a writer, urged him to rewrite the story with a slightly happier ending.

THE GREAT GATSBY

ABOUT THE AUTHOR

F. Scott Fitzgerald lived the life he wrote about. He was born in Minneapolis and attended Princeton, after which he joined the Army in 1917. His first novel, *This Side of Paradise* (1920), was a bestseller and made him a literary star. Its depictions of the wealth, decadence, and excitement of the Jazz Age attracted a great deal of attention.

Fitzgerald married Zelda Sayre, and they lived a glamorous and decadent life in New York, Paris, the Riviera, and Rome. After an unsuccessful attempt at writing a play, Fitzgerald needed more money and craved critical acclaim. *The Great Gatsby* was his calculated effort to generate both. During Fitzgerald's lifetime, the novel had only mixed reviews and mediocre sales; he only dreamed of the success that *Gatsby* would ultimately achieve. In the late '50s, many critics began to recognize it as a classic, and it has since become one of the most assigned books in high school and college.

After writing *The Great Gatsby*, Fitzgerald became an alcoholic, and his wife suffered a nervous breakdown. He wrote a number of short stories and a few more novels, and made sporadic efforts to become a highly paid screenwriter. He died at age forty-four while working on *The Last Tycoon*, a novel about Hollywood.

THE BIG PICTURE

Fitzgerald's *The Great Gatsby* is a story of power and wealth, and those who use power and wealth for their own ends. The narrator—Nick Carraway—provides us with a strong symbol of morality in this strange world of greed, lies, and lust; it is through his eyes that we see this world's lack of substance.

Why you're reading this book:
- It reflects a particular era in American society, one in many ways repeated in the 1980s.
- It shows the corruption of the American Dream.
- It asks basic, important questions: What is success? What is the meaning of Life?
- The subject matter is truly entertaining.

Your teachers are looking for:
- The role of the narrator:
  - He forces us to become involved in the story—the novel's events and characters become more meaningful when seen from Nick's point of view.
  - He acts as a reference point for the reader in an otherwise foreign and confusing world.
- The lack of purpose and responsibility among these rich, elite people.
- Racism and how the characters use it to put down people unlike them.
- Symbolism:
  - The use of colors throughout the book as symbols.
  - The shifts from West to East representing the shift from decency to decadence.
  - Tom's frequent use of physical force to push people around, symbolizing this society's brutality and lack of decency.
  - The ash heaps, symbolizing the decay and waste of Gatsby's world.
  - Wolfsheim's cuff links made of human teeth, symbolizing how people prey on and use each other.

The fact that *The Great Gatsby* is both easy and fun to read should not keep you from looking for its big ideas and serious literary value.

KEY CHARACTERS

Nick Carraway: The narrator, an earnest middle-class young man from the Midwest. Nick is the moral barometer that everyone is measured against. As he describes himself, he is "the only honest person in the book."

Tom Buchanan: A Yale graduate who was born wealthy. He played football in college and has sought to recreate that feeling ever since. He is callous, cruel, and brutal. Tom is married to Daisy and has Myrtle as his mistress.

Daisy Fay Buchanan: Nick's cousin and Tom's wife. She is Gatsby's dream, but remains unattainable. Daisy is a spoiled rich girl, unable to plan any further ahead than the next party.

Jordan Baker: A semi-professional golfer. A good friend of Daisy's, she acts as go-between for Gatsby. Nick falls in love with her despite the fact that she is a compulsive liar.

Jay Gatsby: A racketeer by trade, Gatsby has devoted his life to attaining what he can't have: Daisy. His parties attract the attention of the wealthy East Eggers, yet he always seems aloof, a spectator rather than a participant in the decadence around him.

George Wilson: Myrtle's husband and the victim of Tom's cruelty. He eventually kills Gatsby.

Myrtle Wilson: A shabby woman with dreams of grandeur. She is Tom's mistress only to pull herself up to the class she dreams of being part of.

Meyer Wolfsheim: A gambler and racketeer; Gatsby's business associate and our only link to Gatsby's professional life.

ESSAY IDEAS

- How does Fitzgerald use the narrator to bring us into the story?
- What are the meanings of the key symbols in the book—the eyes of T. J. Eckleburg, the light on Daisy's dock, the movement from West to East?
- Do you feel sorry for Gatsby? Why?
- Nick is the only character who changes; the book is really about him. Do you agree or disagree?
- How is Fitzgerald's life similar to Gatsby's?
- Compare the relationships of Nick and Jordan, Gatsby and Daisy, and Tom and Myrtle.

A SAMPLE ESSAY IN OUTLINE FORM

Symbolism in *The Great Gatsby*
- Wolfsheim's cuff links made out of human teeth, symbolic of the way people prey on one another.
- Cars as the symbol of irresponsibility.
- Nick's descent into the bowels of the subway.
- The use of color.
- Movement from East to West.
- Gatsby's orange juice machine, a symbol of enormous wealth.
- Tom's pushing people as a symbol of his brutality.

Fitzgerald's use of symbols communicates far more than plot alone ever could. Rather than placing symbols arbitrarily, he carefully integrates them into the story, elevating the book to a higher level of meaning.

PLOT SUMMARY

Chapter 1 The entire structure of the book is established by the first chapter. Nick Carraway, the narrator of the book, is fresh from the Midwest, a place that Fitzgerald uses to signify all that is good about America.

Nick has taken a small house in West Egg, the less fashionable of the two Long Island towns that are the setting of the book. His cousin Daisy lives with her husband Tom in East Egg, a "fashionable" town filled with "white palaces." East and West Egg are based on towns on the east end of Long Island, summer communities for wealthy New Yorkers.

Most of the chapter revolves around Nick's reintroduction to his cousin Daisy and to Tom, a former Yale football player with "arrogant eyes" who's always searching for the "dramatic turbulence of some irrecoverable football game." Tom is a cruel man, and we learn that he has a three-year-old child and a mistress as well. He and Daisy are quite wealthy, having just returned from a year spent in France "for no particular reason."

We see that Daisy is a self-centered rich girl, drifting from one diversion to another, unable to plan even an afternoon's activity. Daisy introduces Nick to her friend Jordan Baker, a semi-professional golfer. Nick is attracted to Jordan but seems a bit puzzled by the aimless drifting of those he's met. Daisy is careful to ask about Nick's "engagement" to a girl in the Midwest, but Nick assures her that there is no engagement.

Finally, we hear a bit about Gatsby. He rents a house that costs "twelve or fifteen thousand a season" while Nick's costs eighty dollars a month. Daisy seems fascinated by Gatsby.

When Nick returns home late that night, he sees Gatsby standing on his lawn, entranced by a green light that shines to him from across the bay. The author is foreshadowing much of what is to come in the rest of the book.

Chapter 2 In Chapter 2, one clearly sees the author's deliberate writing style at work. Every word is used for a reason, and every image supports his story. The chapter begins as Tom brings Nick to meet his mistress, Myrtle Wilson.

The first image in the chapter is that of ashes: we are in a section of the city burnt out by fire, where ash-grey men seem to rise up from the debris in waves. The second image is of an abandoned billboard for an optometrist: the all-seeing eyes of Dr. T. J. Eckleburg. This frightening image of gigantic eyes watching over the decadence of Tom and New York starkly illustrates the novel's moral message.

Tom's mistress is married to George Wilson, who runs a dumpy car repair garage and dealership. Tom frequently visits under the pretext of selling George a car, but is always teasing the man and never follows through on his promises.

Myrtle Wilson is a driven woman. She desperately wants to move from the middle class to Tom's class. She doesn't care about her husband, and she doesn't seem to care that Tom treats her poorly, more like a possession than a person.

Tom and Nick meet Myrtle at the Wilson's garage, and the three of them take the train to New York, with Myrtle riding in a separate car. The author uses irony when he describes the precautions Tom takes in case a neighbor is on the train: everything else in Tom's behavior makes it obvious that he's having an affair and that he doesn't really care who knows.

Myrtle buys a tiny little dog from a man on the street. This is an affectation of the rich class of people she aspires to. They arrive at the apartment that Tom keeps for Myrtle.

After a few calls from Myrtle, people come over (including Myrtle's sister) and Tom throws a party. Myrtle changes her clothes for the third time since we've met her.

The author uses images rather than simple description to describe the drunken party that follows. Things move in and out of focus, and our sense of time is distorted because we're watching the party through Nick's eyes. Tom and Myrtle have a fight and Tom breaks her nose. The careless way that he abuses the woman is a vivid illustration of his personality.

The chapter ends as Nick descends into the depths of the filthy, cave-like Penn Station and waits for the train to take him home. Nick is alone and in bad surroundings, but in a way, he started that way as well—both Tom and Myrtle are self-absorbed and morally corrupt.

Chapter 3 Gatsby is a mysterious figure who has entered Long Island society by creating a non-stop party at his West Egg mansion. The first images we see are the action at Gatsby's—guests all the time, with great attention given to their coming and going at all hours.

Then the author goes into detail about Gatsby's orange juicing machine, which swallows huge numbers of fresh oranges and returns a constant stream of juice. This image serves to highlight Gatsby's wealth (fresh orange juice was quite a luxury) as well as the machine-like nature of his parties—processing the hundreds of guests who walk through his house.

Nick gets an engraved invitation to the party from Gatsby's chauffeur. Soon after he arrives, he's pleased to run into Jordan. They share some speculation on Gatsby's background, and Nick decides to seek out his host and neighbor to thank him for the invitation and to introduce himself.

They look in the library and find a drunken man who crows about the thousands of books there. They're real, but they have never been opened. The drunken man finds this perfectly acceptable—one more comment on the importance of appearances over substance in this society.

Back at the party, Nick sits next to a man who says they met during the war. The man turns out to be Gatsby, and Nick is surprised and embarrassed. Gatsby's smile is described in detail; it is just another prop, but an important one; when it disappears, he becomes a simple roughneck, picking his words with care. "Old sport" is a favorite expression. We still know nothing of his background, his career, or why he throws these parties.

Gatsby is called to the phone, and Jordan shares her opinions of Gatsby with Nick. Jordan has little information on Gatsby, but doubts that he's an Oxford man, as he claims to be. Jordan closes the subject with, "Anyway, he gives large parties...and I like large parties."

As soon as the orchestra stops playing, the forced gaiety of the party abruptly ends. Husbands and wives begin to fight, and it becomes obvious that the party was about appearance, not substance. The people at this high-class party are as crude as those we met at Myrtle's party in the previous chapter.

Jordan is summoned to a mysterious hour-long meeting with Gatsby. Afterwards, we see the guests leaving. Gatsby stands alone on the stairs, the only one at the party not drinking, the only one without a girl swooning on his shoulder.

As one of the cars pulls out, it crashes into a wall. The car crash suggests the failure of these wealthy people to take responsibility for their actions—particularly since cars are a symbol of wealth in America. The driver gets out and says, "Did we run outa gas?," not even realizing that he's had an accident.

After the party, Nick reflects on his interactions with Jordan and decides that he's falling for her, despite her incurable dishonesty (she even cheated in a golf tournament). He decides that the honest thing to do is to break off his vague understanding with his girl out West.

Finally, Nick ends the chapter by going to his job on Wall Street. We learn little about his work, but Nick's shadow goes "westward" when he's at work, which reinforces the image of the East as decadent and the West as standing for hard work and decency. (Note the relationships between Chicago and New York City; New York City and Long Island; and West Egg and East Egg.)

Chapter 4 The chapter opens at Gatsby's latest party, where the guests include Leech, Belcher, Smirk, Blackbuck, Whitebait, Flink, Hammerhead, and Beluga, the tobacco importer. Every name Fitzgerald chooses has some significance.

Finally, we begin to learn a bit more about Gatsby. His car, one more accessory of his wealth, is described as monstrous and triumphant. Gatsby tells Nick that he is the son of wealthy parents from the Midwest (San Francisco[!]). He has spent much of his inheritance living throughout Europe, collecting rubies, and hunting big game.

Gatsby continues to build bigger exaggerations, finally claiming that he was decorated for bravery by the nation of Montenegro. Nick is incredulous, then relieved when Gatsby shows him the medal, as well as a photo taken of him at Oxford. Nick seems once again taken in by Gatsby, ready to believe his fabricated legend.

Gatsby and Nick drive to New York, and again we see the ash heaps, as well as a funeral procession, as they cross the bridge into New York. Nick then meets Gatsby's associate, Meyer Wolfsheim. Straight out of a gangster movie, Wolfsheim has cuff links made from human teeth and talks like a parody of a 1920s mobster. Gatsby proudly informs Nick that Wolfsheim is the man who fixed the 1919 World Series.

We learn about Gatsby through different means than we learn about the book's other characters. While everyone else in the book is described by Nick, we only see Gatsby through the eyes of his associates and himself. Gatsby assured Daisy that he was able to support her in the way to which she was accustomed, and Daisy fell in love. Gatsby was called away to fight, and before he returned, Daisy lost patience and was to marry Tom. Jordan tells us about the night before the wedding, when Daisy got drunk and realized that she really wanted Gatsby, and was compromising her real desire for the comfort and wealth that Tom could offer her.

We finally learn what Gatsby is about. He has moved into the house and hired the servants and given the parties in the hope that Daisy will someday bump into him and see that he has arrived. Everything in Gatsby's life has been aimed toward this one goal. Unlike every other character in the story, Gatsby has a purpose to his life. He wants to regain a vivid moment from his past, to turn back the clock and have Daisy again.

The chapter ends with a brief look at Nick's relationship with Jordan. Nick is human too, and he is willing to go along with Jordan's schemes to get Daisy over to Gatsby's house; he's quite pleased with the kiss and embrace that it earns him.

Chapter 5 Gatsby arranges to have Nick invite Daisy for tea so that he can "coincidentally" stop by and see her. He offers Nick a bribe for setting the meeting up. He has the florist deliver flowers and sends a man over to mow Nick's lawn. When he arrives (an hour early), he's wearing a white suit, silver shirt, and gold tie. This certainly isn't the display of wealth that Daisy was raised to expect, but it is the best Gatsby can do, given his background.

This chapter is an emotional high point of the novel. After many years of struggle, Gatsby is finally at the moment he's worked for. He's quite high strung and totally dependent on Daisy's approval for everything he's done. Every shirt he's bought, every room he's decorated, were all in the hopes of impressing Daisy at this meeting.

Ultimately, Gatsby will realize that the dream was *better* than the goal, and that nothing, not even Daisy can be as wonderful as he had planned and hoped for. The chapter ends with an appearance by Klipspringer, a boarder who freeloads from Gatsby and offers him absolutely nothing in return.

Chapter 6 The chapter begins by foreshadowing what is to follow: a reporter comes to Gatsby's door and asks if he has anything to say.

Fitzgerald interrupts the flow of events with a flashback, told through Nick's voice, that reveals Gatsby's true past and completes the portrait of him. The son of immigrant parents, he changed his name from Gatz when he was seventeen and began his lifelong charade. He was always fascinated by wealth, and he finally found his chance when he happened on a man named Dan Cody. (Note that Dan Cody is a totally American name, like Buffalo Bill Cody.) Dan Cody came from the West, where he made his fortune, then came East to squander it.

Gatsby signed on to be Cody's right hand man. He learned how to talk, how to act, how to live like a wealthy man. Gatsby was able to totally erase his real past and to adopt a new personality. When Cody died, Gatsby was on his own again.

After this flashback, we see the first real meeting between Gatsby and Tom. Gatsby feels awkward but manages to treat Tom with grace—a direct contrast to the way Tom treats *his* mistress's husband. Tom's brutality, a constant throughout the book, is made more obvious here.

Later, Daisy and Tom attend their first party at Gatsby's. This is the first sign that Gatsby's dream is falling apart. Daisy is unimpressed by the gaudiness and wealth, and Tom is particularly critical of everything that he sees.

This scene is full of irony. Tom is critical of Gatsby's party, while his own party (described earlier) could hardly compare. Daisy is not having a good time, but she *is* impressed by one of the guests, a famous movie star escorted by her director. Daisy comes from old money, so she's not impressed by large amounts of money, but she is shallow enough to be impressed by celebrity.

After the party, Gatsby tells Nick that Daisy didn't like the party. The only reason for Gatsby's parties has been to attract and please Daisy, and his failure to charm her with his ostentatious spending is a disappointment to him.

Finally, Gatsby tells Nick about the moment that changed his life one evening as he walked with Daisy, in Louisville. Unlike everything else about Gatsby's life, and about the book, this moment seems real—something actually touched him. He saw in that moment a way to climb to the moon, to work and struggle and reach the top. Then he turned to Daisy and kissed her, and embodied his goal not in achievement and hard work, but in having Daisy. Now his search is for a recreation of that moment—to have Daisy announce that she never loved Tom, to turn back the clock four years and start again.

Chapter 7 This chapter marks the climax of the book. It begins with Nick describing the end of Gatsby's parties. Daisy has returned to him, and Gatsby has fired the servants, turned down the lights, and stopped entertaining the neighborhood. Instead, Daisy spends her afternoons at Gatsby's house, alone with him.

Next, we see a recreation of the first scene in the book, with Nick, Jordan, Tom, and Daisy at the Buchanan house. Daisy and Jordan are even wearing the same clothes, and Tom is on the phone with his mistress again. This time however, Gatsby is there as well.

When Tom leaves the room, Daisy kisses Gatsby, another demonstration of her carelessness. Again we are shown the emptiness of Tom and Daisy's life; the introduction of their daughter is particularly telling. Daisy sees her as a doll to play with occasionally, and Tom ignores her. Gatsby sees the girl as a living, breathing sign that he *can't* turn back the clock and start over with Daisy.

Despite the oppressive heat, the five decide to follow Daisy's suggestion and go into New York. Tom criticizes Gatsby's car, one more element that builds tension between them. After driving past the ash heaps again, they soon reach the neutral ground of the Plaza Hotel. Tom chooses this location to have it out with Gatsby. Ironically, a wedding is taking place just under their window.

Daisy is forced to choose between the two men. Her ideal solution is *not* to choose, to have them both doting on her. When forced, she admits that she loves Gatsby. Gatsby presses however, and wants her to announce that she never loved Tom. This is too much for her, and she admits that she must stay with Tom, shattering Gatsby's dream forever.

Nick realizes that today is his thirtieth birthday. This personal input from the narrator marks a passing in the book: just as

Nick has left his childhood, Gatsby has left his.

The climax is completed on the drive home. Daisy and Gatsby are driving home in Gatsby's car, with Daisy driving to calm her nerves. Myrtle Wilson recognizes Daisy as they drive past the gas station (in the ash heaps) and runs out to talk with her. Daisy panics, runs her over—killing her—and drives on.

Following close behind, Nick, Tom, and Jordan come upon the accident scene. Tom talks with George Wilson, telling him that he knows who was driving the car. Jordan, looking forward to going to dinner with Nick, is completely unaffected by the incident. This event ends Nick's affection for her, forcing him to realize how self-centered and cold she is.

The chapter ends with a shattered Gatsby, standing guard outside Daisy's window, prepared to come to her aid if Tom abuses her. Gatsby is willing to take responsibility for the crash to protect Daisy. Despite his failure to completely attain Daisy, he still clings to his dream, perhaps because he has nothing else to hold on to.

Chapter 8 Gatsby's dream has been shattered, yet he still hangs on, hoping that Daisy will come to him. Summer is clearly over, fall is in the air, and Gatsby is a broken man, standing alone in his mansion with Nick. Nick leaves Gatsby and heads off to work in the city. He ends his relationship with Jordan, and one more thread is broken.

George Wilson is distraught about the death of his wife. His neighbors are comforting him, but to no avail—George has decided that he must discover who killed her and have his revenge. Fitzgerald describes Wilson's motions in great detail, culminating in his murder of Gatsby and his own suicide. Nick feels that Gatsby had "paid a high price for living too long with a single dream."

Chapter 9 This chapter wraps up the book's loose ends and provides the final step in Nick's growth. Tom and Daisy flee New York, avoiding conflict. Nick, on the other hand, demonstrates his maturity. He arranges for Gatsby's funeral; beside Gatsby's father and the nonsensical drunk man in the library, he is the only person at the funeral.

Once again, we see the symbolism of East and West. Gatsby's father refuses to take the body West to be buried, since, "He rose up to his position in the East."

Nick goes to see Wolfsheim, who shows him an old notebook of Gatsby's. In it we see the goals and dreams of youth, the hard work and spirit of America. This is clearly contrasted this with the mess that was made in West Egg. The only hope left at the end of the book is Nick's willingness to see what's happened around him, and to return to the West and recapture the American spirit.

GULLIVER'S TRAVELS

ABOUT THE AUTHOR

Born in Dublin, Jonathan Swift (1667–1745) published his first major work, *The Tale of the Tub,* in 1704. This controversial satire criticizing the Anglican Church brought public attention to Swift's work.

In the years between publishing *The Tale of the Tub* and completing *Gulliver's Travels* in 1725, Swift was a political commentator, writing for a Tory newspaper called *The Examiner.* He was known for his literary discussions with renowned figures of his time.

Gulliver's Travels, Swift's most popular work, is a culmination of his political experiences and literary creativity. This work is deceptive, because although it appears to be a simple children's adventure tale, it is really a brilliant and insightful historical analysis.

The years following the publication of *Gulliver's Travels* were dismal for Swift. His wife died, while he became physically ill and gradually slipped into madness. By the time he died in 1745, his body and mind had withered away.

THE BIG PICTURE

Swift is best known for his political commentary, and *Gulliver's Travels* is no exception. It is a brilliant work of symbolic satire, poking fun and suggesting change to the English society of the time. While reading *Gulliver's Travels*, be on the lookout for the symbolic meaning—and enjoy a wonderful story.

Why you're reading this book:
- It is one of the most eloquent satires in English literature—by using a make-believe situation, Swift is able to make sharp attacks on his own society.
- It provides an interesting historical view of eighteenth-century English society.
- It is a highly imaginative work; its fantastical characters and adventures make for entertaining reading.

Your teachers are looking for:
- The way the narrator's views of English society change as a result of his adventures abroad.
- How Gulliver gives us different perspectives on society when he is either much bigger or much smaller than those around him.
- The narrator's obsession with bodily functions and his grotesque descriptions of certain body parts.
- The symbolic function of the dirty Yahoos in Book IV, who are repeatedly compared to Gulliver and mankind.
- The use of the Houyhnhnm race to establish the author's ideals on virtue and morality.
- The satirical section on the island of Laputa and the symbolism Swift uses here:
  - The significance of the name "Laputa" for the island.
  - The community's lack of social skills.
  - The poor marital relationships of the workaholic husbands and their sex-starved wives.

KEY CHARACTERS

Captain Lemuel Gulliver: The narrator of this first-person adventure tale. Unable to find satisfaction at home, Gulliver leaves his wife and family in England to seek excitement abroad. Traveling to remote islands, Gulliver views different cultures and species and returns a changed man.

Emperor of Lilliput: Leader of the tiny, militant race of people called Lilliputians. After torturing and scrutinizing Gulliver, he decides to accept him into the community. The emperor is cruel and manipulative, and shows kindness to Gulliver only when he finds it beneficial to do so.

Reldresal: The Secretary of Private Affairs of Lilliput. He is a true friend to Gulliver, warning him that danger awaits him on the island. He helps Gulliver escape before he is punished.

Flimnap: The Lord High Treasurer of Lilliput. He is jealous of Gulliver, who has sparked his wife's interest, and does everything he can to make Gulliver miserable. He is a malicious, unsympathetic character.

Glumdaclitch: Gulliver's attentive nine–year–old nurse in Brobdingnag, land of the giants. She protects Gulliver, often saving him from death, and becomes his bodyguard.

Queen of Brobdingnag: Takes Gulliver into her care when he appears to be wasting away. Like Glumdaclitch, she mothers Gulliver and keeps him secure.

King of Brobdingnag: Inquisitive about Gulliver's home country and culture. When Gulliver provides anecdotes about England, the King determines that the English are "the most pernicious race of little odious vermin that nature ever suffered to crawl upon the surface of the earth."

King of Laputa: Unsociable, eccentric leader. He is so absorbed in his scientific and mathematical thoughts that he barely acknowledges Gulliver's presence. Unlike the other rulers, he is not very curious about Gulliver's background.

Governor of Glibdubdrib: Has a magical power of reviving dead spirits. Upon Gulliver's request, the governor brings ancient rulers and thinkers back from beyond.

Master of Houyhnhnms: Gulliver's idol and role model. Takes Gulliver under his care and teaches him Houyhnhnm customs and values. He ultimately decides that Gulliver can no longer live among the Houyhnhnms.

Sorrel Nag: Houyhnhnm servant who aids Gulliver during his stay on the island, protecting him from Yahoo attacks and advances. He grows to love Gulliver despite Gulliver's similarity to the Yahoo animal.

ESSAY IDEAS

- How do Gulliver's values and beliefs change from the beginning of his adventure to the end?
- Is Gulliver a heroic figure? Why or why not?
- Describe the various uses of symbolism in Book III, the voyage to Laputa. How do they tie in with the larger themes of the novel?
- The author graphically describes bodily functions and the dirtiness of human flesh. What significance does this have in the novel and why is it emphasized?
- Is this a moralistic novel, a satire, or some combination of both? Explain your choice.
- The author attempts to show us the world from different perspectives. Cite some examples and describe the author's intentions.
- What is the author's purpose in contrasting the Houyhnhnms and the Yahoos?

A SAMPLE ESSAY IN OUTLINE FORM

Contrast the Houyhnhnms with the Yahoos.

- The Houyhnhnms:
  - A perfect race of horses.
  - Embody every virtue the narrator values: cleanliness, honesty, sobriety, and peacefulness.
  - Masters of the uncivilized Yahoo race.
  - Gulliver's ideal; he becomes obsessed with becoming a horse.
- The Yahoos:
  - A dirty and savage-like race of humans.
  - Often violent; when enraged, they shoot excrement.
  - Oversexed, overindulgent creatures with no sense of moderation.
  - Gulliver despises these animals, ignoring any similarities between himself and the Yahoos.

Contrasting these two races reveals Swift's cynical message that human beings are closer not only in appearance, but in nature as well, to the Yahoos. Gulliver's attempt at becoming a horse, and at denying the similarity between himself and the Yahoos, is hopeless.

PLOT SUMMARY

BOOK I

Chapters I–III The novel opens with a brief autobiographical account by the narrator, Captain Gulliver. We are told that Gulliver is an adventure seeker, and almost immediately, he abandons his domestic lifestyle in England to travel abroad.

Early into the first voyage, the ship faces complications, and Gulliver ends up swimming alone to a remote island. Exhausted, he lies down in the grass and takes a nap. He awakens to find himself bound by thousands of strings and surrounded by six-inch tall creatures, the Lilliputians.

Swift begins the novel by showing how important perspective is to the understanding of a social situation. Swift reveals his talent for demonstrating different perspectives: once placed on this island called Lilliput, Gulliver changes from a normal-sized human being to a giant-sized creature.

Although the Lilliputians are miniature, their logic is just as substantial as human beings'. Like the English, these individuals have warring tendencies, and can be greedy as well as manipulative. At the same time, the Lilliputians have the potential for generosity, which is shown by their tireless efforts to meet Gulliver's demanding needs.

Many details of Lilliputian custom and ceremony are explained in the third chapter. Although the Lilliputians regard their political traditions and army drills as serious business (just as the English do), Swift presents the events humorously. He mocks the actions which are normally regarded as heroic displays of power.

Finally, Gulliver is given a list of rules to follow, which are written to protect the Lilliputians. Compared to Gulliver, these creatures are frail, so they live in constant fear of being accidentally trampled on by him.

Chapters IV–VIII In Chapters IV and V we are introduced to the people of Blefuscu, who live on the neighboring island. The emperor of Lilliput explains the ludicrous origin of the ongoing war between the two groups. Apparently, there was difference of opinion over the proper way to break an egg, and the argument that followed escalated into a war.

Obviously, the dispute that sparked

combat was ridiculous, and the continuing grievances are satirized by the author. Swift is making fun of mankind's tendency to start major battles over minor disagreements.

After gaining recognition as a hero by helping Lilliput win a battle against Blefuscu, Gulliver soon finds himself in an uncomfortable position. When the King's palace was accidentally set aflame, Gulliver urinated on the building to put the fire out. Although he meant no disrespect by this gesture, which he thought was the best possible solution, others consider it disgraceful.

Later on, Gulliver's enemies use this incident and others to increase his unpopularity. In Chapter VII, Flimnap, the Treasurer, composes a list of treasonous acts that Gulliver has allegedly committed. He ultimately convinces the Emperor that Gulliver should either be punished or banished.

To avoid being blinded and slowly made to starve—the punishment decided on by the committee—Gulliver escapes the island and goes to Blefuscu. Unhappy there, he decides to head back to England, where he remains only two months before boarding another ship.

BOOK II

Chapters I–IV As in Book I, Gulliver becomes shipwrecked early in his voyage. He lands on Brobdingnag, an island where every object and person is greatly magnified, making him a minuscule creature in comparison.

Gulliver quickly begins to appreciate how intimidated the Lilliputians must have been when he stood towering over them like a giant. Just as the Lilliputians were extremely cautious, Gulliver has to be on guard at all times in Brobdingnag. Playful cats and rambunctious children are threatening forces, and a harmless piece of crust almost kills Gulliver when he falls over it.

Gulliver is initially adopted by a farmer, who finds him struggling in a giant cornfield. To gain fame and fortune, the farmer treats Gulliver as a circus freak, making him perform tricks and stunts at the market. When Gulliver becomes seriously ill from the strenuous, humiliating work, the Queen buys him from the farmer and nurses him back to health.

The King becomes fascinated by this tiny, rational creature, Captain Gulliver. He asks Gulliver to provide details about his background and home country, which Gulliver does throughout Chapter III. Gull-iver offers a derogatory account of English customs and practices in areas such as trade and warfare; as his experiences abroad increase, his memories of English society become more tainted.

A disturbing element of Chapter IV is Gulliver's description of a woman's cancerous breast. The narrator paints a gruesome picture of large sores and gaping holes strewn across a gigantic breast. Swift suggests here that the human body is repulsive when viewed too closely.

Chapters V–VIII Chapter V gives numerous examples of Gulliver's traumatic experiences on the island. He almost gets killed by a falling apple, a dog snatches him in its mouth like a bone, and a monkey nearly knocks him unconscious. These are just a few of the frightening, although humorous, incidents that occur because of Gulliver's size.

Once again, the King inquires about English affairs, and Gulliver further explains the nature of his country. Gulliver's description about the use of destructive force in England completely shocks the King, who states that England is comprised of "ignorance, idleness, and vice." In Brobdingnag, matters are settled far more rationally and with minimal brutality. Swift, through the King, expresses his idea of how a state should be run: according to the principles of virtue and reason, and without secret diplomacy.

Gulliver develops a close relationship with the King, whose views he highly respects. As a result, Gulliver begins to view English society more unfavorably. At this point, we see a change in Gulliver's character, and his anger toward contemporary English society gets more aggravated as the novel progresses.

Gulliver winds up leaving the island because of a freak accident. The protective box that Gulliver is carried in whenever he is taken through town is picked up by an eagle. During a scuffle with another eagle, the eagle holding Gulliver drops him into the ocean, and from there Gulliver is picked up by a passing ship.

When Gulliver arrives at home, he is disoriented from living among giants for so long. His family thinks he has gone crazy, and they argue that he should never venture off in the future. But once again, he does.

BOOK III

Chapters I–V After battling stormy weather for days, Gulliver's ship is unlucky enough to be overtaken by pirates. As punishment for making bold comments, the pirates send Gulliver adrift in a small canoe. Finally, after hours of struggling, he approaches a flying island (Laputa) and is carried to safety by some of its inhabitants.

The inhabitants of this island are not unique because of their size. What makes them distinct is their odd personalities and distorted physical features. Gulliver explains that "their heads were all reclined either to the right or the left; one of their eyes turned inward, and the other directly to zenith."

As opposed to the previous leaders Gulliver has met, the King of Laputa is an antisocial being. The King always has a servant called a flapper by his side, who is responsible for smacking the King whenever he becomes overly concentrated and unaware of people around him.

Gulliver soon realizes that the male leaders of Laputa define everything in mathematical or scientific terms, including people, food, and other elements of society. As a result of their narrow focus and interests, the people of Laputa suffer from lack of communication, which in turn leads to poor marital relationships.

Like its wacky inhabitants, the island itself is a bit unsteady. The narrator gives a long and complicated explanation about how the island's shape and size contribute to its lack of balance.

The self-centered inhabitants of Laputa show no interest in Gulliver. Unlike the other island leaders, these rulers have no desire to learn about Gulliver's background and home life. Neglected and bored, Gulliver leaves for Balnibari.

The former Governor of Balnibari, Lord Munodi, shows Gulliver around, and Gulliver notes the waste and filth that pervade the town. Everything is in ruins, according to Lord Munodi, because of disastrous town projects that destroy the community instead of improving it.

Chapter V provides a detailed description of the Grand Academy of Lagado, founded by a group of men who had visited Laputa and "gotten educated." Upon their return, they insisted that an academy be built. Unfortunately, the Academy only sponsors projects that have lethal consequences. No worthwhile inventions or environmental improvements are ever made by the Academy.

Chapters VI–XI Disgusted with these crazed projects and the lunatic minds behind them, Gulliver decides to take a short voyage to Glubdubdrib. He meets with the town Governor, who happens to possess magical powers. Gulliver asks this sorcerer to reanimate Alexander the Great and other famous historical figures that intrigue him. He converses with many revered ancients and is enraptured by their brilliance and virtue.

After such an inspiring experience, Gulliver becomes depressed about modern history, filled as it is with incidents of vice and exploitation. Gulliver views contemporary leaders as cheaters who owe their success to immorality and deception. Meeting the Ancients intensifies Gulliver's negative sentiments about contemporary England.

To revive his spirits, Gulliver decides to sail to another area. He ends up in Luggnagg, where he is brought before the King and made to "lick the dust before his footstool." The King finds Gulliver amusing and welcomes him wholeheartedly into the kingdom.

An acquaintance on the island tells Gulliver about a peculiar breed of people, the Struldbrugs. This rare group is immortal. Instantly excited by the idea of everlasting life, Gulliver passionately tells the reader all that he would do if he were immortal.

Unfortunately, Gulliver's friend from Luggnagg explains that being a Struldbrug is more a curse than a gift. The depressing reality is that these immortals grow old, senile, and miserable, and are stripped of all their rights and privileges at a certain age. These poor creatures must endure the pain of life, knowing that death will never come to relieve them.

Swift offers a bleak view of humanity, and its disgraceful treatment of the elderly, in his story of the Stuldbrugs. Rather than attaining respect and honor, aged Struldbrugs are treated with contempt.

After a three-month stay on the island, Gulliver sets sail to Japan. His stay there is brief, and for the most part unadventurous, so he visits Amsterdam quickly and then goes back to England.

BOOK IV

Chapters I–VI Gulliver remains at home for five months before embarking on his final adventure. Again, he has hardships at sea and ends up alone on a remote island.

Gulliver stumbles upon some strange-looking animals, and gives an explicit description of their queer appearance. Immediately, Gulliver despises these animals, who seem dirty and uncivilized. When the animals suddenly spot Gulliver, they become fearful and enraged, and shoot excrement on Gulliver's head from a tree directly above him.

Gulliver hates the Yahoos, as they are called, but is fascinated by the dignified and clever race of horses that approach him soon after. These horses, the Houyhnhnms, are unlike the brute European horses: they are rational creatures with the ability to communicate. Gulliver attempts to converse with them, while they scrutinize his every move, ultimately deciding to bring Gulliver back to the Houyhnhnm household.

While inside the Houyhnhnm house, Gulliver notes how clean and organized the horse section is, as compared to the area designated for the Yahoos, who are the Houyhnhnms' slaves. Much to Gulliver's dismay, the master horse continually notes similarities between the Yahoo's features and his own. Gulliver's redeeming feature, as far as the Houyhnhnm master can tell, is that he is a cleaner and more intelligent creature than the Yahoo animal.

The Houyhnhnm master is anxious to learn more about Gulliver and his place of origin. After learning the Houyhnhnm language, Gulliver provides numerous details about Englishmen and their culture. He tells a disturbing story of how harshly horses are treated, and the master is sickened by what he hears.

When Gulliver finishes his speech about England, the master determines that man is even more despicable by nature than the irrational Yahoos, since man has the ability to reason but uses his intelligence for evil purposes. The Houyhnhnms, we are told, have no notion of evils such as "murder, theft, poisoning, robbery, perjury...etc.," which Gulliver claims are abundant in England.

Chapters VII–XII Gulliver falls in love with this peaceful, morally ordered country. He hopes to remain among the Houyhnhnms and imitate their virtuous ways. The chances for Gulliver's integration and total acceptance in the community grow slimmer and slimmer as Gulliver relays more horrible tales about English folk. The master and others begin to view Gulliver as more closely related to the Yahoos than the Houyhnhnms.

Chapter VIII provides vivid descriptions of Yahoo eccentricities. For one, we learn that the Yahoos eat rat meat and "devour pieces of ass" as part of their daily diet. The incidents Gulliver relates reveal the Yahoos as overly passionate, wild creatures.

In contrast, Gulliver describes the dignified Houyhnhnm culture, exploring their pragmatic education and marriage policies and honorable values. The Houyhnhnms are governed by reason, while the Yahoos follow their lustful instincts.

Another attractive attribute of the Houyhnhnms is their immunity to most diseases. Gulliver describes them as clean, well-bred animals, unlikely to get sick. Gulliver attempts to purify his diet and habits so that he too can become free of illness.

The longer Gulliver lives among the Houyhnhnms, the more he begins to resent European culture. He starts to envision his family and the rest of Europe as Yahoos, which fills him with disgust. It is ironic that he views all Europeans other than himself as sharing Yahoo vulgarities.

Gulliver has a rude awakening when the Houyhnhnm master suddenly directs him to leave the island and rejoin his people. Many of the Houyhnhnms have grown resentful of having this "rational Yahoo" live royally among the ruling class. The assembly pressures the master Houyhnhnm either to banish Gulliver or to make him live with the Yahoos.

Reluctantly, Gulliver leaves and rejoins his family in England. Considering himself a Houyhnhnm now, he spends more time conversing with the horses in his stable than with friends and family. The sight and smell of his "Yahoo family" make him ill, so he avoids them as much as possible. Gulliver becomes an antisocial, disturbing character by the end of the novel, completely distancing himself from society and his "Yahoo" readers.

HAMLET

ABOUT THE AUTHOR

Although the works of William Shakespeare (1564–1616) are abundant, facts about his life are rare. Born in Stratford-on-Avon, Shakespeare received very little formal education. At age eighteen, he married twenty-six-year-old Ann Hathaway.

By 1592, Shakespeare was in London pursuing a career in theater. Drama was quite popular during the reign of Queen Elizabeth. In addition to his talent as a playwright and poet, Shakespeare also made a name for himself as an actor.

His contribution to the building of the Globe Theater in 1599 was instrumental to the theater's later success. Here, many of his plays were performed. About twelve years later, he returned to Stratford-on-Avon to continue writing in retirement.

As a playwright, he wrote 37 works, including tragedies (such as *Hamlet*), comedies, and histories. He also experimented extensively with poetry, writing more than 150 sonnets. Interestingly enough, Shakespeare's works were not published during his lifetime.

THE BIG PICTURE

Hamlet is one of Shakespeare's most celebrated plays, and also one of the most-performed. Very few casual readers of drama do not know the "To be or not to be" soliloquy. There is good reason for *Hamlet's* fame—it is a work of genius in its plot, its characters, and its intense psychological portrait of a young man torn by his father's death.

Why you're reading this book:
- Its soliloquies are among the greatest

and most famous in English literature.
- It illustrates universal themes that are still relevant today: revenge; disguise; moral choices; outward goodness vs. inner evil; sanity vs. madness; illusion vs. reality; and action vs. inaction.
- Its use of symbolism.
- Its intense, believable portrayal of one man's inner psychological state.

Your teachers are looking for:
- The significance of the long speeches given by several of the characters—Hamlet, King Claudius, etc.
- Theme of Revenge:
  - Hamlet's revenge on Claudius for his father's death.
  - The Ghost of Hamlet's revenge on Claudius for his own death.
  - Young Fortinbras' revenge on Denmark for his father's death in the war against Denmark.
  - Laertes' revenge on Hamlet for his father's death and his sister's suicide.
  - The risks and rewards of revenge.
  - The deceit and deception in *Hamlet* and the various ways characters try to trick one another; poisoned blades, switched letters, etc.

Shakespeare's plays are clearly a challenge to read. Sometimes it is best to read them in brief, but concentrated, periods of time. Don't let yourself get bogged down in his elaborate and difficult style.

KEY CHARACTERS

Hamlet: The tragic hero, or protagonist, of the play. Prince of Denmark, he is the son of Queen Gertrude and the late

King Hamlet. Avenging his father's death is his central quest in the play.

Claudius: The antagonist, he is deceitful and selfish. Having secretly murdered his brother, he now occupies the throne of Denmark. In addition, he has married his late brother's wife.

Gertrude: Widowed Queen of the former King Hamlet and present wife of Claudius. One of the more passive characters of the play who seems to be very much confused by the chaotic events.

Ghost: The ghost of the elder Hamlet, former King of Denmark. His brother Claudius poisoned him in order to become King. Returns to his son and urges him to take revenge.

Polonius: Counsel to the King. Plays a central role in the division of sides in the conflict between the King and Hamlet. Contributes to the romantic subplot by discouraging his daughter's interest in Hamlet. Killed by Hamlet.

Laertes: Polonius' son, he also disapproves of his sister's relationship with the Prince. Returns from France to avenge his father's death. Eventually killed by Hamlet in a "play" duel.

Ophelia: Daughter of Polonius. Her love for Hamlet is discouraged by her family. After Hamlet murders her father, she wavers between deep depression and insanity.

Horatio: Hamlet's friend and fellow student. The only true and trustworthy confidant to Hamlet.

Rosencrantz and Guildenstern: Members of the King's court and childhood friends of Hamlet. Claudius has them spy upon Hamlet.

Fortinbras: Prince of Norway. Although he does not have a central role in the play, his character is very important. He is intent upon conquering Denmark, and, like Hamlet, he is very much caught up in his mission to avenge his father's death.

ESSAY IDEAS

- Consider the play's recurrent motif of things hidden or concealed.
- Discuss the significance of the play's various symbols or images.
- Examine the role of the women in *Hamlet*.
- Is Hamlet mad? Defend your answer.
- Discuss the imagery of Denmark as sick or diseased.
- Analyze Hamlet's famous "To be or not to be" soliloquy (III,i). How is it relevant to Hamlet's struggles throughout the play?
- Compare and contrast the characters of Hamlet and Laertes (1) as sons, and (2) as men of action.

A SAMPLE ESSAY IN OUTLINE FORM

Disguise and deceit in *Hamlet*.
- Characters who conceal:
  - Claudius:
    - His inner wickedness is concealed by his status as King.
    - He secretly poisoned King Hamlet.
    - He secretly conspires to poison Prince Hamlet.
  - Polonius:
    - Conceals Hamlet's love for Ophelia from her.
    - Tries to obtain information about his son in an indirect, deceptive manner.
    - Physically hides himself behind a tapestry to eavesdrop.
  - Hamlet—he refuses to reveal where he has buried Polonius.
  - The Ghost of the late King—he conceals himself from most of the play's

characters.
- Symbols or Images of Concealment:
  - Hamlet's switching of the letters to trick the King.

PLOT SUMMARY

Act I, Scene i Set at Elsinore, Denmark's royal castle, the play begins with the changing of the guards at midnight. Horatio recounts the details of Denmark's war with Norway to the sodiers. In his explanation, he glorifies the victory of the late King Hamlet over the Norwegian King Fortinbras. We learn that Fortinbras was slain by the King of Denmark, and now, his son, the young Fortinbras, plans revenge and a recovery of the lands Norway lost. The castle is now being guarded from any possible attacks.

In this first scene, the late King appears to Horatio and the soldiers in ghost form. Though he remains silent and his stays are brief, his appearance is very important as it sets up the plot of the avenging of his death and brings up the question of illusion versus reality, one of the play's major themes. The men decide to take action and report this sighting to Hamlet.

Act I, Scene ii The second scene provides a more personal and detailed introduction to the main characters and their roles in the play. The scene contains several soliloquies. In his first, the newly crowned King Claudius sends a message to young Fortinbras' uncle in hopes of avoiding war. Fortinbras is only one of the youths that Claudius tries deceitfully to manipulate. Laertes, who has come from France for Claudius' coronation, requests permission to return there. The atmosphere at the castle is happy.

We then meet Hamlet. Still in mourning for his father's death, and unhappy with his mother's rash decision to marry the late King's brother, (the newly crowned King Claudius), Hamlet dampens the light mood. The King's second soliloquy addresses Hamlet's behavior. Claudius has no tolerance for the young man's melancholy disposition, accusing him of stubbornness and "unmanly" behavior. He suggests that Hamlet return to school, and seems to be trying to get rid of Hamlet from the start. The Queen disagrees with Claudius and asks that Hamlet remain in Denmark. When the court finally leaves, Hamlet expresses his somberness and resentment.

Horatio and the officers of the night watch enter to tell Hamlet their incredible tale. Hamlet decides to sit watch with them the following night and await the Ghost's return. We see some foreshadowing at the end of the scene: Hamlet senses his father's ghost has come because a wrong has been committed.

Act I, Scene iii In this scene, Laertes and Polonius advise Ophelia to abandon her interest in Hamlet. They claim that while his signs of affection for her may be genuine, she should be wary that he is young and his feelings may be fleeting.

Here, Ophelia takes their advice and locks it in her heart, claiming that only Laertes "shall keep the key of it." Shake-speare portrays her as a weaker character, one who blindly follows others' advice. The other important event in this family exchange is Laertes' leaving for France. With his departure, his family will begin to fall apart.

Act I, Scene iv Hamlet joins Horatio and Marcellus (an officer) for the night watch in hopes of encountering the Ghost. Here, Hamlet has a long speech condemning Claudius' behavior, especially his excessive drinking.

He goes on to explain that this infamous

habit of the King is characteristic of Denmark as a whole. Its reputation as a nation of drunkards has stigmatized it, almost like a disease. This scene contains other images of Denmark as rotted or unhealthy.

The scene's high point is the appearance of the Ghost of Hamlet (the late King). The Ghost is still silent, but he gestures to Hamlet to follow him. Hamlet leaves his friends and follows.

Act I, Scene v Hamlet and the Ghost share a crucial exchange. In a powerful soliloquy, the Ghost reveals the deceit and foul play surrounding his death. Hamlet's father is believed to have died by being poisoned by a snake in the garden. The Ghost reveals that it was Claudius, his own brother, who poisoned him. Here, Shakespeare draws a parallel between Claudius and the Serpent in the Garden of Eden, the ultimate symbol of evil and deceit.

Finally, Hamlet's friends catch up with him. He does not tell them what he has discovered. However, he and the others swear to keep the Ghost's existence secret; to himself, Hamlet swears revenge upon Claudius.

Act II, Scene i As the second act opens, our focus shifts to Polonius. He is sending out a messenger to find out about the doings of Laertes in France. As deception is a theme repeated throughout the play, it is important to note the roundabout methods Polonius uses to gain his information.

Ophelia, distressed by Hamlet's unusual and melancholy behavior, comes to her father for advice. Polonius believes that Hamlet's strange behavior is a result of Ophelia's rejection of him. Through Ophelia's accounts, Hamlet's manner is defined as unnatural. Polonius decides to report Hamlet's peculiar conduct to the King.

Act II, Scene ii The King has sent for Rosencrantz and Guildenstern, Hamlet's two childhood friends, to find out what has caused such a dramatic change in Hamlet. Polonius then enters the scene with a dual purpose. First, he announces that Fortinbras' uncle has proposed a treaty with Denmark; it seems that Claudius has successfully sidestepped the young Fort-inbras.

Polonius' second point concerns Hamlet's behavior. Polonius declares that this lunacy stems from Hamlet's unrequited love for his daughter. Claudius and Polonius decide to spy upon Hamlet and Ophelia to determine Hamlet's true state of mind.

Hamlet enters the scene, and Polonius converses with him to try to discover the reasons behind his unusual conduct. Rosencrantz and Guildenstern then approach Hamlet with the same intention. Hamlet is wary of their visit, and he questions them. Rosencrantz and Guildenstern admit they were sent for by the King and Queen, but, like Hamlet, they do not know why.

Talk of theater diverts the conversation. Rosencrantz and Guildenstern inform Hamlet of a theater group coming to perform for the King. Within this discussion, Shakespeare comments on the new fashion of the satirical stage, child actors. This emphasis on theater also reinforces one of the important themes of the play: the question of what is truth or fiction.

The players arrive and the mood turns to excitement. Hamlet asks for a brief show of their talents from one of the actors. Hamlet and the actor begin a famous speech from the *Aeneid*. He chooses the speech deliberately—the tale he recites parallels the situation in Denmark. The characters of the story represent Hamlet's family: Pyrrhus represents the cruel and vicious Claudius; Priam is his late father Hamlet; and Hecuba, Queen Gertrude.

Hamlet requests that the actors perform a specific play for the court. At the close of

Act II, one of Hamlet's famous soliloquies reveals his intentions for the play. He will watch the King and Queen's reaction to the fictional murder in the play. Hamlet hopes Claudius' response will reveal his guilt.

Act III, Scene i Rosencrantz and Guildenstern have little to report to the King and Queen. Hamlet himself recognizes the change in his behavior, they say, but its cause is still unclear.

Polonius sets up an encounter between Ophelia and Hamlet. Hamlet enters, reciting his most famous soliloquy of the play, the "To be or not to be" speech. This speech expresses Hamlet's desperate inner struggle between taking action (murdering Claudius and avenging his father's death) and remaining passive. He despairs over the choice he has to make between suffering in his mind and taking up arms against his enemy. He questions his conscience and what it means to be a coward.

Ophelia enters, and the two converse. But they are not alone: Claudius and Polonius are eavesdropping. It is important to note that Hamlet and Ophelia's interactions always take place in the presence of other characters. This raises the question of who actually controls their relationship.

In this dialogue with Ophelia, Hamlet's change in behavior becomes strikingly obvious to the reader. First, he doubts Ophelia's good nature, questioning her integrity and truthfulness. He professes that he does not love her any longer and rudely advises her to escape this horrible world and join a convent. He encourages her not to marry. Men are only monsters, he tells her.

After Hamlet leaves, the King and Polonius come to comfort Ophelia. They now confirm that Hamlet is mad. The King determines that the best solution for someone as dangerous as Hamlet is to send him off to England.

Act III, Scene ii In this scene, the play within the play is performed. Although the play is fictional, its plot illustrates very real events, once again blurring the distinction between illusion and reality. This scene is the turning point of the play.

Before the performance, Hamlet advises the actors. He offers specific instructions to the actors to insure that the play will effectively achieve his goal: it must be acted just right to elicit reactions from the King and Queen.

Hamlet, in yet another great soliloquy, reveals his plans to Horatio. Hamlet is sure that Claudius will be unable to conceal his guilt when the murder occurs on stage.

The play proves to be a close reenactment of the actual happenings in Denmark. At the point in the play when the strange man poisons the sleeping King, Claudius can bear no more. Dismayed, the King makes a quick exit with his court.

Hamlet and Horatio remain and discuss the King's reaction. Rosencrantz and Guildenstern enter and comment upon the King's strange behavior. They also bring a message from the Queen, who has requested Hamlet's presence in her chambers.

We should be aware of Hamlet's attitude throughout this scene. He trusts no one and closes himself off from the other characters. He doubts the sincerity of Ophelia's feelings; he is also suspicious of the intentions of Rosencrantz, Guildenstern, and Polonius. Hamlet believes that they will say anything to keep him from taking action against his uncle.

Act III, Scene iii The King sets the plans in motion for Hamlet to go to England with Rosencrantz and Guildenstern. Rosencrantz and Guildenstern begin to side with the manipulative King. Unaware of the truth, they pity the King, whose wife's son's deranged conduct has placed him in an uncomfortable situation. They believe that as King, Claudius has the responsibility to the safety of the people to send Hamlet away.

Polonius plots to hide in the Queen's chambers to overhear the dialogue between the Queen and Hamlet.

We finally witness the King admitting his crimes to himself. Hamlet's trap has worked and gotten to the King's conscience. He wishes to repent, but wants dearly to hold on to all that he has gained: his throne and his Queen.

Hamlet also gives a speech. He sees the King alone and, at once, he draws his sword. However, he remembers that his mother awaits him and he refrains from killing. Hamlet's mother stands in the way of his revenge on two levels: first, she is literally awaiting his arrival, and second, his love for her conflicts with his desire for revenge. He is torn between his love for her and his need to betray her by killing her husband.

Act III, Scene iv Hamlet meets the Queen in her chambers. He speaks angrily to her. The scene erupts as the Queen becomes increasingly fearful of her son's belligerent comments. As her call for help is echoed from behind a curtain, Hamlet, thinking the voice is the King's, makes a rapier thrust toward the curtain and slays the spying Polonius.

Then Hamlet reveals to his horrified mother all that Claudius has done. The Ghost returns for his final visit, possibly for the purpose of preventing Hamlet from killing his own mother. But Hamlet is the only one who can see and speak with the Ghost. The Queen sees Hamlet talking to no one, which confirms her belief that he has gone mad.

Hamlet, meanwhile, begs her to repent for her sins. He asks that she not return to Claudius, and she agrees. Finally, Hamlet announces a plot to destroy Claudius' plan to send him to England.

Act IV, Scene i Believing Hamlet has gone insane, the Queen reports the killing of Polonius to the King but does not reveal what Hamlet has divulged about the King. She seems to have some doubts about Claudius, but she still fears her son. The King calls upon Rosencrantz and Guildenstern to speed up the preparations for England.

Act IV, Scene ii Rosencrantz and Guildenstern approach Hamlet to retrieve the body of Polonius for burial. Hamlet speaks in puzzles and ignores their request for the body. Instead, he asks them to bring the King to him.

Act IV, Scene iii The King meets with Hamlet, who will not reveal what he has done with the body of Polonius. We see that Hamlet learns to play the King's game; he, too, can keep things concealed.

The frustrated King announces that the preparations for Hamlet's trip to England have been made. He sends Rosencrantz and Guildenstern to watch over him with the greatest of care. Hamlet says good-bye to his mother and leaves. When the King is alone, we learn that he has prepared letters which plan for Hamlet's murder upon his arrival in England. Deception and secrecy continue with a new, heightened intensity.

Act IV, Scene iv Shakespeare now shifts the focus of the play by introducing a completely new character. Young Fortinbras of Norway lands with his men upon the coast of Denmark. He sends his captain to announce his arrival to King Claudius. Ironically, along the way, the captain enounters Hamlet and his two escorts.

Before boarding the ship, Hamlet gives another soliloquy about his course of action. Fortinbras' presence causes him to think about his actions. He likens the havoc within his family to war. He questions his own character—is he a beast or a coward? How can he stand by idly when so much injustice has been committed? The question remains of whether Hamlet's passionate thoughts will lead to equally passionate action.

Act IV, Scene v Ophelia speaks with the King and Queen. The young woman, devastated by her father's death and the loss of her true love, begins to act very strangely, continually singing. When she does speak, she talks only of the men in her life who have left her alone: Polonius, Laertes, and Hamlet. Her life seems to be completely out of order. She declares that she will inform Laertes of what has happened in Denmark.

The King believes that Ophelia now suffers from the same madness as Hamlet. Ironically, Claudius defines this madness as a poison, the very method he used to kill his brother. In a speech to Gertrude the King foreshadows events to come, saying that Polonius' death and Ophelia's madness can only be bad signs.

The return of Laertes brings more disturbance. He is enraged at the news of his father's death. His father has not only been murdered, but his body has not been given the proper burial rites. He promises, like the other sons in the play, to avenge his father's murder.

Laertes becomes even more angry and confused when he sees Ophelia. She continues her singing and speaks in irrational sentences. Her family has fallen apart.

Act IV, Scene vi In this brief scene, Horatio receives a letter from Hamlet. Hamlet, on his way to England with Rosencrantz and Guildenstern, has escaped from the ship. He has also intercepted Claudius' letters and altered them. Hamlet tells Horatio of his plans to return to Denmark to divulge the truth. The letters symbolize the deception and the manipulation of truth that occur throughout the play; Hamlet must be deceptive to bring himself closer to the truth.

Act IV, Scene vii The King and Laertes confer about the chaos in the court and in the city. They also discuss Laertes' crusade for revenge. A messenger brings a letter from Hamlet announcing his return to Denmark. Unpleasantly surprised, the King begins to devise a plan to destroy Hamlet. Laertes will fight a play duel with Hamlet. He will secretly replace his practice blade with a real sword and kill the young Prince. To insure Hamlet's death, the King will also lace Hamlet's drink with poison.

The scene ends with the report of another loss of life. The screams of the Queen interrupt the King and Laertes' plans: Ophelia has committed suicide by drowning herself. Laertes is horrified, and his desire for revenge has intensified.

Act V, Scene i Set in an old churchyard, this scene is full of images of death. Two gravediggers are digging a grave for Ophelia. They are discussing the death as a suicide. In those days, suicide was considered a sure way to damnation.

Hamlet, having just returned to Denmark, is unaware of Ophelia's suicide. Entering the graveyard with Horatio, he speaks with one of the gravediggers about the remains of the bodies he is pulling from the earth. These skulls represent the past for Hamlet. This discussion contains Hamlet's famous recognition of the skull of an old court jester he used to play with: "Alas, poor Yorick!" illustrates Hamlet's horror at the idea that death reduces everyone to nothing. Yorick's skull reminds Hamlet of his father's death, and he is overwhelmed by the tragedy that has separated them.

Hamlet is disguised in this passage. The

gravediggers do not recognize him, and thinking he is a stranger, they speak of his madness. Hamlet conceals himself further as Ophelia's funeral procession arrives. He and Horatio take cover.

As the priest performs the ceremony, Hamlet discovers that the body is his fair Ophelia's. Unable to suppress his emotions, he leaps from his hiding place to grieve over her. Laertes, incensed, attacks Hamlet.

The men are pulled apart and Hamlet pronounces his deep love for Ophelia. His overflow of emotion is interpreted by the King and Queen as yet another sign of his madness. The King secretly comments to Laertes that the madman's time is running out.

Act V, Scene ii The final scene of *Hamlet* is considered one of Shakespeare's best. It begins with an exchange between Hamlet and Horatio. Hamlet reveals how he got hold of the letters the King planned to send to England with instructions to murder Hamlet. Hamlet rewrote these letters, instructing that Rosencrantz and Guildenstern (the bearers of the letters) be murdered instead.

Hamlet also reveals to Horatio the truth about Claudius and his mother. Osric, a messenger, interrupts the dialogue. Osric announces that the King has set up a play duel between Laertes and Hamlet. Hamlet accepts the offer.

A banquet and feast have been prepared for the play duel. First, there is an exchange of formalities and greetings. Hamlet plays with the King and Laertes by acknowledging that two Hamlets exist, one of which is the mad Hamlet. Hamlet explains that it is this evil side of himself that has caused Laertes such grief. Laertes accepts the apology, but avoids a true reconciliation.

Claudius explains the rules and the fighting begins. This play duel is another examination of fiction and reality; a play within a play. During the duel, the King places a pearl into a poisoned cup of wine, identifying it as the vehicle of Hamlet's death.

The Queen, however, claims the cup and drinks from it. Here, the scene lapses into utter chaos. Laertes, having cheated by using a real sword, mortally wounds Hamlet. In the scuffle, the swords change hands and Hamlet mortally wounds Laertes. As the fighting becomes a matter of life and death, the Queen, poisoned, falls down dead.

Hamlet kills Laertes. As Laertes lies dying, he reveals the truth about Claudius: he was responsible for the murder of Hamlet's father. Claudius' poisoning the late King Hamlet is avenged in a particularly fitting way as young Hamlet uses Claudius' own poisoned sword to kill him.

The King and Laertes die. Finally, Hamlet is free. As young Fortinbras approaches, Hamlet, dying, drinks the little poison left in the cup. Hamlet's final words are a plea to Fortinbras to carry on Hamlet's voice. The connection between the two young men and their respective quests for revenge come full circle.

Fortinbras enters only to discover that the nation he has conquered has already been destroyed. We also learn that Rosencrantz and Guildenstern are dead. The chaos, the blood, and the death cause Fortinbras to realize that, indeed, revenge is bittersweet. Horatio offers to explain the events to Fortinbras. The play ends as the two young men exit. With corpses strewn all over the stage, Shakespeare leaves a final, devastating image of death.

HENRY IV

ABOUT THE AUTHOR

See page 111.

THE BIG PICTURE

Henry IV is another work of dramatic genius by the Bard. More historical in tone and subject matter than *Hamlet* or *Macbeth*, it nonetheless contains well-drawn (and some very witty) characters. The play depicts the rise of Prince Henry of Wales, or Hal.

Why you're reading this book:
- It contains one of the most comic and complex characters in English literature, Sir John Falstaff.
- In traditional Shakespearean style, it combines tragedy, wit, and very well-drawn characters.
- It raises important questions about the meaning of kingship, honor, and responsibility.
- Its portrayal of the "generation gap" between Prince Hal and his father still holds true today.

Your teachers are looking for:
- The aspects of *Henry IV* that make it a "historical" play.
- Prince Hal's relationship with his father, Henry IV, compared to his relationship with Falstaff.
- How Prince Hal changes and develops throughout the play.
- How Shakespeare's language changes to represent different ideas or lifestyles.

KEY CHARACTERS

The royal family:

King Henry IV: Prince Hal's father. He earned his crown by killing Richard II. He is a fair, brave ruler, but he is quite rigid and stuck in the old order.

Prince of Wales: Prince Henry, or Hal. The play's central figure. Somewhat of a wild prince, he is on bad terms with his father for most of the play.

Prince John of Lancaster: Prince Hal's younger brother, he is portrayed as a brave soldier in the battle at Shrewsbury.

Sir Walter Blunt: A nobleman and aide to the King.

The Percys (rebels against the King):

Henry Percy: Referred to as Hotspur, he is Northumberland's son and the nephew of the Earl of Worcester. He is the young warrior who leads the northern rebels.

Henry Percy, Earl of Northumberland: Hotspur's father, he is the head of the most powerful family of the northern territories. A hostile, cold man.

Thomas Percy, Earl of Worcester: The brother of the Earl of Northumberland and the uncle of Hotspur. A troublemaker.

Sir Richard Vernon: A nobleman who serves the Percys.

Katherine Percy: Hotspur's wife.

Others:

Owen Glendower: A Welshman and the head of another rebel faction against the King. He is rumored to have supernatural powers.

Edmund Mortimer, Earl of March: Leader of the King's troops of Herefordshire in the battle against Glendower's Welsh troops.

Archibald, Earl of Douglas: A Scotsman who led the forces that were defeated earlier by Hotspur. He now fights against Henry IV.

Sir John Falstaff: A rogue and a friend of Prince Henry, he drinks and steals. He has a sharp wit which helps him out of many sticky situations.

Poins, Peto, Gadshill, Bardolph, Francis the Drawer: Some of Falstaff's wild companions.

ESSAY IDEAS

- Why do you think Shakespeare gave the three major players in this drama the same name—King Henry, Henry Percy (Hotspur), and Prince Henry (Hal)?
- Describe Falstaff, using examples of his speeches and conversations to illustrate and/or back up your descriptions. Why is he known as one of the most complex figures in English literature?
- In the fight between Hotspur and King Henry, who do you think is more "correct"? Make a case for either one, using as much evidence from the play as you can.
- Do you see any similarities between the thugs' planning of the robbery at Gadshill and the Percys' planning of the revolt against King Henry? What are they?

A SAMPLE ESSAY IN OUTLINE FORM

Trace the development of Prince Hal's relationship with his father, Henry IV.
- Hal is at first rebellious:
  - Alienated from his father.
  - Spends time with robbers and thugs, particularly Falstaff.

- Seems to be ignoring his duties as Prince.
- Confrontation between Prince Hal and Henry IV:
  - Prince Hal is severely scolded.
  - His father compares him to the enemy, Hotspur.
- Hal finally proves himself worthy of his father's expectations:
  - Tries to redeem himself in battle.
  - During battle, Hal saves his father from Douglas.
  - Kills both Douglas and Hotspur.
- Father and son reconcile

At the end of the play, Prince Hal accepts his responsibility and comes into his role as a leader. However, despite their reconciliation, it is clear that Hal and his father are from entirely different generations, and that Hal will define his role as King in a more modern way.

PLOT SUMMARY

Act I, Scene i The setting is the court of the King of England. The King, the Lord John of Lancaster, the Earl of Westmoreland, and others enter. The King speaks of a war against the Welsh, and asks Westmoreland what his council has decided to do to end the war. Westmoreland tells the King that they have received news from Mortimer, who is leading the King's men against Owen Glendower's troops. A thousand of the King's men have been killed. Westmoreland goes on to tell the King that Hotspur, Harry Percy, and Archibald, all allies of the King, had a bloody battle at Holmedon.

The King tells the others that Sir Walter Blunt has brought good news: the Earl of Douglas, the King's enemy, has had several of his men taken prisoner. The King asks Westmoreland to return the following Wednesday, when the council will meet again. All exit.

Act I, Scene ii Prince Henry of Wales (Hal) and Sir John Falstaff enter. Friendly bantering goes on between the two, and the reader soon finds out that the men are partners in crime; stealing is their hobby. Poins, one of the Prince's companions, enters. He informs Falstaff and Henry that tomorrow morning at Gadshill, Pilgrims with much money and goods will be going to Canterbury, as will other men on their way to London. Prince Hal says he will not take part in the theft. Poins asks Falstaff to leave so he may talk to the Prince to persuade him to take part.

Poins tells the Prince that they will not rob the merchants themselves; they will rob their friends after they have secured the loot. They plan to go with their friends to the scene where the robbery will take place, then split up, saying they will meet up with them later. The scene closes with a soliloquy in which Prince Hal tells the audience that a day will come when he will throw off his evil ways and rise to his duty as Prince of Wales, shocking everyone around him.

Act I, Scene iii The King, Northumberland, Worcester, Hotspur, and Walter Blunt enter. The King announces that he will not tolerate any rebelliousness. Worcester reminds the King that it was their help that enabled him to win the throne. The King orders Worcester to leave.

Northumberland talks to the King, reassuring him. The King is also angry at Hotspur for not showing up when he was called upon. Walter Blunt tries to explain Hotspur's absence, but the King remains angry. The King thinks that Worcester wanted to use the war captives to bargain for ransom money for the Earl of March. When Hotspur defends March, the King refuses to listen any more and leaves.

Hotspur and Worcester confer, and we learn that they are part of the rebel contin-gent, the Percys. They devise a plot against the King: first, they will give him the war captives to appease him., and then they will confront him.

Act II, Scene i Two carriers, getting ready to leave for London, complain about the inn at Rochester. Gadshill, a thief, asks if he can borrow their lantern; the carriers say no and leave. Gadshill calls a chamberlain, who tells him that a middle-class landowner with three hundred marks in gold will be one of the travelers leaving from the inn.

Act II, Scene ii Prince Hal and Poins are together on the highway close to Gadshill. Poins runs off with Falstaff's horse, leaving Falstaff whining for him. Hal offers to find Poins for Falstaff.

Gadshill, Bardolph, and Peto arrive. The people whom the group plans to rob are approaching from the hill. The thieves put on their masks. Prince Hal instructs everyone but Poins to meet the travelers in the narrow lane, and tells them that he and Poins plan to wait in a different spot down the hill. Falstaff hesitates but complies. Hal and Poins leave, putting on disguises to help them carry out their plan.

The travelers are robbed, and the thieves collect the booty. When the group is about to examine the goods, Hal and Poins attack them. Bardolph and Peto run, but Falstaff stays. Seeing that he is outnumbered, he flees, leaving the goods.

Act II, Scene iii At Warkworth Castle, Hotspur is reading a letter from a man who was asked to join the fight against the King. The man has refused the invitation to join. Hotspur worries that the man might tell the King of their plans and betray them.

Lady Percy enters, worried about her husband. He has been neglecting her and acting strangely. Hotspur ignores her concerns; he only tells her that she will see him at an unnamed place soon.

Act II, Scene iv Prince Hal and Poins are at the Boar's Head Tavern. Hal gets Francis, one of the tavern workers, to play a game. Hal and Poins take turns calling Francis, who runs up and down the stairs of the tavern, trying to answer both of their calls.

Falstaff and his group arrive, and Falstaff tells how he bravely fought his attackers that night, exaggerating grossly. Hal recounts what really happened and challenges Falstaff to tell why he has lied. To cover up his lie, Falstaff says he knew it was really Hal, and would never have killed him. Falstaff is pleased: he knows Hal has the goods that were robbed.

One of the King's messengers comes. Hal tells Falstaff to make him leave. Falstaff returns with news that the Percys are revolting, and Hal seems unconcerned. He must go see his father, the King. Falstaff and Hal play-act a scene between Hal and his father, in which Hal plays the role of the King and Falstaff plays the role of Hal.

Suddenly, the sheriff arrives at the tavern. Hal tells Falstaff to hide, and tells the sheriff that the "fat man" isn't around. The sheriff leaves. Falstaff is asleep where he has hidden.

Act III, Scene i The scene is Glendower's castle in Wales, where the rebel leaders are meeting. Hotspur and Worcester speak with Glendower and Mortimer. Hotspur and Glendower are arguing over a land dispute; to settle the problem, the rebels split a map of England into three parts to be divided among them after they have overthrown the King. The northern parts will go to the Percys, the West to Glendower, and the South to Mortimer. Mortimer says he will set out with Hotspur and Worcester to meet Northumberland at

Shrewsbury. Glendower will need to join them later.

Hotspur is unhappy with the division—he wants a bigger portion. Glendower is hesitant, but the two of them manage to reach a compromise. Mortimer and his wife are trying to say good-bye; however, they don't speak the same language, so she sings a Welsh song instead. Hotspur tells his wife to join him and prepares to leave for Shrewsbury in two hours.

Act III, Scene ii Prince Hal comes to the palace in London to speak to his father. The King scolds his son for taking part in thievery and ignoring his stature as a prince. The King suggests that perhaps God is punishing him for something. Hal insists that accounts of his activities have been exaggerated.

Hal is told that his younger brother has taken his place in the political arena. Hal argues that his father should not believe the people who have told the King to dismiss him in such a way. Pleading his case, he tells his father he will prove his loyalty by fighting Hotspur. Ecstatic, the King tells Hal that he will be the commander of the royal forces. The King, Westmoreland, and Prince John will lead another brigade that will meet Hal's troops in the North. Walter Blunt arrives and tells the King and Hal that Douglas and the rebels have gathered their troops at Shrewsbury.

Act III, Scene iii Falstaff is bitter about his overweight state. A comment from Bardolph on his obesity prompts a speech concerning Bardolph's red nose. Mistress Quickly, the mistress of the tavern, enters. Falstaff accuses her of having searched his things and refuses to pay the bill for his food and clothing. When she mentions Hal, Falstaff calls him a Jack, or a rogue, and says he would hit him if he were there.

Hal enters with Peto. Falstaff continues

his argument with Mistress Quickly until Hal tells him that he was the one who searched his pockets. Falstaff forgives Mistress Quickly. Falstaff is unhappy to hear of Hal's reconciliation with his father. The young Prince gives orders to Bardolph, Peto, and Falstaff, enlisting them to fight the rebels.

Act IV, Scene i The scene is the rebel camp at Shrewsbury. Hotspur, Worcester, and Douglas enter. The Earl of Northumberland brings news that Hotspur's father is sick and cannot lead his men to Shrewsbury. News of the King's armies arrives. Prince John and the Earl of Westmoreland are leading seven thousand soldiers towards Shrewsbury, and the King has another army as well.

Hotspur, however, is not scared—he is eager to fight the royal army. He asks the whereabouts of Prince Hal. Vernon informs him that Prince Hal is ready to fight. He also says that Glendower needs time to gather his strength for the battle. Hotspur, fearless, eagerly awaits the battle with the King's men.

Act IV, Scene ii Falstaff and Bardolph are with their soldiers on a road near Coventry. Falstaff tells Bardolph to replenish the supply sack and to tell Peto to meet him at the end of town. He doesn't want to march his men through the town, since they are dressed in rags. Prince Hal and Westmoreland meet him and comment on how the soldiers are dressed. Hal reminds them to hurry, as Hotspur is already in the field, ready for battle.

Act IV, Scene iii Worcester and Vernon try to convince Hotspur that the rebels should hold off on their attack. Hotspur, however, wants to attack immediately, and Douglas agrees with him. A trumpet is heard, announcing a meeting. Walter Blunt enters.

Hotspur tells the story of how the Percys aided King Henry when he returned from his forced exile and how he took the throne. Hotspur says that the King has shown that he is ungrateful. In the morning, Hotspur will send Worcester to hear the King's terms and to announce their own.

Act IV, Scene iv The Archbishop of York—a clandestine ally to the Percys in their struggle aginst King Henry—instructs one of his men to bring vital information to the rebels. He has heard that Hotspur will face the King without the help of Northumberland, Glendower, and Mortimer. The Archbishop is frightened that the Percys will lose and that the King will discover his role in the conspiracy to overthrow him.

Act V, Scene i The Earl of Worcester and Sir Richard Vernon go to the King's camp outside of Shrewsbury. The King, Prince Hal, Prince John, the Earl of Westmoreland, Sir Walter Blunt, and Falstaff are all there. Worcester announces the position of the Percys. Their first demand is the King's abdication of the throne. Prince Hal responds by offering to fight Hotspur one on one to settle the battle once and for all, but his father refuses to let him. The King offers the rebels pardon if they put down their arms.

Worcester and Vernon leave, and Prince Hal says that Hotspur and Douglas will definitely reject the offer. The King agrees, and tells all to get to their posts. Falstaff has no desire to risk his life, and asks Hal to watch out for him. He gives a soliloquy about not finding any merit in being a dead war hero.

Act V, Scene ii At the rebel camp, Worcester says Hotspur must not be informed of the King's offer to pardon the rebels if they don't fight. Vernon agrees to stay silent on the subject. Worcester tells

Hotspur that the King is ready to fight. He also says that Prince Hal expressed a desire for head-to-head combat with Hotspur. Hotspur sounds the trumpets as the conflict is about to begin.

Act V, Scene iii On the field, Walter Blunt, who is wearing the same uniform as the King, meets Douglas. Douglas thinks that the King is before him and demands his surrender. Walter does not reveal his identity, and when the two fight, he is killed. Hotspur enters, praising Douglas until he realizes that the fallen man is not the King. Hotspur and Douglas reenter the battle.

A sudden attack leaves Falstaff alone. He sees Blunt and gives a soliloquy about the doubtful merits of seeking wartime honor. All but a few of his troops have been killed. Prince Hal enters. He scolds Falstaff for being idle and asks for his sword. Falstaff lies about his courageous behavior, even saying he killed Hotspur. Hal tells him that Hotspur is alive.

Falstaff refuses to give Hal his sword, but offers his "pistol" instead. It is a bottle, not a gun, that he takes out. Hal grabs it, scolds Falstaff again, and throws the bottle at him. Falstaff says he will kill Percy. Yet he is certainly not too willing to go after him if he will end up like his friend Walter Blunt. Falstaff makes it clear that he would be happy just to stay alive, no matter who wins or loses the battle.

Act V, Scene iv The King tells his sons Hal and John to rest. John won't rest, and Hal praises his younger brother's toughness.

Douglas enters and is confused when he sees the King. He demands to know the real identity of this man. Henry and Douglas now battle. The King is in real danger until Prince Hal enters the scene and challenges Douglas. Douglas turns and runs for his life. The King is moved by his son's courage.

As the King leaves, Hotspur enters and engages Prince Hal. Falstaff cheers the prince on. Douglas returns and tries to fight Falstaff, who falls down, playing dead. Douglas leaves, and Hotspur is wounded and falls. Hotspur begins to deliver his own eulogy but dies before he can finish. Prince Hal completes it for him.

Hal then sees Falstaff, who is seemingly dead. He recites a eulogy in his honor and leaves. Falstaff gets up after Hal leaves. He expresses his fear that perhaps Hotspur is faking his death just as he himself did moments ago. To be sure, he stabs the already dead Hotspur. He takes the body onto his back as Hal and John enter. John is confused because Hal has just told him that Falstaff is dead.

Falstaff says he would like to be made an earl or a duke. He acts shocked when the prince says that he killed Hotspur. A trumpet announces that the rebels have lost. The two princes leave to see how their allies have fared, and Falstaff follows to receive his reward.

Act V, Scene v King Henry calls for the deaths of Worcester and Vernon. The other rebels' fates will be decided later. Prince Hal intercedes on the behalf of the Earl of Douglas. His life is not taken, and Prince John sets the Scotsman free. The King announces he will divide his forces. One group, led by John and Earl of Westmoreland, will fight against the forces assembled by Northumberland and Archbishop Scroop in northern England. Accompanied by Prince Hal, the King will march to Wales to fight Glendower and Mortimer.

HUCKLEBERRY FINN

ABOUT THE AUTHOR

Mark Twain (1835–1910), born Samuel Langhorne Clemens, is one of the most well-known writers in American literature. He wrote some of America's most important fiction.

Twain was born in Florida, Missouri, near the Mississippi River. The river's steady parade of colorful characters made a great impression on Twain and his view of the world. He was first employed as a printer at the age of 16, but he soon decided to give riverboat piloting a try. When he eventually returned to printing and newspaper work, it was with a new set of observations about human nature and a new drive to write humorous fiction.

His career as a writer of popular fiction began in 1865 with the short story "The Celebrated Jumping Frog of Calaveras County." A series of popular books, beginning with *The Innocents Abroad* in 1869, soon changed the face of American literature. With books like *Tom Sawyer, The Prince and the Pauper,* and *A Connecticut Yankee in King Arthur's Court,* Twain introduced a loose, simple writing style that approximated natural American speech and made his writing accessible to the average American.

His influence grew over the years, peaking with *Huckleberry Finn* (1885), a book so powerful that Ernest Hemingway noted, "All modern American literature comes from *Huckleberry Finn.*" Twain died a bit more cynical than in his youthful Mississippi days, but no less popular or talented. Mark Twain is widely acclaimed not just as a comic author, but as one of American literature's central figures.

THE BIG PICTURE

Huck Finn is the satirical masterpiece of Mark Twain, one of the most widely read American authors. It is the story of the misadventures of the young runaway Huck Finn and his friend Jim, an escaped slave. During the course of the novel, Twain introduces us to many different characters and customs, many of them comic, all of them distinctly American.

Why you're reading this book:
- It is a very funny and entertaining satire of human nature and American culture.
- It is one of the first examples of the American "road" genre, where two people travel around the country having interesting experiences together.
- It presents a view of slavery that, while it may seem offensive to us, actually existed in our country.
- It interestingly blends the conventions of "boys' stories" with sharp satire.
- It contains themes common to all American literature.

Your teachers are looking for:
- How the book reflects American culture at the time it was written.
- How the river functions as a symbol.
- Racism and how it is treated by various characters.
- The meaning of "good boy" versus "bad boy."

You may question why you are reading a book that is unquestionably racist. This criticism has plagued the book for decades, and is most difficult to answer. What's your opinion?

H
U
C
K
L
E
B
E
R
R
Y

F
I
N
N

KEY CHARACTERS

Huckleberry Finn: The narrator of the story and a very free-spirited youth. Huck defines himself as a "bad boy" to free himself from the social conventions associated with being "good." He seems to do the right thing most of the time, however.

Jim: The slave that escapes on the same night as Huck. He joins him on his journey up and down the river, looking for freedom. Jim acts as both a surrogate brother and parent to Huck. Jim is very superstitious, but essentially gentle-hearted and good-natured.

Tom Sawyer: Huck's best friend and a self-styled authority on adventures. Tom complicates Huck's life and river adventures, since his romanticism clashes with Huck's practicality. On shore, Huck and Jim let him get his way every time.

Pap: Huck's father, a nasty scoundrel. He is one of the reasons Huck believes himself to be bad at heart. Pap attempts to steal Huck's money and be better than him, but he fails.

The duke and the dauphin: A pair of con men. The younger claims to be the exiled English Duke of Bridgewater and the older claims to be Louis XVII, the deposed King of France.

Mary Jane Wilks: A girl conned by the duke and the dauphin into believing they are her uncles. Huck develops a crush on her and finally tells her the truth about himself. With his help, she manages to set things right.

Aunt Sally: Tom's aunt. She believes that Huck is Tom and that Tom is Huck's brother Sid. She tries and fails to keep the boys out of trouble. She is very kind, though, and Huck feels real affection for her.

ESSAY IDEAS

- Define Huck and Jim's relationship.
- How does Huck as narrator color the story he tells?
- Huck finally gives up on himself and defines himself as an eternally bad boy. How does this change him?
- What significance does the river have in this story?
- How is the issue of slavery handled? Compare Jim with some of the other slaves in the book.
- What satirical points does Twain make through the duke and the dauphin?
- What does the novel say about American culture at that time?

A SAMPLE ESSAY IN OUTLINE FORM

Compare and contrast the characters of Huck Finn and Tom Sawyer.
- Huck Finn:
  - Poorly educated.
  - His intelligence is practical.
  - Caring of others.
  - He saves Jim.
  - Inventive.
- Tom Sawyer:
  - Well-read.
  - His book learning takes him on periodic flights of fancy.
  - More concerned with his own welfare and reputation than with Huck.
  - The famous fence-whitewashing incident.
  - Wildly imaginative.

While Tom is better educated than Huck, it is Huck's practicality that saves the day. He is less full of himself and more caring than Tom. Through Huck, Twain celebrates the rough-hewn, simple American; he portrays Huck's good, basic values as more important than Tom's book smarts.

PLOT SUMMARY

Chapters 1–2 Huck introduces himself to us in these chapters. He summarizes some of the events from *The Adventures of Tom Sawyer* and updates us on some of the characters in that novel.

Huck is staying with the Widow Douglas and her sister, Miss Watson. They try to teach him to be civilized, but he resists them. He finally scandalizes them by saying that he thinks he would probably prefer hell to their heaven.

Huck meets up with Tom and they sneak out past a sleeping Jim. Jim thinks that what Huck and Tom do when they sneak out is the work of devils, and he eventually becomes famous for the tale of possession that he invents. Huck and Tom go to a cave and form a robber band with some of their friends. There is much discussion of the rules of the band. Tom, as always, is the authority on the proper conduct of robbers.

Chapters 3–4 Huck says that he doesn't see the point in praying. He hears that his father has been drowned, but he doesn't believe it. The robber band breaks up, because they don't really rob or kill except in Tom's imagination.

Huck gets more used to life with Widow Douglas and Miss Watson. We can see that they haven't changed him much, though, because he still holds on to his superstitions. Huck begins to worry about the bad luck in his future. He sells his six thousand dollars to the Judge for a dollar so that nothing will happen to it, and he asks Jim to predict his future. Chapter 4 ends with Huck discovering his father in his room.

Chapters 5–6 Huck's father is angry because Huck has learned to read and write, and he doesn't want Huck to better him. He demands Huck's money, but Huck has already given it to the Judge.

Huck's father tries to convince another judge that he has reformed, but later gets drunk at a party and breaks his arm. He finally kidnaps Huck, holding him in a shack in the woods. He gets very drunk and goes on a tirade about free black men and the government, saying how unfair it is that he should be looked down upon more than a black man. When he passes out, Huck takes his gun and guards him.

Chapters 7–8 Huck falls asleep, and in his dream he tells his father that he was trying to keep someone away from their shack. This gives Huck an idea for his escape. He fakes his own murder, steals the provisions, and escapes in a boat he has found on the river.

The whole town searches for Huck's body in the river, but he is hiding out on Jackson's island. There he discovers Jim, who is running away from being traded and sent to New Orleans. They have a talk about Jim's bad luck with money.

Chapters 9–10 Huck and Jim find a cave. During a heavy storm, they see a house floating down the flooding river, with a dead man inside. Luckily there are plenty of provisions in the house.

Jim is bitten by a rattlesnake, the first of many misfortunes Huck and Jim blame on the bad luck they got when Huck handled a snakeskin. Huck decides to go to town dressed as a girl to find out how much trouble they are in, and his first stop is an old woman's house.

Chapters 11–12 Huck finds out from the old woman that both his father and Jim are wanted for his murder. Then he blunders, giving his identity away. She sends him off saying that her husband is searching Jackson's island for the two suspects.

Huck returns to the island before the husband, and he and Jim leave on a raft they have rebuilt. After a few days of pleasant drifting, they find a wrecked steamboat, onto which Huck coaxes Jim aboard, for the adventure. They find a murderous gang on board. Jim hangs back, but Huck moves closer to get a better look. When Huck goes back for Jim, they find that their raft has washed away.

Chapters 13–14 Huck and Jim steal the gang's skiff and find the raft, but Huck feels guilty for stranding the gang on the island. He lies to the boat's watchman to get him to go back to the boat and rescue the men, but by the time he gets there the boat is sunken and dark.

Jim and Huck sit on the raft and have one of their deep discussions, this time about kings and the "wisdom" of Solomon and Frenchmen.

Chapters 15–16 The travelers head for Ohio, a free state, but get lost in a fog. They are separated for an entire night. When Huck finds the raft again, he tries to trick Jim into thinking that the whole night was a dream, but Jim gets angry.

Huck and Jim can't find Cairo, the town where the river to Ohio meets the Mississippi, and Huck begins to wonder if he should "do the right thing" and turn Jim in. At this point they run into two men searching for runaway slaves. Jim hides and Huck tells them a lie about his family having smallpox to keep the men away from the raft. To soothe their consciences, the two men give Huck forty dollars. Huck decides that doing the right thing is a waste of time and resolves to do whatever comes easiest to him, which, for the most part, is the "wrong thing."

They discover that they have gone past the junction for Ohio, and as they head back they are run over by a steamboat. Huck loses Jim and swims for shore.

Chapters 17–18 Huck is taken in by the Grangerfords, an aristocratic family. He meets their son Buck, who is his age, and learns about Buck's sister Emmeline, who wrote poetry about dead people before her own death. Huck tries to write her a poem, but it doesn't seem to work.

The Grangerfords are feuding with another family, the Shepherdsons. Huck goes back after church to get young Sophia Grangerford's Testament, and he sees a note in it from Harney Shepherdson. Sophia and Harney run away together, and there is a gun battle between the families. All the Grangerfords are killed in a very violent scene. Huck heads back for the Grangerfords' house and finds that Jim has been taken in by their slaves and has repaired the raft. Huck and Jim head back down the river.

Chapters 19–20 Floating slowly down the river, Huck and Jim meet the duke and the dauphin, who flag them down for a ride and then claim royal heritage aboard the raft. Huck sees through this, but knows that it is easier just to agree with their lies. He creates his own lie about owning Jim but having to hide during the day because no one will believe him. The duke and the dauphin try to think of a way for all of them to be able to travel in daylight.

The two con men practice their Shakespeare in preparation for a show at the next town. They take Huck to town with them. The dauphin takes Huck to a revival meeting, where he claims to be a pirate who has reformed on the spot. He passes a hat around and makes them some money. Meanwhile, the duke has come up with a scheme to explain Jim's being on the raft with them. He says Jim is a runaway that they have captured, and he makes a handbill to prove it. Back on the raft, Jim asks the dauphin to speak some French, but he claims to have forgotten it.

Chapters 21–22 The duke and the

dauphin practice *Romeo and Juliet* and *Richard III*. The duke gives his rather cracked version of Hamlet's soliloquy. They advertise their show in a very drab little town.

There are many layabouts in this town. One drunken man rides up and down the street, cursing a man named Sherburne, who tells the drunk that he will only tolerate the drunk's behavior until one o'clock. At that time, the drunk continues to rant and Sherburne shoots him. Surprised and excited by the shooting, the townspeople decide to lynch Sherburne. He makes a very grand speech about the cowardice of the average man, and the crowd leaves him alone and goes to the circus.

Since no one attends the duke and dauphin's show, they change their advertising tactics. They write on their new posters for the Royal Nonesuch, "Ladies and Children not Admitted."

Chapters 23–24 The two cons perform their show for a full house; their show consists only of the dauphin, painted and naked, jumping about on stage. The audience rises up to attack the players, but one of them says that to preserve their dignity, they should recommend the show to the rest of the town for the next night—that way, they won't look like fools for spending their money to see the show. The same thing happens on the second night, but on the third, when both audiences show up to pelt the duke and dauphin with rotten fruit and dead cats, the two skip town with the ticket money.

On the raft, Jim asks Huck if all kings are as bad as the dauphin. Huck says that he is about normal for a king. Then Jim remembers how he once hit his small daughter for not obeying him and then found out that she was deaf. Jim cries for his lost family. Huck thinks that this is unusual for a black man.

The duke decides to disguise Jim as an Arab, for a change of plan. The dauphin finds out that someone named Peter Wilks just died and that his brothers, a Reverend and a deaf-mute, are expected from England. Since no one in town knows what they look like, the duke and the dauphin disguise themselves as Wilks' brothers.

Chapters 25–26 The town and Wilks' orphaned daughters fall for the trick. The two "brothers" are left $6,000, which they give to the girls as a show of good faith. The family doctor doesn't buy their accents, but the girls still believe them. To prove their faith, Mary Jane, the eldest, gives all the money back to her "uncles."

Huck plays their servant. He talks with the younger daughter, but he keeps getting his story wrong. She challenges him and the other two girls defend him. He resolves to save their money from the two crooks, and swipes it from the duke and dauphin's room.

Chapters 27–28 Huck hides the money in Wilks' coffin, but he doesn't have time to check for it before the burial, so he is not sure if it is there or not. The dauphin announces that they wish to take the girls to England as soon as everything is sold. The duke and the dauphin sell the family's slaves, separating a slave family. The girls are very upset and Huck decides that he should comfort them. The dauphin finds that the money is gone and asks Huck about it. Huck hints that it was taken by the sold slaves.

Huck finally tells Mary Jane the true story. He arranges for her to hide out until he can expose the duke and the dauphin. Huck seems to be developing a crush on Mary Jane. He tricks the other sisters into going along and gets ready for the day of the auction. Just before the auction is to start, the real brothers appear.

Chapters 29–30 The heirs are surprised

to find impostors. A witness steps forward and says that he saw Huck and the duke and the dauphin up the river in a canoe. The dauphin doesn't have the money anymore, so more suspicion falls on him. They then fail a handwriting test, and the true brother challenges the dauphin to describe the tattoo on his dead brother's chest. The dauphin hazards a guess, and the tattoo that the real brother describes wasn't seen by the pallbearers. To settle the matter, they decide to exhume the body. They find the money and in the confusion, Huck escapes.

He runs to the raft, and he and Jim celebrate being rid of the con men. But the duke and dauphin soon catch up with Huck and Jim. The con men blame each other for losing the money and ruining the scheme, but they make up.

Chapters 31–32 After the excitement dies down for a few days, the two crooks go back to scheming, but nothing seems to work very well. Huck and Jim resolve to get rid of them, so Huck goes to town with them and runs away. When he gets back to the raft, he finds that Jim is gone. A passerby tells him that the dauphin sold Jim as a runaway slave.

Huck has a crisis of conscience here. He wants to help Jim, but the "right thing" for him to do is to let Jim be returned to his owner. Huck decides to help Jim, even though he thinks he will probably go to hell for it.

Huck finds the duke and tells him that the raft is gone. The duke is setting up the Royal Nonesuch scam again; he gives Huck three days to find Jim. Huck reaches the farm where Jim was taken and is mistaken for the owner's nephew. Upon learning that the owner's nephew—who is expected very soon—is none other than Tom Sawyer, Huck pretends to be Tom and tells

them all about home before trying to intercept Tom.

Chapters 33–34 Huck finds Tom a little way from the farm. After he explains what has happened, he gets Tom to help him steal Jim back. So that Huck will be able to stay disguised as 'Tom Sawyer,' Tom goes to his aunt's and pretends to be Sid, Tom's brother.

At dinner, Huck and Tom learn that the town has figured out the duke and dauphin's tricks and plans to get them that night. When Huck and Tom go for a walk that night, they see the duke and the dauphin, tarred and feathered, being run out of town on a rail.

Huck and Tom find Jim in a shed in the yard. They decide to dig him out, since that is the most adventurous way. Huck is surprised that a boy with breeding as good as Tom's would ever want to steal a slave, but Tom tells him that it isn't important. Another slave lets them in to see Jim, and they let him in on the plan to steal Jim.

Chapters 35–36 Tom Sawyer, with his love for the dramatic, decides that Jim needs to be freed properly—which means by the most complicated means possible. However, Tom's elaborate plans are too difficult. Finally, in the interest of speed, they get more practical. The slave attending Jim thinks he's bewitched.

Chapters 37–38 Tom, again drawing on his view of how a "prisoner" should be, decides that Jim needs a number of things before he is a legitimate prisoner: a plant, a pet, and his "coat of arms" whittled in the wall of the shack that serves as his prison. Huck and Tom steal various things from the house. Tom's Aunt Sally begins to miss the things, but Tom confuses her enough to get her to stop asking questions. Tom and Huck make more prisoner provisions for Jim, and Tom has many rules for prisoners. Jim disagrees with most of his ideas.

Chapters 39–40 Huck and Tom catch vermin for Jim to befriend in captivity (another important requirement to be a 'real' prisoner). The creatures, however, get loose in the house as well, driving Aunt Sally crazy.

Finally all the preparations are complete. After all that fanfare, all Huck and Tom have to do is steal the key to the shack and ride down the river with Jim. Tom decides the plan is too easy and tips off the locals with an anonymous note saying a desperate band of Indians are going to try and free Jim. It works so well that on the night of the escape, fifteen farmers with rifles fire on Huck, Jim, and Tom as they run for the river. Tom is shot in the leg, and Huck goes for a doctor.

Chapters 41–43 As Huck gets the doctor, he runs into Tom's uncle. The two men return to a very worried Aunt Sally. The two wait the night out for the doctor to return with news of Tom.

Tom does not return until the morning. He is fine, but exhausted and a little feverish. The doctor tells everyone what a help Jim was in tending to Tom; however, despite this, Jim is locked up once again.

When Tom wakes up, he tells Huck that Jim had been free all along—his mistress had set him free in her will. Tom's Aunt Polly shows up at the farm and tells Aunt Sally that "Tom" (actually Huck) and "Sid" (actually Tom) had been tricking her. Despite the revelation, the boys do not get into serious trouble.

Jim is freed and treated well, and Tom makes him rich with a gift of forty dollars. Huck finds out that his father is dead—his body was the one he saw in the floating house—so he can get his six thousand dollars back. Aunt Sally wants to adopt Huck, but he wants to see the frontier and get away before he gets "sivilized."

THE ILIAD

ABOUT THE AUTHOR

The exact identity of Homer is a matter of great debate. One school of thought believes that Homer was a single poet writing in the eighth or ninth century B.C. Another school believes that the name "Homer," a possible variation on the Greek word for man, is simply the convenient pen name for a number of authors. Both the *Iliad* and the *Odyssey* are attributed to Homer.

Both works are written in verse, and both are transcriptions from a long-standing oral tradition. Before playwrights or novelists, there were bards, storytellers who would tell or sing their tales professionally. Rhymed and metered verse was not only more pleasant to listen to, but it was also easier for the bards to memorize.

Regardless of his actual identity (or identities), it is certain that Homer's works, the *Iliad* and the *Odyssey,* are cornerstones of modern literature. Homer's understanding of human nature, combined with the scope and range of his epics, make his work a foundation for virtually everything you will read.

THE BIG PICTURE

The *Iliad* recounts the story of the Greek war hero Achilles. Its central theme is the relation between gods and men and the roles both play in man's destiny. It closely parallels the *Aeneid* both in its style—epic poem—and the story it tells—the adventures of a man leading a nation.

Why you're reading this book:
- It is an epic poem, the precursor to the novel.

- The prominent role of the gods provides a good overall view of the importance of mythology in Greek and Roman culture.
- Historically, it paints a sweeping picture of the Trojan War. The tale of the Achaian*–Roman conflict is an enduring one.
- The character of Achilles is a forerunner to the "tragic hero," who appears in the works of many later authors, including Shakespeare.

Your teachers are looking for:
- Achilles as a tragic hero, and his "fatal flaw."
- How the actions and attitudes of the gods affect the story.
- The Greek definition of heroism.
- The fact that the story is essentially an oral history—the effect this has on the story.
- The characteristics and language of the epic genre of literature.

KEY CHARACTERS

Achilles: A fierce Achaian warrior. The *Iliad*, more than anything else, is the story of his development.

Hektor: The Trojan war leader. Receives Achilles' full wrath when he kills his friend Patroklos.

Agamemnon: The Achaian war leader. Heady and proud, his argument with Achilles nearly costs the Achaians the war.

Helen: Wife of Menelaos. Her capture at the hands of the Trojan, Paris, caused the Trojan War.

Paris: Son of King Priam, brother of Hektor. He often hides from the battles his actions cause.

*The people known today as Greeks used to be called Achaians.

Diomedes: An Achaian soldier. He is courageous and strong, receiving the assistance of the gods more than once in battle.

Nestor: An Achaian soldier. He is noble and wise, the creator of many shrewd plans.

Priam: The King of Troy and Hektor's father.

Zeus: The King of the gods. He dictates much of the immortal intervention in the story.

Hera: Zeus' wife. Through many different devices, she is able to manipulate her husband to her advantage. More than anything else, she wants to see the Trojans defeated.

The many gods who intervene in the fighting and other human affairs. Some of the more prominent: Athena, Apollo, Aphrodite, Ares, and Poseidon.

ESSAY IDEAS

• How does Achilles fit the role of a tragic hero? What is his fatal flaw?
• Compare/contrast Achilles and Hektor.
• Why do you think the intervention of the gods is such a prevalent theme in the *Iliad*?
• What role does Nestor serve?
• There seems to be a code of honor throughout the *Iliad*. Who adheres to this code? Who departs from it?
• Trace Achilles' development from egotistical warrior to understanding conqueror. How much change do you think he truly undergoes?

A SAMPLE ESSAY IN OUTLINE FORM

Discuss Achilles as a forerunner to the "tragic hero" of later literature.
• Achilles' heroic qualities:

• Strength and bravery in battle.
• Intelligence (particularly in battle).
• Support from the gods.
• Achilles tragic flaw, pride:
  • He is too headstrong in his first confrontation with Agammemnon.
  • Pride nearly causes the Greeks to lose the war.
  • Pride causes the death of his good friend Patroklos.
• Similarities between Achilles and later tragic heroes:
  • He has a mixture of tragic and heroic qualities; he is not all good or all bad. (This is true of Shakespeare's tragic heroes and almost all the heroes of modern literature, through to the twentieth century.)

PLOT SUMMARY

Book I   Before beginning his story, Homer asks the Muse of Poetry for her assistance. This is the traditional opening to any epic poem; it also introduces the idea of the gods being actively involved in human life, an important theme in the *Iliad*.

The Achaians and the Trojans are at war. As the story begins, we are introduced to Achilles, the Achaians' strongest soldier, and Agamemnon, the commander of the Achaian army. Achilles is trying to help his friend Menelaos save his wife Helen, who has been taken by the Trojans. Achilles and Agamemnon have received from their troops two "war prizes": Chryseis and Briseis, beautiful Trojan women.

Chryseis' father, Chryses, begs Agamemnon to release his daughter, but Agamemnon will not hear of giving up his prize. Chryses, a priest of Apollo, asks his god for help. Apollo complies, sending a plague that kills scores of Achaian warriors.

After a week of plague, Achilles demands that a soothsayer explain its cause.

When it is revealed that the plague is the fault of Agamemnon, the commander is enraged at having been shown up in front of his troops. He says that he will return Chryseis to the Trojans only if Achilles gives him Briseis. At this, Achilles becomes enraged. Only the soothing words of Nestor and intervention from the goddess Athena prevent him from attacking Agamemnon. He proclaims that he will do as Agamemnon wishes; however, neither he nor any of his troops will fight for the Achaians.

Later, while walking alone by the seashore, Achilles is visited by his mother Thetis, a sea nymph. He asks that she persuade Zeus to help the Trojans defeat the Achaians; then the Achaians will realize they have made a mistake in insulting Achilles.

Thetis visits Zeus in the palace of the gods. Despite his fear that his wife, Hera, will be greatly angered, Zeus agrees to help the Trojans.

Book II Zeus sends a dream to Agamemnon that convinces the Achaian leader that he must attack the Trojans in full force the next day. Agamemnon awakes and begins preparing his troops for battle.

Agamemnon decides to test the troops' loyalty: he tells them that they have been at war long enough and can now return home. The test of loyalty fails: all the soldiers cheer and rush to the ships. Odysseus and Nestor, however, persuade the troops to stay and fight for the honor of taking Troy. The Achaians prepare for battle.

Hektor, the Trojan commander, has heard of the Achaians' plans, and readies his soldiers as well. The Trojan army sets itself on the field outside Troy.

Book III As the two armies face off, the Trojan prince, Paris, steps to the front and dares anyone to fight him. Paris' challenge is quickly met by Menelaos, husband of the abducted Helen. Despite his outward bravado, however, Paris tries to hide from Menelaos. His brother Hektor scolds him for his cowardice. Ashamed, Paris agrees to a duel with Menelaos. A truce is called. Agamemnon and the Trojan King Priam work out the details of the truce and make a joint sacrifice to the gods.

Menelaos quickly gets the better of Paris in the duel, wounding the Trojan. Before Paris can be taken prisoner, however, he is saved by the goddess Aphrodite. She takes him to his bedroom, to Helen. Agamemnon declares Menelaos the winner of the fight and demands that Helen be returned.

Book IV The truce is short–lived. The gods convene in Olympos, and Hera argues that the fighting must continue: she wants to see Troy destroyed. Zeus gives in and sends Athena to resume the battle.

Athena convinces the Trojan warrior Pandaros to kill Menelaos. He fires an arrow at Menelaos, severely wounding him. The furious battle resumes.

Book V A wounded Achaian soldier, Diomedes, prays to Athena for help. She answers his plea, giving him courage and the ability to tell the difference between gods and men on the battlefield. He is not allowed to fight with any gods, with one exception. He may fight Aphrodite—who, as the goddess of love, should not intervene in battle—if she tries to engage him.

Diomedes reenters the fray and is a fighting machine. He tears through the Trojan ranks, wounding Aphrodite's son Aeneas. When Aphrodite comes to help Aeneas, Diomedes attacks and wounds her as well. She runs to Zeus, crying, but the god has no sympathy for her. Because Aphrodite is the goddess of love, Zeus feels that she should stay out of battle; love and war, while remarkably alike, should remain separate.

Back in the battle, Ares, the god of war, has decided to help the Trojans. His power is felt, and the Achaians begin to lose. Both Hera and Athena intervene, however, and give the Achaians new life. Inspired by Athena again, Diomedes attacks Ares and wounds him. Ares, as well as Athena and Hera, leave the battle.

Book VI The battle is now being fought solely by mortals, and the Achaians begin to push the Trojans back. A soothsayer tells Hektor to make a sacrifice to Athena to regain her favor. Hektor goes back into the city to prepare a sacrifice.

The two armies are now taking a break from fighting. Diomedes challenges a Trojan warrior, Glaukos, to one-on-one battle. However, before they fight, they realize that their grandfathers were once friends. They decide to avoid harming each other in honor of that friendship and exchange armor.

Hektor, within the walls of Troy, tells his mother Hekuba to go to Athena's temple to make a sacrifice. He then goes to find Paris, who is hiding from the battle again, this time with Helen and her female attendants. Hektor again demands that Paris fight, and the warrior agrees to rejoin the battle.

Before Hektor returns to the fray himself, he is met by his wife Andromache. She begs him to stay in the safety of Troy. Hektor, although he knows that he will eventually die in battle, refuses: his fate is the will of the gods, an irresistible force. He meets Paris and the two leave the city.

Book VII Athena and Apollo, watching from Olympos, decide to stop the day's fighting. They arrange a duel between Hektor and Ajax. The two soldiers are evenly matched, however, and neither can win the duel. Night approaches and the battle is left until the next day.

That night, Nestor proposes that a truce be called to allow for the burying of the dead on both sides. A truce is called, and the next day both armies bury their dead and feast peacefully. The Achaians use the time to build walls around their ships, a plan suggested by the indispensable Nestor.

In the gods' camp, Zeus has proclaimed an end to immortal intervention in the battle. He threatens dire consequences to any god or goddess trying to help either side. Zeus does, however, allow Athena to give advice to the Achaian camp.

Book VIII When fighting begins anew the next day, the Trojans quickly gain an advantage and push the Achaians from the battlefield. Hera tries to enlist the aid of Poseidon against the Trojans, but the god is mindful of Zeus' warning.

As the Achaians are being pummeled, Hera and Athena try to sneak down to help. They are caught by Zeus, who again tells them that no gods shall intervene in the battle. The Achaians are on their own.

Darkness is again falling, and the Achaians retire for the night, nearly defeated. The Trojans set up camp by the walls protecting the Achaian ships so that the enemy cannot sail off during the night.

Book IX In the Achaian camp that night, Agamemnon breaks down, believing that all is lost. His despair is shared by his men, and the troops begin to talk of leaving for home. At this, Diomedes states that even if all leave, he will stay alone and fight. He proclaims that Troy is destined to fall. His fiery speech rallies the Achaian army, and all agree to fight.

Nestor tells Agamemnon that the Achaian army is faring so poorly because of the loss of Achilles and his men. Agamemnon finally suppresses his pride and agrees. He sends two soldiers with gifts and promises to appease Achilles and bring his might back to the Achaian fold.

However, Achilles is not so quick to put aside his ego, and refuses Agamemnon's offer of reconciliation. He says that his pride is too hurt to return; he and his troops will sail away from the Achaian camp in the morning.

Book X Later that night, Agamemnon, unable to sleep, calls a meeting of his advisers. Here, Nestor suggests that spies be sent into the Trojan camp. Agamemnon agrees, and Diomedes and Odysseus make their way to the enemy camp.

They capture a Trojan spy, Dolon, who tells them the troop placement and battle plans of the Trojans. More important, he tells them of the camp of the warriors from Thrace. The camp is unprotected and holds a beautiful team of horses. After killing Dolon, Diomedes and Odysseus make their way to the Thracian camp. They kill a number of sleeping soldiers, steal the horses, and get away unharmed, returning to the Achaian camp laden with booty.

Book XI In the morning, the Achaians at first have the advantage in battle. But again, the Trojans begin to bludgeon their opponents, wounding many soldiers, including Agamemnon.

Achilles, watching from afar, decides to send his friend Patroklos for news of the battle. Patroklos finds Nestor, who recounts the day's events (and rambles on at length about many other battles). Nestor suggests to Patroklos that he dress up in Achilles' armor and join the battle. At the sight of Achilles' armor, the Trojans might think that the powerful soldier and his troops have returned to the fight. This might help to turn the advantage to the Achaian side.

Books XII–XV The Trojans, who have won the favor of Zeus and are receiving his aid, break through the Achaian defenses. They are now at the Achaian ships, and it appears they will win. Agamemnon, again in despair, argues that the Achaians must try to board their ships and escape.

But help for the Achaians is on the way. Zeus, satisfied that his intervention has insured a Trojan victory, forgets the battle. Poseidon, noticing the inattention of Zeus, moves to encourage the Achaians. Hera helps to divert Zeus' attention even further: she visits him clad in Aphrodite's magic girdle and seduces him.

Books XVI–XVII In Achilles' camp, Patroklos begs the warrior to allow him to wear his armor and put Nestor's plan into action. Achilles at first opposes the idea, but he relents when he sees the Achaian ships being burned by the Trojans. He warns Patroklos only to rescue the ships, for he fears that Patroklos will be killed if he attacks Troy.

Patroklos, accompanied by his troops, enters the fray. The combination of fresh troops and the fear of Achilles sends the Trojans into quick retreat. Patroklos chases the Trojans toward Troy.

He should, however, have listened to Achilles' warning. Apollo appears in the fight and knocks Patroklos' helmet off. A Trojan warrior wounds Patroklos with a spear; Hektor adds a spear to the belly and Patroklos dies.

After Patroklos falls, Menelaos tries to drag his body to safety. Hektor stops him and takes Achilles' armor off the corpse. The two sides battle for possession of Patroklos' body. The Achaians rescue his body and bring it back to their camp for a proper burial.

Book XVIII The death of Patroklos hits

Achilles hard and he cries loudly and openly. His mother Thetis hears his sobs and comes to him. She tells Achilles that if he tries to seek revenge for the murder of his comrade, he may be killed as well. Achilles is bent on avenging the death of Patroklos, however, so she promises to help him.

Achilles goes to the battlefield. At the sight of Patroklos' dead body, he lets out a bloodcurdling cry. The Trojans retreat in fear and awe, and Achilles vows to destroy Hektor.

Thetis goes to the god Hephaistos and asks him to fashion new armor for her warrior son. After hearing her recount Achilles' exploits, Hephaistos makes an incredibly beautiful and strong suit and shield. Thetis returns to her son bearing the gift.

Book XIX As soon as he dons his armor, Achilles calls a war council. He proclaims his feud with Agamemnon over and calls for immediate engagement. Odysseus says that the attack will have to wait: the troops are too tired from constant fighting to rally so soon. Achilles decides to fast until he is allowed to seek his revenge.

Preparing for the attack, Achilles accuses his horses of allowing his friend to be killed. One of his horses replies that it was fate that caused Petroklos' demise, a fate that will soon meet Achilles. Achilles says that he is well aware of the dangers he faces, but he must avenge his friend.

Books XX–XXI Zeus proclaims that gods are now allowed to intervene in the battle on any side they choose. As the battle opens, it appears that Achilles is the true god: he slaughters scores of Trojans, and would have killed Aeneas if not for the protection of Poseidon.

A group of Trojan soldiers tries to escape from Achilles by hiding near the River of Xanthos. Before they can traverse the river, Achilles overtakes them and kills them, leaving the water strewn with bloody bodies. The god Xanthos sends huge waves at Achilles, and for a moment the warrior falters. However, other gods come to his aid, and Xanthos is neutralized.

The battle is now in full force, with both mortals and immortals joining in the fight. Hera defeats Artemis; Ares and Aphrodite fall to Athena. Throughout, Achilles is an ever-present force. The Trojans, in full retreat, hide in the city of Troy.

Book XXII The entire Trojan army is now safe in Troy, save Hektor, who awaits Achilles outside the city walls. Like Paris, his courage falters when he sees Achilles, and he runs away. The gods finally persuade Hektor to face Achilles.

Before the two duel, Hektor asks that Achilles above all treat his dead body with respect. Achilles, full of bloodlust, refuses. The two clash, and Achilles kills Hektor with a spear wound to the throat. The Achaian army crowds around the fallen Trojan commander. Achilles tears off Hektor's armor and drags him by his horses off the battlefield. The entire city of Troy grieves at this horrible death; Achilles' revenge is complete.

Book XXIII After a night of feasting, the Achaians prepare a funeral pyre for Patroklos. His body, along with the bodies of twelve Trojan soldiers, is burned. Achilles then begins a series of athletic events in honor of his dead friend.

Book XXIV Each day for more than a week after his death, Achilles drags the corpse of Hektor around the grave of Patroklos. The gods preserve Hektor's body until they decide that he must be given a proper burial. Zeus sends Thetis to explain to Achilles that he must return Hektor's body to Hektor's father Priam.

Priam is led into the Achaian camp that night by Hermes. He pleads with Achilles to return the body of his son. Achilles, his anger quenched, shares in Priam's mourning for the dead and agrees to return the body. Priam and Achilles eat together. Hektor is given a proper funeral in the city of Troy, complete with eulogies and a great feast.

ABOUT THE AUTHOR

See page 111.

THE BIG PICTURE

Julius Caesar, Shakespeare's dramatic rendering of the rise and fall of the Roman leader, focuses on power and treachery as its main themes. Brutus and Caesar, the play's central characters, are prime examples of Shakespeare's tragic heroes.

Why you're reading this book:
- The language and imagery, as with all of Shakespeare's works, are beautifully crafted.
- It provides a grandiose, theatrical view of politics in Roman times.
- Julius Caesar and Brutus are classic examples of the tragic hero.
- The play's central ideals—putting one's country before oneself, fighting against tyranny—still apply today.
- Shakespeare raises important questions concerning the use and abuse of power and authority.

Your teachers are looking for:
- The abuses of power by each of the characters in the play.
- Modern-day equivalents to the power struggle in Rome.
- Shakespeare's use of foreshadowing (Calpurnia's dream, for example).
- What makes certain characters in the play tragic heroes.
- Images or events repeated three times, and why they are significant.

KEY CHARACTERS

Julius Caesar (Caesar): Leader of the Romans, he is much loved by the people he governs. He is not a perfect man, however—he is beset with physical difficulties (epilepsy and deafness) and is too prideful.

Octavius Caesar (Octavius): A member of Caesar's triumvirate, he joins with Antony to avenge Caesar's murder.

Marcus Antonius (Antony): Caesar's protégé and a noble and loyal man. He is also very shrewd, an attribute that helps him avenge his mentor's death.

Marcus Brutus (Brutus): A well-meaning but misguided noble. He is convinced by Cassius that Caesar is too power-hungry and must be murdered.

Cassius: Hungry for personal power, he dupes Brutus into leading the conspiracy against Caesar.

Calpurnia: Caesar's wife. She tries, in vain, to warn him of the murder plot against him.

Portia: Brutus' wife. She is a meddler, constantly trying to discover her husband's plans.

Soothsayer: Warns Caesar of the impending conspiracy and the murder plot against him.

ESSAY IDEAS

- Why is Julius Caesar a good example of a tragic hero?
- How can Brutus be considered a tragic hero, and how does he differ from Julius Caesar in this respect?
- Compare Antony and Octavius' leader-

ship to that of Cassius and Brutus.
- Do you feel sorry for Caesar? For Brutus? Why or why not?
- Discuss the significance of events grouped in threes.
- What do you think Shakespeare is saying about power through this play?
- Discuss the roles played by the women in the play. Are they important?
- Where do you see situations similar to *Julius Caesar* in our world?

A SAMPLE ESSAY IN OUTLINE FORM

Discuss Brutus as a tragic hero.
- Brutus' heroic qualities:
  - His loyalty and love for his country.
    - His funeral oration for Caesar.
    - His dying speech.
  - His high ideals:
    - He wants only what is best for the Roman people
    - The people of the state should come before the rulers.
- Brutus' tragic flaw:
  - He is too trusting of others.
    - He allows himself to be swayed by Cassius.
    - The message thrown through his window.
    - He allows Antony to speak after him.

Brutus is a tragic hero whose high ideals make him susceptible to deception. Because he is completely committed to the Roman people, he turns against Caesar when Cassius convinces him that Caesar will bring great harm to the Roman state. A man of his unselfish ideals that is too trusting is easy prey for the opportunistic Cassius.

PLOT SUMMARY

Act I, Scene i This scene establishes the political atmosphere of the play, set in ancient Rome. Flavius and Marullus, members of the Republican nobility, are asking the commoners to explain why they are not at work that day. One answers seriously, but the other teases them with puns, a popular form of humor in Shakespeare's day.

Through this exchange, we learn that a holiday is being celebrated; Julius Caesar has returned from defeating Pompey's sons, who are also Romans. Marullus is disgusted, because these commoners used to cheer for Pompey. Flavius tells the people to go cry over their fickleness until their tears overflow the rivers.

Flavius then asks Marullus to help him remove from the statues the decorations honoring Caesar. He is afraid that Caesar will think himself more than a man and become a tyrant. This is the biggest fear of the nobles, but the commoners seem to support Caesar as their ruler.

Act I, Scene ii Caesar enters Rome before the celebration race and calls for his wife, Calpurnia. He asks that Marcus Antony not forget to touch her as she runs past, because doing so will cure her of sterility. Right after this, a soothsayer tells him three times to "beware the Ides of March," but Caesar ignores him. This shows that Caesar considers himself invincible, which is his "tragic flaw."

Caesar and most of the crowd leave to watch the race, but Brutus and Cassius stay behind. Cassius asks Brutus how he feels about the change in Caesar; Brutus, although he is Caesar's best friend, responds that he is troubled by Caesar's becoming a dictator. Cassius points out that Caesar is no god, but is human like them, and that he could not tolerate such a man being his absolute ruler. He then reminds Brutus that he is a nobleman, with an obligation to Rome to do the right thing. This is Brutus' concern, and he will be the one person to act truly for the benefit of his country.

Caesar returns and remarks to Antony that he senses Cassius is up to something, "Cassius has a lean and hungry look; He thinks too much, and such men are dangerous." But because he is Caesar, he does not actually fear Cassius. As he exits, Brutus and Cassius stop another noble, Casca, to ask him what happened during the race.

Casca tells them that Antony offered Caesar the crown three times, and that each time his refusal became more reluctant. After being offered the crown, Caesar had an epileptic seizure. His epilepsy and his deafness are signs that Caesar has human weaknesses.

The three nobles decide to go and think over the day's events, and Cassius is left alone. In his soliloquy, he states his plan to get Brutus to join him in a conspiracy against Caesar.

Act I, Scene iii Cicero and Casca meet that night, and Casca tells Cicero of the strange and violent storm raging outside. Eerie events have also taken place. Cicero leaves and Cassius enters, saying that he interprets these things to mean that Caesar, as tyrant, will destroy Rome. He persuades Casca to join him in his conspiracy, but there are moments in his speech where it is obvious that his rebellion is not for the Republic, but for himself. Another conspirator, Cinna, joins them, and agrees that Brutus' support is important to their cause. They agree to meet with the others at Pompey's Theater. There, they will try to win Brutus over.

Act II, Scene i Brutus, standing in his orchard, calls to his servant Lucius to light a candle in his study. Brutus delivers a soliloquy explaining that while he has nothing personal against Caesar, he does fear that Caesar will become a tyrant if he is crowned. As Brutus debates with himself, his servant returns with a message thrown through the window. Cassius has planted this letter, but Brutus takes it to be the voice of the Roman people asking him to save them from Caesar.

Right on cue, the conspirators arrive. Brutus agrees to join them, and Cassius proposes that they swear an oath. Brutus, however, is now so committed that he says honorable men who are working for such a just cause have no need for oaths. It is debated whether Cicero should join them, and Brutus persuades them to leave him out. He also objects to killing Antony along with Caesar, because then their "course would be too bloody." This decision will later bring about Brutus' downfall. When that decision is made, the clock strikes three.

The plan set, the conspirators now leave. Portia, Brutus' wife, enters and expresses her concern over the change in his behavior. She begs him to tell her what is troubling him. Brutus says that he will tell her soon.

Act II, Scene ii Caesar, at home, comments on the strange events of the night, and tells how Calpurnia cried out three times in her sleep, "Help, ho! They murder Caesar!" She had dreamt that her husband had been killed and the murderers had washed their hands in his blood. He sends a servant to ask the priests to make a sacrifice to the gods to find the meaning of all these signs. Calpurnia begs him not to leave home, as the message in her dream is clear to her. He tells her that he is a man, so he is going to have to die someday.

The servant returns, saying that the priests have advised him not to go to the Capitol today as he had planned; they could not find a heart in the animal they sacrificed, an ominous sign. Calpurnia finally persuades him to stay home. Decius enters, and Caesar decides to send a message through him. Decius asks why Caesar is staying home, and Caesar tells him of Calpurnia's dream. Decius is a conspirator, so he re-interprets the dream in a positive light. He tries to get Caesar to go to the Capitol by praising him and his power.

Decius adds that if the people think Caesar listens to his wife, they might change their minds about his strength as a ruler. His manly pride pricked, Caesar agrees to go to the Capitol. The other conspirators enter. Antony enters as well. Caesar asks Trebonius (unbeknownst to Caesar, also a conspirator) to stay by his side. Trebonius, in an aside, says that he will be so close, Caesar's "best friends will wish he had been farther."

Before they leave, Caesar asks these people, whom he thinks are his friends, to drink with him. In another aside, Brutus sadly comments that Caesar does not know that some of his friends are enemies. His saying this reminds us that he does not hate Caesar; he only wants to act in the best interest of his country.

Act II, Scene iii On a street near the Capitol, Artemidorus waits for Caesar. He has a letter that will tell Caesar of the plot against him as well as the names of the conspirators. He says that if the Fates wish Caesar to live, this letter will save him. This short scene is a reminder that many people, including nobles, still support Caesar.

Act II, Scene iv Portia has not been calmed by Brutus' words. She decides to send Lucius out to find out the reason for her husband's strange behavior. The Soothsayer enters again, and he tells her that he is on his way to watch Caesar walk to the Capitol. He says that he fears there may be a plot against him, but he is unsure. The Soothsayer leaves to find a good spot from which he can hail Caesar. Portia finally sends Lucius off, asking him to give her greetings to Brutus, and to see what he has to say in reply.

Act III, Scene i Caesar, Antony, and the conspirators are now just outside the Capitol. Caesar sees the Soothsayer and arrogantly tells him the Ides of March have come with no harm to him. Artemidorus tries to give him the letter, but Caesar refuses to take it and invites him to enter the Capitol.

Inside, Trebonius leads Antony away so that he cannot interfere. On the pretense of begging for the end of his brother's banishment, Metellus Cimber draws closer to Caesar. Caesar refuses his plea, and the others close in pretending to plead the cause, kneeling and kissing his hands. Caesar's refusals show his pride. He also compares himself to the gods; this likening of oneself to the gods is the traditional tragic flaw, and is the worst thing a Roman can do. Casca stabs him, as do the rest, but the blow that kills him is Brutus'. Caesar dies saying, "Et tu [you too], Brutus?"

The conspirators then try to calm the people, saying they have ended tyranny for the people's benefit. Trebonius enters the chaotic scene and says that Antony has fled to his house in a panic. Just as in Calpurnia's dream, the conspirators stoop to wash their hands in Caesar's blood, crying "Liberty! Freedom! Tyranny is dead!" Only Brutus seems disgusted.

A servant of Antony's comes to Brutus, telling him that Antony wants to speak to the conspirators. Brutus grants the request, saying that he will explain all. Antony enters and laments the death of Caesar. Shrewdly, he pretends to be reconciled with the conspirators, and shakes them all by the hand. He asks to speak at the funeral as Caesar's friend, and over Cassius' objections, Brutus tells him he may. Brutus is now considered to be the leader of the conspirators.

All but Antony exit, and he apologizes to Caesar's body for appearing to have agreed with his murderers. Swearing revenge, Antony predicts a civil war between the two groups. Antony knows Brutus is mistaken in thinking the people will believe that Caesar was killed for their benefit. A servant enters, and Antony tells him of his plan to persuade the people with his funeral speech. The servant agrees to monitor how the crowd reacts, and the two carry out Caesar's body.

Act III, Scene ii Brutus and Cassius enter the forum before the people, who are demanding an explanation for Caesar's death. Each takes half the crowd, but we only hear Brutus' speech. He begins by asking people to judge the case with reason rather than with their emotions. He explains that he killed Caesar because the good of Rome was more important to him than his friendship. He killed him because Caesar was too ambitious a ruler, and he would have tyrannized them. Antony has now arrived with Caesar's body, and Brutus tells the crowd that Antony was not part of the conspiracy. He closes by saying he is ready to kill himself if his death would benefit Rome. The crowd is now on his side, but he asks them to listen to Antony as well.

Antony's funeral oration begins with the famous line, ``Friends, Romans, countrymen, lend me your ears." Like Brutus, Antony asks the people to judge Caesar's so-called ambition with their reason. He

asks them whether Caesar's generosity with the loot he won for Rome or his work with the poor was ambition. He reminds them that Caesar refused the crown not once, but three times. Antony then says he has Caesar's will, but will not read it because it will sadden them too much. He hints that there is something in it for them. The crowd insists that he read it.

He hedges, telling them he has already said too much. He says that he does not want to dishonor the men who killed Caesar. But the crowd is now calling the conspirators murderers. Antony shows them Caesar's wounds, pointing especially to the one inflicted by Brutus, calling it "the most unkindest cut of all." The crowd is incensed and begins to leave, seeking revenge.

The people are about to go on a rampage, but Antony calms the crowd by reminding them of the will. They stay, and he reads that Caesar has left every citizen of Rome 75 drachmas, plus all his personal woodlands, walks, and orchards for the public use. The crowd then sets out after the conspirators.

A servant comes to Antony to tell him that Octavius Caesar, an ally, has arrived in Rome, and is with Lepidus in Caesar's house. The servant also tells him that Cassius and Brutus have fled the city.

Act III, Scene iii The angry citizens intercept Cinna the poet on his way to Caesar's funeral. Hearing his name, they confuse him with Cinna the conspirator. He tries to explain that he is not the same person, but they kill him anyway. They then go to burn the houses of the other traitors. This scene shows how Antony's words have moved the populace to violence against the conspirators.

Act IV, Scene i Antony, Octavius, and Lepidus are in Antony's house. They have formed a second triumvirate. They are devising a plan for consolidating their power and removing those that oppose them. They are more farsighted than the conspirators—the conspirators had only planned the assassination of Caesar, not what to do afterward. They even agree to the deaths of some of their relatives: Lepidus will lose his brother, Antony his nephew.

Lepidus leaves to get Caesar's will, as they have decided to reduce some of his bequests. While he is gone, Antony tells Octavius that he thinks Lepidus is not a strong enough leader to rule a third of the world. While Octavius does not disagree, he does point out that Lepidus is a good soldier; Antony retorts that so is his horse. We see that Antony is very ambitious himself, willing to sacrifice Lepidus for more personal power.

Antony then tells Octavius that Brutus and Cassius are preparing for war, and they must ready themselves. This civil war is the focus of the rest of the play.

Act IV, Scene ii We now see the conspirators' camp near Sardis, where Brutus is standing outside his tent. Cassius' servant comes to tell Brutus that his master is coming. The two leaders are involved in a petty squabble of some kind: Brutus has been offended by something Cassius said but thinks that Cassius can explain. Cass-ius enters, and the two agree to speak in Brutus' tent, so that they do not show disunity before their armies. The conspirators are now the emotional, not the rational, party.

Act IV, Scene iii Cassius is angry because Brutus has condemned Cassius' friend despite his pleas that he be let off. Brutus replies that Cassius is wasting his time defending an unjust cause. He then accuses Cassius of selling offices because he has an "itching palm." Not only is Cassius forgetting the ideals for which they killed Caesar, he has also refused to send the money that Brutus requested for his troops. Cassius says that if he has been dishonest, he will kill himself. Brutus believes Cassius' claim, and they reconcile.

Titinus and Messala enter, and they discuss how Octavius and Antony's armies are advancing. According to Messala, they have killed a hundred senators, but according to Brutus, only seventy. Messala tells Brutus that Portia has died. Brutus proposes that they march to meet the enemy, but Cassius wants to wait for the enemy to come to them so that their armies remain fresh. Cassius eventually concedes; this, like Brutus' decision to let Antony live, is an error.

Brutus invites the leaders to sleep in his tent, and has Lucius play some music to soothe them. Everyone falls asleep quickly, except Brutus. He is visited by the ghost of Caesar, who calls himself Brutus' "evil spirit." He tells Brutus that he will see him at Philippi, which is where Antony and Octavius' armies are.

Act V, Scene i Octavius and Antony are waiting at Philippi with their army, and they are pleased that the approaching enemy is playing into their hands. A messenger comes to tell them they should prepare, as Cassius and Brutus are very close. The opposing sides begin the battle by mocking each other, and Octavius eventually says they should stop talking and fight.

Cassius speaks to Brutus of omens that have occurred that day that do not bode well for the conspirators. However, he is still willing to fight. He and Brutus bid farewell in case they never see each other again. Brutus swears that he will not be led captive into Rome.

Act V, Scene ii Brutus sends a message with Messala to Cassius, telling him to engage Octavius' army before they get in a better position.

Act V, Scene iii In another part of the field, Cassius' army is retreating. Brutus' own troops, having beaten back Octavius, are looting rather than coming to help Cassius. Cassius sends Titinius out to discover which troops are approaching him and asks Pindarus to watch his progress. Pindarus sees Titinius surrounded by cheering soldiers, and Cassius assumes he has been captured. Disheartened that he has done this to a friend, Cassius asks Pindarus to stab him. Cassius dies with the words, "Caesar, thou art revenged, even with the sword that killed thee."

The sad irony is that Titinius was not captured, but was being greeted by Brutus' triumphant soldiers. He returns with Messala to tell Cassius that Brutus has defeated Octavius' army, and they find Cassius' body. Messala goes to tell Brutus, and Titinius says he will look for Pindarus. Instead, he kills himself with Brutus' sword.

Brutus enters with the others and delivers a eulogy for his friends. Then, at the fateful hour of three o'clock, he sends the men off to fight again.

Act V, Scene iv Brutus enters the thick of battle with Lucilius and Young Cato, and inspires his soldiers to fight well. Cato dies, and Lucilius is captured. Lucilius pretends to be Brutus, to try to buy his master time. Lucilius is presented to Antony, to whom he admits his true identity; he tells Antony that they will never take Brutus alive. Antony sends his soldiers to find Brutus. Antony and Octavius are now winning the battle.

Act V, Scene v Brutus enters with some members of his army. Clitus and Dardanius both refuse Brutus' whispered request that they kill him. Brutus tells them that he has seen the ghost of Caesar for the third time, and he knows that it is time for him to die. They hear the enemy approaching, and Clitus pleads with Brutus to flee. Brutus sends his soldiers ahead of him and bids them good-bye. Strato remains, and he agrees to hold Brutus' sword so that Brutus can run upon it and kill himself.

An alarm sounds, indicating that Brutus' army has been defeated. Octavius, Messala, Lucilius, and the army find Strato with Brutus' body. Antony gives a brief eulogy for Brutus, saying that he was "the noblest Roman of all": he was the only one that did not raise his hand against Caesar for spite, but for the good of the people. Octavius agrees, and promises that Brutus will be buried with honor.

KING LEAR

ABOUT THE AUTHOR

See page 111.

THE BIG PICTURE

King Lear is considered to be one of Shakespeare's finest plays. It is a tragedy of full-scale emotion and powerful characters that revolves around the timeless themes of loyalty versus treachery and truth versus deception. In Lear, Shakespeare created perhaps his most highly developed character ever.

Why you're reading this book:
• *King Lear* is considered one of Shakespeare's finest plays and one of the greatest tragedies ever written.
• The language, while sometimes difficult, is beautiful and descriptive.
• King Lear is a highly complex and moving character.
• The play makes important statements about central human themes:
  • Appearance vs. reality.
  • The meaning of "power."
  • Man's relationship with nature.
  • Family relationships.
  • Betrayal.

Your teachers are looking for:
• The main themes of the play—deceit vs. honesty, pride vs. loyalty, appearance vs. reality—and the ways in which Shakespeare illustrates them.
• How characters develop and change throughout the play.
• Lear's faults and strengths; his tragic flaw.

• An appreciation and understanding of Shakespeare's language.
• The depth and scope of experience that Shakespeare puts King Lear through.
• How Gloucester's plot parallels and reflects King Lear's.

KEY CHARACTERS

King Lear: The King of England and the central character of the play. Father of Cordelia, Goneril, and Regan. He is proud and quick to anger, traits that lead him into grave mistakes.

Cordelia: Lear's loyal daughter. Although she is banished by Lear at the beginning of the play, she returns to fight for her father's safety and kingdom.

Goneril and Regan: Lear's conniving and deceptive daughters. They plan to weaken Lear and gain control over his kingdom.

The Earl of Kent: Banished by Lear at the beginning of the play. Like Cordelia, he remains loyal to Lear to the end.

The Earl of Gloucester: Lear's good friend and counsel, he is also a victim of Lear's temper. Like Lear, he endures many hardships because of his lack of insight. The "subplot" of *King Lear* revolves around him.

Edmund: Gloucester's illegitimate son. He conspires to discredit his brother Edgar, then joins the forces against King Lear.

Edgar: Gloucester's legitimate son. Noble and loyal, he is forced to hide in the woods when Edmund frames him as a traitor. He still remains true to his father, however, disguising himself as a beggar to help him.

The Fool: Lear's companion. His constant commentary provides insight into Lear's behavior.

The Duke of Albany: Goneril's husband. Unlike the rest of the conspirators against Lear, he is noble and ends up helping Lear.

The Duke of Cornwall: Regan's husband. He is cruel and hardhearted.

Oswald: A steward to Goneril, he acts as a messenger for many of her treacheries.

ESSAY IDEAS

- Discuss the theme of sight/insight vs. blindness/ignorance.
- Do you think Lear is a tragic hero? If so, what is his tragic flaw?
- Compare/contrast Edmund and Edgar.
- What role does the Fool play for King Lear? Is he really a fool?
- Discuss the use of disguises (i.e, Edgar and the Fool). How do these disguises function in the play?
- What is the role of Nature in the play?
- Examine Lear's conception of kingship and how it changes throughout the play.

A SAMPLE ESSAY IN OUTLINE FORM

Throughout the story, Lear's fatal flaw is his anger. Discuss how that anger blinds him and brings about his downfall. How is he saved?

- Lear's original banishment of Cordelia:
  - Blind rage.
  - Fails to see that Goneril and Regan are his true enemies.
  - Also banishes his good friend Kent.
- Lear's rage when he is treated poorly by Goneril and Regan:
  - Causes him to end up in woods during storm.

- Lear's anger, and the events it brings about, begin to push him towards madness.
- Near the brink of madness, Lear finally begins to achieve some insight into his own character.
- He is saved from destruction by Kent and Cordelia, the very people at whom he directed his anger to begin with.

Lear continually falls prey to his anger, and it shapes the events that lead to his downfall. To save himself from the predicament he is in, he must come to terms with his anger and the way it has blinded him to the truth.

PLOT SUMMARY

Act I, Scene i The play opens with a conversation between Gloucester and the Earl of Kent in King Lear's castle. They are talking about the fact that Lear is planning to divide his kingdom. During the conversation, it is revealed that Gloucester has two sons, one of them illegitimate.

King Lear enters. He is with his daughters, Goneril, Regan, and the unmarried Cordelia. Lear instructs Gloucester to receive two of Cordelia's suitors, the King of France and the Duke of Burgundy. He then announces that he has decided to divide his kingdom among his three daughters in proportion to their love for him.

Lear asks each of his daughters how much she loves him. Goneril and Regan shower praise on their father and pledge their love and respect. However, Cordelia responds that she loves him only as a daughter is expected to love a father. Lear, enraged, banishes Cordelia and gives her portion of the kingdom to her two sisters. Kent tries to make Lear see the error of his rash action, but the King will not hear of it, and in a rage he banishes Kent.

Gloucester returns with the King of

France and the Duke of Burgundy. The two are informed of Cordelia's punishment. The Duke is quick to back out, but the King of France wants her as his bride nonetheless. Cordelia explains why she did not praise her father as highly as her sisters: she did not want to engage in false flattery.

Cordelia then leaves with the King of France, suspicious of her sisters and their "love" for King Lear. Her suspicions are not unfounded; the scene ends with Goneril and Regan plotting to reduce their father's power.

Act I, Scene ii Edmund, Gloucester's illegitimate son, is plotting to trick his legitimate brother Edgar out of his inheritance. He has written a false letter to serve that purpose.

Gloucester enters, and Edmund makes a great show of hiding the letter. When Gloucester asks to see the it, Edmund is happy to oblige. The letter, supposedly written by Edgar to Edmund, plots the death of Gloucester so that the two brothers can collect his inheritance. Gloucester becomes very upset and leaves.

Edgar enters. Edmund tells him that their father is very angry at him, and offers to bring Edgar to him to find out why. He also warns Edgar to carry a weapon for protection.

Act I, Scene iii Goneril's steward, Oswald, has been struck by the King. Goneril takes this as another example of Lear's weakness, and tells her steward not to wait on him. If the King asks for Goneril, the steward is to say that she is ill. Goneril is scornful of King Lear; her flattery in the first scene was merely to insure her portion of the kingdom.

Act I, Scene iv The loyal Kent has returned to King Lear in disguise, hoping to serve him again. Impressed by the "new

man's" honesty, Lear allows him to stay in the court.

Lear's court is not as it once was, however. Oswald is disobedient, Goneril is not in attendance, and even the Fool is unhappy since Cordelia has left. King Lear calls Goneril and the Fool to him. The Fool insults him with jests, showing Lear's lack of power and his mistake in banishing Cordelia. Then Goneril enters and insults the King even more deeply, suggesting that his advanced age has taken its toll and demanding that he reduce the number of people in his court. The King angrily decides to leave and go to Regan's house.

Goneril's husband, the Duke of Albany, enters and tries to calm the King. Lear will not be calmed, however; he is beginning to see that he has made a grave error in choosing Goneril over Cordelia. His rage only increases when he discovers that Goneril has dismissed fifty members of his court. He leaves for Regan's.

Goneril tells Oswald to take a letter to her sister. She then insults her husband for his conciliatory attitude towards Lear.

Act I, Scene v Lear sends Kent ahead to Regan's home in Gloucester. The Fool tries to cheer him with comic antics, but Lear is distraught and wonders aloud about his sanity. The scene ends as the small party prepares to go to Gloucester.

Act II, Scene i Edmund is again conspiring against Edgar. He has learned that there will probably be a battle between Cornwall and Albany over Lear's kingdom. Cornwall will arrive that night.

Edmund convinces Edgar, who has been in hiding, that he must leave the castle. He tells Edgar that Cornwall suspects him of treason. When Edgar leaves, Edmund wounds himself in the arm. Seeing Edmund's wound, Gloucester is convinced that Edgar is a villain and Edmund is his true son. When Cornwall and Regan enter the scene, they too are convinced of Edgar's treachery. Cornwall invites Edmund to join his camp.

Regan and Cornwall then ask Gloucester for advice on how to deal with the angry Lear.

Act II, Scene ii Kent, still disguised, and the impudent steward, Oswald, arrive at Gloucester's castle at the same time. Kent, angered at the mistreatment of his beloved King Lear, draws his rapier and attacks Oswald. Their shouts bring first Edmund, then Regan, Gloucester, and Cornwall to the scene. Cornwall, upon finding out that Lear's messenger is actually the Earl of Kent, orders him to be put into the stocks. Gloucester protests, but the order is carried out.

Later, in the stocks, Kent reads a letter from Cordelia. In it she says that she appreciates all that he has done for her father, and that she is worried about Lear.

Act II, Scene iii This scene consists of a soliloquy by Edgar. He has escaped by hiding in a tree, and will now avoid capture by posing as a beggar, Tom O' Bedlam.

Act II, Scene iv Lear arrives at Gloucester to find the Earl of Kent in the stocks. Fuming, he goes off in search of Regan. He returns with Gloucester, who explains that the punishment was ordered by the Duke of Cornwall. Lear demands to see the Duke and Regan.

The Duke and Regan enter, release Kent from the stocks, and greet Lear as if nothing had happened. Lear tells Regan of his problems with Goneril. Rather than agreeing with Lear, she suggests that Lear return to Goneril and apologize. Lear refuses and curses Goneril angrily.

Goneril enters, and it becomes obvious to the King that his two daughters are con-

spiring to reduce his power. The two ask him why he needs even one follower, when he can be taken care of by their servants. They are treating Lear like a powerless old man. Finally, Lear rages off into the countryside into an impending storm. Regan says that she would take him in, but not his followers. Goneril is far harsher; she believes that Lear is getting what he deserves. Even as the storm continues to grow stronger, the two do not seem concerned over their father's plight.

Act III, Scene i The Earl of Kent, still disguised, meets a Gentleman in the storm who tells him that Lear is wandering around in the storm, alone save for the Fool. Kent tells the Gentleman of the rift between the Duke of Albany and the Duke of Cornwall. He also tells him that the King of France plans to invade England to restore King Lear to his position. He tells the Gentleman to travel to Dover to get support for Lear. He gives the Gentleman a ring to give to Cordelia in the hopes that the Gentleman will find her in Dover; Cordelia will then know that the Gentleman is loyal to the King and she will tell him the Earl of Kent's true identity.

Act III, Scene ii Lear is caught in the savage storm. Seeing the storm as yet another insult to him from his daughters, he rails against their false praise of him. Kent enters, and tries to persuade Lear to take shelter. He then goes back to Gloucester's castle to try to persuade the daughters to let Lear return.

Act III, Scene iii Back at the castle, Gloucester is talking with Edmund. He complains that Goneril and Regan will not let him help Lear in any way. The devious Edmund acts sympathetic, leading Gloucester to confide in him: Gloucester has learned that help is on the way for Lear. He resolves to find Lear and to try to help him. Once alone, Edmund reveals that he will betray his father to Cornwall.

Act III, Scene iv Kent tries to get Lear to seek shelter in a hovel, but the troubled King says that the storm in his head makes him oblivious to the storm going on around him. He urges the Earl and the Fool to seek shelter. Outside in the harsh elements, he begins to feel remorse for the underprivileged people whose suffering he did not allay during his reign.

Suddenly, the Fool tears out of the hovel, screaming that it is haunted. At the urging of Kent, the "ghost" shows himself: it is the disguised Edgar. Lear sees "Tom" as his companion in suffering and tears off his clothes to be as humble as he.

Gloucester enters. Against the wishes of Lear's daughters, he has helped Lear by finding a farmhouse for shelter. Seeing Lear near madness reminds Gloucester of his own "ungrateful" offspring; he does not realize that Tom O' Bedlam is the innocent Edgar.

Act III, Scene v Edmund has betrayed Gloucester to Cornwall, and is rewarded with his father's lands. Cornwall sends Edmund to find Gloucester and find out more information.

Act III, Scene vi Gloucester, Lear, the Fool, Kent, and Edgar all arrive at the farmhouse. Gloucester leaves to find food for the company.

Lear is beginning to lose touch with reality. He decides to put Goneril and Regan, whom he represents with two stools, on trial. He appoints Edgar and the Fool judges. Worried, the Earl of Kent gets Lear to lie down and rest.

Gloucester returns with bad news: there is a plot to kill Lear, and he must be taken to safety at Dover immediately. All leave except for Edgar. Despite his own troubles, he prays for Lear's safety.

Act III, Scene vii This scene highlights the cruelty and violence of Regan and Cornwall. Cornwall has learned that the army of France is in Dover. He sends a letter to Albany via Edmund and Goneril urging him to join forces with him against King Lear.

Gloucester is dragged in by Cornwall's men; Oswald has found out that he sent Lear to safety in Dover. Cornwall punishes Gloucester by scratching one of his eyes out. Regan urges him to scratch out the other. However, a servant of Cornwall's, disgusted by his master's cruelty, pulls his sword and wounds the evil Duke. Regan immediately kills the servant.

Enraged, Cornwall scratches out Gloucester's second eye. The blinded man cries out for his Edmund, only to learn from Cornwall that it was Edmund who betrayed him. Gloucester finally realizes Edmund's treachery and prays for Edgar's safety. Cornwall then throws Gloucester out of the castle and leaves with Regan.

The remaining servants are horrified by the cruelty of Cornwall and Regan. They decide to find the beggar, Tom O' Bedlam, and get him to bring Gloucester to wherever he wants to travel.

Act IV, Scene i Edgar, alone, is hopeful that his condition will soon improve. On cue, a servant arrives with Gloucester and asks that Edgar lead him to Dover. He provides Edgar with fresh clothes.

Gloucester speaks of Edgar, his faithful son that he misjudged. Edgar resists the temptation to reveal his true identity. Gloucester asks the "beggar" only to lead him to the cliffs of Dover.

Act IV, Scene ii Edmund arrives at Albany's castle. Goneril asks Oswald about her husband, and he answers that the Duke of Albany seems very changed: he is pleased at the arrival of the King of France and very displeased with the poor treatment of Lear. Goneril decides that she must take matters into her own hands. Hinting that she wants Edmund as her lover, she tells him to return to Cornwall to marshal their forces.

Albany enters. He argues with Goneril over her and Regan's actions against their father, but Goneril remains cruel. They are interrupted by a messenger, who informs them that Cornwall has died from the wound inflicted by his servant. Albany takes this as a sign of a higher power, but Goneril only considers what this turn of events means to her strategy. In an aside, Goneril wonders if she and Edmund can now have the whole kingdom—if the newly widowed Regan does not attempt to seduce him.

Act IV, Scene iii Kent learns from a Gentleman that the King of France has returned to his country, leaving a Marshal in command. He also learns that Cordelia knows of her father's plight and is deeply saddened. Lear, however, does not want to see his daughter because of his shame at his treatment of her. Kent tells the Gentleman he will bring him to Lear. There, Kent promises to reveal his true identity.

Act IV, Scene iv Cordelia is now commanding the French troops who seek to restore King Lear to his proper position. The King, meanwhile, has completely degenerated. A doctor reassures Cordelia that he can restore Lear's health and sanity. First, however, Lear must be rescued from danger.

Act IV, Scene v Oswald, who is searching for Edmund to deliver a letter to him from Goneril, goes to Regan's. Regan demands to see the letter, and decides to send her love to Edmund by way of Oswald as well. A rivalry is developing between the two sisters over Edmund.

Edmund has set out to find Gloucester and kill him. Regan urges Oswald to do the same.

Act IV, Scene vi Edgar and Gloucester are now outside Dover. Edgar leads his father (who is now beginning to recognize the "beggar's" voice) up a small hill. He convinces Gloucester that the hill is the cliffs of Dover, and Gloucester jumps off.

After he survives his "fall," Gloucester is persuaded by Edgar that his survival is a sign from the gods, that he must go on living. Gloucester is filled with renewed strength and a will to live.

Lear enters, wildly dressed and raving. A search party from Cordelia then catches up to him, but he escapes. A man in the search party tells Gloucester and Edgar that the fight is about to begin.

Oswald enters, declaring Gloucester a traitor. Despite Edgar's warnings, he attacks. Edgar defends Gloucester and kills the steward. Oswald, dying, gives Edgar Goneril's letter to Edmund, in which she tells him she wants him to kill Albany and marry her.

Act IV, Scene vii Kent finally removes his disguise, showing himself to Cordelia. Lear is brought in, only half-awake, and his daughter kisses him lovingly. At first, Lear cannot believe his eyes, but he recovers himself and begs Cordelia for forgiveness. He is still somewhat muddled, however, and the doctor recommends that they not talk about the past quite yet. Lear is led away.

Kent learns that Edmund is now commanding the opposition. He says that they must prepare for battle; although the battle will be bloody, he is ever loyal to his King.

Act V, Scene i In the opposing camp, Regan is making advances toward Edmund. She questions him about his relationship with Goneril, and Edmund denies any involvement with her.

Goneril and Albany enter. Albany has decided to join Goneril and Edmund's side and fight against the French. When the two sisters and Edmund leave, Edgar delivers Goneril's treacherous letter to Albany and tells him to read it before the battle. He exits.

Before Albany can read the letter, however, Edmund reenters and tells him that Cordelia's forces are fast approaching. Albany exits, and Edmund reveals his devious plan. He does not know which sister he will take; however, he does know that once the battle is won, he will kill Albany, Lear, and Cordelia.

Act V, Scene ii At the start of the battle, Edgar brings Gloucester to safety and leaves to fight. He returns, however, with terrible news: Cordelia has been defeated and she and the King have been captured. At first, Gloucester reacts to the news by giving up all hope, but Edgar manages to get him up and moving again.

Act V, Scene iii Edmund has sent Cordelia and Lear to prison and plans horrid punishments for them. Albany, Goneril, and Regan enter. Albany demands that the prisoners be given over to him, and tells Edmund that he is of low stature. When Regan defends Edmund, Goneril is greatly angered at her sister's treachery. Albany says that Goneril and Edmund are traitors; Regan starts to die, a result of poison given to her by Goneril.

Edgar enters, declaring Edmund a traitor and engaging him in battle. Edmund loses the duel, admitting his guilt just before he dies. Edgar then finally throws away his disguise and is praised by Albany for his honesty and valor.

The conspiracy against Lear is fully extinguished; Goneril, after admitting that she poisoned her sister, has killed herself. Kent enters, saying that he wants to take leave of the King and Cordelia. Albany realizes that he has not yet secured their safety, and sends out an officer to get them and stop Edmund's officers from carrying out his execution order.

But it is too late—Lear enters with the dead form of his beloved Cordelia. She has been hanged. In his grief, Lear does not even recognize Kent. Bent over Cordelia, trying somehow to revive her, King Lear dies of grief.

At the close of the play, Albany asks Edgar and Kent to try to restore order to Lear's kingdom.

LORD OF THE FLIES

ABOUT THE AUTHOR

William Golding (1911–   ) was born in Cornwall, England in 1911. He was trained to be a scientist, but after two years at Oxford he began studying English literature. Golding joined the Royal Navy when World War II began and finished his naval career as a lieutenant in command of a ship.

Golding described World War II as "the coldest of cold-blooded genocide." His wartime experience shattered his idealistic belief that man was "perfectible" and essentially good. This bleak view of human nature inspired his first novel, *Lord of the Flies* (1955), as well as his later novels.

Lord of the Flies was a great success both in England and the U.S. It was followed over the next three decades by several more novels, including *The Spire* (1964), *The Scorpion God* (1971), and *Rites of Passage* (1980). Golding has described his novels as an attempt to trace the defects of society back to the basic defects of human nature.

Golding was awarded the Nobel Prize for Literature in 1983.

THE BIG PICTURE

Lord of the Flies tells the story of a group of military school boys stranded on an island after a shipwreck. Their attempt to live on the island and create a "civilization" leads to disaster. The novel provides a disturbing and powerful picture of the dark underside of human nature.

Note: When reading *Lord of the Flies*, it is helpful to draw parallels between the boys' world and the adult world. The world the boys create on the island takes its lead (and its mistakes) from our society.

Why you're reading this book:
- It offers several levels of interpretation:
  - On a political level: democracy vs. dictatorship.
  - On a psychological level: the id (self-gratifying, anarchic impulse) vs. the ego and the superego (moral, stabilizing forces).
  - On a basic level: a fantastic tale of a group of boys.

Your teachers are looking for:
- The question of whether man is predatory by nature, or simply responds to his surroundings.
- The boys' desire to either rule, be ruled, or live without rule
- The relevance of the boys' ages: are their acts ones that men of any age might also have committed?
- The degree of evil humans are capable of; the circumstances which drive humans to certain behavior.

KEY CHARACTERS

Ralph: A decent, considerate boy. He represents democracy and fairness and realizes that the boys must all work together on the island in order to survive.

Piggy: The brains of the group. He is fat, has asthma, and is extremely nearsighted. He is loyal to Ralph. Piggy represents the human spirit. He knows nothing is safe on this island and tries to do the best he can.

Jack: Authoritarian and power-hungry, he represents dictatorship and conflicts with Ralph's democracy. Loves adventure and excitement. Jack is especially cruel to Piggy.

Simon: Obedient and helpful, he never raises an argument. He is introspective and mature, and avoids controversy. He fears speaking in front of the assembly. The others see him as somewhat queer, or funny.

Sam and Eric, or Samneric: Identical twins who are completely dependent upon one another. Essentially, they are one and the same.

ESSAY IDEAS

- Why do you think Golding chose the characters in the story to be English schoolboys (even more ironically, choirboys)?
- In your opinion, why do things "come apart" on the island? Find episodes in the book to support your ideas.
- What is really the "beast" on this island? Is there more than one beast?
- Would things have been better or worse with an adult on the island? How might they be different?
- Is this a realistic story? Why or why not?
- Given the group's state of mind, are the fates of Simon and Piggy understandable?
- What do you think the parachutist symbolizes?
- How are Jack, Ralph, and Piggy representative of three very different modes of thought? Could one argue that any one of them is "better" than the others?

A SAMPLE ESSAY IN OUTLINE FORM

Discuss the use of symbolism in *Lord of the Flies*. How does it enhance the book?
• Symbolism in things:
  • The conch as power.
  • Fire as hope.
  • Piggy's specs as truth, rationality.
• Symbolism in people:
  • Ralph as democracy.
  • Jack as dictatorship/fascism.
  • The painted boys as anonymous soldiers.
• Symbolism in the book as a whole:
  • The island as a mirror of adult society.
  • The story as a commentary on human nature as a whole:
    • The need to create systems of government.
    • The desire to wield power over another group.

The book's symbolism causes us to see each person, thing, or situation in the book as representative of a larger idea. This allows us to read the story on more than a basic level and to see it as a commentary on mankind rather than just a story.

PLOT SUMMARY

Chapter 1: The Sound of the Shell The reader infers from the opening paragraphs that the boys are on a tropical island. They are survivors of an accident of some sort. Two boys, Ralph and the "Fat Boy," are exploring their surroundings. They wonder where the other boys from the crash are as they inspect the debris that has fallen on the island. Piggy, the Fat Boy, suggests having a meeting. Ralph approaches the water, quickly looks it over, and dives in. Piggy dips one toe in and declares it is too hot.

We find out that Ralph's father is in the Navy, and that the cause of the accident involved an atom bomb. Ralph is sure his dad will find them. Piggy insists on trying to find the others. Ralph grows thoughtful and pensive from Piggy's talk.

The boys find a shell, a conch, which Piggy fears he will break. He suggests using it to call the others for meetings. Ralph blows it, and one boy shows up. Other boys start making their way over too. A party of boys approaches, dressed in black choir robes, marching in parallel lines. Merridew, or Jack, is their leader. In a key exchange, the question of whether there are any grown-ups on the island is raised. The conclusion is that the boys will have to look after themselves.

A few of the boys decide to go on an expedition to explore the island. Jack insults Piggy and tells him he's not wanted on their trip. Jack declares himself the chief, and Roger calls for a vote. Ralph wins the election. It is decided that Jack and his choirboys will be the hunters.

Jack, Ralph, and Simon leave to determine if they are on an island without any connection to a mainland. The others are ordered to stay. The three are enjoying the trek through the lush forest when they hear a pig squeal. Jack poises his knife to kill it, then lets it go. Foreshadowing the events to come, he promises to do it the next time.

Chapter 2: Fire on the Mountain Ralph blows the conch to call a meeting again in the afternoon. He tells the group that they are on an island. There are no footprints, no boats, and no people. Jack also needs an army for hunting the pigs that inhabit the island. They establish the conch rule, which states that whoever is holding the conch has the floor to speak. Jack wants to establish many rules so he can punish any

lawbreakers. Piggy tells the group that no one knows they are there, while Ralph expresses an interest in having a good time while on the island.

A "littlun," one of the small boys, is crying, and the boys are laughing at him. Piggy listens to what the boy is saying, then relays it to the group. The boy is worried about the "beastie." The boys try to reassure him, and probably themselves, that it was just a nightmare. Jack announces that if there is a beastie he will kill it.

Ralph, having knowledge of the seas from his naval father, tells the group of the Queen's maps of the vast seas and islands. It is decided that a fire must be kept lit on the mountain to alert any rescuers. All follow Jack, except Piggy, who grudgingly gives in and catches up to the group. They attempt to start a fire using logs and dried leaves when they realize in embarrassment that they have no matches.

They try to use the lenses of Piggy's specs to ignite a fire, but it doesn't work. Jack turns on Piggy in frustration. Maurice suggests using green branches to make smoke. The fire starts and gets totally out of control. The scene grows chaotic, and the boys start arguing and bickering over who gets the conch to speak. Piggy realizes there is one child missing, the child who was worried about the beastie. The chapter closes with the fire creating a sound similar to a drum roll that seems to be coming from the other side of the mountain.

Chapter 3: Huts on the Beach While Jack is doubled over on the ground, covered with debris from the exploding trees and fire, he finds a path for pigs. Jack is described like a primitive native, naked and carrying a stick. He is hunting. He finds Ralph, and asks him for some water. Ralph barely recognizes him

Ralph displays his work of the past few days, two shelters. He explains that only he and Simon have been building while all the others have been playing. He asks for meat, and Jack answers that he will get it next time. He makes excuses and promises for the future. They talk of the need for shelters, because the littluns are scared. Ralph talks of being rescued, while all Jack can talk about is killing a pig. He goes on and on about the methods and schemes he will use. Ralph is angry, because Jack doesn't notice the huts he's built. He claims that because Jack likes to hunt, it's not hard work for him as building is for himself. Jack offers to help a little, and Ralph says not to bother.

Simon has walked into the forest to pick fruit for the littluns and to wander on his own. He leaves the littluns and walks on a secluded path. He checks to see if he is alone, and buries himself amidst the leaves and the creepers. He listens to the sounds of the island as the evening approaches. After a time, he gets up and places the leaves back in their place. Meanwhile, the others notice he is missing.

Chapter 4: Painted Faces and Long Hair This chapter begins with a general description of all the young boys on the island, some playing, some crying. All are carefree. Henry and Roger amuse themselves with various activities. Jack summons Roger, who comes and meets the twins, Samneric, and Bill by a small pool. Jack shows them the white and red clay he has collected in two large leaves. Jack paints the clay on himself as if it were warpaint. He laughs, sings, and dances, hiding eerily behind this new face he has created for himself.

Piggy sits with Ralph under some palms and suggests that the boys make a sundial to tell the time. Ralph rejects the idea and returns to the pool, where Maurice and Simon are swimming. Ralph spots smoke on the horizon and concludes that it is a ship. Piggy wonders if the boys have any smoke to be seen by a passing ship. Ralph runs to check if the fire on the mountain is burning, and Simon, Maurice, and Piggy follow. Ralph shouts for Piggy's specs to start a fire. When they turn to the horizon, the boat is gone. Ralph curses the fire.

Jack and a small procession of boys enter the scene. The twins are carrying the carcass of a pig on a stake. They are chanting what will become their ritual hunting chant: "Kill the pig. Cut her throat. Spill her blood." The hunters describe the kill. Ralph tells Jack that he has let the fire burn out. Piggy joins in, scolding Jack for his irresponsible behavior, and Jack punches Piggy. His spectacles fly off and one lens shatters. Simon retrieves them from the rocks. Jack apologizes to Ralph for letting the fire out. The boys return to the mountain to light a new fire, Ralph using Piggy's one good lens to ignite it. Jack hacks the pig, and the meat is cooked. When Piggy asks for meat, Jack taunts him for not earning his meal by helping in the hunt. Simon tosses Piggy some meat out of pity. The hunters reenact their kill, singing and chanting in a murderous fervor. Overwhelmed by the intensity of the "dance," Ralph calls for an assembly.

Chapter 5: Beasts From Water Ralph declares that the meeting he has called will be business-oriented, not fun and games. This scene shows the boys' weariness and decay: irritated, sunburned skin; dirty hair; and ripped or no clothing. The boys sit and wait for the meeting to begin. The mood is grim because of the incident of the boat passing when no fire was lit on the mountain. Ralph establishes the need for a serious assembly, to straighten out the business and get things done. He complains about people not doing what they've promised. Ralph talks of the makeshift lavatory that's been set up, the duty to collect water, the chore of building huts, and finally the fire issue. He tells them that it is essential to always to have a fire burning. He laments about things breaking up on the island, how everyone is now frightened and no longer enjoying themselves.

Jack scolds the littluns for being sissies. They talk of the beast, and there is speculation as to whether it really exists. A littlun stands and tells of fighting with the creepers, or "twisty things." All insist it was a nightmare, and he insists it was real. He also says he saw a large horrid thing in the bushes.

Simon steps up to admit that it was he who was in the bushes. Another littlun, Percival, comes forward, and seems to be losing his strength and his sanity. Jack speaks for him to the assembly; the child tells of a beast from the sea. Arguments ensue about the beast, and a power struggle begins for the attention of the group. Insults fly.

In an important passage, Ralph declares that the rules are all that the group has got. Jack says that they are strong and can hunt; if there is a beast, they will simply hunt it down and kill it. Piggy wonders what the grown-ups would say about all of this. The meeting is out of control and chaotic, although the boys are desperately trying to have the orderliness of grown-ups. Piggy expresses a fear of Jack, and a desire for Ralph to rule over Jack. The boys ask for a sign from the grown-up world, a grim omen of what is to come in the next chapter.

Chapter 6: Beast From Air Ralph and Simon pick Percival up from a nightmare and bring him to a shelter. As if in answer to the previous chapter's plea for adult signals, there is an explosion in the sky. A figure drops to the ground with a parachute.

He hangs twisting and turning in the wind, caught up in the trees and the rocks.

The twins, Sam and Eric, are at watch at the fire, tending it to make sure it doesn't go out. The boys spot the body and run away gripped with fear, thinking it is the beast everyone has been speaking of. They wake Ralph from his dreams of home, telling him of their sighting of the "beast." They plan an assembly at dawn. Ralph holds the conch, not blowing it. The twins relay the story of the beast to the group. They try to devise a plan to find the beast. They ask Jack if there is any part of the island he has not seen. He answers that there is one part, the tail end, which he has not seen.

Jack leads this theatrical hunt for the beast, followed by Simon, and then Ralph. Another power play ensues between Jack and Ralph, each one testing the other's bravery and fearlessness. Ralph goes ahead of the other two, checks the area, and takes note of the vast sea below him. He is overwhelmed. He sees no beast but realizes the fire is out. Frustrated and scared, he insists that the fire be rekindled. The boys are tired and annoyed, and Jack leads the way down and back to the bottom of the mountain.

Chapter 7: Shadows and Tall Trees Feelings on the island are tense and fearful. Ralph quietly surveys the situation as the boys, dirty and unkempt, sit down to eat their usual fare of fruit. Ralph and Simon are discussing leaving the island. In a bizarre mood, Simon predicts that Ralph will get back all right.

Ralph daydreams of home, of corn flakes, of the warmth and security of England. He thinks of the symbols of his youth, for example his books about trains and ships. He has now been thrown into an adult world with adult responsibilities. Ralph's thoughts are interrupted by a chase for a pig. Excited, he takes a swipe at the boar. He decides that hunting is good after all. This change in Ralph represents the group's shift toward anarchy and chaos.

Ralph and Jack again battle it out for the attention and admiration of the group, Ralph with his swipe at the boar, and Jack with his very impressive flesh wound. Jack and Ralph start playing, jabbing at Robert as he squeals like a pig, play acting. Robert begins to wail in earnest as the jabs get more painful. Someone cries to hold him down while they all jab at him with their spears. The boys begin their chant, and the desire to hurt Robert overtakes them. The group stops, practically foaming at the mouth with their desire to rip flesh.

The boys trek on in search of the beast. Piggy is now alone on the other side of the island. Simon offers to go tell him that the hunting group will not be returning until after dark. Jack, Ralph, and Roger start up the mountain to find the beast while the others prepare for sleep. Jack taunts Ralph about being scared to go up, and ends up going alone. Jack, seeing the bulge of the parachute, runs back to Ralph and Roger, and the three go up together to see the beast. They find the body of the parachutist and flee in terror.

Chapter 8: Gift for the Darkness Ralph tells Piggy he has seen the beast. He is scared and wonders what should be done. They think the beast doesn't want the boys to be rescued because it sits by the fire. Ralph feels they are beaten.

Ralph insults the hunters, and Jack is personally offended. They have an assembly, and Jack announces the sighting of the beast. Ralph and Jack accuse each other of cowardice, each asserting his own strength and courage in the search for the beast. Jack questions the group's desire to have Ralph as their leader, and declares that he

is no longer on Ralph's side. He leaves and retreats into the forest. Simon takes the conch and announces that the group should climb the mountain and confront the beast, for the simple reason that there is nothing else to do.

Ralph's camp decides to keep a fire lit at the bottom of the mountain by the camp, since the beast will prevent any fire from staying lit at the top. The boys work to build a fire, and their mood is one of panic. Ralph notices some of the "biguns" are missing and wonders if they have joined Jack's camp.

Piggy and some others collect fruit for Ralph to have a victory feast of sorts. Simon is missing: he's gone again to his special place up on the mountain, and buries himself in his screen of leaves. The air feels threatening to him, where before it simply felt hot.

Jack has collected his group of hunters, which has spread out to hunt for pig. He spots a fat sow with piglets sucking at her nipples, and poises his spear for an attack. He hits her, and she runs. She eventually falls from the heat, and the hunters converge and attack. Jack guts her, and the boys dance and squeal, play acting as pigs. The hunters realize they need fire to cook their feast, and it is decided that they must raid Ralph's camp to steal the fire. The hunters place the sow's head on a stick as an offering for the beast.

Simon, semi-delirious from the heat and his fragile state of mind, finds the sow's head on a stick. It is covered with bugs, earning the title Lord of the Flies. Back at camp, Ralph and Piggy sit and discuss that Ralph is right in feeling the way he does about the fire—that it should be kept lit in the hopes that a passing boat will see it. They determine Jack to be the reason things have fallen apart on the island. Their discussion is abruptly interrupted as the hunters come flying out of the bushes to steal fire with their sticks. They invite the others to come join their clan of hunters, to have fun and feast. Ralph collects his sparse group together to discuss the importance of the fire. His attendants sense a weakness on Ralph's part.

Simon, in his delirium, hears the Lord of the Flies "speak" to him. In a powerful speech, the sow's head tells Simon, "Fancy thinking the beast was something you could hunt and kill!" For the reader and for Simon, the "beast" takes on new meaning. It is not only a monster roaming the island; it is the monster within each one of the boys. Simon faints and loses consciousness.

Chapter 9: A View to a Death The weather has grown fittingly ominous, with building clouds and air that is ready to explode. Simon awakens and wanders, still half-crazed. He finds the beast with the parachute blowing in the breeze and flies covering the face and body. Sick from the sight and smell, Simon realizes what it is and frees the lines of the parachute from the rocks. He looks down at the beach and at the boys around a fire.

Ralph is bathing. All the boys except Ralph, Piggy, and Simon are at Jack's feast. Ralph gives in, and suggests to Piggy that they might go join the others. They approach the party and see the pig roasting with its fat dripping. Jack and Ralph confront one another about who will join whose side. Ralph declares that the group appointed him chief. It begins to rain and Ralph asks Jack where the hunters will go for shelter, since Ralph has rights to the shelters. He, after all, built them.

Jack, in a frenzy, orders his hunters to begin their hunting chant. Thunder and lightning crash around them. Something is crawling out of the forest. It is dark. The thing, which is really Simon, crawls into the circle, where he is attacked in a mad frenzy by the group. He is heaped in a bloody mass by the water, where he is eventually dragged out to sea. In the same grotesque, terrifying moment, the parachutist's body slips through the rocks and trees, falling to its watery grave.

Chapter 10: The Shell and the Glasses
Piggy and Ralph question what should be done. Piggy suggests calling an assembly. They discuss the murder, and Piggy tries to justify the boys' actions as an accident and a result of fear. He says that Simon was batty. Piggy rationalizes that Simon was batty anyway, and that he asked for it. He goes on to say that he and Ralph were outsiders and therefore not guilty for the murder. Sam and Eric claim they left the scene of the crime early.

Roger climbs the mountain to Jack's fortress and is stopped by Robert, Jack's lookout guard. Within his cave, Jack expresses his fears of the beast returning, even though they have offered it the head of a pig. He again talks of the need to steal fire from Ralph's camp. Maurice, Roger, and Jack plan to raid the other camp.

At the bottom of the mountain, Piggy and Ralph feel the need for fire for a different purpose, comfort. Asleep in the shelter, Ralph dreams of home, whimpering. He's told to keep it down. Sam and Eric are battling it out, and they too are told to be quiet. The boys hear a noise outside, like a stick crackling. Voices taunt Piggy, and out of anxiety he has an asthma attack. The group of three hunters attacks the hut, and Sam, Eric, Piggy, and Ralph fight them off. The hunters withdraw and escape back to their hide-out. They have, however, stolen Piggy's glasses.

Chapter 11: Castle Rock Ralph, Sam, Eric, and Piggy are gathered around the remains of the ashes from their fire. The four have their own assembly. They plan to clean themselves up, get spears, and ask the hunters for Piggy's specs back. As they prepare to approach Jack, Piggy wants to hold the conch as a sign of strength. As they near Castle Rock, Jack's fortress, Ralph blows the conch to tell them he's having an assembly.

The painted hunters return, and Ralph asks Jack to give Piggy's specs back. Jack tries to spear Ralph, and a chest to chest combat ensues. Ralph insists on the importance of the fire. Jack orders Sam and Eric to stand back and has his hunters tie them up. Jack and Ralph charge each other, and a fight begins. Holding the conch, Piggy, who remains the voice of reason amid the chaotic group, asks the question that has hung over the boys each day they've been on the island: "Which is better, law and rescue, or hunting and breaking things up?"

Roger pushes a boulder off an overhang of rock, which drops down to shatter the conch and pushes Piggy to a forty-foot plunge to his death. Jack stabs at Ralph, who flees. Sam and Eric remain tied up.

Chapter 12: Cry of the Hunters Ralph, fearing for his life, is in hiding. He has the awful realization that as long as they are trapped on this island, Jack will never give him one moment's peace. He hears the tribal dancing of the hunters. He stalks back to Castle Rock to speak to Sam and Eric. They are now guarding the cave against Ralph. They warn him to go before any of Jack's troops see him. They tell him of the signals Jack and the hunters will be using for their hunt, and he departs, telling Sam and Eric where he will be hiding so they know not to look there.

After hiding all night, Ralph awakens to the sound of moving rocks. A deadly cat and mouse game ensues and Ralph is running for his life. Jack's troop is just about on him. Suddenly, the whole band comes upon a naval officer on the beach.

The officer asks if there are any grown-ups on the island. Ralph replies no. The officer wants to know how many have died, who is in charge. The officer surveys the boys' dirtiness and general wild appearance and censures Ralph for not having kept up a "better show" as British boys.

The boys, exhausted and crazed, break down sobbing. Ralph, in the middle of the boys, weeps for "the end of innocence, the darkness of man's heart, and the fall through the air of the true, wise friend called Piggy."

MACBETH

ABOUT THE AUTHOR

See page 111.

THE BIG PICTURE

Set in Scotland in the Middle Ages, *Macbeth* tells the tragic story of one couple's ambition and their eventual destruction at its hands. It is a play both of the natural and the supernatural—events in human life are spurred on by otherworldy influences. And as with all of Shake-speare's works, it is filled with beautifully descriptive language and vivid images.

Why you're reading this book:
- It is a classic example of Shakespeare's tragedy.
- It provides an intriguing picture of medieval politics and society.
- The play's images and ideas are valuable and relevant to readers of any era.
- This play demonstrates Shakespeare's timeless understanding of history and the forces that instigate change.

Your teachers are looking for:
- The witches' statement, "Fair is foul and foul is fair" as one of the play's central themes.
- Images of darkness/night vs. light/daylight.
- The relationship between sleep and death.
- "Manliness" vs. "femininity" in the play.
- Cycles of three throughout the play
- The way the supernatural and the natural intertwine, blurring the distinction between the real and the imagined.

KEY CHARACTERS

Banquo: Macbeth's friend and fellow soldier, he is intelligent and honorable. After he is murdered by a paranoid Macbeth, he comes back as a ghost to haunt him.

Duncan: King of Scotland. A kind, gentle king, he is murdered by Macbeth at the beginning of the play. The murder of Duncan sets the wheels of the tragedy in motion.

Malcolm: King Duncan's son. Acting for the good of the people, he and Macduff lead the rebellion against Macbeth. He ends up being appointed King of Scotland and restores order and trust in the land.

Macbeth: The tragic hero of the play. He begins the play as an honest nobleman, but he soon becomes overtaken by greed and ambition and commits hideous crimes. Although he finally realizes how terrible his actions have been, it is too late to make amends.

Lady Macbeth: Macbeth's cold, callous wife. She coaxes Macbeth into murdering Duncan. She eventually goes insane, and the burden of guilt drives her to her grave.

The three witches: They open the play, setting an eerie tone that will linger throughout. Their prophecies spur Macbeth on to commit his crimes. Although the "Weird Sisters" have few lines, their impact is crucial throughout the play.

Lennox: A nobleman of Scotland. Until he suspects foul play, he is a loyal and true friend of Macbeth's. He winds up joining Macduff's alliance against Macbeth.

Doctor: Examines Lady Macbeth who is assumed to be physically ill. He finds that he is unable to cure her ailments, because what she suffers from are deep mental and spiritual afflictions.

Ross: Delivers the messages of death to Siward and Macduff. He too is initially Macbeth's comrade, but also has a change of heart.

ESSAY IDEAS

- What do the witches and supernatural elements in the play represent?
- Do you sympathize with Macbeth? Why or why not?
- How does Lady Macbeth's character change from the beginning to the end?
- Why is *Macbeth* considered a tragedy?
- Who are the heroic characters in this play?
- Discuss Shakespeare's use of symbols, particularly light versus dark.
- How does guilt manifest itself in the play?

A SAMPLE ESSAY IN OUTLINE FORM

Lady Macbeth's changing character
- Her initial image: Macbeth's emotionless, cold-blooded partner in crime:
  - A desire to "unsex" herself and lose her feminine identity.
  - Lack of maternal instincts—an indication that she is going against nature.
  - Lust for power and prestige at any cost.
  - Her headstrong and rational nature; she is able to make viable excuses for Macbeth when he acts crazy.
  - She is an active, controlling force, dictating Macbeth's actions.
- This strong image cannot hold up and her guilty conscience takes over:
  - She is unable to sleep soundly and begins walking and talking in her sleep.
  - She grows physically and mentally weaker.
  - She hallucinates that there is a permanent bloodstain on her hands.
  - She loses her independent will and counts on Macbeth's strength to get them through the crisis.

Through Lady Macbeth, Shakespeare shows us the impossibility of "unsexing" oneself. Lady Macbeth is incapable of eliminating "feminine" emotions of pain and sorrow, although she may have buried those feelings for a while. Her guilt must inevitably surface in some form.

PLOT SUMMARY

Act I, Scenes i–iii In the short opening scene, we are introduced to the three witches, whose prophecies and spells will haunt Macbeth throughout the play. The witches utter puzzling chants whose words seem to contradict each other, such as "Fair is foul and foul is fair." They are wicked and cunning, but also insightful, creatures.

In Scene ii, a wounded soldier enters King Duncan's camp to deliver news of the battle: under the leadership of Macbeth and Banquo, the Norwegian King and the deceitful Thane of Cawdor have been conquered. On hearing of Macbeth's heroic performance, Duncan decides to bestow the Thane of Cawdor's title on him. As the witches predicted in Scene i, something is "lost and won" in the battle.

The witches meet again, and this time Macbeth and Banquo are present. The witches make more bizarre exclamations, addressing Macbeth by three different names: Thane of Glamis (his present title), Thane of Cawdor (his newly acquired title that he hasn't learned of yet), and King in the future. Also, they tell Banquo that he is "lesser than Macbeth, and greater" and that "thou shalt get Kings though thou be none."

When Macbeth is informed that he is the new Thane of Cawdor, he is excited and stirred by the witches' accurate prediction. Banquo, on the other hand, is more wary about the statements, believing that the curious prophecies will cause trouble and harm.

In his first soliloquy, Macbeth wonders how he will earn the rights of kingship without killing Duncan. Already, Macbeth is consumed by the idea of becoming King. He decides to let fate determine his future for the time being.

Act I, Scenes iv–vii At the King's palace, King Duncan and his son Malcolm discuss how difficult it is to distinguish a traitor from a patriot. Ironically, Macbeth and Banquo enter as this conversation comes to a close. Macbeth is believed to be a patriot, but he turns out to be more treacherous than the first Thane of Cawdor.

The setting switches to Inverness, Macbeth and Lady Macbeth's home. Scene v describes Lady Macbeth's passionate reaction to the letter she has received from Macbeth. The letter explains the prophecy delivered by the witches. Fearful that fate may not follow through, Lady Macbeth decides that she may have to take forceful action to ensure the realization of the prophecy.

Even more ambitious and greedy than Macbeth, Lady Macbeth has no reservations about using violence to make the prediction come to pass. Her only fear is that her husband's weak nature may prevent him from taking the necessary action. She asks the spirits for strength and vows to take control.

The unsuspecting King Duncan comes to Inverness for a friendly visit. Once he arrives and is settled in, Macbeth is left alone to contemplate the King's murder and to consider its consequences. He almost decides against killing Duncan because he realizes the gravity of such an action.

But Lady Macbeth intervenes, provoking him to take action. By offering examples of her own hardness and strength, she indirectly questions Macbeth's manliness and manipulates him into deciding to go through with the murder. Macbeth finally decides that he will kill Duncan in a way that will make Duncan's grooms look guilty.

Act II, Scenes i–ii Before Macbeth commits the crime, Banquo anxiously tells him that he has dreamt the witches' prophecy was fulfilled. Macbeth lies to Banquo, telling him he has not even thought about the witches' prediction. After his confrontation with the honorable Banquo, Macbeth has a horrible hallucination of a bloody dagger.

Macbeth is reluctant about his decision to kill the King, but before he can back out, Lady Macbeth informs him that she already drugged Duncan's grooms. Macbeth goes through with the plan to murder Duncan. Afterwards, a shaken Macbeth tells his wife that during the killing he heard a voice cry "Macbeth does murder sleep...Macbeth shall sleep no more." Only those who are innocent can sleep soundly, and Macbeth will always have this murder on his conscience.

Lady Macbeth, who is still calm and contained, tells Macbeth to wash his bloody hands and to put the tainted daggers beside the grooms. When Macbeth is unable to pull himself together, Lady Macbeth snatches the daggers from his hands and finishes the job herself.

At the end of Scene ii, Macbeth expresses his fear that no amount of water could cleanse his hands. Lady Macbeth mocks his feelings of guilt, but she will suffer similar pain later on. Although Macbeth is presently weak with grief and Lady Macbeth is filled with wicked energy, the roles will reverse as the play continues.

Act II, Scenes iii–iv Macduff and Lennox go to the King's chambers to speak with him, and they discover his body. Macduff exclaims that the King has been cruelly murdered. Soon after that announcement, Macbeth murders the two grooms to cover up his crime, pretending to have killed the men as retribution for killing Duncan. Lady Macbeth faints, and Duncan's sons flee to England. Banquo watches everything with suspicion, suspecting foul play.

In Scene iv, some noblemen discuss the strange occurrences since Duncan's murder. Elements of the natural world are behaving as strangely as the members of society. Nature and society are tied closely together in this play, so when Macbeth disrupts the natural progression of fate, nature is thrown off balance as well.

None of the noblemen can agree about whom to blame for Duncan's death. As of yet, no one has named Macbeth as the murderer. But Macduff has expressed mixed emotions about Macbeth becoming the new ruler of Scotland.

Act III, Scenes i–iii Macbeth and Lady Macbeth are now King and Queen of Scotland. To celebrate this honor, Macbeth invites Banquo to dinner at his castle. Although outwardly friendly to Banquo, Macbeth is jealous and fearful of him.

Macbeth considers both Banquo and his son Fleance as threats to his security as King. He hires assassins to kill them, hoping that his mind will then be at ease. Macbeth has clearly lost all sense of morality; his overwhelming guilt and fear drive him to become increasingly cruel and merciless.

Lady Macbeth realizes that her husband is becoming deeply troubled, and fears his recent plotting is based on paranoid fears. To renew his confidence, she flatters him with words of praise and admiration. This helps his fragile ego somewhat, and he appeals to the spirits of the night to give him blind strength.

On the way to Macbeth's house, Banquo is murdered by the hired killers. This murder, like Duncan's, takes place at night. Fleance manages to escape.

Act III, Scenes iv–v As the guests are being seated for the banquet, one of the murderers provides the details of Banquo's murder to Macbeth. After hearing the news, Macbeth thinks he sees Banquo's ghost sitting in the empty seat where Banquo would have been. The hallucination drives him mad, driving him to blurt out incriminating information about his part in the crimes.

Lady Macbeth takes control again. She makes reasonable excuses for Macbeth's behavior and politely asks the guests to leave. Again, Macbeth feels remorse and wishes that he had never gotten himself into this mess. He decides to ask the witches what the future holds for him.

In Scene v, Hecate, the goddess of witchcraft, is speaking to the three witches about Macbeth's future. Her speech, like the other witches', is uttered in poetic rhymes and puzzles. She provides instructions for their last meeting with Macbeth.

Meanwhile, back at the palace, the noble lords discuss their misgivings about Macbeth. Suddenly, Macbeth is viewed as a tyrant, and the grooms are no longer believed to be Duncan's murderers. Macduff has gone to England to join Malcolm, who has planned to organize an army against Macbeth. This is the beginning of Macbeth's demise.

Act IV, Scenes i–iii Macbeth approaches the witches, who are dancing around the boiling cauldron. Upon his request for new information, the witches chant spells that produce strange apparitions. The spirits offer more baffling proclamations to Macbeth.

First, an armed head appears which warns Macbeth to "beware Macduff." Then a second ghost says that "none of woman born shall harm Macbeth," so he no longer worries about the first premonition. But the witches speak in riddles, so what appears to be comforting information must still be regarded with caution.

The final apparition delivers the message that Macbeth will not be defeated until Birnam Wood moves to Dunsinane. Foolishly, Macbeth also accepts this information with the utmost optimism. It seems impossible to Macbeth that a forest would ever be able to move from one place to another.

Just as the witches disappear, Lennox arrives and tells Macbeth that Macduff has fled to England. No longer fearful of being dethroned or harmed, Macbeth decides to punish Macduff. He sends murderers to attack Macduff's castle and household at Fife.

Lady Macduff and her son are attacked by Macbeth's murderers as they attempt to leave the castle. A messenger had brought warning to the family members, but they were not able to escape in time. The level of violence rises as the play progresses: the murder of a woman and child shows that Macbeth will now stop at nothing.

Scene iii shifts to England, where Macduff and Malcolm are grieving over their homeland Scotland, which is now in great turmoil. They vow to bring it back to its previous glorious state. But just as they become excited about their plans, Ross enters bearing the news that Macduff's family has been murdered.

Act V, Scenes i–ii A doctor is sent to examine Lady Macbeth, who has been walking and talking in her sleep. Before the doctor approaches her room he notices Lady Macbeth pacing restlessly, repeatedly rubbing her hands together, and making jumbled confessions about the murders.

Now Lady Macbeth is traumatized by guilt as her husband was earlier. She rubs her hands in an effort to remove the guilt and blood that stain her conscience. As Macbeth noted earlier, Lady Macbeth is destined to have a disturbed sleep, since she lost her innocence and her clear conscience.

At the end of Lady Macbeth's haunted murmuring, she concludes by saying, "What's done can never be undone." As Macbeth realized earlier, it is too late for her to make amends for the course of action she has taken. She will only find peace in death; the doctor has no cure for the breakdown caused by her guilty conscience.

Near Dunsinane, a combined army consisting of English and Scottish troops are preparing for battle against Macbeth. People who once obeyed Macbeth because of his title now refuse to do so, because no one respects him as the rightful King of Scotland.

Act V, Scenes iii–v When we hear Dunsinane and Birnam Wood mentioned in Scene ii, we are reminded of the witches' prophecy. A servant announces that an army is approaching Macbeth's castle. Macbeth still refuses to give up, although he has no soldiers on his side and is in great distress.

Malcolm instructs his soldiers to cut trees from Birnam Wood to be carried along as a camouflage. It becomes clear that the witches' prophecy about Birnam Wood moving to Dunsinane will indeed come true, and that Macbeth is in grave danger.

In Scene v, we see that time is running out for Macbeth. Seyton delivers the sorrowful message that Lady Macbeth has died, and soon after, another messenger appears to tell Macbeth that Birnam Wood is moving toward Dunsinane. Filled with despair, Macbeth decides that his life has been worthless.

Macbeth suddenly realizes that the prophecy of his doom is being fulfilled. He knows he will probably die, but he refuses to end his life like a coward. He puts on his suit of armor and prepares to battle the opposition alone.

Although Macbeth has committed many crimes throughout the play, he now appears pitiful and sympathetic. As his doom approaches, he behaves more like a confused fool than a cold-blooded killer.

Act V, Scenes vi–viii Macbeth's only hope at this point is that he will find security in the prediction, "none of woman born could harm Macbeth." Young Siward, a soldier fighting with Malcolm, dies under Macbeth's sword. Macbeth is then reassured about his immunity to death.

Macbeth and Macduff soon find themselves in a face-to-face confrontation. Thinking himself invulnerable, Macbeth warns Macduff that no man of woman born can harm him. Macduff reveals, however, that he was "from his mother's womb untimely ripped," and Macbeth's hope is clearly lost.

Macduff attempts to persuade Macbeth to surrender, but Macbeth stubbornly refuses. The two begin fighting and exit the stage.

When Macduff reenters, he is holding Macbeth's severed head. Malcolm is considered a hero and is appointed the new King of Scotland. The honorable new leader proclaims he will restore order and bring harmony and happiness back to Scotland.

MOBY DICK

ABOUT THE AUTHOR

Herman Melville (1819–1891) was born in New York City. At eighteen, he went to sea on a whaling ship. This voyage was to be extremely influential on the young Melville, and serves as the foundation not only of *Moby Dick* but of several of Melville's other works. Melville published *Typee* in 1846, and *Omoo* in 1847. His masterpiece, *Moby Dick*, first appeared in 1851. Melville wrote of *Moby Dick* to fellow writer Nathaniel Hawthorne, "I've written a wicked book, and feel spotless as a lamb."

Melville retired from writing after publishing *The Confidence Man* in 1857, and worked as a customs inspector. His final work, *Billy Budd, Sailor*, was unpublished at his death.

THE BIG PICTURE

Moby Dick is the story of Captain Ahab's single-minded pursuit of the dreaded white whale. The novel is told through Ishmael, a crew member on Ahab's ship, the ship's only survivor. Melville's writing is heavy with symbolism; as a result, *Moby Dick* can be read on many different levels and with many different interpretations.

Why you're reading this book:
- It is considered one of the great classics of American literature—an American epic.
- Melville's use of symbolism is excellent.
- The tension between the ideologies of Queequeg and Ahab provides an interesting commentary on religious differences. Melville seems to be asking us to question who exactly is "the savage" in this story.
- It is not only the story of one man's obsession with a whale, but an allegory of man's relationship with the divine.

Your teachers are looking for:
- Color imagery: Melville's use of light and dark colors, especially in describing characters' appearances.
- Ishmael's role as narrator, and how his view of the world differs from Ahab's.
- Ahab's harsh Christian theology contrasted with the gentler cannibal theology of the tropics.
- Rebellion and obedience:
  - Ahab's demand for obedience contrasted with his own rebellion against his "fiery father."
- What Moby Dick symbolizes for Ahab and the other members of the crew.

Moby Dick is far from easy to read. Remember that the story line is secondary to the writing, and be on the lookout for Melville's underlying messages.

KEY CHARACTERS

Captain Ahab: Captain of the whaling ship Pequod. He is obsessed with the white whale Moby Dick that swallowed his leg in a previous encounter. A very eccentric character, he is described as an "ungodly, god-like man."

Ishmael: A sailor aboard the Pequod, and our narrator. He alone survives the wreck of the Pequod to tell the tale to us.

Starbuck: First Mate of the Pequod. Cautious by nature, oriented toward business, he sees no reason to pursue Moby Dick. Contemplates mutiny against Ahab.

Stubb: Second Mate. The antithesis of Starbuck. Craves danger and cares little for business.

Flask: Third Mate. A little man and a brave whaler.

Queequeg: Ishmael's closest friend and confidant. A harpooner aboard the Pequod, he originally hails from a cannibal island in the South Pacific. Although somewhat Christianized, Queequeg still speaks in broken English and still retains a loyalty to the gods of his youth.

Tashtego: A harpooner aboard the Pequod.

Daggoo: Another harpooner.

Moby Dick: A giant white whale whose existence some whalers in the book doubt. The pursuit of Moby Dick is Ahab's obsession, and the Pequod's voyage revolves around this goal.

ESSAY IDEAS

- Explain how Moby Dick's swallowing of Ahab's leg relates to the larger issues of cannibalism in the book.
- Describe Queequeg and his relationships with the other characters.
- How does Ahab's relationship with his "fiery father" compare to his relationship with the crew of the Pequod?
- Discuss the aquatic imagery in the novel.

A SAMPLE ESSAY IN OUTLINE FORM

Discuss the symbolism of the White Whale. What does Moby Dick represent?
- On a concrete level:

- Ahab's biggest challenge as a whaler.
- The cause of Ahab losing his leg.
- The most dangerous of whales.
- For Ahab and the crew, hunting down Moby Dick is their driving force.

On a symbolic level:
- Much more than just a whale.
- For Ahab, Moby Dick has come to represent all that is evil in the world.
- Moby Dick becomes a symbol for universal ideas: challenge; the enemy; obsession; revenge; the unobtainable.
- The crew members fear Ahab's obsession with Moby Dick more than the whale itself.

Moby Dick is the ultimate opponent to Ahab, and represents all that is evil to him. To the crew, he is more just a danger of the sea, although a very great one. Ahab's obsession with the destruction of Moby Dick in turn leads to the destruction of both him and his crew.

PLOT SUMMARY

Note: For the sake of clarity, chapter numbers are indicated by standard Arabic numbers rather than the Roman numerals that appear in the book.

Chapters 1–5 We meet Ishmael, our narrator, in the first sentence of the book. Ishmael is in a foul mood, in the "November of the soul," and seeks to drive out this malaise by shipping out to sea. Unlike in his past voyages as a merchant sailor, he chooses to ship out on a whaling ship.

Ishmael arrives in New Bedford, Massachusetts, to begin his search for a whaling ship. He carries a carpet bag holding his belongings (Chapter 2 is entitled "The Carpet Bag") and takes lodging at "The Spouter-Inn: Peter Coffin." The Spouter-Inn is a large, wooden, gothic place, full of high arches and the like. Ishmael has dinner and arranges for his night's lodging. The landlord informs him that if he chooses to stay, he will have to share a bed with a harpooner.

In Chapter 3, Ishmael learns that this harpooner hails from New Zealand and is out peddling shrunken heads

Ishmael goes to the room and finds his roommate's belongings, including a small pagan idol. He settles into the hard and uncomfortable bed. Queequeg, Ishmael's roommate, soon returns to the room and performs a short ceremony, sacrificing a biscuit to his little idol. Ishmael awakes and is immediately horrified by Queequeg's appearance. Queequeg is a tall, bald, heavily tattooed man. On further reflection, however, Ishmael concludes that Queequeg does not look so bad, for a cannibal.

Queequeg discovers Ishmael in the bed and pulls out his tomahawk, yelling at Ishmael in broken English dialect to identify himself. Ishmael calls for the landlord, who soon arrives and mediates between Ishmael and Queequeg. They quickly come to an agreement and fall into a sleep that Ishmael describes as the best in his life.

Chapters 4 and 5 take place the next morning. Ishmael wakes to find Queequeg's arm thrown over him. He attempts to wake Queequeg, who eventually rises. They both dress and go to breakfast. They descend to the dining room, where the landlord serves a massive breakfast feast. Whalers of all sorts, hailing from a variety of ports, eat breakfast together in the main room.

Chapters 6–10 Ishmael goes for a stroll through New Bedford, and describes how the character of the town is completely imbued with whaling. The people on the street represent the ethnic mix of the whaling trade. All sorts of groups, from Native American tribes to cannibals from the South Seas, comprise the population of New Bedford.

In Chapter 7, Ishmael makes a Sunday pilgrimage to the whalers' chapel, as he claims all good whalers should. Plaques commemorating sailors lost in whaling expeditions adorn the walls of the chapel. He finds Queequeg seated near him.

Ishmael discusses the importance of the plaques, as the victims of accidents at sea have no other memory. He contemplates the fates of these sailors, and thinks briefly on the idea that the same fate may await him. He concludes, however, that he is not worried because the soul is the larger part of the individual, and what happens to the body is largely unimportant.

Father Mapple, minister of the chapel and a former whaler, delivers a sermon on the biblical account of Jonah and the Whale. He describes how Jonah set out to run around the world to flee the wrath of God, how he brought a storm to the ship on which he had booked passage, and how the crew threw him overboard and he was swallowed by a whale. Father Mapple relates that Jonah then prayed and was delivered from the whale.

Ishmael returns to the inn and finds Queequeg in the room. He describes Queequeg as "George Washington, cannibalistically developed."

Queequeg and Ishmael smoke together, and then Queequeg prepares a sacrifice to his god Yojo. Ishmael, despite his Christian misgivings, aids in the ceremony and places a burnt offering before Yojo.

Chapters 11–15 Queequeg and Ishmael go to bed and lie awake together. Ishmael gives the reader a biography of Queequeg. He tells us that Queequeg was born on the island of Kokovoko and is the son of the High Chief.

Eager to see Christian civilization, Queequeg attempted to book passage on a passing ship. The ship refused his request. He took his canoe to a strait through which the ship had to pass and climbed onto the hull when the ship came through. The captain, after trying to get rid of him, eventually allowed Queequeg to stay on, and the crew trained him to be a whaler.

Queequeg tells Ishmael that he will eventually return to his island, after he feels he can wash away the corruption from the Christian world.

Queequeg and Ishmael check out of the inn. They borrow a wheelbarrow for their belongings and book passage on a ship to Nantucket. Some of the young sailors mimic Queequeg behind his back. Queequeg grabs one of them and tosses him into the air. The sailor lands on his feet, and runs to tell the captain, who warns Queequeg to behave himself. At that moment, the mainsail of the ship breaks loose, and Queequeg jumps in to re-secure it.

Ishmael and Queequeg arrive in Nantucket, and Ishmael describes his theory of why Nantucketeers are the highest form of sailors. Other sailors only build extensions of land onto the sea. The Nantucket whaler, on the other hand, reaps his living from the sea itself.

Chapters 16–20 Ishmael scouts the docks for a suitable ship and finds the Pequod. He talks to Captain Peleg, one of the three principal co-owners of the ship, who questions him about his experience in whaling. Captain Bildad, the second co-owner, arrives, and Bildad and Peleg discuss what portion of the ship's profits Ishmael should receive. Peleg signs Ishmael on at a 300th part of the profits. Ishmael inquires as to where he may find Captain Ahab, the man Peleg and Bildad have named as the commander of the vessel.

Peleg describes Ahab as a "grand, ungodly, god-like man."

Chapter 17 focuses on Queequeg's observance of a religious holiday, which includes fasting and kneeling before the idol for a long time. Ishmael leaves Queequeg doing this in their room in the boarding house. When he comes back from the Pequod, he tries to get Queequeg to let him back into the room, but there is no reply. Ishmael thinks something terrible has happened to Queequeg and tries to get the landlady to break down the door. They find a key to the room and open the door to find Queequeg engaged in his religious observance.

Ishmael implores Queequeg to go get something to eat, but Queequeg ignores him. Eventually, Ishmael goes to bed. Queequeg joins him later and tells him that his Ramadan holiday is over.

Ishmael and Queequeg go down to the ship to sign Queequeg aboard. Peleg and Bildad express their reservations about having a cannibal on board ship. Ishmael says that Queequeg is a deacon of the First Congregational Church, that church to which everyone belongs. Peleg and Bildad seem to accept this. Queequeg then gives them a demonstration of his skills, expertly harpooning a small spot of tar floating on the water. He is offered a 90th fraction of the ship's profits, and signs the paper with a mark. (Chapter 18 is entitled "His Mark.")

In Chapter 19, entitled "The Prophet," a man named Elijah accosts Ishmael and Queequeg, and tells them about the temperament of Captain Ahab, or "Old Thunder" as he calls him. He says he does not think the Pequod is fated for a good voyage.

Chapters 21–25 Queequeg and Ishmael head towards the ship, and are accosted by Elijah again, who asks them whether they thought they saw men moving towards the ship the night before.

They board the ship and find no one awake. They begin to smoke and attract the attention of Starbuck, one of the mates of the ship, who tells them that departure is imminent.

Chapter 22 shows the Pequod pulling out of port on Christmas Day, piloted by Bildad and Peleg. (Ahab, said to be ill, stays below.) Peleg gives a lecture to the mates and crew, and the two return to shore in a launch.

In Chapters 24 and 25, Ishmael talks about whaling. He argues the virtues of whaling with an imagined opponent in mind, and adds the fact that British Kings and Queens are anointed with sperm whale oil.

Chapters 26–30 In Chapters 26 and 27, both entitled "Knights and Squires," Ishmael gives a description of each of the mates of the Pequod, beginning with Starbuck, the first mate. He describes Starbuck as tall, thin, and wiry, but extremely healthy. Ishmael tells us that he is thirty years old and has a wife and child in Nantucket. Starbuck says that he "would have no man in [his] boat who is not afraid of a whale." He looks for a boat crew that can make fair estimations of the dangers of a whale, and will not exhibit foolish bravado. He is practical, organized, and reasonable.

Stubb, the second mate, hails from Cape Cod and chain-smokes pipes. Ishmael tells us that he is neither brave nor cowardly, but takes danger in stride. Ishmael describes Flask, the third mate, from Martha's Vineyard, as a man who misunderstands whales. He tells us that Flask thinks of whales as nothing more than water-rats, and hunts them for the fun of it.

Ishmael then turns to describing the harpooners ("squires") whom the mates have chosen to serve for them during the voyage. Starbuck has picked Queequeg to harpoon for him; Stubb's squire is Tashtego, a Native American from

Martha's Vineyard; and Flask's harpooner is Daggoo, a giant African. Ishmael goes on to describe the crew as a group of isolates federated for this voyage.

Chapters 28–30 introduce Captain Ahab. Ahab emerges from his cabin and stands upon the quarter-deck of the ship. Ishmael describes him as a "high broad form" and compares him to Cellini's bronze statue of Perseus. Ahab has a white scar that runs down the length of his body. He has only one leg, the other having been lost and replaced with an ivory peg.

As the Pequod heads south and the weather gets better, Ahab is seen more and more by the crew, standing or sitting on the quarter-deck or pacing the deck. Ahab paces the deck at night, and Stubb comes up from below to suggest that he use some device to muffle the noise of the ivory leg. Ahab turns on Stubb and insults him. Stubb replies that he will not tamely be insulted. Ahab towers over him, and so intimidates him that Stubb retreats.

Ahab goes to the deck and lights his pipe. He finds that the pipe no longer gives him enjoyment. He meditates on this and determines that pipes are for more serene people. He throws the pipe into the sea.

Chapters 31–35 Stubb is the focus of Chapter 31, telling Flask of a dream he's had in which Ahab kicks him, and he tries to kick back, but Ahab turns into a pyramid. Stubb keeps kicking, until an old merman swims by and asks him why he's kicking. Stubb explains about the kick he received from Ahab, and the merman tells him that kicks from Ahab are honors.

Ishmael devotes Chapters 32 and 33 to a discussion of whales and whaling. He first gives an organized list of the methods of categorizing whales. He goes on to tell us that, in the past, command of a whaling vessel was split between the Captain, who commanded the vessel, and the chief harpooner, or specksynder, who commanded the whaling operations. Ishmael goes on to explain that officers and harpooners live in the aft part of the ship, and the crew lives forward. Chapter 33 ends with Ishmael comparing Ahab to Emperors and Kings.

Chapter 34 is Ishmael's description of a typical dinner in Captain Ahab's cabin with the mates and the harpooners. He describes the manner in which each behaves at the table, and he tells us that Ahab sat apart from the interaction.

In Chapter 35, "The Mast-Head," Ishmael describes keeping watch for whales on top of the mast-head. He tells us that the altitude and the serenity induce thoughtful trances, and that he finds it hard to keep his attention on looking for whales.

Chapters 36–40 Chapter 36 introduces us to Moby Dick. Ahab orders the ship's company assembled in the aft of the ship, and offers a sixteen dollar gold coin to anyone manning the mast-head who spots a white whale. Daggoo, Queequeg, and Tashtego ask Ahab if that whale is Moby Dick. Starbuck asks if Moby Dick is the same whale that crippled Ahab. Ahab answers yes. Ahab tells the crew that their primary mission is to hunt down Moby Dick. Starbuck voices reservations, saying that he will hunt Moby Dick, but only as he would hunt any other whale. The chapter ends with the crew of the Pequod vowing to hunt and kill Moby Dick.

Ahab then ponders his life. He states that he is "gifted with high perception," and lacks "low, enjoying power." He claims that the loss of his leg was prophesied and predicts that he will "dismember [his] dismemberer."

Starbuck, leaning on the main mast, reflects on the manner in which Ahab overpowers him. He reflects, also, on the "heathen" composition of the crew. Stubb, mending a brace, adds his thoughts: he

says that he thinks the fate of the ship is predetermined. He also thinks Ahab somewhat god-like, possessing a "gift." The crew revels, singing, yelling, and sometimes fighting and insulting each other.

Chapters 41–45 Ishmael describes Moby Dick as a giant white sperm whale with a pyramid hump and a crooked jaw. He tells of the whalers who have tried to kill him and the manner in which harpoons appear to have no effect. He then relates the extent of Ahab's hatred for the white whale.

In Chapter 42, "The Whiteness of the Whale," Ishmael draws parallels between Moby Dick and traditional uses of the color white. He points out that white is a royal color, and that both the steed of Indian mythology and Coleridge's albatross are white. He claims that Moby Dick is the incarnation of all things in one, and that this justifies the Pequod's hunt.

One of the sailors mentions to a fellow that he thinks he's heard someone coughing below decks. The other sailor scoffs. Ishmael then describes Ahab in his cabin, pondering over sea charts, attempting to locate where Moby Dick might be located.

In Chapter 45, Ishmael's narrative becomes somewhat technical again, citing several examples to prove that sperm whales are powerful, intelligent, and sometimes malicious.

Chapters 46–50 In Chapter 46, "Surmises," Ishmael tells us that Ahab would like to hunt only for Moby Dick, but in order to maintain command of the ship, he has to make a show of pursuing other whales.

Tashtego, in the mast-head, sights some whales. The boat crews get into their boats to hunt the whales. After a few minutes, however, they lose sight of them. Flask stands on Daggoo's shoulders and sights them. A sudden storm squall disrupts the hunt; the crew of Starbuck's boat, including Queequeg and Ishmael, are tossed overboard when the Pequod, driven by the storm wind, sails over their boat.

Ishmael inquires of his mates whether it is common for boat commanders to chase a whale even in such unfavorable conditions. They reply that it is not only common, but expected.

Ahab, despite his handicap, outfits one of the spare boats for his use. The crew at first believes that the preparations he makes are for the hunt for Moby Dick, not for general-purpose whaling. But Ahab puts the boat to general use. The Pequod picks up an Asian named Fedallah, who becomes part of the crew.

Chapters 51–55 The men occasionally sight a spout during the night, which disappears when they try to chase it. The crew believes this to be the spout of Moby Dick. As the Pequod travels toward the Cape of Good Hope, Ahab constantly walks the quarter-deck, searching for the whale.

Chapter 52 describes the Pequod's encounter with another whaling ship out of Nantucket called the Goney, or Albatross. Ahab shouts to the ship, asking if they've spotted Moby Dick. While attempting to reply, the captain of the Albatross drops his bullhorn. Ahab shouts back to the ship, telling them to tell people in Nantucket that the Pequod is bound to circumnavigate the globe, and that future letters should be addressed to the Pacific. The other ship sails off without replying.

Ishmael describes the customs followed by whaling ships when they encounter each other. He tells us that the ships exchange crews, and that for a time, the two captains will stay aboard one ship, and the two first mates aboard the other.

In Chapter 54, the Pequod encounters another homeward bound whaling ship. One of its crew members tells Tashtego of an encounter with Moby Dick, but swears Tashtego to secrecy. Tashtego, however, talks in his sleep. When he awakens, the crew makes him tell the full story.

The rest of Chapter 54 is Tashtego's telling of the story. The ship the Town-Ho began to take on water, and the hold was being pumped. One of the men told Radney, the first mate, that he would no longer obey orders. The Captain went down into the hold to resolve the situation. The mutineers backed down, but Steelkilt, the ringleader, continued to plot against the Captain. Steelkilt went to murder Radney, the mate, on the quarter-deck. As he was about to do so, the masthead cried out. A large white whale, identified as Moby Dick, had been sighted. Radney harpooned Moby Dick, and was pulled out of his boat. He tried but failed to free himself from the rope tying the harpoon to the whale. Moby Dick turned around and seized Radney in his jaw. Steelkilt severed the rope, and Moby Dick escaped.

The Town-Ho arrived at port, and Steelkilt and his followers deserted. The crew plugged the leak in the ship and set sail for Tahiti to get replacements for the deserters. A few days out, they encountered the deserters, and Steelkilt boarded the ship. He forced the Captain to beach the ship for six days before heading to Tahiti. Steelkilt made it to Tahiti on his own and enlisted on a ship heading for France. The Town-Ho arrived in Tahiti ten days later and enlisted more men.

Chapters 56–60 In Chapters 55–57, Ishmael describes paintings with whales as their subjects. He differentiates true depictions of whales from erroneous ones, and describes accurate pictures of whaling scenes. He then describes works of art depicting whales in whale teeth and other types of material carved by whalers while sailing.

The Pequod encounters a field of brit, a sea organism upon which whales feed. They encounter several whales. Daggoo, in the mast-head, thinks he sees Moby Dick. The boats are lowered. Upon arriving at the spot, the crew discovers that it is only a squid. The squid, however, is an omen: squid is said to be the food of sperm whales. Ishmael discusses the composition of the rope used to ensnare whales.

Chapters 61–65 On a calm day in the Indian Ocean, a sperm whale is spotted. The crew becomes alert, and boats are lowered into the sea. Ahab sees that the whale is unaware of his pursuers and gives orders for stealth. The boats glide up to the whale. Stubb's boat makes the attack, and they hit the whale repeatedly with harpoons until it dies.

In Chapter 62, Ishmael once again takes over the narrative, explaining the importance of the harpooner in hunting whales. He suggests a change to the harpooning system.

The whale carcass is secured to the hull of the Pequod for the night, and whale steaks are prepared for dinner. The sharks in the surrounding water also feed on the secured whale carcass. Ishmael describes the kinds of dishes made from whales.

Chapters 66–70 In these chapters, Ishmael describes what happens after a whale is harpooned. Queequeg and another crewman kill the sharks at the side of the ship. The crew brings the whale carcass aboard and begins to remove the blubber; Ishmael describes the blubber and skin of the whale. The rest of the whale carcass is jettisoned. Ishmael explains how a whale is beheaded.

Chapters 71–75 The Pequod encounters a ship called the Jeroboam, whose captain announces that they have an epi-

demic on board and advises against direct contact. Ahab rows out to talk to the captain. He boards the boat. Captain Mayhew of the Jeroboam tells of their encounter with Moby Dick. Macey, the chief mate, longed to hunt the white whale when he was spotted, and he was plucked out of his boat by Moby Dick.

Queequeg, while attending to the whale with Ishmael, falls overboard. He climbs onto the ship, and the steward offers him ginger water. Stubb comes on deck and yells at the steward. He then offers Queequeg a flask of "strong spirits."

During one of the Pequod's frequent forays through fields of brit, an announcement is made that a right whale will be captured that day. One is sighted, and the boats are lowered. Flask and Stubb take turns stabbing at it with harpoons. Ishmael tells us that hoisting the head of the right whale on the other side of the ship will balance the weight of the sperm whale's head. Ishmael describes in detail first the two whale heads hanging over the side of the Pequod.

Chapters 76–80 Ishmael offers information about the head of the sperm whale. He tell us that the head can be used as a battering ram. The top portion of the head is tendonous and free from bone; the cranium and jaws are in the lower half of the head. Ishmael describes the face of the sperm whale as large, grand, and without a nose, and goes on to describe the whale's brain. While draining the head of its oil, Tashtego falls overboard and is rescued by Daggoo and Queequeg.

Chapters 81–85 The Pequod encounters a whaling ship from the Netherlands called the Jungfrau, or the Virgin. The ship's captain asks for some oil, as they have used up their supply and have not caught a whale. While the ships are next to each other, a group of whales is sighted, one of them old and sick. Both ships lower boats to chase that whale, and the Pequod kills and claims it. The Pequod is unable to hold onto it, however, as it eventually sinks. The Virgin is seen later lowering boats to chase a fin-back, a whale difficult to catch because of its speed.

In Chapters 82 and 83, Ishmael comments on the historical glory of whaling and finds historical flaws in the story of Jonah and the Whale. In Chapter 84, Stubb and Tashtego kill another whale. Ishmael then resumes his own narrative, describing the function and form of the whale's spout.

Chapters 86–90 The Pequod happens upon a herd of whales and lowers its boats. This herd includes a mother giving birth, still attached to her young by the umbilical cord. After several struggles, the crew manages to capture only one of the whales; the rest of the herd escapes.

Ishmael describes how whales travel in schools. He then explains the laws governing the securing of whales to ships, and the regulations that govern the recovery of whales that have become detached from ships. He tells a story of a King and Queen of Britain and a controversy over ownership of a whale; ownership of the whale reverts to the King and Queen in the end.

Chapters 91–95 The crew of the Pequod smells something strange. They happen upon another whaling ship with two whales attached to its side, apparently the source of the odors. The ship is called the Rose Bud, and it hails from France. Stubb talks to the chief mate, who speaks English. They discuss another vessel, whose crew caught a disease from a diseased whale. Stubb persuades the Rose Bud to cast off one of the whales. Stubb goes to it and begins digging into it, finding ambergris, a valuable substance used by druggists. Ishmael discusses the origin and uses of ambergris.

Ishmael discusses Pip, the small black boy in the Pequod's crew. He tells us that the first time Pip lowered with Stubb, he fell overboard; the crew saved him and lost the whale. Stubb tells Pip that if he jumps out of the boat again, he will not go back for him. On the next trip, Pip indeed jumps out of the boat, and Stubb, expecting one of the other boats to pick him up, does not go back for him. No one does pick him up, and Pip is lost.

Ishmael describes massaging sperm blubber and the process of removing the skin from the whale.

Chapters 96–100 In Chapters 96–98, Ishmael discusses details of whaling life. He describes the try-works, where the cooking is done. He tells us that whalers, unlike merchant sailors, have an abundance of oil since they hunt it, and thus have the luxury of lamps. He then describes the process of cleaning up the ship after processing a whale.

Ahab stands on the quarter-deck, looking at the coin he holds up as an incentive for finding Moby Dick. The Pequod meets a ship called the Samuel Enderby, hailing from London. Ahab goes aboard, and finds that the commander, Captain Boomer, has had a run-in with Moby Dick similar to his own. Captain Boomer relates the story of how they encountered Moby Dick rising from the depths while they were chasing a pod of whales. He tells Ahab of being pulled from his boat, caught in Moby Dick's mouth by his arm. Like Ahab, Boomer has lost a limb to Moby Dick. Unlike Ahab, however, he does not want revenge: He says that one limb is enough to give to the white whale.

Chapters 101–105 Ishmael discusses the prominence of Enderby and Sons in English whaling. He then focuses on whales, describing the internal anatomy and skeleton of the sperm whale. He mentions past discoveries of fossilized whale skeletons and tells us that whales have decreased in size with evolution. He talks about the number of whales living and the number harvested by humans, making the argument that whaling will not drive the whales to extinction.

Chapters 106–110 Having damaged his ivory leg on returning to the Pequod from the Samuel Enderby, Ahab orders the carpenter to make a new one. In Chapter 107, Ishmael describes the Pequod's carpenter and his duties, including repairing parts of the ship, decorating and repairing oars, and removing teeth.

The carpenter and the blacksmith work on creating a new leg, and Ahab happens upon them in their work. He talks about their workmanship, and about Prometheus, who forged people and animated them with fire.

Chapter 109 describes an encounter between Starbuck and Ahab. Starbuck comes to Ahab in his cabin to inform him that the barrels of oil are leaking. Ahab is distracted, apparently thinking of Moby Dick. Starbuck insists that the cargo is more important. Ahab tells Starbuck to get back on deck. Starbuck refuses, and Ahab pulls a shotgun on him, telling him that there is "one Captain that is lord over the Pequod." Starbuck backs down, and Ahab orders him to tend to the leaking barrels.

Queequeg is the focus of Chapter 110. While moving barrels around the hold, he contracts a fever and seems near death. The carpenter constructs a coffin for him, and Queequeg demands to see it. He settles into it with his idol, Yojo, and his harpoon. He gets back out, and returns to his hammock. Soon after, he recovers from his illness. He declares that he has decided that he has business ashore, and therefore

could not die at that point. He keeps the coffin, using it as a sea chest.

Chapters 111–115 The Pequod sails from the Indian Ocean into the Pacific. Ahab comes upon Perth the blacksmith, working in the forge. He brings him the stubs of horse-shoe nails and tells him to make a harpoon from them. Perth forges the shank, and then Ahab forges the point. When this is completed, Ahab asks his pagan harpooners for blood to baptize the harpoon. They prick themselves and give him the blood, and Ahab baptizes his harpoon in the name of the Devil.

The crew contemplates the calm Pacific. The Pequod comes upon the *Bachelor*, a Nantucket whaler that has had unprecedented success. When Ahab asks the captain if he's seen Moby Dick, the captain replies that he's only heard of him.

Chapters 116–120 The Pequod happens upon four whales, and Ahab kills one of them himself. Chapters 117-120 show Ahab's growing irrationality and his almost maniacal fervor for his mission to capture Moby Dick. While he and the rest of the crew sleep, Ahab dreams of a hearse. Wakened by his dream, he goes to walk on the deck. There he encounters Fedallah, a crew member who is something of an enigma. Fedallah prophesies that he will die before Ahab, and that Ahab can only die by a rope. Ahab interprets this to mean that he can only be killed by an executioner's noose, and concludes that he is immortal. Frustrated with his fruitless hunt, Ahab destroys his navigational instruments and decides to navigate by dead-reckoning.

The Pequod encounters a thunderstorm, and Ahab claims that the forks of lightning will light the way to Moby Dick. He speaks to the lightning, claiming it as his "fiery father" and declaring that its "right worship is defiance."

Starbuck approaches Ahab with common advice about the ship, which Ahab refuses. Stubb and Flask talk about the danger to the ship from lightning. Tashtego addresses the thunder, asking it for rum. Starbuck enters Ahab's state room to tell him that the storm has subsided. He finds Ahab asleep and his musket on the wall near the door. He contemplates shooting Ahab but decides against it.

Chapters 121–125 The next morning, Ahab comes to the deck and finds his smashed quadrant. He magnetizes a piece of iron from a lance and uses it as a compass. The crew uses a device made of a log and a line to determine the Pequod's position. While doing this, they discover Pip, and they take him aboard.

The crew hears voices in the water, and the life buoy is dropped into the sea. After a while, the buoy needs to be replaced, and Starbuck decides that Queequeg's coffin should be modified and made into a new life buoy.

The Pequod encounters another whaler called the Rachel, whose captain tells Ahab that they engaged Moby Dick the day before. The captain asks if any on the Pequod have seen a whale boat adrift—the boat was lost in the fight and contains his son. He asks the assistance of the Pequod to search for the boat, and Ahab refuses.

Chapters 126–130 The Pequod encounters another ship, and Ahab inquires about Moby Dick. The captain tells Ahab that he lost five men engaging Moby Dick, and that the harpoon that will kill Moby Dick has not yet been forged. Ahab brandishes his weapon. The captain tells him not to fight the white whale.

On a mild, calm day, Ahab speaks to Starbuck, telling him of his life in whaling and of his wife and son. Ahab is tempted to turn around and return to a calm life in Nantucket, but he comes to the decision that he must follow his present course.

Chapter 128 describes the first sighting of Moby Dick. Ahab sights the white whale, and they lower boats to hunt him. Moby Dick thwarts the first attempt and wrecks Ahab's boat. The crew is recovered and lands in Stubb's boat.

Moby Dick is seen again, and a new chase ensues. One of the boats harpoons him, and the boats are tied up in entangled whale line. Ahab's boat gets drawn in and capsizes. When the crew is recovered, it is discovered that Ahab's ivory leg has been broken, and that Fedallah, one of the crew members, is missing. Starbuck insists that this chase is stupid and dangerous and urges Ahab to discontinue it. Ahab refuses.

In the final chapter, Moby Dick is sighted again, and the boats go out to hunt him. After a brief engagement, Ahab sends the other boats back to the ship. He says that one boat and one life are enough to risk for Moby Dick. Ahab manages to harpoon the whale, but the line gets caught. While he is clearing the line, however, he gets plucked out of the boat and is fastened to the whale. Moby Dick sinks, pulling the Pequod and the remaining boat down with him.

Epilogue Ishmael describes how Queequeg's coffin was released from the sinking ship, and how he was able to grab hold of it and survive to tell his tale.

1984

ABOUT THE AUTHOR

See page 23.

THE BIG PICTURE

1984, set in the futuristic country of Oceania, offers a horrifying view of how a totalitarian government uses power and language to control and abolish the individual. Big Brother, Oceania's dictator, manipulates the truth and demands that all his subjects think and speak the way he orders them to. The novel tells the grim story of what happens when the two main characters, Winston and Julia, try to go against Big Brother's order.

Look for ways that truth is malleable for the Party, and how its language, Newspeak, supports this. Notice that appearances aren't always what they seem, especially with the Party. It's also important to note how Oceania society treats the individual.

Why you're reading this book:
- The novel's striking relevance to the world we live in—more than 40 years after it was written, totalitarian governments continue to control the individual just as Orwell described.
- The important lessons Orwell teaches about the use of language and the manipulation of truth.
- The relationship between totalitarianism and the individual.

Your teachers are looking for:
- Orwell's use of near-reality to portray a world that is frightening but believable.
- How Oceania is similar to and different from the world of today.
- The meaning of truth in the novel.
- The role of the individual versus that of society.
- The strength of the human spirit.

KEY CHARACTERS

Winston Smith: Middle-aged and sickly, he can still vaguely remember the time before Big Brother. He is searching to learn about the past, and is hoping for a rebellion.

Julia: She is young and beautiful, and seems to be the perfect Party member, but she is not. She and Winston have an affair.

O'Brien: A member of the Inner Party, he gives Winston the feeling that he is understood. However, he is not the rebel Winston thinks he is.

Mr. Charrington: The shopkeeper from whom Winston buys his black market goods. He is a member of the Thought Police.

ESSAY IDEAS

- What aspects of Julia and Winston's struggles are similar to those in your life?
- Examine the role of the individual in Oceania. How do Winston and Julia react to it?
- Why is the Party so concerned with altering history? Where else did (does)

this happen in the real world? Does it happen in the United States?
- Describe the similarities/differences between Julia and Winston.
- Comment on the role of language and its relationship to truth in the world of *1984*.

A SAMPLE ESSAY IN OUTLINE FORM

Compare the world of *1984* with the real world of the late twentieth century.
- *1984*:
  - Extensive use of propaganda.
  - History altered to fit government policies.
  - Dictatorship.
  - Government enemies flushed out and punished by the Thought Police.
- Our world:
  - Pervasive advertising and television intrusion; views and attitudes are shaped by the media.
  - Many historical events of the last 50 years are similar to the world of *1984*:
    - McCarthy hearings.
    - Watergate.
    - Apartheid.

The world of *1984* and our world share more characteristics than we would like to think. The complete denial of personal freedom seen in *1984,* although not characteristic of the American government, still goes on in many regions of the world; both here and elsewhere, government secrecy and corruption are still rampant. Some would argue that, like in *1984*, technology and the media have depersonalized our society and alienated people from one another.

PART ONE

Chapter 1 Here we see the basic structure of the society of Oceania. The housing conditions are depressing, and everything is rationed. There are posters up everywhere, a reminder that "Big Brother Is Watching You." The face on the posters is described to be like Hitler's—and some aspects of this society do not greatly differ from Nazi Germany or Stalinist Russia. The meaning of the poster is very literal: every room has a telescreen, a huge television-like device, except that the viewer can also be seen. The telescreen can never be shut off, and you never know when they are watching you.

There is a footnote that refers to an appendix on Newspeak. It describes the censorship of language that will give the Government total control. No one will be able to think or speak against the Govern-ment because there will be no words for it. Newspeak is the only language whose vocabulary is shrinking.

The only remaining changes that still need to be made to Newspeak are those that ease pronunciation, because if words are short and easy to pronounce, one can say them quickly never thinking about what they actually mean. However, this language is not targeted to be used exclusively until 2050, so people are still capable of thinking things they shouldn't. That is why the Thought Police and "doublethink" exist.

There are four major sections of the government of INGSOC (English Socialism): the Ministry of Truth, the Ministry of Peace, the Ministry of Love, and the Ministry of Plenty. Each of these is a misnomer, with its purpose the opposite of its definition. For example, the Ministry of

Peace concerns itself with war. The three party slogans—"War is Peace," "Freedom is Slavery," and "Ignorance is Strength"—also show this contradiction of meanings

We then see Winston's apartment. It is peculiar, because there is one space where he cannot be seen by the telescreen. Here he sits and begins to write a diary, which is a "thoughtcrime." Winston is aware that he eventually will be caught, but thinks he can evade the Thought Police for a while.

He has a hard time writing until he remembers the incident that had happened that day, during the Two Minutes Hate (which is directed at the enemy of the Party, Emmanuel Goldstein). O'Brien's eyes had met his in such a way that although Winston didn't know him, he felt sure O'Brien shared his hatred for the Party. Also during the Hate, a woman, who we later find out is Julia, had sat behind him. Winston hates her and is certain that she is a member of the Thought Police. Ironically, the opposite is true.

Chapter 2 Winston goes to help a neighbor, Mrs. Parsons, and we see what kind of children this society raises. The children are wild, and the parents are afraid of them (kids often report their parents to the Thought Police).

Returning home, Winston resumes writing his diary. He recalls a dream he had seven years ago, in which he heard O'Brien's voice saying, "We shall meet in a place where there is no darkness." The telescreen announces news about the war, and Winston thinks of the three principles of INGSOC: newspeak, doublethink, and the mutability of the past. Although unsure that it will be read, he addresses the diary to the future.

Chapter 3 Winston dreams of his mother, of a time when people cared about others and helped them. He also dreams of

Julia, living in a place he calls the Golden Country. Winston wakes up as dictated by the telescreen, and begins his morning exercises. He tries to remember his childhood, but he cannot.

He cannot remember his country not being at war, but he does know that Oceania is now presently at war with Eurasia and allied with Eastasia. While the records have all been changed to read as if it has always been this way, he knows that the alliances have changed four times. This is the reality of the Party: the past is altered to fit the present, as if nothing else ever existed.

The exercise instructor on the telescreen notices that Winston is not working hard enough, and snaps him back to reality. They are always watching.

Chapter 4 Winston is at work at the Ministry of Truth, and we see the process by which history is changed. Not only is history mutable, but people can be entirely erased, too. Big Brother does not care about the individual; he cares only about what makes him look good. This impersonality, and the constant fear that anyone can turn you in, oppresses Winston.

Chapter 5 Winston has lunch with Syme, who is working on the Eleventh Edition of the Newspeak Dictionary. Syme explains more of the theory behind it, adding that once the language is in place, even the Party slogans will change—the concept of "slavery is freedom" cannot exist if there is no concept of freedom. He says that in the future, sticking to the party line will not require thought because it will be inherent in the vocabulary. Winston decides that Syme will probably be vaporized because he knows too much.

Mr. Parsons, Winston's neighbor, sits down and asks him for his contribution, or "sub," for Hate Week. The telescreen says that the Ministry of Plenty was raising the chocolate ration to twenty grams. Winston remembers that only yesterday they had *reduced* it to twenty grams. He looks around him to see if anyone else notices this, and becomes aware that no one matches the standard Party look: young and strong, blond and beautiful, carefree and happy. Most people seem dark and beetle-like. He also notices that Julia is there, staring at him.

Chapter 6 Winston is writing in his diary about the last time he saw a prostitute, a member of the social class of Proles (proletariat). This makes him think about his wife, Katherine, and how the Party has destroyed intimacy between couples. He wishes he could have a loving relationship.

Chapter 7 Winston believes that if rebellion against the Party is to come, it will start with the Proles, who are not under the same kinds of restrictions as the other social classes. Even though the Proles show no indications of revolting, this is Winston's hope. Proles appear to be leading the same kind of life as before the revolution. To learn about life then, Winston reads the Parsons children's textbook. The history in the book reads much like that of the revised history of the world that the Soviets printed in the 1920's. Winston knows there is no way to find out the truth.

On one occasion, Winston possessed the truth after it was officially changed. He accidentally received a newspaper clipping about three Party men who had become "unpersons" after they had been erased; he can even remember seeing the men in the Chestnut Tree Cafe. This was proof that history was being rewritten daily. He had not kept the clipping, but destroyed it.

He questions the party's policy of lies: "I understand HOW: I do not understand WHY." He comes to the conclusion that certain things are always true, and that this diary really is for O'Brien. He closes with "Freedom is the freedom to say that two plus two make four. If that is granted, all else follows."

Chapter 8 Winston goes out for a walk alone, which is considered to be a suspicious act. He walks to the Prole section of London. A bomb lands near him, but afterwards, everyone acts as if nothing had happened. He enters a pub and begins a conversation with a very old man in the hope of learning about pre-revolution history; however, the man's memory is only of specific details in the past. Winston realizes he will probably never learn the whole truth.

He continues wandering and ends up at the shop where he originally bought the diary. He purchases another object, a paperweight. The owner, Mr. Charrington, takes him up to see a spare room. Prompted by a picture on the wall, Mr. Charrington recalls the beginnings of a rhyme about old London churches, the St. Martin rhyme. Winston will piece this rhyme together throughout the book. Returning home, Winston thinks about what will happen to him after he is captured for his thoughtcrime.

PART TWO

Chapter 1 Julia falls in the hallway, and when Winston helps her up, she slips him a note that reads "I Love You." He waits until he can sit with her in the cafeteria, and they make arrangements to meet after work. In their later meeting, Julia has a plan for them to meet in the country on Sunday.

Chapter 2 They meet in the woods, in a situation that is just like Winston's dream of the Golden Country. While their embrace is an act of rebellion against the Party, they do have genuine feelings for each other. Sadly, their love for each other will doom them both.

Chapter 3 Winston and Julia have now been seeing each other about two months. Julia is different from Winston in that she puts up a better front as a good Party member. She does not have his general hatred of the Party. She does not think it can be overthrown, and scoffs at the idea of the existence of the Brotherhood, the rumored resistance group. She is from a generation after Winston—she has no memories of what life was like before the Revolution.

Julia tells Winston that the Party represses sexuality because it is dangerous to them. This is comparable to the way the Party affects the family: family has been changed into an extension of the Thought Police, to change a threat to the Party to something that supports it.

Winston is more realistic about their inevitable capture. She understands this, of course, but still seems to feel "that it was possible to construct a secret world in which you could live as you chose." Winston sees the couple as being already doomed; Julia says they are not dead yet.

Chapter 4 Winston rents the upstairs room from Mr. Charrington. The idea came to Winston because his love for Julia is so urgent that he wants to be with her all the time. While they are digging their own graves, they have fallen in love—this gives them a naive hope.

They create a private world in the room, with Julia smuggling in goods stolen from the Inner Party, who do not have the same rationing as they do. The paperweight is a symbol of this little world. Noticing the picture Winston saw earlier, Julia adds another part to the rhyme about the churches, and the closing line, but the link-

ing line is still missing. The print itself is a symbol of the existence of the past.

There is also a reference to Winston's fear of rats, foreshadowing the couple's demise.

Chapter 5 Winston's prediction about Syme comes true; he has vanished. Everyone is especially busy in preparation for Hate Week. Even the Proles are getting involved.

Knowing the room exists has a calming effect on Winston. He and Julia speak of finding the Brotherhood, but Julia doubts its existence. In some ways, she understands the Party better than Winston; however, she only questions the Party line when it affects her adversely. Her view is very practical, whereas Winston considers the whole picture. Her interest is not in the benefit of the generations after herself, but in making her present life more comfortable.

Chapter 6 O'Brien runs into Winston in the hall, and engages him in a conversation about Newspeak. He makes a references to Syme, which Winston takes as a sign that they are alike in their feelings against the Party. Later, he will find out that he is sadly mistaken. O'Brien offers a copy of the new dictionary as a way to give him his address.

Winston thinks that the conspiracy does exist, and is now ready to move from words to actions.

Chapter 7 Winston has a dream about his mother, and comes to a full understanding of the society that the Party has created: it is a society that does not allow room for true, self-sacrificing love. The Party makes one think that human feelings are not important, that individuals are powerless. All Julia and Winston want is a life where they can be free to be together and show their feelings, but the Party will never allow such things to exist. The couple make a pact that when they get caught, they will not betray their feelings for each other. However, this will not be the case.

Chapter 8 Winston and Julia go to O'Brien's house. It is the first time that Winston has seen the opulence of an Inner Party home. What is most astounding is that O'Brien can turn his telescreen off. Believing that they are unobserved, Winston tells him that they have come because they think he is a member of the Brotherhood. O'Brien admits that he is, and they make a toast to the Brotherhood leader, Emmanuel Goldstein.

O'Brien then asks what they are prepared to do, and the couple agrees to do anything but separate forever. O'Brien then outlines the Brotherhood, explaining that they will be working alone, with no other contacts. At times it will seem as if they are accomplishing nothing. He also tells them they will be caught.

O'Brien promises to deliver a copy of Goldstein's book to Winston, and says they will meet again, "in a place where there is no darkness." Winston asks him if he has ever heard the St. Martin rhyme, and O'Brien is able to complete it for him.

Chapter 9 In the midst of Hate Week, the book is delivered to Winston. But he has no time to read it; because the enemy has changed, all of history must be changed accordingly. Oceania is at war with Eastasia, and Eurasia is the ally, and that is how it has always been. Anything else was a trick by Goldstein.

Eventually, Winston is able to start the book. The book explains how the present society came to be, but does not answer Winston's question of why. In fact, it does nothing more than restate what he already knows. But it does make Winston feel that his thoughts were not insane, and he falls

asleep with the idea that "sanity is not statistical."

Chapter 10 When Winston and Julia wake up, they contemplate the domestic simplicity of a Prole woman who is singing by the window. She is full of life, vibrant, while they are as good as dead. Winston says this aloud, and Julia echoes it—then, a third voice concurs. It has come from behind the picture; they have been caught. Mr. Charrington is a member of the Thought Police.

Behind the picture is a telescreen, and Charrington repeats the last line of the church rhyme, "Here comes a candle to light you to bed, here comes the chopper to chop off your head." The Police then storm in and destroy the room. In the process, the glass paperweight gets thrown to the floor and is shattered. From now on, the story focuses on Winston and O'Brien.

PART THREE

Chapter 1 Winston is now in a cell, presumably in the Ministry of Love. He has not eaten since he arrived, but he cannot tell how long that has been, since the lights stay on all the time. This is "the place where there is no darkness" to which O'Brien had referred. Orwell describes the prison in detail. People keep coming in and out, and Winston notices that the common prisoners, the Proles, are very different from the political prisoners, who are members of the Party. Room 101 is spoken of many times. We never learn what is in it, but from the tone in which it is spoken of, it must be something horrible.

Winston thinks of Julia. His love now seems like a fact rather than an emotion. Two people that he knows, Ampleforth and Mr. Parsons, are in the cell briefly. Parsons was turned in by his own daughter, and he seems very proud of her for doing it. A man who looks like a walking skeleton is put in there, too. This is what Winston will soon look like.

Finally, Winston is called and taken by O'Brien, who will be his torturer and reformer.

Chapter 2 Winston is now lying on a bed near O'Brien and another man. So far, he has been repeatedly tortured and he has confessed, but that was only a preliminary. He is now being brainwashed. He has the feeling that it has been O'Brien who has been directing everything, who both hurts him and saves him. He still sees O'Brien as a friend, which is the key to this kind of brainwashing.

O'Brien explains why he is taking so much time with him. He says that Winston's problem is that he has a defective memory. O'Brien then reminds him that "who controls the present controls the past," and that the actual past does not exist. Memory does not exist. He then begins to teach Winston, using a torture device, that two plus two equals what the Party says it does. Winston has to learn not to believe what he sees; he must believe what the Party says he sees.

O'Brien further explains that their goal is to make Winston fully loyal to the Party. Then, fully brainwashed, Winston will beg for his own death, thinking it a service to the Party. This way, there will no longer be any martyrs, as there have in other totalitarian regimes. O'Brien then administers a drug to show Winston that he can be made to think correctly; however, its effects are temporary. At the close of the session, O'Brien allows Winston to ask him some questions. Winston learns that Julia has betrayed him and that Big Brother is not actually a person but a personification of the Party. His final question is "What is in Room 101?" O'Brien ominously replies that

Winston already knows.

Chapter 3 O'Brien now tries to make Winston understand the motive behind the Party's actions, to answer his question of "why." The Party makes no secret of the fact that it seeks power for power's own sake. It seeks to control men, not things, so that the actual reality that exists is of no importance. The way to control people is to make them suffer. Truth is also controlled by the Party, so whatever is advantageous to the Party is true, and as these things change, truth itself is also changeable.

Winston still thinks that the "Spirit of Man" will revolt against them. O'Brien makes him take a look at himself, naked, in front of the mirror. He is emaciated and completely worn down. O'Brien tells him that he is the last specimen of humanity.

Chapter 4 Winston is now allowed to regain his health, and is given better accommodations. He has accepted everything, but his mental processes are still not as automatic as they should be. He has a dream of Julia; he still does not love Big Brother. Winston thinks they can only control his mind, not his spirit. This is unacceptable to the Party; Winston must not only obey Big Brother, but love him as well. O'Brien sends him to Room 101.

Chapter 5 Room 101 contains the ultimate torture, which is individual for each person. In Room 101 is Winston's biggest fear: rats. At first, Winston is not sure what they want him to do. Panicking, he realizes that he must get someone else between him and the rats, and he screams that they should torture Julia instead. He has now betrayed the person he loves. His transformation and acceptance of Big Brother is complete.

Chapter 6 As he is no longer a threat,

Winston has been released. It has been nine months, and he has been "reborn" in the love of Big Brother. His life is just like Rutherford's, Aaronson's, and Jones' after their conversion. He has a secure position and spends most of his time drinking in the Chestnut Tree Cafe. He even cries at the same song.

He has an encounter with Julia, and they admit their betrayal of the other. There is no reawakening of their love, as neither can feel anymore.

The final moment of Winston's conversion happens during a news broadcast about a victory in the war. He slips into a dream where he is back in the Ministry of Love. With his mind now fully purified, he accepts and even welcomes his death, because it is good for the state. He looks into the face of Big Brother, and with a sense of homecoming, realizes that he lives in him.

THE ODYSSEY

ABOUT THE AUTHOR

See page 132.

THE BIG PICTURE

The *Odyssey* is a story of one man's struggle to return home after an age of war. Both mortals and gods play their parts, creating a tale of many fantastic stories and adventures. Like its predecessor, the *Iliad*, it deals with human faults and their consequences.

Why you're reading this book:
- It is one of the primary foundations of Western literature; the epic form it uses serves as a model for many later works.
- Its action-packed narrative and its focus on one character's individual struggle make it a precursor to the novel.
- Its central theme—one man's struggle to fulfill his duty—is still relevant today.
- The *Odyssey* is a valuable historical text and an essential key to understanding ancient Greek culture:
  - It provides an understanding of Greek mythology, which shaped the morals and ethics of the Greeks and determined how they viewed the world.
  - It contains historical facts about actual kings, warriors, families, and events.

Your teachers are looking for:
- The relationship between the gods and the mortals.
- The system of justice in Homer's world.
- Odysseus and his education through his travels.
- Homer's notion of heroism.
- The characteristics and style of the epic genre.

As you read the *Odyssey*, it will be helpful to keep the basic beliefs of Greek mythology in mind. Unlike in Judeo-Christian mythology, the Greek gods share the same weaknesses and temptations as mortals. In the Greek world, human affairs mirror those of the gods, human events have cosmic significance.

KEY CHARACTERS

Odysseus: King of Ithaca, hero of the Trojan wars, and long-time wanderer. Odysseus is sly, wise, brave and virile. Odysseus longs for an end to his endless travel and a return to his kingdom and family.

Penelope: Odysseus' wife. In his twenty-year absence she has delayed the advances of numerous suitors who have invaded her home. She awaits the return of Odysseus, but fears the worst.

Telemachus: Odysseus' son. Telemachus has endured the suitors' presence in his home for many years. He too longs for the return of his father. His journey to find his father is a journey toward manhood.

Athena: The Goddess of wisdom and Odysseus' guardian angel. She also helps Telemachus.

Nestor: King of Pylos, friend of Odysseus.

Menelaus: King of Sparta. Brother of Agamemnon and friend of Odysseus.

Menelaus aids Telemachus in his search for his father. His hospitality does not go unnoticed by the gods.

Agamemnon: The dead former captain of the Greeks in the Trojan war. Agamemnon is dead by the time of the Odyssey, and appears only in the final chapter, in Hades.

Calypso: A sea nymph (daughter of Atlas) who falls in love with Odysseus when he washes up on her island. She keeps him in her smooth caves for nine years before Zeus forces her to "release" the hero.

Circe: Goddess on the island Aeaea, known for turning men to swine. Odysseus, assisted by a gift of an herb (Moly) given him by Hermes, resists her spell. In the process, she too falls in love with the hero.

Tiresias: The blind prophet whom Odysseus consults in Hades for advice on how to placate the wrathful Poseidon.

Poseidon: God of the seas. Poseidon has cursed Odysseus with wandering as vengeance for the blinding of his Cyclopean son, Polyphemus.

ESSAY IDEAS

• In what ways, if any, does Odysseus grow in wisdom throughout his journey?
• Are we to take all the events in Odysseus' adventure literally?
• Trace Telemachus' development from boy to manhood.
• How do you think Homer would define manhood? Justice? Wisdom? Give examples to back up your arguments.
• Is there a universal right and wrong in Homer's world?
• Does Penelope's waiting twenty years for Odysseus' return make her virtuous or pathetic?

A SAMPLE ESSAY IN OUTLINE FORM

Trace Telemachus' passage into "manhood." Is Homer's concept of manhood different than ours?

• At the opening, Telemachus is passive, boyish:
  • Urged by Athena to take action.
• Begins to assert authority:
  • Calls assembly to reprimand suitors.
  • Decides to go in search of father, Odysseus.
• Finds Odysseus upon return to homeland:
  • Again, aided by Athena.
  • Helps father regain his kingdom.
• Characteristics of rite of passage (Homer):
  • Ability to act decisively in father's absence.
  • Manhood proven at father's side in battle.
• Today's "rite of passage":
  • Ability to think clearly and act on one's own (but without divine aid).
  • Manhood/adulthood proven by maturity and success in the world, not necessarily in battle.

The rite of passage into adulthood in Homer's age has some elements in common with that of today. A boy growing both physically and mentally into a man is a theme found in much of today's literature. However, Homer's epic uses prowess in battle as a standard for manhood, a concept that is rare today. And the divine intervention that is essential to Telemachus' development has disappeared from today's conception of valor and manhood.

PLOT SUMMARY

Book I Homer begins his epic work with the traditional invocation of the Muse of Poetry, the goddess of artistic inspiration.

He states that he plans to tell the story of a lone man, Odysseus, wandering through the difficult world, unable to return home. Having achieved great fame and glory in the Trojan War, Odysseus is the only surviving Greek left unaccounted for after the war. We learn that he is now stuck on an island with the nymph seductress Calypso, Atlas' daughter. Odysseus cannot return home because Poseidon, the god of the sea, dislikes him.

Zeus calls a general meeting of the gods on Mount Olympus. Luckily, Poseidon is busy attending sacrifices and rituals in the far East and cannot attend. Athena petitions Zeus on Odysseus' behalf. She feels that he has suffered unfairly, and asks that Hermes, the messenger of the gods, be sent to Calypso to demand Odysseus' release. Zeus agrees. Athena then visits Ithaca.

Odysseus' wife Penelope has been swamped with marriage offers during her husband's twenty-year absence. The suitors, including Ithacan princes and noblemen, loiter around the grounds, gambling, feasting, and generally wasting Odysseus' money. Athena, disguised as an old friend of Odysseus (Mentes), urges Odysseus' son Telemachus to find out for himself whether his father is dead. Athena, by urging Telemachus out of his passivity, is urging him to manhood.

Book II Inspired by Athena's words, Telemachus holds an assembly the next morning. It is the first of its kind since Odysseus' departure for war. Telemachus shames the assembled suitors for their lecherous loitering. The most vocal of the suitors, Antinous, shouts back that Penelope is the one to blame for their behavior. Antinous explains how Penelope has promised to remarry when she finishes her weaving, but keeps her suitors waiting by unraveling her work every night.

Telemachus promises revenge for the suitors' behavior. To add weight to his words, two eagles (Zeus' birds) swoop down upon the panicked assembly. Despite this obvious omen, not all of the suitors get the message.

Telemachus promises the suitors that he will give his mother's hand away to a new husband only when he is certain that his father is dead. He plans to journey for news of his father, and asks the suitors for a ship and crew for this task. Athena, disguised as his friend Mentor, promises to help him procure the ship and crew. Telemachus secretly sets sail during the night.

Book III Telemachus and Mentor reach the port of Pylos, where they are met by King Nestor and his sons. The fatherly Nestor tells Telemachus the sad story of Agamemnon's homecoming after the wars. Unlike Penelope, Agamemnon's wife Clytemnestra was unfaithful in her husband's absence. Upon his return, King Agamemnon was tragically murdered by his wife's new lover.

Nestor explains that before his death, Agamemnon and his brother Menelaus had parted ways. When last seen by Nestor, Odysseus was leaving Menelaus to join Agamemnon. Menelaus might have seen him last. Nestor recommends that Telemachus ask Menelaus about Odysseus' whereabouts. He gives him a chariot and his son Peisistratus as a companion for his journey to Menelaus' kingdom of Sparta.

Mentor departs, and all at the feast suddenly recognize him as Athena in disguise. Nestor sacrifices a gilt-horned bull in honor of her.

Book IV Telemachus arrives in Sparta. A huge feast is underway in celebration of the double wedding of Menelaus' son and daughter. Not realizing his new guests' identity, Menelaus speaks longingly of Agamemnon and Odysseus. When Telemachus begins to cry, Menelaus recognizes the physical likeness of the boy to his father. Indeed, the similarities go further, as the father's homeward journey will mirror his son's odyssey toward manhood.

After the feast Menelaus tells the boy of his profitable adventures after the Trojan war, and about how he first heard about both Agamemnon's murder and Odysseus' captivity on Calypso's island. The aged Menelaus speaks sadly about the loss of his friends. Like Nestor, age has given the warrior a gentler outlook on what is important in life.

Meanwhile, back in Ithaca, Penelope's suitors realize that Telemachus has gone to find his father. Realizing that the young prince poses a threat to their desires, they plot an ambush. Penelope worries for her son, but Athena sends her a soothing dream.

Book V Back on Olympus, the gods are again in meeting. Athena restates her case for helping Odysseus, and mighty Zeus again agrees to send Hermes to Calypso. Calypso is madly in love with Odysseus and has promised him eternal life if he stays with her. She has kept him in her smooth caves for years. Nevertheless, she complies with Zeus' orders, and promises Odysseus that she will finally help him return to his kingdom.

Although we have heard much of Odysseus already, this is the first time we actually see him. We find him weeping for his family. When first told by his captor of her desire to set him free, Odysseus is doubtful that she will finally let him go. Cleverly, he assures her that he leaves out of duty only. She gives him her veil as a protective talisman. He builds a boat and sets sail.

Poseidon returns just in time to find Odysseus at sea. In his wrath, he creates a storm, ripping Odysseus' tiny boat to shreds. Clinging desperately to a floating board, the half-dead hero is guided by Athena to the shores of the island of Scheria, land of the Phaeacians. Exhausted, he passes out on the beach.

Books VI–VIII Athena visits a princess on the island in a dream and convinces her to travel to the shore. Stumbling across the half-drowned Odysseus, the princess brings him home to her family. They feed and clothe him and send him on to the city, where he is graciously received by the King and Queen. This island is a paradise of beauty and hospitality, the ideal spot for Odysseus' recuperation. The grace of the islanders' hospitality is enhanced by their ignorance of his fame.

Even without his fame, Odysseus is a heroic character, proving his wit, athletic ability, and temperament at a banquet. When he at last informs the islanders of his name, he tells the story of his past adventures. Odysseus proves himself in deed before he allows his name and history to speak.

Book IX Odysseus tells the tale of his adventures after the Trojan War. His story begins immediately after his narrow escape from Troy.

Storms keep him at sea for many days, finally landing his ships upon the land of the Lotus-Eaters. Those who eat the opiate Lotus become lethargic and forgetful. Odysseus and the other abstaining crewman have to drag their weaker, drugged shipmates from the island by force.

Next, the ships sail to the islands of the Cyclops, a primitive and brutish clan of one-eyed giants. Trapped with his men in one of their caves, Odysseus is forced to sit by while the giant Polyphemus eats handfuls of his men for meals. Odysseus comes up with a clever plan to introduce himself to Polyphemus as "Nobohdy" and get the giant drunk on strong wine. Together with his men, Odysseus pokes out the eye of the sleeping Cyclops with a sharpened mast. When the other Cyclops, rallied by the screams, ask who was responsible, Polyphemus answers, "Nobohdy." The others assume that this means it was the work of the gods.

Polyphemus guards the cave exit to catch those responsible. Because he can no longer see, he touches each of his sheep as he lets them pass to graze. Odysseus and his men escape by clinging to the bellies of these sheep.

While the escape is perfect, Odysseus makes a grave error. As he rows away from the island, he yells out his true name. Polyphemus calls upon his father Poseidon to punish this Odysseus for his injury. Odysseus' subsequent wandering is his punishment.

Book X Odysseus continues his story with the tale of his next stop, the island of Aeolus, King of the Winds.

As a parting gift, Aeolus gives Odysseus a bag containing all the winds unfavorable to sailors. With these winds safely out of the way, Odysseus can finally expect a clear journey home.

Odysseus' ship is within sight of the Ithacan coast, almost at the end of his journey. But Odysseus' sailors, certain that Aeolus' bag contains treasure, greedily rip it open while Odysseus sleeps. The ensuing wind storm blows the ships back to Aeolus, who refuses to accept Odysseus' apology and banishes him from the island. So, like Odysseus' pride on the Cyclops' island, the sailors' greed has grave consequences for the journey.

The ships make their way to the next island, that of the Lestrygonians. An attack by these guileful cannibals destroys all but Odysseus' ship.

This solitary ship lands next on the island of Aeaea, home of the goddess Circe. A team of men is sent to investigate the island, but only one man returns, telling Odysseus of the beautiful seducing goddess who turns men to swine. Odysseus goes to investigate and is met on the way by the messenger Hermes disguised as a mortal. Hermes offers him advice in dealing with Circe, as well as an herb to ward off her spells.

Odysseus confronts Circe. When she is unable to turn him into a pig, he forces her to return his men to human form. She complies and falls in love with this powerful hero. The affair lasts for a year until, as she has promised, she must help Odysseus and his men back to their homeland. She sends Odysseus on a journey toward the edge of the world to enlist the aid of Tiresias in Hades.

Book XI At the world's edge the crew makes the appropriate sacrifices and awaits the blind oracle Tiresias. Made hungry by the smell of sacrificial blood, the dead rise from the earth.

Tiresias rises too, and tells Odysseus that his misadventures have only just begun. Tiresias outlines Odysseus' upcoming adventure. He tells him that his return to Ithaca is impossible without a full reconciliation with Poseidon. When Odysseus finally does return, he will do so as an unknown and friendless man.

In this chapter, the hero crosses the line between mortals and gods, life and death. In the course of his adventures and trials, we see that Odysseus is very much a mortal; he struggles and fails, succumbing to temptation and pride. But this symbolic voyage into death and back takes him beyond the limits of the mortal and gives him super-mortal status.

Book XII Odysseus and his crew return

to Aeaea to bury one of the sailors and restock their supplies. Circe gives Odysseus advice on his upcoming perils.

As Circe and Tiresias prophesied, the ship passes the islands of the Sirens, bird-like women whose beautiful songs lure sailors to their deaths on the perilous rocks. While Odysseus blocks his men's ears with beeswax to save them from temptation, he insists on being lashed to the mast so that he may experience their rare song without danger. This typifies the nature of Odysseus' adventuring: he is torn between longing for home and a longing for adventure. In the process, he lives fully, if not happily.

The ship safely passes the Sirens and moves on to the next obstacle, a narrow strait between Scylla, a six headed monster, and Charybdis, a whirlpool. While safely avoiding the latter, the ship looses six sailors to Scylla.

The ship survives this peril only to face another. It lands at the island of the sun god Helios. Despite the warnings of both Circe and Tiresias, the hungry crewmen slaughter the oxen of the sun. The act is unforgivable, and the ship and all its crew are destroyed by a thunderbolt from Zeus. Only Odysseus survives, washing up after nine days at sea upon Calypso's island. Thus ends Odysseus' tale; the rest of the story we know from Homer.

Books XIII–XVI The Phaeacians, charmed by Odysseus, give him gifts and a magic ship to bear him to Ithaca. This act of kindness will later bring Poseidon's ruinous punishment upon the Phaeacians.

At long last Odysseus reaches his homeland. Suddenly, the fantastic difficulties of his adventures around the globe are replaced by domestic problems.

Odysseus is greeted on the shore by Athena. She disguises him as a beggar so that he may observe the situation unnoticed. He heads for the mountains to find his trusted servant, Eumaeus. Telemachus, meanwhile, has returned from his travels and also seeks Eumaeus. Father and son are reunited and Odysseus reveals his identity to his son.

While Telemachus' efforts abroad have not speeded Odysseus' return, they have provided the broadening experiences which bring manhood. Telemachus has returned as a mature man in his own right, one worthy of his father's return.

Together, father and son plot Odysseus' return to his household and revenge upon Penelope's suitors. In order to most effectively achieve this end, they agree to keep Odysseus' identity a secret, even from Penelope and Odysseus' father, Laertes.

Book XVII Telemachus returns to his home and greets his mother, telling her of his adventures. She greets him excitedly but sadly; the situation at home has grown intolerable. Despite a soothsayer's accurate synopsis of Odysseus' disguised return, Penelope's faith in his return is waning.

Odysseus and Eumaeus return to town, passing on the way Odysseus' emaciated but still faithful dog. Clearly, the kingdom has fallen on hard times. The disguised Odysseus begs for food at the suitors' banquet. All present donate except for Antinous, who strikes him and sends him away. The impending revenge on these suitors, particularly this man, shall be sweet and well-deserved. Penelope displays her hospitality, as well as her fidelity to her missing husband, by asking the beggar for news of Odysseus.

Book XVIII The suitors pit the disguised Odysseus against a more favored beggar in a boxing match. While neither man wants the fight, Odysseus ends up breaking the man's jaw.

Penelope addresses the crowd of suitors, chastising them for arranging the fight. Her anger grows, and she scolds them for drinking away her husband's wealth. While many of the suitors are ashamed, none leave.

The evening ends in the suitors' drunken mockery of the disguised, and secretly enraged, Odysseus. All present, from maid-servants to suitors, prove themselves worthy of contempt with their lack of hospitality toward the lowly.

Book XIX The suitors retire to bed, and Odysseus and Telemachus lock up the extra weapons in the household. Penelope returns and confides in the "beggar." She tells him of the difficulty she has endured in Odysseus' absence. Odysseus is torn with sympathy but realizes that secrecy is necessary to his successful return to power. Instead of giving his true story to his wife, Odysseus tells her a tale which soothes her pain. Touched, Penelope asks an old and trusted maidservant to bathe the beggar's feet for him before he retires. When she does so, she recognizes her old master by a tell-tale scar on his foot. Odysseus insists that the maidservant keep her secret from Penelope.

Penelope returns to inform Odysseus of her plan to choose a suitor. She intends to marry the man able to shoot an arrow through a row of twelve axes, a feat which her Odysseus was capable of. While this decision is not a happy one, it is necessary for the survival of the kingdom.

Odysseus agrees that the challenge is fitting for her suitors, but predicts that her husband will return before the contest comes to an end. Despite the dreams Athena brings to her, Penelope cannot believe the beggar's words. She retires and cries herself to sleep.

Book XX Odysseus is barely able to sleep with his rage for the suitors. He attempts to determine which of the servants are still loyal to him and which pander to the suitors. Athena comes to him to calm him. As always, she will help in his revenge. Penelope cannot sleep either, and she prays to the gods to spare her from remarriage.

Athena allows the suitors to behave as offensively as possible, so as to stir further rage in Odysseus. At a luncheon the next day the suitors step up their barrage of insults toward their host Telemachus. Proving that he is no longer the weak boy they once knew, Telemachus stands tall and predicts that the suitors' days are numbered. Athena makes the guests break into painful and uncontrollable laughter. This omen is read by a fortune teller as a sign of impending death, but the suitors laugh his words off. The tension mounts as the suitors await the contest for Penelope's hand and Odysseus awaits his revenge.

Book XXI Penelope takes Odysseus' great bow from its locker and is flooded by sensual memories of her husband. In the great hall she announces the beginning of the contest for her hand in marriage. The suitor who can send an arrow through twelve lined axes will win.

Telemachus sets up the axes with wonderful skill. With revenge so close at hand, he can barely contain his joy. He goads the suitors toward their doom, inviting them to step up, string the bow, and win the prize.

Telemachus himself tries to string the massive bow and stops short only at the silent command of Odysseus. Demonstrating a sharpness of wit comparable to his father's, he steps back to leave the task to the "real men." The most offensive of the suitors, Antinous, goads the others on toward this challenge. The irony of the situation is clear: Antinous is pushing everyone to step up and string the massive bow—the same bow that Odysseus will use to kill the suitors.

Odysseus, meanwhile, takes his two most trusted servants aside and reveals his true identity. As they weep for joy, he cuts them short to enlist their help in the upcoming revenge. The servants are to give Odysseus the bow, protect the women, and lock the gates to ensure that the revenge is complete.

Antinous has decided to postpone stringing the massive bow until the next day. Odysseus steps forward and offers to try his hand. Antinous threatens vile punishment if the beggar should touch the bow. But Penelope interjects, pointing out that the reputation of the suitors has been far more soiled by their behavior in Odysseus' home than it could be by the beggar's success. Penelope generously promises that, if successful, the beggar will receive an outfitting and an escort. This act demonstrates not only her gracious and gentle manner, but also her understanding of the importance of a man's freedom.

Telemachus also demonstrates his power over the situation. In Odysseus' absence, he has matured into a prince worthy of a king such as Odysseus. Filled with pride in her manly son, Penelope retires to her bedroom. Athena soothes her tear-filled eyes with gentle sleep.

Despite the protests of the suitors, Odysseus is given the bow. He checks it thoroughly, then smoothly strings it and sends an arrow through the axes. Zeus sends a single thunderclap through the air and Odysseus chuckles inwardly. Needless to say, the suitors have lost their festive mood. Still disguised as a beggar, Odysseus calls Telemachus to his side. The father and son prepare for their ensuing triumph.

Book XXII   Odysseus methodically reaps his long-awaited revenge. The first on his list is Antinous; Odysseus buries his arrow deep in the foul suitor's neck. Antinous' golden cup, full of Odysseus' own wine, falls clanging to the floor. The meat and bread from the overturned table soak in a widening puddle of blood. Homer uses these images of the suitor's "free lunch" to lend irony to Odysseus' revenge.

The suitors are angered by what they feel was a wild shot. But when Odysseus reveals his true identity, their anger turns to groveling terror. Odysseus ignores their pleas and excuses; one by one, the suitors are slain by his arrows as they hide in his banquet hall. Telemachus joins his father in the fight.

Odysseus is a man who knows the significance of human death; his slaughter is not mindless, but rather decisive. When the last of the suitors has been killed, Odysseus orders the women of the house who were disloyal to carry the bodies away and scrub the courtyard clean of the blood of his enemies. Odysseus then hangs these women. As his servants fumigate the house with fire and brimstone, Odysseus weeps. He is finally at home in his kingdom.

Book XXIII   Penelope is informed of Odysseus' homecoming by her faithful servant Eurycleia. She rushes to the hall to see him for herself. Dressed like a beggar, covered in blood, and changed by his twenty years of adventures, Odysseus does not immediately appear to be the husband that Penelope remembers.

To ascertain Odysseus' identity, she slyly tests him by ordering Eurycleia to move the wedding bed into the hall. Odysseus recognizes the trick; the bed is carved out of a giant stump that is still rooted in the ground. When Odysseus states that the bed cannot be moved, Penelope is convinced of his identity.

The reunited husband and wife spend the long evening making love and informing each other of their twenty years' adventures. Athena delays the dawn until Odysseus is satisfied and exhausted.

The contrast between the behavior of Odysseus and Penelope over the twenty years they have spent apart may seem peculiar to the modern reader. Odysseus' sexual adventures with goddesses and women go unchallenged by Penelope, while her chastity, in spite of twenty years of intense courtship by hundreds of men, is expected.

Odysseus wakes his sons and attendants in the morning. He is going to visit his father, Laertes, in the country. Athena cloaks the men in darkness as they walk.

Book XXIV The scene shifts to Hades, where we see the famed ghosts of the Trojan War and other inhabitants of the underworld speak of their past adventures. Hermes brings in the ghosts of Penelope's slain suitors. Agamemnon asks why Ithaca's best have all been delivered to the underworld simultaneously; one of the suitors replies with the story of Odysseus' return. Impressed by the faithfulness of Penelope, Agamemnon sings her praises.

We return to the mortal world, where Odysseus finds his father working as a woodsman. Concealing his identity, he asks the old man about the fate of Ithaca and its king. These questions bring visible pain to the old man, who still believes his son to be missing. Finally, Odysseus can disguise himself no longer and rushes into his father's arms. Laertes asks for proof of Odysseus' identity. Odysseus shows a telltale scar and the two men fall into tears.

The Ithacans hold assembly to assess the new situation on their island. While many of the Ithacans wish for a peaceful settlement between Odysseus and the slain suitors' families, several of the families plan revenge. Having heard of Odysseus' visit to his father, they go to seek their revenge at Laertes' home.

Athena asks her father Zeus for his judgment on the matter. Zeus believes Odysseus' actions were justified and grants Athena permission to continue her protection of him. Zeus' judgment helps to settle the ambiguous questions of right and wrong that arise in this revenge-based system of honor and justice. As his power is highest, he has the last word.

Athena comes down to intervene between the warring parties. She helps Odysseus' side to get a few good kicks in before ordering a complete truce. The townspeople run in terror at the sight of Athena, and Odysseus begins to give chase. He is clearly hesitant to give up his traditional role of warrior. Athena demands that he control himself. The finality of her order is backed up with another thunderbolt from Zeus.

When Odysseus at long last puts down his weapons it is a great relief; this act seems to signal a new era for the man. Athena, disguised again as Mentor, negotiates a lasting peace for the island. The struggle is finally over.

OF MICE AND MEN

ABOUT THE AUTHOR

See page 74

THE BIG PICTURE

John Steinbeck is best known for his unblinking view of American hardship. *Of Mice and Men*, the story of two ranch workers and their fight to stay alive and stay together, is one of the finest examples of Steinbeck's style—it is beautifully written and poignant, while at the same time depicting the harshness and cruelty of life.

Why you're reading this book:
- It is an excellent example of realism: it shows characters struggling to survive in a cruel, merciless world.
- Characteristic of Steinbeck's works, it is both tragic and uplifting at once.
- It is an accurate, human portrait of a particular era in American history and society.
- Steinbeck's characters are realistic and compelling.

Your teachers are looking for:
- Class conflict and racism in this book, and how they relate to the situation and treatment of Lennie.
- The importance of the characters' names.
- Steinbeck's use of dialogue.
- The varying degree of sympathy we have for the sole female character in the novel.
- Lennie as both a human being and an animal.
- The distinction between reality and illusion in the novel.

KEY CHARACTERS

Lennie Small: A huge, goodhearted man with the mental capacity of a child. He wanders with George from ranch to ranch, where he is accepted because he has George to speak for him and because he is an exceptional laborer. Lennie is the center of this novel.

George Milton: Cares for and travels with Lennie. George has put the idea of buying a small farm into Lennie's head. He is both impatient and kind to Lennie in turns, and in the end must make the crucial decision about Lennie's fate.

Slim: He is, in a sense, prince of the ranch where the story takes place. Slim is wise, rather ageless, and described as "godlike." He is the incarnation of reason and goodness.

Candy: An old man, referred to as "the skinner." He does unspecified jobs on the ranch. He lost his hand in an accident long ago and is incapable of hard work.

Curley: The boss' son. An ex-boxer, he is mean, insecure, and weak-spirited. Curley is married to a "tart" of a woman, whom he constantly suspects of infidelity. He has it in for Lennie because Lennie is a "big guy."

Carlson: Slim's buddy on the ranch. Large and loud, he is quick to follow the suggestions of others. Gets easily excited about violent occurrences.

Curley's wife: Although nameless, she is a crucial character in this novel. She is portrayed as lonely and mistreated but at the same time represents evil temptation.

Crooks: The "stable-buck," a black stable worker at the ranch. He is the voice of cynicism. He is described as having a "head lined with pain."

Whit: Another man who works at the ranch.

ESSAY IDEAS

- Each chapter is "framed" by a description of the natural surroundings. Why does Steinbeck do this?
- What do the rabbits symbolize to Lennie?
- How much of what happens in the story is the fault of Curley's wife? How is she portrayed in the novel?
- Discuss morality and responsibility as they are portrayed in *Of Mice and Men*.

A SAMPLE ESSAY IN OUTLINE FORM

Steinbeck often contrasts the setting with the action in this story. Why do you think he uses this device? Give examples to support your answer.

- The action is tough, often cruel:
  - Racism, class prejudice, and sexism.
  - Lennie and George's lost dreams.
  - The death of Lennie.
  - Steinbeck describes the action in a gritty and realistic style.
- Setting:
  - Beautiful landscapes.
  - Nature is a noble, uplifting force.
  - Steinbeck describes the natural setting in a poetic style.

The contrast between the novel's harsh action and its beautiful natural setting shows that there are two sides to all human experience. Even the harshest events have some beauty in them. The presence of nature shows that characters and events in the novel are part of a larger order.

PLOT SUMMARY

Chapter One We meet Lennie and George on their way to find work at a ranch in California. It is clear that George, described as "defined" and "quick," both cares for and dominates the "shapeless," mentally deficient Lennie. They have been forced to leave their last job because Lennie "felt a girl's dress" and frightened her. Because he was so alarmed by her cries for help, he didn't let go. The ensuing controversy forced them to leave. Lennie unintentionally harms almost everything he touches—from mice to people—and yet he tries pathetically hard to be tender, and dreams of living in a house with rabbits that he can care for.

George feels trapped to have Lennie always with him—he cannot have the normal, solitary life of other roving ranch-workers. Because of this, and the fact that his companion often accidentally causes him problems, he is bitter toward Lennie. However, his bitterness is constantly checked by Lennie's kindheartedness and childlike dependency.

In a clearing near their new job, Lennie asks George to tell him again the story of their future: how someday they will save up their money and have a little house with a vegetable garden and rabbits. George tells Lennie that if he ever gets into trouble at this new ranch, he should come back to this very spot and wait till George comes to him. They go to sleep with Lennie still talking about rabbits.

Chapter Two Lennie and George arrive at the ranch the next morning and are taken to the bunkhouse. George is extremely sharp: after finding a can of insecticide by his bed, he suspiciously questions Candy, an old ranch hand, about the quality of the place. He also has all the right answers, some of which are lies, to the boss' questions. The boss is wary of Lennie and George from the start because they have arrived a day late, and because George does all the talking even when Lennie is pressed to answer.

We meet Curley, the boss' son, an ex-lightweight boxer with a "little man's" complex. He immediately goes after Lennie because Lennie is a "big guy" and, as Candy explains, "Curley hates big guys." Candy also tells George and Lennie that Curley is even worse than usual since he got married. Curley's new wife, described by Candy as "pretty, but a tart," becomes the subject of discussion. George makes Lennie promise to stay as far away from Curley as possible.

Soon, Curley's wife comes and stands in the doorway, proving Candy's description correct. She flirts and lingers with the men. Finally she goes, leaving behind a sense of unease. The ranchers come in from their morning shift. Carlson and Slim discuss the litter of puppies Slim's dog has just had, and this sparks Lennie's interest. When the men go to lunch, George says he'll try to get Lennie one of the puppies. Curley pokes in and menacingly asks after his wife. Lennie and George go off to lunch too.

Chapter Three George and Lennie appear to have established themselves at the ranch by the first evening. George talks to Slim about Lennie. Everyone is curious about why he and Lennie travel together. Slim listens carefully; he is quiet and respected. He witnesses the interchange between Lennie and George when Lennie comes in with the puppy hidden under his coat. George immediately knows what Lennie is up to. He sends Lennie back out to the barn to put the puppy back, and Slim remarks "Jesus, he's jes' like a kid, ain't he."

Carlson complains about how horrible Candy's old dog smells, saying that Candy should just put him out of his misery and

shoot him. Candy refuses until Slim, whose 'opinions were law,' gently suggests that the dog is too old to live. Candy seems helpless without an ally.

Whit comes in and changes the subject, telling the others about a letter he has found in a magazine written by a guy who used to work at the ranch. Carlson, however, does not forget the old dog, and he offers again to shoot him. Finally, Candy sadly agrees, and Carlson takes the dog out of the room. Afterwards, George and Whit play cards and talk about the whorehouses in town and Curley's "looloo" wife.

Carlson comes back, soon followed by Curley, who demands if anyone has seen his wife. He leaves with his suspicions aroused when he hears that Slim has just gone out to the barn with Crooks to tar a mule's hoof. Almost everyone goes out to see the fight they expect between Curley and Slim.

George stays and talks to Lennie again about the place they're going to get, and his description is so comforting that it draws Candy out of his misery and leads him to ask if he can go in on it, too. Because Candy has money saved up, the dream that had never been realistic suddenly looks as if it could actually happen. It is a beautiful idea: having a place, "living off the fat of the land," and being free to do whatever they please. They agree to keep their plan a secret. Candy, now taken into George's confidence, confesses that he wishes that he, not a stranger, had killed his dog.

Just then, everyone comes back into the bunkhouse. Curley is apologizing to Slim for accusing him of messing with his wife—he is obviously very respectful of Slim. But his humiliation finds a target in Lennie. Accusing Lennie of laughing at him, Curley attacks him. Lennie cries and Slim is about to go after Curley, but George orders Lennie to fight for himself. Lennie only grabs at Curley's fist, but he is so strong that he crushes the hand completely. He doesn't know his own strength, and is terrified at being attacked.

Lennie is still shaking when Slim takes control and orders the ranchers to get Curley to the hospital. Slim makes Curley promise not to tell what has happened; if he did, Lennie and George would get fired. Everyone knows that Lennie is not at fault. However, by displaying his superhuman strength, he has left everybody quite shaken and awed.

Chapter Four This chapter offers us a close-up view of Crooks, the ranch's black stable hand. He is solitary, and he likes—or pretends to like—being that way. The other men have gone to town, leaving Lennie behind. Lennie, seeing the light on in Crooks' room, comes to him for company. Crooks at first tries to send Lennie away, but eventually he gives in and invites him to sit down. Lennie talks about the house and the rabbits, but Crooks takes it to be crazy gibberish. Crooks talks to Lennie about his childhood.

Crooks starts off being kind, but as soon as he sees how easily Lennie is upset, he vents all his pent-up anger on him. Crooks asks Lennie what would happen if George didn't return from town tonight, a tormenting thought for Lennie. What if George got hurt or killed, Crooks asks. Lennie, who interprets everything literally, gets angry at the suggestion that someone might have hurt George. He menacingly approaches Crooks, who sees he has pushed too far and reassures Lennie that George is fine.

Crooks has made his point though: he wants Lennie to see how it feels to have no one. As a black man, Crooks is completely isolated and alone. He talks about how a man can go crazy being left alone to think about everything. Candy enters, and Crooks continues to voice his harsh cynicism, telling them that their dream of getting a piece of land will never come true. He reminds Candy and Lennie that every man who passes through has the same dream, and it is never realized. As Candy indignantly insists that they have the money saved and the land picked out, Crooks starts to want to believe in the dream too and offers his help to Lennie and Candy.

Curley's wife interrupts their conversation, again "looking for Curley." She finds only the "leftovers" of the ranch: Crooks, the hunchback black stable buck; Lennie, the idiot; and Candy, the old cripple. A neglected, lonely woman, Curley's wife herself could fit into this group of "leftovers." But she knows how to take control, and the men are afraid of her. She makes searing comments about Candy and especially Crooks. She also admits to Lennie that she knows he busted Curley's hand and that she's glad for it. When she finally leaves, the dreamy mood that had overtaken the men has been destroyed by her presence.

The ranchers return from town. George restores order by taking Lennie out of Crooks' room. Candy suddenly feels uncomfortable there and decides to leave too. Crooks tells Candy to forget what he said about going in on the deal with the house.

Chapter Five Lennie is alone in the barn on a Sunday, and though the day and scene are described as pleasant, death is in the air. Lennie has accidentally killed the puppy he had tried so hard to treat gently. Curley's wife comes into the barn and talks to Lennie; she is dressed up nicely and it is obvious that she is lonely. It is not hard for her to persuade Lennie to talk to her, even though he has promised George he wouldn't. He admits he's upset because now that he has killed his puppy, George won't let him tend the rabbits. He mustn't do anything bad, so he mustn't talk to her.

This makes Curley's wife angry, and she complains that nobody will talk to her. She tells Lennie that she shouldn't be stuck here married to a man she hates—she should have been in "the pictures." This is her dream, just as the house with rabbits is the men's dream. Lennie keeps talking about rabbits, and when Curley's wife announces that he is crazy, he explains that he just likes to touch soft things. Curley's wife says she understands this.

Eventually, she invites Lennie to touch her hair. She gets scared when Lennie doesn't stop, but he doesn't understand. She screams, and Lennie gets frightened. He tries to hush her, and she struggles and screams even more. Lennie's terror builds and causes him to use more force. He loses control, and before he knows it, he has broken the woman's neck.

All he can think to do is to run to the brush where George told him to hide if there was any trouble, and wait for him. He half covers Curley's dead wife with hay and runs away, taking the dead puppy with him.

Candy discovers the body in the barn and calls George to come in. George and Candy know they must find Lennie, because Curley will have him killed when he learns what has happened. The death of Curley's wife destroys their dream of getting a home, and she, as always, becomes the target of blame.

Candy gets all the men to come to the barn. Immediately Curley riles everyone up to find and shoot Lennie. He is driven by pure anger, not by grief for his wife's death. Only Slim stays calm; George talks to him about how Lennie didn't do this out of meanness, and Slim understands. Slim also knows that there is nothing they can do. The sympathetic characters in the story—Candy, George, and Slim—pity Lennie and don't blame him. They are in the minority, though, and everyone except Candy leaves to find Lennie.

Chapter Six Lennie has gone back to the brush, and his guilt plays tricks on him. He sees the form of his Aunt Clara, who took care of him before George. The image speaks with George's voice. It reminds Lennie that, as hard as he tries, he always messes things up for George.

Then Lennie's conscience appears to him in the form of a gigantic rabbit, which speaks to him in his own voice. It tells him that he is not good for anything, including tending the rabbits. The rabbit image repeatedly insists that George is going to leave Lennie now.

But soon, George comes to Lennie and reassures him that he will not leave him, and that he was never angry. George himself seems to understand this now for the first time. But he also knows what he has to do. He tells Lennie to look out over the water. George talks to him for the last time about the place they are going to have together. His words are full of sadness, regret, and obligation.

When Lennie asks if they can go and make a home right now, George says yes, then shoots Lennie in the back of the head. We are reminded of the way Candy's dog was shot.

The other men hear the gunshot and run to the clearing. They find Lennie dead and George with the gun. Only Slim understands what it was, exactly, that George needed to do. George has, in a sense, shot his dog: his companion, his responsibility, and his best friend. The other men stare after Slim and George as the two walk off together, Slim reassuring George that he has done the right thing.

THE OLD MAN AND THE SEA

ABOUT THE AUTHOR

Ernest Hemingway (1899–1961) is considered to be the principal literary spokesman of the "lost generation" of the 1920s, characterized by its decadence and lack of roots or direction. The travels and activities of which Hemingway wrote were based chiefly on his personal experience.

Born in Oak Park, Illinois, Hemingway began his writing career in the newspaper business. During World War I, Hemingway served as an ambulance driver on the Italian front until he was injured and discharged. In 1921 Hemingway moved to Paris, where he was received by the large expatriate community of celebrated writers and artists there, including F. Scott Fitzgerald, Gertrude Stein, and Ezra Pound.

Hemingway's third book, *The Sun Also Rises*, was his first American success. His many subsequent novels such as *Men without Women* (1927) and *A Farewell to Arms* (1929), based on his Italian war experiences, further solidified "Papa" Hemingway's position as a preeminent American writer. Sportfishing in Key West and Cuba, big game hunting in Africa, and bullfighting in Spain, Hemingway continued through the 1930s to live and write about the traveling sportsman's life with which his works are associated.

The fascinating adventure and variety of his later occupations, including his reporting of the Spanish Civil War and World War II and his service as a U-boat hunter in the Caribbean, served both to shape Hemingway's popular image as a figure of rugged romanticism and to provide fascinating material for such classic novels as *For Whom the Bell Tolls* (1939) and *The Old Man and the Sea* (1952). The latter won Hemingway the Pulitzer prize in 1953. In 1954 he received the Nobel Prize in Literature.

Hemingway struggled with depression and alcoholism for the majority of his adult life. He committed suicide in 1961 at his hunting lodge in Ketchum, Idaho. Today, Ernest Hemingway is one of the most widely read American authors.

THE BIG PICTURE

Hemingway's *The Old Man and the Sea* is a tale of survival. On a literal level, it tells the story of the humble fisherman Santiago's battle with the ocean and the elements; on a more symbolic level, it represents all the battles man must fight to survive.

Why you're reading this book:
- More than just the story of an old fisherman who proves himself through persistence, it is an analogy for the struggle of the individual in the world.
- The novel portrays the triumph of universal human strengths:
  - Overcoming adversity.
  - Remaining true to one's ideals.
  - Maintaining faith in oneself and in life.
- t addresses the timeless question of how much man can truly control his fate.

Your teachers are looking for:
- Santiago's speaking aloud to the animals, and the function this has in the novel.
- The juxtaposition of the human condition with that of the animals.
- The important role the ocean plays for Santiago:

- Source of life; food; beauty; danger; the adversary.
- Mysterious and unpredictable, it parallels fate in many ways.
- Parallels between Santiago and Christ.
- The importance of faith in the book.

Upon first reading *The Old Man and the Sea*, many readers are confused by the relative simplicity of its plot and language—its short sentences, basic vocabulary, and simplistic title make it in some ways similar to a children's book. Don't be fooled—this deceiving simplicity is one of the reasons this book is so effective, and beneath it lie important themes and symbolism.

KEY CHARACTERS

Santiago: The novel's hero. An old fisherman and the boy Manolin's mentor. He is calm and contemplative and has a simple yet profound appreciation of nature. Because of his age and recent bad luck, Santiago is mocked by the younger fishermen. Only Manolin has retained faith in Santiago, and he is the old man's only link with the rest of the community. Santiago, however, holds on to his pride.

Manolin: The boy, Santiago's attendant and fishing companion. He has learned all he knows about the philosophy and practice of the sea, as well as the art of fishing, from Santiago. For this Manolin is grateful, and gives Santiago the respect and loving care a disciple gives an aging mentor.

ESSAY IDEAS

- Discuss Santiago's relationship with animals in the novel.
- Is Santiago a religious man? Explain. Based on this novel, what do you think Hemingway's definition of religion might be?
- What is the relationship between Santiago and the great fish?
- Discuss the book as a metaphor for the journey of life. Is Santiago a successful "traveler?" Explain.
- Discuss the relationship between Santiago and Manolin. What does each provide for the other? How does their relationship fit in with the rest of the community?
- How would you characterize Santiago's attitude toward DiMaggio? How does this relate to how Santiago views himself?
- What do you think is Hemingway's concept of "the hero"? How does Santiago fit into this? DiMaggio? Christ?

A SAMPLE ESSAY IN OUTLINE FORM

Santiago as "hero"
- Santiago is a simple, humble man, but in many ways heroic:
  - Manolin's great love and respect for him.
  - Santiago's fishing exploits that we learn of through his talking to himself.
  - Respect and love for nature and the sea.
  - His strength and courage in the fight with the marlin.
  - His respect for the marlin, and other fish, both as companions and competition.
  - His love and care for Manolin.

Santiago is more than an ordinary fisherman. He lives by his own set of ideals that he refuses to compromise. He manages to persevere despite the community's ridicule and doubt, and this makes him a hero.

PLOT SUMMARY

Santiago, an old fisherman fishing alone in a small boat in the Gulf Stream, has not caught a fish in eighty days. His skin is wrinkled and scarred from hard years of fishing in the sun. His boy companion for the first half of this dry spell has been ordered by his parents to a luckier and more modern fishing boat. The community doubts his ability; they feel he is finished as a fisherman, and ridicule him for not realizing it.

Santiago's only companion is the boy Manolin, who loves and respects the old man. He fears, however, that Santiago is too weak, and perhaps truly unlucky. Manolin tricks the owner of another fishing boat to fish close to the old man in case he catches a fish too large for his aging strength. Although his father no longer allows him to help Santiago with his fishing, Manolin helps the old man with encouragement and provisions. Santiago has taught Manolin all that he knows about the sea and the art of fishing, and for this the boy loves him. Their relationship is simple yet powerful.

The old man has faith in his fishing ability and the bounty of the sea. He is proud of his past abilities, yet shows humility. His shack is simple and barren, adorned only with two Christian religious icons left in respect for his deceased wife.

Santiago maintains an optimistic outlook on life. Rather than complain of the obvious burdens of his age, poverty, and poor luck, the old man speaks instead of the glories of the current American baseball heroes, especially Joe DiMaggio. Santiago believes profoundly in the greatness of such heroes. While he realizes that DiMaggio alone cannot bring the Yankees victory, he has great faith in the passion with which one great man may inspire a community.

Manolin prepares a meal for Santiago each night, and each night Santiago pretends that he has already prepared his own food. Santiago is in fact dependent upon the boy but refuses to be an obtrusive burden to him. He thus gives Manolin the opportunity to stop his care. The exchange between the two men is touching and humorous. The boy acts like a father to the old man, covering him up with a blanket while he naps before fetching the food.

When Santiago wakes they talk of baseball, and again of DiMaggio. The old man's faith is not injured when he learns that the Yankees have lost. Again, DiMaggio's individual greatness is enough to maintain Santiago's faith in the entire team.

Santiago and Manolin's conversation moves from baseball heroes to fishing heroes. Manolin flatters Santiago's fishing abilities, but the old man speaks humbly of better fishermen. Although he recognizes that age has limited his strength, Santiago has faith in his own great skill and determination. The boy leaves for the night, and Santiago sleeps. His dreams are always of the pure white beaches and virile African lions he saw from ships in his youth.

Santiago wakes before dawn. Despite the darkness and chill, he looks forward to the upcoming row out to sea in his little skiff. The old man wakes the boy at his parents' house. The boy is too tired to go out, but the old man is understanding. Santiago has taught him that suffering is a necessary aspect of being both a fisherman and a man.

Santiago rows alone into the predawn sea, acutely aware of the natural beauty around him: the flying fishes, the birds, the phosphorescent sea weed. Santiago's deep respect for the ocean's greatness and wisdom keeps him dedicated to her even when she seems cruel.

Santiago prepares the baits and fishing

lines. The description of this process is poetic and extremely detailed, reflecting Santiago's skill as a fisherman and the delicacy of his technique.

While fishing, Santiago speaks aloud to himself. His acute observations inform the reader of his extensive experience as a fisherman. He talks about the balance of nature, about how things are born and die in a natural and necessary cycle. In characteristic Hemingway style, Santiago speaks of death with poetic beauty.

Santiago has high hopes for this day's fishing. He has faith in his skill as a fisherman, and feels it is only luck which he needs today to succeed. It is significant in both a symbolic and a literal sense that Santiago is further out to sea today than ever before.

When the floats on Santiago's skillfully set lines begin to move, Santiago knows exactly what is happening; 100 fathoms (6800 feet) down, a marlin is nibbling his bait. There is much suspense as Santiago waits for the big fish to swallow the bait; when at last it does, Santiago can feel the enormous weight of the fish. He is unsure of exactly how large it is, but he knows it is too large for him to move it with the line.

In fact, quite the opposite begins to happen; the fish pulls the little boat through the water. Santiago welcomes the fish to tire itself out this way, but is worried that the fish might dive. If this happens, Santiago knows that he will either lose the fish or sink with it.

The towing continues for hours, seemingly without the fish getting tired out. Santiago both pities and respects the struggling fish. Although he is exhausted, Santiago's tone has not changed; he is still observant and appreciative of his natural surroundings.

The struggle with the marlin is often slow and provides much opportunity for contemplation. Santiago's thoughts about aspects of the human condition, such as the loneliness of old age, are juxtaposed with natural images such as frolicking couples of dolphins. Schools of fish, particularly dolphins and the flying fishes, are referred to as Santiago's friends and brothers. Santiago has been ostracized by his human community, but he is certainly at home in nature.

Through Santiago's simple situation, Hemingway is able to explore various aspects of man's destiny. As Santiago is pulled by the marlin through the star-dotted night, many facets of human experience come into play: the intellect (Santiago's skill at navigating); faith (the stars and Santiago's spirituality); fate (Santiago's luck at catching fish); and basic physical needs. Hemingway explores the question of whether a man has control over his own fate, or if nature is leading him on a random course. In this sense, Santiago's ordeal with the marlin parallels the struggle of a man's life. This is poignantly demonstrated when Santiago must release his other successful fishing lines, or opportunities, in order to pursue the great fish.

Santiago emerges as something of a saint through his patient and understanding suffering. Although he loves the fish, he will not hesitate to kill them for food if necessary. He speaks in the manner of St. Francis to a bird which has landed on the tight fishing line. Santiago asks questions of the bird in a fatherly and sympathetic manner; he seems to know more about being a bird than the bird itself does. Santiago sends this bird away with the sage phrase, "Then go in and take your chance like any man or fish or bird." When Santiago cuts himself on the tight line, the fish seems to feel his injury, finally jumping with the pain.

The marlin surfaces as Santiago had hoped, filling its air sacks and rendering itself unable to dive again. Santiago is finally able to see the incredible size of the fish; it is larger than the boat. The fish is described beautifully and colorfully, its tail cutting through the water like "a great scythe-blade." Upon seeing the immense fish, Santiago prays for a little help from God. Although he is not a religious man, Santiago, like many men, turns to religion when he recognizes the size of the struggle before him.

Santiago's battle with the fish also becomes a battle with himself: his own cramping hands, his hunger, and his fatigue. His struggle with his rebellious cramping hand is carried out as patiently and philosophically as his struggle with the marlin. As this is his second day with the marlin, Santiago is careful to maintain his strength by eating raw fish. He would also like to sleep a bit for strength but, as he needs to remain alert, he cannot.

Throughout his struggle, Santiago tries to live up to the heroism embodied in his hero DiMaggio. Santiago recalls his own former feats of endurance and strength, such as a twenty-four-hour arm wrestling match against "the Negro from Cienfuegos."

Santiago catches another dolphin for food, and notices that, as the marlin has slowed his course, he must be tired as well. The struggle of man against fish which we see above the water is paralleled by the fish's struggle against man beneath the surface. Like Santiago, the fish too must "pull until he dies."

Exhausted, Santiago finally dozes off. He dreams of miles of splashing dolphins, of the white beaches and lions of Africa, and of his youth when he still had his strength. These dreams are interrupted by a jump from the marlin which pulls him roughly to the bow. Although he is exhausted and weak, and his hands are horribly cut by the line, his resolve remains firm. Even under such duress Santiago still takes stock of simple and sustaining pleasures such as the breeze.

Santiago watches the movements of the fish carefully; after hours of circling, the marlin comes close enough to the skiff to be harpooned and killed. Santiago lashes the giant fish to the side of his boat. As he does so, he realizes for the first time that the fish is worth a great deal of money. Santiago's interest in the great fish was for its sustenance and vitality, not its monetary value. As he navigates his return to the distant harbor, we sense that Santiago has transformed himself from a failure to a hero.

The story takes a tragic turn when attacking sharks are drawn by the trail of marlin blood. Santiago fights them with everything he has; his hooked iron gaff, then his knife tied to a board, and finally with oars themselves. It is no use; the sharks are unrelenting. We sense, as Santiago does, that to struggle against them is futile. Exhausted, he gives up and spits into the water at the sharks so that they may eat his saliva and "dream they've killed a man."

The weary Santiago returns to his harbor with only the skeleton of the enormous marlin. He leaves the boat and skeleton in the water and, Christ-like, walks to his shack bearing the heavy mast of the skiff like a cross over his shoulder. He falls five times on this trip home, paralleling the five times Christ fell on the road to Calvary. In a further parallel to the Christian resurrection story, Santiago has returned to the harbor on the third day after he set out.

As the old man rests, Manolin attends to him. He assures the exhausted Santiago that his battle against the great fish was successful and impressive. In town, the word has spread about the great skeleton lashed to Santiago's skiff. Santiago dreams peacefully of the white beaches and lions.

OLIVER TWIST

ABOUT THE AUTHOR

See page 85.

THE BIG PICTURE

Oliver Twist is Dickens' novel about an orphan and his many trials and setbacks. In the story, we see the seamy side of the lower class in Dickens' world: a world of thieves, manipulators, and con artists. However, we also see Dickens' faith in humanity, as his title character rises above his upbringing to achieve success.

Why you're reading this book:

- Dickens' painting of characters is remarkable. They are caricatures without being clichés.
- Like most of Dickens' works, it places us right in the middle of nineteenth-century British society.
- It is a lifelike portrayal of an important time in the social history of England.
- Its humorous style and larger-than-life characters make it entertaining to read.

Your teachers are looking for:

- Dickens' social commentary on the classes, both through his first–person involvement as narrator and through more subtle tactics.
- The author's use of sarcasm, irony, wit, and black humor to set the mood.
- How the tone and style of writing changes when different characters are being discussed.
- The importance of the characters' names.

KEY CHARACTERS

Oliver Twist: The novel's main character and hero. An orphan who experiences incredible hardships and poverty, but who ultimately finds the good life he deserves.

Mr. Bumble: A power–hungry beadle. He works for the poorhouses where Oliver spends his childhood. He eventually marries Mrs. Corney.

Fagin: An old Jewish thief who exploits boys, women, and anyone else he can to get him money. Oliver ends up in his clutches.

Bill Sikes: An evil, violent thief who works with Fagin. He and Nancy have a relationship, although it is difficult to define. Eventually he kills Nancy for betraying the thieves.

Nancy: A young woman who works for Fagin and lives with Bill Sikes. She has a soft spot for Oliver and secretly tries to help him.

Betsy: A close friend of Nancy who also works for Fagin.

The Artful Dodger (John Dawkins): A boy who is Fagin's number one pickpocket. He finds Oliver and introduces him to Fagin. The Dodger seems much older than his age and is very intelligent. However, he is eventually caught and sent to prison.

Charley Bates: Another apprentice to Fagin. He has a loud, boisterous sense of humor.

Flash Toby Crackit: A house–breaker who works with Sikes. They use Oliver to break into the Maylie house.

Mr. Sowerberry: An undertaker who takes Oliver from the workhouse to be his apprentice.

Mrs. Sowerberry: The undertaker's wife. She is a cruel and cold woman.

Noah Claypole: A charity–boy who works for the Sowerberrys. He abuses Oliver and instigates the incident that makes Oliver run away. Noah, too, eventually runs away to London, and joins up with the thieves. He ultimately turns the thieves in.

Charlotte: The Sowerberrys' servant. She runs away to London with Noah.

Mrs. Corney (later Mrs. Bumble): She runs the workhouse where Oliver was born and has many secrets about Oliver's history.

Monks: Oliver's half–brother. He and Fagin work together to try to keep Oliver away from the kind, rich people who care for him.

Mr. Brownlow: A kind old gentleman who is the victim of the young thieves' robbery and as a result ends up meeting Oliver. Unbeknownst to both of them, he is very important in the history of Oliver's family, and eventually, he ends up adopting the boy.

Mrs. Bedwin: Mr. Brownlow's servant. She takes an instant liking to Oliver when he comes to the house, and nurses him back to health.

Mr. Grimwig: A friend of Mr. Brownlow's with an obnoxious but goodhearted personality.

Rose Maylie: Mrs. Maylie's ward. Rose is of questionable parentage, but is incredibly kind, good, and pure. She is in love with Harry Maylie, Mrs. Maylie's son, but is reluctant to marry him because of her lowly background.

Mrs. Maylie: An old, wealthy lady whose home is the site of an attempted robbery by Sikes and Crackit. Oliver comes into her life when he is used in the robbery and shot by her servant, Giles. She takes him under her wing.

Harry Maylie: Mrs. Maylie's son. A charming, up–and–coming young man who is madly in love with Rose.

Giles: The Maylies' butler who shoots Oliver when he is forced to break into the house.

Mr. Losberne: The Maylies' doctor and close friend. He is well–meaning, although a bit hot–tempered.

Barney: A young Jewish thief who works for Fagin.

Tom Chitling: One of Fagin's less intelligent boy–apprentices.

Little Dick: A poor, sick orphan and close friend to Oliver. He has a great deal of childlike wisdom.

Agnes Fleming: Oliver's mother and Rose's sister.

ESSAY IDEAS

- What is the role of the women in this novel?
- What is Dickens' apparent opinion of the British class system?
- How does Dickens portray the rich? The poor?
- How much control does Oliver have over the events of his life, and over the path the novel takes?
- How does Oliver change throughout the book? What does he learn?
- How does Dickens create the dark mood of the story?
- Discuss the anti-Semitism in the novel. How does it affect Fagin? Other characters?
- Discuss the significance of some of the symbols in the book: the clock heard by those who are about to be hanged; the bridge where Nancy meets Rose.
- What is the importance of the presence of things like thunder, darkness, and rain? How do these features act to set the stage, almost as if in a play?
- This story has "good" bad guys and

"bad" bad guys. Who are they? Which ones do we sympathize with and why?

- What does Little Dick symbolize?

A SAMPLE ESSAY IN OUTLINE FORM

What kind of control does Oliver have over the movement and development of the plot?

- On the level of plot, Oliver is not master of his own destiny:
  - He is not present in many of the scenes; much of the story happens when he is absent.
  - Other characters decide his actions for him:
  - He is sent to a workhouse.
  - The robbery when he is shot.
  - He is a child, often unwillingly controlled by a world of adults as if he were a piece of merchandise.
  - There is almost no action he can take that can change his situation.
- Oliver is not an active force in the novel:
  - He rarely speaks; Dickens does not offer us much insight into his thoughts.
  - Although his influence is crucial to the novel, it is not due to any conscious action on his part.

Although the book is about Oliver Twist, he has very little control over any of the events in his life. Our sympathetic image of him results from the mistreatment he endures and his tenderhearted reaction to his situation, rather than from his character as an individual. Rather than a strong, active force in the novel, Oliver Twist is a passive character acted upon by his environment—and manipulated by Dickens. The book is more about what society does *to* Oliver Twist than about Oliver Twist himself; Dickens uses Oliver's plight to make a social commentary.

Chapter 1 We meet Oliver, who is born in a workhouse to a nameless mother who dies just after his birth. This foreshadows the cruel and harsh life which Oliver will live, but as we can guess by his loud cries of protest, he may fight against it.

Chapter 2 Oliver's early childhood is presented to us through a general description of all the orphans, lumped in with theirs. This narrative method shows how unnoticed and indistinct Oliver is. We see Oliver again on his ninth birthday: he is small, high-spirited, and presently locked in the cellar as punishment. Mr. Bumble, the beadle and parish officer, takes Oliver to a workhouse since he is too old to remain at Mrs. Mann's awful orphanage.

"The Board," the rich men who govern the workhouse, are introduced. We see how they thin out the workhouse population by essentially starving the inmates. In addition, they justify their actions amongst themselves by calling them humane treatment.

Meanwhile, three months after Oliver arrives at the workhouse, he asks for more food. This request outrages everyone, including "The Board," who decides to pay five shillings to anyone who will take Oliver.

Chapter 3 Oliver is kept in a dark cell for a week, taken out only to be beaten and made an example of to the other boys. He is almost given away to Mr. Gainfield, a brutal, poor chimney sweep, but is saved when the magistrate who is to sign Oliver over to him notices how frightened the boy is. The next morning, the sign is up again to give Oliver away.

Chapter 4 "The Board" wants to send Oliver to work at sea, where they are convinced he would die, but Mr. Sowerberry, the undertaker, takes him off their hands instead. After tears and words of loneliness, Oliver arrives at his new home. We immediately see that Mrs. Sowerberry, who is much less warm than her husband, is the true master of the house.

Chapter 5 Oliver is awakened in the morning by Noah Claypole, a "big charity boy" who right away abuses his position of superiority and uses every opportunity to pick on Oliver. Charlotte, Mrs. Sowerberry's servant, is Noah's slightly more sensitive cohort.

Mr. Sowerberry, a relatively kind man, decides that Oliver would be a good prop at children's funerals, and begins to take Oliver along with him on his rounds. Their first stop is a rat–infested slum where a mother has died, of which Dickens gives a vivid, horrifying description. After a rainy burial, Oliver expresses his dislike of the undertaking business.

Chapter 6 Oliver reaches a turning point when, after Noah teases him about his dead mother, he flies into a rage and manages to beat Noah up. Noah exaggerates his injuries and gets Charlotte and Mrs. Sowerberry to violently subdue Oliver; but Oliver remains undaunted, even when they throw him in the cellar and send for Mr. Bumble.

Chapter 7 Noah returns from the workhouse with Mr. Bumble, who does not affect Oliver's new, bold mood. But when Mr. Sowerberry returns, he beats Oliver brutally. Maintaining his pride, Oliver does not cry until late that night when he is alone and the events of the day weigh heavily upon him. As soon as the first light of morning comes, Oliver runs away. He passes the farm where he first lived and sees an old friend, Little Dick, who blesses Oliver on his way.

Chapter 8 Oliver decides to go to London, even though it is seventy miles away. After a week of walking, he arrives exhausted and starving in a town, where he meets the Artful Dodger. The Dodger feeds him and offers to get him shelter with a "'spectable gentleman" in London. This gentleman, whom we meet soon, is Fagin, an old Jew who has a group of boys as "pupils."

Chapter 9 Still half–asleep in the morning, Oliver watches Fagin as he uncovers and inspects a collection of jewels and riches he keeps hidden away. Fagin catches the boy looking, but after Oliver reassures him that he has not seen where the treasures are kept, Fagin relaxes. The Dodger and his friend, Charley Bates, return from a morning of "hard work" with two pocketbooks and four pocket handkerchiefs. Oliver is too naive to know that the goods are stolen. The two boys and Fagin play a pick-pocketing game, and then Betsy and Nancy come in. After everyone but Fagin and Oliver leaves, the old man begins to teach Oliver how to pick pockets.

Chapter 10 Oliver finally gets permission to go to work with the other boys, never realizing what this means. He is shocked when he sees his two companions stealing, and he ends up being the one who gets caught as the thief. Oliver, the gentleman who was robbed, and a policeman go to the station after a man stops Oliver from escaping by punching him in the face.

Chapter 11 Mr. Brownlow, the victim of the robbery, is reluctant to press charges, because he is unsure that Oliver is the thief. Just as the magistrate is about to sentence Oliver to three months' hard labor, the bookkeeper who owns the stall where the robbery occurred comes and declares Oliver's innocence. Kindly, Mr. Brownlow and the bookkeeper take the boy, who has fainted, away in Mr. Brownlow's coach. Mr. Brownlow has been struck by the expression on Oliver's face, which reminds him of someone.

Chapter 12 Mrs. Bedwin, Mr. Brownlow's servant, slowly nurses Oliver back to health from a bad fever. After several days, Mr. Brownlow comes to see Oliver. Standing in the parlor, he notices the uncanny likeness of Oliver's face to that of the woman in the portrait on the wall.

Chapter 13 This chapter takes us back to the thieves. The Dodger and Charley return home, and Fagin is furious at hearing of Oliver's arrest. We meet Bill Sikes, another criminal. They all decide they must get Oliver out of prison before he gives them away. Nancy is sent to the police, where she learns he has been taken by "the gentleman." The thieves hastily set out to find him and kidnap him back.

Chapter 14 Oliver talks again to Mr. Brownlow, who promises not to desert him if Oliver never gives him cause to. The boy is about to tell his history when Mr. Grimwig, Brownlow's friend, comes to tea. Later, Oliver is sent to return some books with a five pound note. The two gentlemen bet on whether Oliver will return or go back to the thieves and rob Mr. Brownlow of all he has sent Oliver out with. They wait a very long time for him to return.

Chapter 15 Oliver gets lost on his way to the bookstall, and Nancy finds him. She and Bill carry him away despite his cries for help. Meanwhile, everyone at the Brownlows' is still waiting for Oliver's return.

Chapter 16 Bill and Nancy take Oliver to a new hideout where they meet the other thieves. They strip Oliver of money, clothes, and books, while Oliver begs that everything be returned to Mr. Brownlow. As soon as he gets a chance, he tries to escape, but he is caught and beaten. This is a turning point, where Nancy suddenly becomes very sympathetic toward Oliver: we see that she is caught between good and bad.

Chapter 17 This chapter takes us back to Mr. Bumble. We also see Little Dick, who is dying and has some very insightful things to say. Mr. Bumble goes to London and sees an ad placed by Mr. Brownlow, who is looking for Oliver. Mr. Bumble runs to the gentleman and ruins Oliver's reputation by telling his own terrible version of Oliver's history.

Chapters 18–22 After being alone in the dirty hideout for a week, Oliver begins spending time with the boys and Fagin again. Fagin attempts to drag Oliver into a criminal lifestyle by breaking down his defenses. Fagin, Nancy, and Sikes discuss a house–breaking plan in which they will put Oliver through a small space and he will open the door. Nancy is back on the thieves' side again. She takes Oliver to Sikes' place and warns him to be good, for her sake and his, because she has already gone out of her way for him.

In the morning, Oliver and Sikes leave for the robbery. They travel all day until they arrive at a rundown house. Two more thieves, Barney and Toby Crackit, wait for them at the house. Late that night, Toby and Sikes take Oliver to the appointed house, where he finally realizes with horror what is about to happen. He is given a gun and told to shoot anyone who may get in the way. Paralyzed with fear, he is shoved inside the window, there is a flash of confusion, and two servants appear. Oliver is shot in the arm and carried away by Sikes as the alarm bells go off.

Chapters 23–24 Dickens takes us back again to Mr. Bumble, who is now with Mrs. Corney, the attendant of the workhouse where Oliver was born. They flirt ridiculously. Just as Mr. Bumble makes a serious advance, an old pauper woman arrives and announces that a woman is dying and will not rest until she gives Mrs. Corney a piece of information.

The dying woman tells Mrs. Corney that it was she who nursed Oliver's mother in childbirth, and that she stole something made of gold from the young woman when she died. She is about to say something important about the gold object, but she dies before she has a chance.

Chapters 25–26 We return to Fagin and the boys playing cards. Toby Crackit enters and says that he and Sikes left Oliver alone in a ditch after he had been shot. Fagin, frantic, goes to the Three Cripples Inn in search of a shadowy character named Monks, whom we know nothing about, and leaves a message at the bar. He then goes to Sikes' apartment to talk to Nancy. He finds her drunk and depressed, and in an argument, Fagin accidentally hints at a villainous plan involving Oliver. He returns to his place, where he and Monks discuss Oliver secretly. Monks thinks he sees the shadow of a woman pass, but Fagin assures him that no one has heard their conversation.

This chapter is important, not only because of its plot developments (some which will only become obvious later), but also because it is an excellent example of Dickens's descriptive, mood-setting writing style.

Chapter 27 After searching through Mrs. Corney's belongings and assuring himself that she is sufficiently rich, Mr. Bumble proposes and she accepts. Then he goes to tell Mr. Sowerberry about the body of the dead pauper woman, but instead finds Charlotte feeding oysters to Noah Claypole.

Chapter 28 Oliver awakens in the ditch where Sikes left him, and makes his way to the very house he was forced to break into. The servants are overjoyed at having "caught one of the thieves," but Miss Maylie, whose guardian is mistress of the house, orders that Oliver be brought to bed and the doctor sent for.

Chapters 29–30 The doctor, Mr. Losberne, arrives and tells the women of the house, Rose Maylie and Mrs. Maylie, to come see "the thief." The women instantly take pity on Oliver after hearing his miserable story. The doctor tries to get the boy off the hook by persuading the servants that they cannot swear that this boy was the thief.

Chapter 31 Mr. Losberne creates a plot to convince the police that Oliver is innocent. Mr. Losberne disarms the servant, making it look as if no one could have been shot during the break–in. The police leave, and Oliver is now in the caring hands of the doctor and the two Maylie women.

Chapter 32 Oliver's life improves as he lives with the Maylies. His goodness and love of simple beauty are apparent when he goes with them for a three–month stay at a country cottage. Oliver's only sadness occurs when the doctor takes him to visit Mr. Brownlow and they discover that he has gone to the West Indies. Oliver desperately regrets not being able to explain why he never returned on the day the thieves kidnapped him.

Chapter 33 Oliver's health flourishes with the lush summer weather. In contrast, Rose Maylie (Mrs. Maylie's ward) falls deathly ill, and Oliver runs into a "madman" in town who curses him and wishes "death on his shoulders." The chapter culminates with Rose coming close to death. But good wins over evil: Rose survives, and her brush with death has a maturing effect on Oliver. These incidents reflect Dickens's hidden optimism and his fundamental faith in goodness.

Chapter 34 Mrs. Maylie's son, Harry, comes when he hears of Rose's illness. He announces his intention to tell Rose of his long and undying love for her, but his mother has reservations. She fears that Rose will refuse him. Rose begins to recover quite rapidly, and life improves, until one evening Oliver falls asleep studying and wakes to find Fagin and the madman he met in town peering in through his window. We assume now that this madman must be Monks.

Chapter 35 Harry, Mr. Losberne, Giles (the servant who shot Oliver), and Oliver all search for Fagin and Monks, but find no trace of them. Harry declares his love to Rose, who humbly says she returns his love, but that she cannot be his partner because of her "stained" background. Notice the conflict between love and social class.

Chapter 36 After asking Oliver to write once every two weeks to report how his mother and Rose are doing, Harry leaves with the doctor to return home to London. Rose sadly watches him leave.

Chapter 37 This chapter mocks the Bumbles' unhappy married life. Mr. Bumble feels impotent and Mrs. Bumble gains control. She beats him when he says men should command and women should obey. Later, she degrades him by giving him a tongue–lashing in front of the paupers.

Depressed, Mr. Bumble goes to a bar where Monks questions him about the woman who nursed Oliver's mother the night he was born. She is dead, but Mr. Bumble tells Monks that someone else may have information. Monks pays Bumble, and they agree to meet the next day.

Chapter 38 The woman with information is Mrs. Bumble herself. After demanding to be paid, she tells Monks the secret: the old woman who nursed Oliver's mother stole a locket with the name Agnes engraved on it from her when she died. Mrs. Bumble says she got the necklace from a pawnbroker after finding a receipt in the nurse's hand when she died. Monks takes the locket and throws it in the river.

Chapter 39 This chapter describes the everyday life of the thieves. (Note the language and dialogue Dickens uses to portray them.) Nancy goes with Fagin to get money to pay off Bill, and while they are there, Monks arrives. He and Fagin go to another room to talk, and Nancy sneaks after them to listen. She hears their conversation and it greatly upsets her, but she still gives Sikes the money.

Chapter 40 In this chapter, we see an important bonding between two women despite their different social positions. It also shows women playing an active role in the progression of the novel. Nancy goes to Rose Maylie and tells her that she heard Monks say that Oliver is his brother, and that he destroyed all evidence that would prove it. He also said that he will do everything he can to harm Oliver, even if it means extorting money from the Maylies.

Rose begs Nancy not to return to the thieves, but to redeem herself. Nancy says it's too late; she loves Bill, and no matter how cruel he is, she must return. She promises, though, that she will go to a certain bridge every Sunday night so that Rose can find her if she needs anything.

Chapter 41 Oliver accidentally learns that Mr. Brownlow is living in London, and he tells this to Rose. She sees this as her chance to help Oliver and goes directly to Mr. Brownlow. A "committee" of Rose, Mrs. Maylie, the doctor, Mr. Brownlow, Harry, and Mr. Grimwig is formed. They will try to save Oliver and secure him his inheritance. They decide that they must first find Monks, since he is the key to the puzzle.

Chapter 42 Noah Claypole and Charlotte have left the Sowerberrys and gone to London. They end up at the Three Cripples Inn, where Fagin and Barney eavesdrop on their conversation. Hearing that Noah is interested in thieving, Fagin talks to him about joining his band. After Noah gives himself and Charlotte the aliases of Mr. and Mrs. Morris Bolter, Fagin leaves.

Chapter 43 Noah meets Fagin, and during their discussion, we learn that the Artful Dodger has been caught and is going to be "transported for life." Noah is sent to the courthouse to find out what's going on. He sees the Dodger, who, after a great performance in court, is taken to a cell and locked away.

Chapter 44 Nancy feels awful; she is caught between her loyalty to the thieves and her traitorous discussion with Rose. Sunday night comes, but Bill won't let her go out. Fagin, who witnesses Sikes' treatment of Nancy, and Nancy's resulting desperation, becomes determined to find a way to manipulate her weakness and control her.

Chapters 45–46 Fagin hires Noah to follow Nancy; on Sunday night when she finally goes out, Noah follows. Nancy meets Rose and Mr. Brownlow at the bridge and gives them a description of Monks so they can find him. Mr. Brownlow recognizes Nancy's description of a scar on his neck and a nervous twitch. Rose and Mr. Brownlow again offer Nancy a life away from the thieves, but she refuses. Noah, having heard everything, runs back to tell Fagin.

Chapter 47 Fagin tells Bill that Nancy has betrayed them, and Bill goes home and beats her to death. This is a brutal, violent chapter, where the strange shadow of death that Nancy sensed earlier in the night becomes real.

Chapter 48 Sikes runs away to the country, terrified by the act he has committed and the idea of being caught. Nancy's dead eyes seem to follow him everywhere. After wandering for about a day, he returns to London and hides there. Knowing that his dog has always been seen with him before, he decides to drown it. But the dog runs away, as if to suggest that even he knows that Bill Sikes is a murderer.

Chapter 49 Mr. Brownlow captures Monks and takes him to his house. Here we learn that as a young man, Mr. Brownlow had been in love with a woman who died before they could marry. The woman's younger brother, who became an intimate friend of Mr. Brownlow, was forced to wed a woman ten years his senior. They grew to hate each other, and after having a son, Monks, they separated.

Monks' father (Brownlow's friend) met a beautiful young woman, Agnes, and was going to marry her after acquiring a huge sum of money, when he suddenly died of illness. Because there was no will, the money fell to his first wife and Monks.

Oliver, Agnes's son, was born in poverty and received nothing.

Mr. Brownlow accuses Monks of villainy and association with murderers, and Monks promises to swear in court what he knows and to give Oliver his share of the inheritance. Sikes and Fagin are about to be caught.

Chapter 50   At an old hideout, Toby, Tom, and another thief discuss Fagin and Bill. That night, Bill comes to the house. The thieves say he can stay, but Charley Bates arrives and swears to turn Bill in for the murder of Nancy. Just then, the angry crowds and the police arrive. Trying to escape, Bill accidentally hangs himself from the chimney. It is ironic that the crowd reacts so violently to the murder of Nancy; when she was alive she was considered sinful and dirty.

Chapter 51   More details of Oliver's history are revealed. Rose Maylie is Agnes's lost younger sister, and thus Oliver's aunt. Harry returns and says that he has given up his life of high society and wealth. This leads to his engagement to Rose. Sadly, we also learn that Little Dick is dead.

Chapter 52   Fagin has no sympathizers, and is sentenced to death. In his cell, he grows crazy with "fear and wrath" waiting for Monday, when he will be hanged. Mr. Brownlow and Oliver visit him to find out where he has hidden some papers that Monks gave him. Fagin tells Oliver where they are, then tries to use the boy to escape. However, he is unsuccessful.

Note how Fagin is simply called "The Jew" all the way through the book, especially in this chapter. The furious crowd is no doubt even more swayed against him because of his religion.

Chapter 53   Dickens concludes the lives of all the "good" people in the book: Harry and Rose marry, Mr. Brownlow adopts Oliver, and even Charlie Bates, repulsed by Sikes' murder, turns to an honest life. Dickens attributes this good fortune to God's mercy, and the book ends with the image of Agnes' spirit appearing in the church.

OTHELLO

ABOUT THE AUTHOR

See page 111.

THE BIG PICTURE

Shakespeare's *Othello* is the story of a Venetian general and his downfall at the hands of his treacherous officer Iago, and finally, his own blinding jealousy. Othello is one of Shakespeare's most compelling tragic heroes; he is noble and courageous, the epitome of soldier and man. His lofty stature makes his failure to see the truth about Iago all the more tragic.

Why you're reading this book:

- Although set in an era long gone, its themes are timeless and universal: good vs. evil; appearance vs. reality; loyalty; honor; deceit.
- Shakespeare makes his characters thoroughly real and human through minute, exquisite detail.
- Its very clever use of irony to demonstrate the insignificance of appearances over reality. The play illustrates that things or people may not be what they seem.
- Shakespeare is unrivaled as a poet and as a dramatist.

Your teachers are looking for:

- Ironic descriptions, such as repeated references to "honest Iago."
- Shakespeare's treatment of racism against the Moor.
- ago's methods of trickery.
- Clues to Iago's motives; his explanations to the audience for his actions.

KEY CHARACTERS

Othello: The Moor (Arab). He is a general in the service of Venice. He is highly intelligent, honorable, and generous. He is also fiercely passionate, which eventually causes his tragic downfall.

Iago: Othello's seemingly faithful officer. His deceptive trickery brings many of the play's characters to ruin. He is the ultimate infidel; he lacks any virtue and is described as a demon and a serpent. His soul is devoted to evil without any apparent causes or motives.

Brabantio: A senator, and Desdemona's father. A racist, he is somewhat severe and abusive to Othello. He had ideas for his daughter to marry into more acceptable hands.

Gratiano: Brother to Brabantio.

Lodovico: Kinsman to Brabantio.

Cassio: A gentleman and Othello's lieutenant. Noble yet somewhat arrogant, he unknowingly falls prey to Iago's web of lies.

Roderigo: A Venetian gentleman. He is a simple, foolish man. A fop and a gullible pushover.

Montano: A good friend of Othello's, he is the governor of Cyprus when the Turks decide to attack the island.

Desdemona: Daughter of Brabantio and wife of Othello. She is a compassionate and gentle woman. Desdemona is so innocent that she cannot conceive of evil in others.

Emilia: Wife of Iago, maid to Desdemona. A perfect portrait of common life, she has strong sense yet low intelligence. She is vulgar and, with the exception of the play's final scene, has weak principles.

Bianca: Mistress to Cassio. She lacks refinement and is portrayed as an obtrusive, somewhat annoying character.

ESSAY IDEAS

- Compare and contrast Iago to a modern-day villain.
- What is the irony of the nickname "Honest Iago?"
- Is Othello a noble man? Why or why not?
- Is it possible for a person to be as evil as Iago yet still feel sorrow and/or guilt for his or her actions?
- How does Desdemona's naivete contribute to Othello's downfall?
- What instances in the play address the theme of false appearances? (For example, Brabantio's warning to Othello about Desdemona.)
- What details about specific characters help paint clear pictures of their personalities (i.e. style of speech, mode of conduct, etc.)?

A SAMPLE ESSAY IN OUTLINE FORM

Honesty, or lack of honesty, as a central theme in *Othello*
- The dominance of appearances over reality throughout the play.
- The irony of the nickname "Honest Iago."
- Instances in which honesty is an issue:
  - Iago's betrayal of virtually everyone.
  - Desdemona's "betrayal" of her father.
  - Othello's dishonesty in dealing with Desdemona (withholding information from her)
  - Emilia's dishonesty in giving Iago Desdemona's handkerchief.

The play makes it difficult to distinguish between what *appears* to be "honest" or "dishonest" behavior, and what actually is—as exemplified by the nickname "Honest Iago." In the end, Iago is not the only character guilty of dishonesty; he is able to entangle the play's other characters in the web of lies he has created, making even the most virtuous characters act dishonest. All the characters in the play both use, and are used by, lies. This obscuring of the truth is what causes the play's tragic outcome.

PLOT SUMMARY

Act I, Scene i The play opens at night on a street in Venice. Roderigo and Iago are discussing the Moorish (Arab) general of the Venetian forces, Othello. Othello has overlooked Iago, his ancient, for the position of lieutenant, and has instead given the position to Cassio. Iago is greatly angered, and tells Roderigo that although he must still serve the Moor, he only does so out of obligation, with no true sense of love or devotion. As he tells Roderigo, "I am not what I am." Iago urges Roderigo to wake Brabantio, the father of the beautiful Desdemona. Desdemona and Othello have been secretly married, and Iago wants to make this known to Brabantio in an insensitive and cruel fashion. Referring to the marriage of Desdemona, Iago and Roderigo begin yelling to the old man that he's been robbed by thieves, and that "half his soul has been lost."

When Brabantio is fully aroused and at the height of his anger, Iago conveniently tells Roderigo that he must slip away, for it would look bad if Othello found out that he had caused this disturbance. The scene closes with Brabantio calling for a house to house search for his daughter, Desdemona.

Act I, Scene ii Iago has run to Othello, although he doesn't mention the chaotic scene from which he's come. He asks Othello about his wife and warns him that Desdemona's father is angry about the relationship. Iago fails to mention that it was he and Roderigo who pushed Brabantio into such a furious state.

Cassio, Othello's lieutenant, enters with a few officers. He tells the Moor that Othello is needed in Cyprus; the Turks are planning to attack the island and Othello's forces must defend it. Iago informs Cassio of Othello's marriage to Desdemona. Brabantio, Roderigo, and several officers enter. Brabantio confronts Othello, accusing him of using evil mysticism to woo Desdemona into his arms. He calls for Othello's imprisonment. Othello explains that even if he were to obey Brabantio's orders, he has been called to Cyprus on important business by the Duke. Brabantio brushes this off as trivial and calls for Othello to be taken away.

Act I, Scene iii In a council chamber, the Duke, senators, and officers are discussing a Turkish fleet's approach to Cyprus. A sailor rushes in, reporting that the Turkish fleet is headed for Rhodes. The senator protests that this change of course is really a ruse staged to fool Othello's army. He argues that since Cyprus is so much more important to the Turks than Rhodes, it simply would not make sense for them to neglect Cyprus and attack Rhodes. The Duke agrees with the senator.

A messenger enters, confirming the senator's suspicion that the Turks are actually planning to attack Cyprus, not Rhodes. Brabantio, Othello, Iago, Roderigo, and several officers enter the chamber. Brabantio announces the purpose of his visit, which is to find his daughter and determine if Othello's story is true or false. Othello again asserts his innocence and reminds those in the room that Desdemona has fallen in love with him of her own will.

Iago is sent to find Desdemona so that she may tell her story herself. She returns with Iago. Brabantio asks Desdemona to explain her position, obviously feeling confident that his suspicions about Othello will be confirmed. Desdemona explains that her devotion is to the Moor. Brabantio nobly bows out, admitting his error.

The Duke and Othello begin to discuss the Turks' plans for an attack on Cyprus. It is decided that Othello will go to Cyprus, assume the position of governor from Montano, and defend the island against the Turks. Desdemona wants to go to Cyprus with Othello; the Moor decides that she will travel with Iago. Before Othello and Desdemona exit, Brabantio warns Othello that Desdemona has deceived her own father, and that she may do the same to him.

Iago and Roderigo are left alone. Roderigo confesses his fondness for Desdemona, and the two begin to discuss Roderigo's pain in seeing her leaving with Othello. Iago repeatedly urges Roderigo to put money in his purse in preparation for the day when Desdemona will tire of Othello and perhaps run to Roderigo. The true motive behind Iago's advice is to take the money for himself—he would never advise anything unless it proved profitable for him.

In the closing soliloquy, Iago, alone on stage, reveals his plans of trickery. In an attempt to earn Cassio's position and make himself look noble, he will make Cassio appear to have had an affair with Desdemona. He knows that the trusting Moor will be easily convinced of the infidelity by his "friend" Iago.

Act II, Scene i The scene opens on a platform at a seaport in Cyprus. Montano and a gentleman are surveying the extremely rough waters, predicting that the Turkish fleet will drown if they are not protected. A third man enters to tell of the destruction of the Turkish fleet that a Venetian ship has seen. Cassio is said to be onshore. The men discuss Cassio's worries about Othello's safety. Cassio then enters, assuring the men of Othello's strength and expertise. Montano and Cassio discuss Desdemona's beauty and worth.

Desdemona, Emilia, Iago, Roderigo, and some attendants enter. Desdemona asks Cassio for news about Othello. He replies that he has none, but is confident that Othello is fine. Cassio greets Emilia and a witty exchange begins between Iago and Desdemona. Iago explains his theories about women, his wife in particular. Desdemona asks Iago how he would describe her. Iago answers with a rhyme about fairness, wisdom and wit. Iago continues the game with more poems. Cassio and Desdemona chat while Iago looks on, plotting to set Cassio's trap.

Othello and his attendants enter. Desdemona and Othello greet each other passionately. Iago, bitter, comforts himself in the knowledge that he will soon be destroying this happy scene.

Othello, Desdemona, and attendants exit, and Iago tells Roderigo that Desdemona is in love with Cassio. Iago explains that Cassio possesses everything the Moor lacks: beauty and manners, among other things. Roderigo protests that Desdemona is too noble for that kind of infidelity. To prove his point, Iago twists the smallest indications of friendship between Desdemona and Cassio into lusty passion plays.

Roderigo exits, and Iago gives a soliloquy about his passion for Desdemona. He suspects the Moor of having an affair with Emilia, his wife, and that he must take revenge, "wife for wife." Iago goes on to speak of his plans to destroy Cassio and have Othello love him.

Act II, Scene ii On the street, a herald enters with a proclamation. He announces Othello's call to celebrate his wedding and his defeat of the Turks.

Act II, Scene iii In a hall in the castle of Cyprus, Othello, Desdemona, Cassio, and attendants enter. Othello advises Cassio to be on the lookout for the evening. Cassio agrees to do so, and Othello leaves with Desdemona and his attendants.

Iago enters, and Cassio tells him of their guard duty for the evening. Iago talks of Desdemona's charming ways, implying that she is perhaps not as honest as all believe her to be. Cassio innocently agrees with Iago. Iago encourages Cassio to drink in celebration; he at first protests, but Iago persuades him, and Cassio leaves to call in Montano and other men to drink with them. Iago plays along with the charade of celebrating with the men, all the while planning to get the others drunk. Cassio, very drunk, leaves to do his duty for the evening, assuring the others of his sobriety. Roderigo enters, and Iago sends him after Cassio.

Cassio runs back in, chasing Roderigo. He accuses him of being a knave for trying to teach him his own duty. A fight ensues between Montano and Cassio as Montano tries to hold him back.

Othello hears the noise and enters. Iago claims he doesn't understand what the cause of the skirmish is, when in actuality he had deliberately sent Roderigo out so that an argument between him and Cassio would begin. This plants the seeds of doubt and mistrust in the mind of Othello, who now thinks he sees a side of Cassio he has not seen before. Othello thanks Iago for his honesty in trying to help him clear up the matter.

Cassio speaks to Iago of his lost reputation, the most valuable thing he possesses. Iago assures Cassio that reputation means nothing. Cassio tells Iago he will talk to Desdemona in the morning to try to clear up the matter; he hopes that Desdemona will put in a good word for him to Othello. Left alone, Iago reveals how Cassio's talking to Desdemona plays into his plan: it will allow Iago to convince Othello that Desdemona is defending Cassio because of her love for him. Iago ends his soliloquy saying that he will use Desdemona's good will towards Cassio to destroy them all.

Roderigo enters to tell Iago that he is returning to Venice because he has no money left. Iago persuades him not to go, and tells him to relax and get some sleep. Iago plots his evil influence on Othello; he plans to arrange the meeting between Cassio and Desdemona in such a way that Othello will see Cassio visiting Desdemona and his suspicions will be aroused.

Act III, Scene i At the castle, Cassio, a clown, and some musicians enter. The clown jokes with the musicians and then tells them that the general would prefer that they leave, as he does not want to hear their music. Cassio asks the clown if he's heard or seen Iago, because he needs to speak with Emilia, his wife, about talking to Desdemona. The clown exits, and Iago enters. Cassio asks him to send in Emilia so he may ask for permission to speak with Desdemona. Iago complies, telling Cassio he will even help get Othello out of the way so that he and Desdemona can speak easily. Iago exits.

Emilia enters, and Cassio asks to speak with Desdemona alone. Emilia permits him to come in.

Act III, Scene ii Othello, Iago, and other gentlemen are in a room in the castle. Othello gives letters to Iago to give to a "pilot," thus fulfilling an obligation to the senate. Iago agrees to deliver the letters. Othello asks to see his troops' fortification, and the gentlemen answer that they will serve their leader however he wishes.

Act III, Scene iii Desdemona, Cassio, and Emilia are in the castle garden. Desdemona assures Cassio that she will do all she can for him when talking to Othello. She promises Cassio she will have his friendship with Othello patched up soon.

Cassio voices his concern that Othello will forget his love and devotion. Desdemona again assures Cassio that she will work tirelessly to have Othello forgive him. Emilia tells Desdemona that Iago is approaching, and Cassio tells her that he must leave. Desdemona asks him to stay, but he tells her he is uncomfortable and must go.

Othello and Iago enter. In this crucial segment of the scene, Iago turns to Othello and tells him of his "suspicions" about Cassio and Desdemona. Iago has begun to poison Othello's mind against Cassio.

Desdemona greets Othello and tells him of her visit with Cassio. She pleads for Othello to forgive Cassio, and asks Othello to call him back to speak to him. Othello tells her he will do it some other time. Desdemona again asks Othello when he will speak to Cassio. Othello twice tells Desdemona he will not deny her wishes, yet he wants the matter to rest until a later date. Desdemona stubbornly persists, confused as to why Othello is not respecting her wishes. Othello's anger grows. Desdemona leaves with Emilia, telling Othello that whatever his wishes are, she will respect them.

A crucial exchange takes place between Othello and Iago. Iago shrewdly implies his suspicions about Cassio and leads Othello into a jealous, paranoid state. Othello urges Iago not to withhold any knowledge he had concerning Desdemona and Cassio. In one of the most famous passages in the play, Iago warns Othello of "jealousy...the green-eyed monster."

Othello seems to come to his senses,

reassuring himself that Desdemona chose him, and that before he accuses her of anything, he must see it for himself. Iago acts as though he is pleased with this statement. Yet he reminds Othello that Desdemona deceived even her own father.

Iago acts apologetically to Othello, claiming that he is sorry to cause him such grief, but that it is simply his love for his leader that drives him to do it. Othello says good-bye to Iago, reminding him to let him know if he hears anything. Before leaving, Iago tells Othello not to worry about Cassio unless Desdemona makes an attempt to see him, in which case Othello should be worried. Alone, Othello speaks of his inadequacies. He also curses marriage, and claims he would rather be a toad and live in a dungeon than have his wife be with others.

Desdemona and Emilia enter, and Desdemona tells Othello it is time for dinner. Othello tells her of his headache, and Desdemona hands him her handkerchief, which he pushes away. It drops to the floor, unnoticed. Desdemona and Othello leave together. Emilia picks up the handkerchief, which was the first gift Othello ever gave to Desdemona. She stashes it away to give to Iago, remarking that he has asked her to steal it from Desdemona many times, although she doesn't know why and doesn't seem to care.

Iago enters, and Emilia tells him of her find. She asks Iago what he needs the handkerchief for, and he grabs it, avoiding the question. Emilia exits. Iago explains what he plans to do with the handkerchief: he will leave it for Cassio to find. Othello will then find out that Cassio has it, and his suspicions will grow even stronger. Othello enters near the end of Iago's speech, managing to hear Iago say that Othello will never again have the security and contentment that he knew such a short time ago. Othello questions Iago, telling him it is bet-ter to know the awful truth than to be left in the dark knowing nothing.

Othello warns Iago that if he is wrong about Desdemona and Cassio, his punishment will be hell, to which Iago responds that his own honesty has been wrongly turned against him. Fooled by Iago's apparent innocence, Othello feels guilty and asks Iago to stay. He pours out his insecurities to Iago, telling him how unsure he is about both Desdemona and Cassio. He again asks Iago for proof of Desdemona's disloyalty.

In an outright lie, Iago tells Othello of a night he slept by Cassio and heard him cry out in his sleep for Desdemona. Othello is torn apart by this. Iago further enrages Othello by telling him that he has seen Cassio with Desdemona's handkerchief. Othello talks of violent revenge and asks Iago to take care of Cassio's death. Iago tells him it is as good as done. He also tells Othello to let Desdemona live. The two exit together.

Act III, Scene iv Desdemona, Emilia, and a clown are before the castle. Desdemona asks the clown to go find Cassio. She then asks Emilia about her missing handkerchief. Desdemona tells Emilia it is a good thing Othello is not jealous; otherwise this missing handkerchief would cause quite a stir.

Othello enters, greets Desdemona, and takes her hand. Referring to her friendly heart and "free" spirit, he talks of how moist and warm they are. He is, of course, making insinuations about the affair that he believes she is having.

Knowing Desdemona doesn't have her handkerchief, Othello asks her for it, testing her. He angrily questions her about the lost handkerchief; she answers nervously that it's not lost, wondering about his abrupt change in character. In the midst of his anger, as he yells for the handkerchief, Desdemona asks that Othello speak to Cassio. Othello exits angrily.

Emilia comments that Othello is very jealous, and Desdemona says she has never seen him this way. Emilia comments on men's mistreatment of women. Cassio and Iago enter, and Cassio tells Desdemona he has given up trying to win Othello's favor. Desdemona urges him to be patient. Iago, pretending he knows nothing of Othello's rage, asks if Othello is angry, saying he will go after him to settle the matter. Iago exits.

Desdemona wonders aloud what is wrong with Othello, guessing it is something unrelated to her that has caused his anger. Emilia tells Desdemona to hope it is not jealousy that causes Othello to act this way. Desdemona innocently responds that Othello has no reason to be jealous. Desdemona and Emilia exit.

Bianca, Cassio's mistress, enters. He asks her to copy the pattern on the handkerchief he has found—Desdemona's handkerchief. Bianca thinks it is a gift from another mistress, and accuses Cassio of keeping two lovers. Cassio insists he has no other lover, and Bianca calms down. Bianca asks to stay with Cassio, but he says he is too preoccupied with business to see her. She understands, and they leave.

Act IV, Scene i Othello and Iago discuss the handkerchief. In a rage of frenzied questioning about Cassio, Othello falls into a trance-like state. Iago, to the audience, speaks of the "medicine" that he has used on Othello to make him so confused. Cassio enters, wondering what is wrong with Othello. Iago warns him of the Moor's trance-like state. Cassio advises him to rub his temples to wake him. Iago urges Cassio to leave, as the Moor would be angry to see him when he awoke.

Cassio leaves, and Othello wakes up, asking Iago if Cassio has confessed to his affair with Desdemona. Iago tells Othello

that while he was "asleep," Cassio entered the room, and Iago asked him to return later. Iago plans to engage Cassio in a conversation about Bianca, his mistress. To further his plan, Iago will let Othello overhear the conversation, telling him it is Desdemona they are discussing, not Bianca.

Othello, as planned, listens in on Iago's and Cassio's conversation, fuming at the notion that it is Desdemona they are discussing. Bianca enters, screaming at Cassio about the handkerchief he gave her to copy the pattern from. Othello sees the handkerchief, and his fury grows even greater. Bianca assumes because of the handkerchief that Cassio has another mistress, and she is furious. She leaves, and Cassio soon follows. Iago and Othello discuss the conversation between Iago and Cassio, Iago all the while helping to convince Othello of Desdemona's "crime."

Lodovico, Desdemona, and attendants enter. Desdemona tells Lodovico about the falling out between Othello and Cassio and asks him to help resolve it. Lodovico asks about it, and Desdemona innocently mentions her love for Cassio and her desire to have things between him and Othello patched up. Othello, infuriated by Desdemona's response, hits her.

Othello bids Desdemona to leave, then calls her back to taunt her in front of his guests. She leaves, completely upset and ashamed for something she knows nothing about. Lodovico expresses disgust and shock at Othello's actions. Iago and Lodovico discuss the "changes" in Othello; Iago advises Lodovico to watch Othello's behavior closely in the future.

Act IV, Scene ii Othello questions Emilia about Desdemona and Cassio. Emilia denies the suspected love affair between them and says she would lay down her soul to defend Desdemona's honesty. Othello asks Emilia to get Desdemona so he may speak to her.

Desdemona enters and asks Othello what is wrong; he is at his wit's end trying to determine if his wife is honest or not. Othello asks bizarre questions, while Desdemona grows confused and nervous from her husband's odd behavior. Othello cries that Desdemona is dishonest, while she insists she is innocent.

Emilia enters the room to hear the final words of Othello's speech. He accuses Desdemona of being a whore and leaves the room. Emilia, shocked by his behavior, questions Desdemona about it. Desdemona is utterly lost, and asks Emilia to place her wedding sheets on her bed that night.

Emilia exits, thinking this an odd request. She reenters with Iago so that Desdemona may talk with him. She asks Iago what has driven Othello into such a frenzy. Iago feigns ignorance, claiming that he couldn't possibly imagine what has caused Othello's craziness. Iago assures Desdemona that business matters are probably the cause. Desdemona and Emilia exit.

Roderigo enters and chides Iago for lying to him all the time. He claims he will not put up with it anymore. Iago is amused by Roderigo's small display of insight and tells Roderigo of his plan to win Desdemona. Iago explains that there is an order from Venice for Cassio to replace Othello in rank. This would mean that Othello and Desdemona would leave Cyprus. But, Iago tells Roderigo, if Cassio for some reason couldn't take the position, then Othello and Desdemona would have to remain. Thus, Iago plans to have Roderigo murder Cassio. The two exit, Iago further explaining the plan.

Act IV, Scene iii Othello, Lodovico, Desdemona, Emilia, and attendants enter another room in the castle. Before Othello and Lodovico leave to take a walk, Othello tells Desdemona to get to bed immediately, and to dismiss Emilia. Desdemona agrees, and tells Emilia of his request for her to leave.

Emilia is surprised, yet tells Desdemona she has laid the wedding sheets on the bed as Desdemona requested. Desdemona, half joking, tells Emilia that if she should die this evening, she should be wrapped in the wedding sheets. Emilia dismisses this as foolishness. She helps Desdemona prepare for bed while Desdemona sings a sad song, an omen of the events to come.

Desdemona, revealing her absolute innocence, asks Emilia if she thinks there are women who abuse their husbands by lying or cheating on them. Emilia replies yes. The two women discuss if they would commit such sins for "all the world." Desdemona says she would not. Emilia claims it is a husband's fault if a woman cheats. Desdemona bids Emilia good night.

Act V, Scene i On a street in Cyprus, Iago prepares Roderigo for the murder of Cassio. Roderigo mentions that he doesn't really know why he is going to murder Cassio. Iago, in an aside, claims that regardless of who dies, he will benefit. Cassio enters, and Roderigo attempts to strike him. Cassio draws his sword and wounds Roderigo. Roderigo cries out, while Iago wounds Cassio and exits. Cassio cries out and falls.

Othello enters as Cassio calls for help and is joyous over Iago's "honesty and bravery." He exits after anticipating out loud the horrors to come to Desdemona. Meanwhile, Cassio and Roderigo continue to call for help.

Iago reenters with a light. Iago, Lodovico and Gratiano find the injured Cassio, and Iago pretends to have no idea who has done this. Iago calls to Lodovico and Gratiano to aid Cassio, while Roderigo also calls for help. Cassio points to Roderigo as his attacker, and Iago stabs Roderigo.

Roderigo curses Iago as the dog that he is.

Cassio, in the meantime, has a severed leg, for which Iago offers his shirt as binding. Bianca enters, asking about the disturbance. Iago tries to tie Bianca in with Roderigo's attempt on Cassio's life. Cassio had eaten at her house that night and Iago argues that she was conspiring to kill him. Emilia enters, asking what the disturbance is. Iago explains that Cassio has been hurt by Roderigo and others, and that Roderigo is now dead.

Iago asks Emilia what she knows of Cassio's whereabouts before the incident. She replies that she doesn't know where he went after he ate at Bianca's house. The two accuse Bianca of conspiring to have Cassio killed. Bianca insists that she is innocent.

Act V, Scene ii Desdemona is asleep in her bedchamber in the castle. Othello enters and gives a monologue about his tormented heart. He contrasts Desde-mona's beauty and purity with her deceitful ways. Desdemona awakens. Othello makes a reference to killing, which Desdemona nervously picks up on. She still does not know the cause of his torment.

Desdemona asks for mercy, desperate in her confusion. Othello tells her to confess her sins, which of course do not exist. Othello asks about the handkerchief that was in Cassio's possession, and she replies that he must have found it.

Othello accuses her of lying, calling her a strumpet. The tragic momentum of the scene builds as he begins to strangle her. Emilia hears noises and begs Othello to let her in; when he finally unlocks the door, she tells Othello of Roderigo's murder. Desdemona tries to speak, and Emilia, astonished, wonders where this cry comes from. Desdemona is alive to utter her final statement that she and her lord, Othello, are both innocent.

Desdemona dies. As Othello explains her "whorish" ways, Emilia realizes that he has killed her. He tells Emilia that Iago knew of Desdemona's affair with Cassio all along, and that he was the one who told Othello of Desdemona's misdeeds. Emilia, knowing of Iago's dishonest, cruel ways, is appalled. She cries murder.

Montano, Gratiano, Iago, and others enter. Montano asks what the matter is. Emilia asks Iago if he has told Othello of Desdemona's "wrongdoings." Emilia scorns Iago for lying, and all are struck by the horror of the situation.

Emilia curses Othello for killing sweet Desdemona. Othello explains that the knowledge of the affair between Desdemona and Cassio, which he claims Cassio admitted, led him to murder her. Emilia, incredulous of Othello's explanation, insists that she will tell the truth.

Iago tries to stab Emilia to prevent her from revealing his misdeeds. Othello, realizing his awful mistake, runs at Iago, while Iago stabs Emilia from behind and exits. Gratiano sees what Iago has done, while Emilia falls. Before dying, she reminds Othello of Desdemona's purity and innocence.

Lodovico, Montano, Cassio, and officers reenter with Iago, the prisoner. Othello wounds him, and Iago spitefully taunts Othello with the fact that he is merely wounded, not killed. Othello expresses pleasure in this notion, as he would rather have him alive to experience the pain.

Othello asks Cassio how he got the handkerchief. Cassio tells him that he found it in his chamber. Othello, now sure of his horrible mistake, stabs himself and falls upon Desdemona's bed.

Lodovico closes the drama addressing Iago, telling him that the "tragic loading of this bed" has been entirely his doing.

PLATO'S REPUBLIC

ABOUT THE AUTHOR

Plato (ca. 438–348 B.C.) was born in Athens, Greece, which was at the time at war with Sparta. After living through many revolutions and governments, Plato finally came to the conclusion that government existed only to serve itself.

A major influence on Plato was Soc-rates, his friend and teacher. Socrates is considered one of the foremost philosophers in all of history, and is an almost mythic figure. He and Plato would engage in long philosophical arguments; these became the basis for much of Plato's writing. Socrates was put to death by the Athenian government in 339 B.C. Plato wrote of the death of his teacher in the *Apology* and *Phaedo*. It is generally thought that the Socrates of the *Republic* speaks for Plato.

Plato also founded the Academy, a school designed to educate future rulers. (Plato's ideas on the education of rulers make up a large part of the *Republic*.) His most famed student was Aristotle.

THE BIG PICTURE

Plato's *Republic* is a philosophical discussion centered around Socrates. Plato used this dialogue form to set forth many of his philosophical beliefs. *The Republic* is not just a dry academic discussion, however; it is a lively and often witty debate on the meaning of life.

Why you're reading this book:
- With its colorful images and back-and-forth discussions, the *Republic* is the most accessible philosophy you may ever read.

Your teachers are looking for:
- Analogies: Plato uses analogies to explain his ideas and arguments. Look for them throughout the book. If you can grasp the analogies (not always an easy task), you will grasp Plato's philosophy.
- Plato's Ideal State.
- Plato's class divisions.
- Plato's use of questions to answer and explain arguments.

The *Republic* is unlike most literature you will ever read—neither a story, nor a play, nor a dry philosophical essay. It is a discussion mostly among three men (Glaucon, Adeimantus, and Socrates) that takes place in one room. The *Republic* presents Plato's ideas on the philosophy of government; he speaks through Socrates, his real–life teacher.

Note: it is very interesting to compare Socrates's "ideal state" in the *Republic* with some of the more modern "ideal states," or dystopias, discussed in novels reviewed in this book. See *Brave New World* (page ooo) and *1984* (page ooo).

KEY CHARACTERS

Socrates: The central figure in the book. He was Plato's teacher and friend; it is through him that Plato illustrates his own philosophy.

Adeimantus and Glaucon: Plato's older brothers, they are his partners in discussion for most of the book. Their main function is to ask questions and pose arguments.

Thrasymachus: A Sophist, one of the breed of philosophers that Plato detested.

The Sophists demanded money for their "wisdom."

Cephalus: The old businessman in whose house the discussion takes place. He only appears at the very beginning.

Polemarchus: Cephalus' son. He also participates minimally in the discussion.

ESSAY IDEAS

- What role does Thrasymachus play in the Republic?
- What do you think of Plato's Ideal State? Is it a realistic model of society?
- Explain the use of analogies in the Republic.
- What do you think of Plato's class divisions? Are they fair?
- Discuss the education of Guardians. Is it complete? In your opinion, would this education produce the best rulers?

A SAMPLE ESSAY IN OUTLINE FORM

Explain Plato's analogy of the "cave of belief" and what it illustrates.

- Plato uses the analogy of the man living in the cave to illustrate the four levels of the human knowledge, from lowest to highest:
  - Belief of images.
  - Belief of actual things.
  - Knowledge of Forms.
  - Knowledge of Goodness.
- As the man goes from the cave into the outside world, he passes through four stages of mental capacity:
  - In the cave: only able to see shadows on the walls (belief of images—the lowest level of knowledge).
  - As he leaves the cave: able to see things outside, but not sure they are real (belief of actual things).
  - Outside the cave: able to see that the things outside are real (knowledge of Forms).
  - Understanding that the sun makes seeing things possible (knowledge of Goodness—the highest level of knowledge).
- Plato argues that men who achieve the highest level of knowledge must "return to the cave" to show others. It is their responsibility as philosophers to the rest of the people.

PLOT SUMMARY

BOOK I

Section I The *Republic* begins in a room in Cephalus' house, where the characters will remain throughout the book. Socrates and Cephalus are having a discussion about morality and wealth. Cephalus' stand is that money makes morality easy: if you are rich, you have no need to resort to lies and crime. Socrates disagrees, saying that morality and justice are not as simple as just telling the truth and avoiding crime. He gives the example of a man who borrows a knife from a friend. One day, the friend returns, very angry at someone, and asks for the knife back. Obviously, it would be wrong for the man to give the knife back to his friend, but to keep it away from him would require lying.

Cephalus doesn't take Socrates' bait and bows out. Polemarchus, however, is up to the challenge.

Section II The conversation becomes more focused; Polemarchus attempts to define Justice, a central theme throughout the book. Polemarchus and Socrates banter back and forth until Polemarchus comes up with his final definition: "Justice" means helping one's friends and hurting one's enemies.

Socrates goes to work on that statement quickly. He argues that we ourselves are not necessarily the people who can best help our friends in every situation. For example, in the event of illness, it is the doctor; in the event of building a house, it is the architect. The person best qualified to help our friends changes with every situation. Thus, Polemarchus' definition does not work as a code for "just" behavior.

More important to Socrates, we have no way of telling if our friends are truly good and our enemies truly evil. Polemarchus asserts that we can help evil people as long as they are our friends. He scrambles to redefine: he says that Justice is helping our friends as long as they are good, and hurting our enemies as long as they are evil.

But Socrates argues that in no circumstances is it acceptable to return wrong for wrong. By being evil to evil men, you can only make them more evil—certainly an unjust thing to do. Polemarchus' definition of Justice does not pass the test.

Section III Thrasymachus, who has been listening to Socrates' and Polemarchus' conversation and making annoying remarks, now demands that Socrates come out and tell the men his definition. Socrates says that he does not have a definition; he wants to hear one from Thrasymachus. The Sophist finally gives in and offers his "wisdom."

Justice, Thrasymachus contends, is defined by the interests of the ruling party. The laws of those in power are Justice; those beneath the ones in power must obey them. This argument, Socrates argues, hinges on the rulers always knowing what laws will be in their own best interest. Taking human error into account, this is an unlikely assumption. Thrasy-

machus, however, is not as quick to yield as Polemarchus. He says that rulers cannot make a mistake; they must always act in their own best interest or they will cease to become rulers.

Socrates then challenges the entire premise of Thrasymachus' conception of Justice. He argues that just as a doctor must help his patients, so must a ruler rule his subjects. "Ruling" includes acting in the best interest of one's subjects. Thrasymachus' flimsy treatise is quickly shot down.

Section IV Thrasymachus, not content with being outwitted by Socrates, expounds upon his view of Justice. He feels that Justice is something pursued by the ignorant; for intelligent men, Justice is not particularly useful. Thrasymachus states that it is the despot who enjoys the best life— by taking all resources and making his subjects slaves, he insures his own success. Thrasymachus finishes his speech and tries to leave.

But Socrates will not let him get off that easily. First, Socrates argues that even among the most unjust, there must be some justice (e.g., loyalty in a band of thieves), or there would be total chaos. He then states that everything in life must have a function—for instance, an eye's function is to see. Everything must also have a quality that enables it to perform its function—an eye has the quality of sight.

Man's "function" is to live. Now, how will he best fulfill that function? Certainly not by being unjust; that has already been shown to create chaos. Therefore, it must be by pursuing Justice. Socrates' arguments in this section are questionable at best. However, Thrasymachus realizes that he is quite overmatched and does not speak for the rest of the book.

Section V Glaucon and Adeimantus pick up the argument where Thrasymachus left off. Glaucon begins, first saying that he would like to be convinced that Justice is better than injustice, as he has not been swayed by Socrates' previous arguments. He decides to take up Thrasymachus' stand against Justice in the hopes that Socrates will effectively prove him wrong.

Glaucon argues that Justice arose out of necessity: without rules or laws to live by, everyone would live in constant fear. He states that people only act justly out of fear of retribution, because they have to. Finally, he takes issue with Socrates' view that Justice is valuable on its own. According to that argument, a completely just man would lead a perfect life; Glaucon states that many just men lead hard lives.

Before Socrates can answer, Adeimantus chimes in with arguments of his own. Justice is not good for its own sake, he says; people only aspire to Justice because it provides them with a good reputation and other rewards. Adeimantus also says it is impossible to state that injustice will be punished by the gods, who are as corruptible as mortals.

Remember, Glaucon and Adeimantus are only disagreeing with Socrates for the sake of debate. They truly want to believe that Justice is essential on its own. They hope that if they challenge Socrates, he will convince them of the value of Justice.

Section VI Socrates asks the pair if he may first define Justice in a community or state, then return to man. Glaucon and Adeimantus agree, and Socrates begins to outline his state.

First, he says that communities started because people needed each other to live. Thus, everyone in the community must perform a function that is useful to every-one else. With the needs of the community met, we can expect everyone to lead full and contented lives.

Before Socrates can look for Justice in his newly created "state," Glaucon interrupts. He argues that a state must do more than meet the basic needs of its subjects; it must have other amenities and luxuries, such as entertainment. Socrates agrees. But now our state has become so large, Socrates says, that we will begin to expand, perhaps into the territory of the state next to us. This will lead to conflict, and for this we will need soldiers.

These soldiers (called Guardians) will have to be the most physically strong of men, completely trained in all aspects of warfare. They must also be fully educated in order to know how to utilize their training wisely.

BOOK III

Sections VII–IX The Guardians, whom Socrates sees as the rulers of the state, must start their education early to prepare them for their duty. First, they must be told only stories that teach morality, and no stories that encourage cowardice. These stories must not be in the form of plays, because plays almost inevitably have evil characters. If an actor plays these parts well, he will take on some of the evil qualities associated with them.

Socrates also prescribes the kind of music Guardian trainees can hear—they must only be allowed to listen to music that is morally uplifting. The focus of Socrates' training program is to create a group of people with a full appreciation of the beautiful and moral things in life. Socrates spends only a small amount of time on the physical education of the Guardians. He argues that the education they will have received will make good health an obvious pursuit.

Section X Socrates now brings these Guardians back into his state. The wisest Guardians will be the actual rulers. The lesser Guardians, called Auxiliaries, will serve as the upholders of law and order. The final class will be made up of people not of the ruling class, but of the workers and artisans.

A problem arises with this new, class-based society: how are people kept performing their duties in their respective classes without trying to "jump" to other classes? Socrates turns to mythology for his answer.

He proposes a sort of theology for this new state, called the Myth of Metals. The myth states that each class has a certain alloy in its veins. For Rulers, it is gold; for Auxiliaries, silver; and for everyone else, bronze and iron. Therefore, one is born into one's class with no way of moving up or down. Socrates, while acknowledging that complete belief in this myth could take many years to achieve, hopes that it will insure each man's loyalty to his assigned position.

Socrates returns to his Guardians. To protect them from corruption, he states that they must have no excess money or properties. All that the Guardians have will be provided to them by the people they rule.

BOOK IV

Section XI To Adeimantus, it seems that the Guardians are getting a rather bad deal: they are the ruling class, but have none of the trappings of a governing body. Socrates agrees, but states that their happiness need not come from external wealth. Besides, this society has been created for the purposes of finding Justice; therefore, all classes must function for the benefit of the state as a whole. It would contradict the function of the community if the ruling class unjustly held all the wealth while the lower class had nothing. Socrates goes on to say that because its citizens are well educated, his state will need only a few laws.

Section XII Now that Socrates has created his "perfect" community, he says that we should be able to find in it the four virtues of courage, wisdom, discipline, and Justice. The first two virtues are found easily enough; wisdom in the highly educated ruling class, and courage in the Auxiliary class, the soldiers.

Discipline, unlike wisdom and courage, cannot be found in one class. It is found in the way the classes relate to one another: an orderly class system creates a disciplined society.

Socrates now turns to Justice. Without Justice, he argues, the first three virtues could not exist. So to find the existence of Justice, we have to discover which conditions made the first three virtues possible.

This is clear enough: all of the virtues could not exist unless each person does the job that he was born to do. It is that order—each individual doing the one thing he is best suited for—that brings about Justice. If different classes interfere with each other's work, injustice will ensue.

Socrates' reasoning, although highly involved and confusing, satisfies Glaucon and Adeimantus. He then sets out to discover Justice in man.

Section XIII We now realize why Socrates first insisted on discovering Justice in the state before man: his society built on three classes serves as a direct parallel to a man's mind. Socrates says that the mind has three distinct sections. First, the rational part (corresponding with the ruling class in the state); then, the emotions (the auxiliary class); and finally, desire (the working class). Just as in the state, the ruling class (reason) serves to govern the other two classes (emotions and desire).

We should be able to find courage, wisdom, discipline, and Justice in man as well as in the state. Wisdom is found in reason; courage is found in emotions; and discipline is found in a man whose reason rules his emotions and desire. Justice results from the orderly relationship of all three parts of man's mind. If each part of a man's mind performs its function, he will be a just man.

BOOK V

Section XIV Socrates, while defining Justice, has not answered the original question of whether Justice is essential for its own sake. To answer the question, Socrates decides to first contrast justice with injustice. Before he can go on, Polemarchus and Adeimantus interrupt, wanting to know more about the women and children in Socrates' state. Socrates now digresses from his definition of injustice to outline his community.

Women, like men, will be classified. They can be members of the ruling class. However, male and female Guardians will be kept separate, and there will no longer be any families. This is to prevent family quarrels and problems. Children will be raised together in nurseries, creating one single huge family.

To solve the problem of procreation, Socrates proposes festivals where men and women will be matched up according to class, then allowed to mate. It is obvious that Socrates, above and beyond anything else, wants order in his state.

Section XV The men in the room now take issue with Socrates. His state seems too farfetched to be useful. Socrates, how-

ever, argues that for their discussion they needed an ideal state, not necessarily a realistic one. He says that a perfect state will never come to pass "till philosophers become rulers in this world, or till those we now call kings and rulers really and truly become philosophers, and political power and philosophy thus come into the same hands." Glaucon presses Socrates to explain himself further, so Socrates begins to define "philosopher."

A philosopher, says Socrates, is one who is interested in knowledge, not belief. To illustrate the difference, he uses many different analogies. One of them is the analogy of Size. Size itself is unchanging, but relationships of size vary constantly—for instance, a man can appear huge next to a mouse but small next to a boat. This perception of size is belief; understanding the reality of size as constant is knowledge. This "Size" is called a Form of a quality, its abstract and unchanging reality (Beauty, Justice, and Goodness are other examples of Forms).

BOOK VI

Section XVI Because the philosopher has an understanding of Forms, he is best qualified to be a ruler. A person with a grasp of the Forms will always rule in the interest of the state, rather than in his own best interest.

Adeimantus, however, disagrees. He says that all the philosophers he knows are either completely useless or are con artists (like the greedy Thrasymachus). Socrates agrees, but he lays the blame on society, not philosophy. Society, with its corrupt politics and emphasis on material wealth, discourages the pursuit of knowledge. Socrates does state that while there may be no philosopher fit to rule at the present time, this does not mean that it could not happen in the future. A true philosopher could end "the troubles of states."

Section XVII It is clearly established that the philosopher is best suited to rule. Socrates then decides that his Rulers need to be even better trained, as they will be called upon to be both highly intelligent and highly principled. Their training will completely familiarize them with all Forms.

Glaucon then asks Socrates what he feels the most important Form is. Socrates answers that Goodness takes precedence over all other Forms. But what exactly is Goodness? Goodness, explains Socrates, is like the sun. The Sun provides light so that we can see; Goodness sheds "Truth" upon the Forms so that the mind can grasp them.

Section XVIII Socrates further explains Goodness and the different types of knowledge and belief. Goodness is the highest type of knowledge, because it allows all the other Forms to be understood. The next type of knowledge in the hierarchy is that of the Forms themselves.

Belief is divided into two parts; the perception of objects and the perception of images. Objects are things that we see that we can actually identify; images are things that for whatever reason we can see but cannot name.

BOOK VII

Section XIX Socrates explains these four divisions further. He asks Glaucon and Adeimantus to imagine a group of men that have been imprisoned in a cave all of their lives. In the cave, all they can see are the shadows and sounds of people outside projected onto the cave's walls. Their whole reality is these shadows. This state of being is the lowest form of belief.

Now, we take one of the men and show him, through a long tunnel leading into the cave, that there are real men and women that cast these shadows. This is the highest form of belief—he is now perceiving real objects. However, he does not necessarily believe that these "pictures" outside of his cave are real. So then we take that man and bring him outside. After a painful period of adjustment to the sun, he realizes that the objects he saw are real. Now he has achieved the knowledge of Forms. He will eventually understand that it is the sun that lets all these objects be perceived. He will then have achieved the highest form of knowledge, that of Goodness.

Finally, the man is taken back into the cave. This return to the "cave of belief" is necessary for any philosopher; philosophers must not only have knowledge of the Forms, they must also be willing to pass on that knowledge to those still stuck in belief. Glaucon, following Socrates' analogy, says that the man who returns to the cave will have to bear an unfair burden, as he will be unable to see in the dark. Socrates agrees, but points again to the true function of Rulers—they must serve the good of the community, not themselves.

Section XX Socrates then turns again to the education of the Guardians. Their original education, with its emphasis on character and body, is not enough; the education must also exercise the mind to its fullest potential. The Guardians will first be taught the five kinds of mathematics: basic arithmetic, both solid and plane geometry, astronomy, and "harmonics" (the math of musical scales).

Section XXI After grasping the concepts in all areas of math, the Guardians must move on to the more abstract thinking necessary for knowledge of the Forms. They will first learn the science that Socrates refers to as "Dialectic": the science of arguing logically. A full understanding of Dialectic will allow the Guardians a full understanding of Forms; Dialectic questions everything, and is the only way to find the absolute truth. This is the final stage in the schooling of Guardians.

Section XXII Finally, Socrates sums up his proposed education for Guardians as a six-step process. Progression to the next step hinges upon the successful completion of the previous step.

From birth until their late teens, Guardians will receive musical and literary education, as well as some mathematics. After this stage, those who go on will go through intense physical training, a three-year gym period. At the age of twenty, these students (now considered Auxiliaries), begin a ten-year mathematics course. At the end of ten years, those that remain take Dialectic for five years. The fifth step is fifteen years of apprentice ruling in lower-level government positions. Finally, at about the age of fifty, they are full-fledged Guardians.

BOOK VIII

Section XXIII At the request of Glaucon, Socrates leaves the topic of the education of the Guardians to return to Justice. In particular, he addresses the question of why it is better for a man to lead a just life for its own sake.

Socrates begins his argument by outlining the four kinds of unjust states: the timocracy (military rule), the oligarchy (rule by the wealthy), democracy (rule by the people), and the tyranny (rule by one man). The timocracy is the most just of these states; the tyranny, the least.

Socrates goes on to show how each unjust state creates unjust men. In a timoc-

racy, man is ruled by physical impulses; reason has lost control. A man in an oligarchy, while working hard and leading a fruitful life, does so only out of fear. A democratic man will have no rules and will only pursue the pleasures he desires. Finally, in a tyranny, man is controlled by only one thing, the lust for power. This lust will eventually drive him insane, as there is no way to satisfy it fully.

BOOK IX

Section XXIV Having shown the four kinds of unjust men, Socrates goes on to show why their lives are worse than those who lead just lives. First, a just man is balanced. He cannot be ruled by any one emotion, such as the tyrant's lust for power. Socrates then compares the three sections of the mind—reason, emotion, and desire—to the just man, the man in a timocracy, and the men in the three other unjust states.

If asked who had the best life, any of these men would answer, "I do." But it is only the just man who has the knowledge to accurately say that he has the best life. The other men are still "in the cave" and therefore unable to truly appreciate life. Finally, Socrates states that all the comforts of an unjust life are not real; only the comforts of the just man, who has full knowledge, are true pleasures.

Socrates' argument is complete (although the reader may not be anywhere near sifting through his logic). The just man, with his wisdom and balance, is guaranteed a happy life.

BOOK X

Section XXV This section, in which Socrates gives a criticism of the arts, is a departure from the rest of the book. Artists do not create things, he argues. A painting is just the presentation of an image, even further removed from its original Form. These representations appeal to the lowest part of the human mind, because they are mere illusions.

Socrates turns his criticism to theater. Drama, he says, tries to elicit emotion by showing other people's experiences on stage. If we give in to this emotion during a show, we will be unable to react correctly to our own experiences. Socrates concludes by saying that art has no place in his Ideal State.

Section XXVI Socrates now turns to the afterlife and the rewards that await the just man. Glaucon interrupts, asking if Socrates truly believes that the soul is immortal. Socrates answers that he does, and offers proof.

Things that decay, like the body, have a particular cause for their decay. For the body, it is old age. We have already seen that the most destructive thing to a man's soul is injustice; however, injustice does not destroy a man's soul. Therefore, nothing can, and the soul is immortal.

Section XXVII Socrates uses the myth of Er, a soldier who was killed in battle but came back to life, to illustrate the just man's rewards. Er, when he died, went to a place of four chasms. Two of them led to Heaven, two of them to Hell. Spirits in between the chasms told each soul that entered where to go; the upper right-hand chasm for just men, the lower left for unjust men. Just men traveled to Heaven; unjust men traveled into the bowels of the earth, where they paid for their sins many times over.

Once souls came out of the chasm, they went to the Fates, who gave them the choice of lives they would lead upon being reincarnated. The unjust would choose badly, while the just would choose a new life that promised peace and happiness; for instance, the famous warrior Odysseus chose the life of an ordinary man. These souls then drank from the River of Forgetfulness, so that they would not bring news of the afterlife into the world. Er was allowed to return without drinking, and was revived on his own funeral bed.

THE RED BADGE OF COURAGE

ABOUT THE AUTHOR

Stephen Crane (1871–1900) lived an exciting but tragically short life. Born in Newark, New Jersey, he was the youngest of fourteen children. Although his father, the Reverend Jonathan Crane, kept a strict Methodist household, Crane's earliest ambition was to become a professional baseball player. As a teenager, he gained notoriety for his attempts at balancing a pool cue on his nose and other pranks.

Crane first attended Claverach College, then Lafayette College and Syracuse University. He was asked to leave both Lafayette and Syracuse after one semester because his interests in baseball, gambling, and pool took precedence over his academic work.

In June of 1891, Crane moved to the Bowery, a rather seedy New York City neighborhood. He survived by doing freelance reporting for papers such as the *New York Tribune*. From his experiences in the Bowery, Crane wrote his first book, *Maggie: A Girl of the Streets*. He published the first edition under a pseudonym in 1893.

In December 1894, *The Red Badge of Courage* first appeared in serial form in several newspapers. It received little attention. When he published it as a full-length novel in the fall of 1895, however, it became an incredible success. Critics today cite *The Red Badge of Courage* as one of the great American novels.

During the last five years of his life, Crane traveled around the globe reporting for various newspapers. Some of his biographers claim it was an obsession with death that brought him repeatedly to war-torn countries, notably Greece during the Greco-Turkish war and Cuba and Puerto Rico during the Spanish-American war. While in Florida, he met and fell in love with Cora Howorth Stewart, the proprietor of a Jacksonville brothel. Crane died of tuberculosis five months before his twenty-ninth birthday while living in England with Cora.

THE BIG PICTURE

The Red Badge of Courage is a detailed psychological portrait of Henry Fleming, a soldier in the Union Army during the Civil War. It is a story not only of the horrors of war, but also of Henry's coming of age through his experiences.

Why you're reading this book:
- It captures the essence of an important historic period, the American Civil War.
- Crane's writing style is an early example of modern "realism" in fiction.
- ts use of symbols and color create intense, vivid imagery.

Your teachers are looking for:
- Symbolism:
  - War as a machine or beast.
  - Red and black representing courage, war, and death; yellow as cowardice and sickness.
  - Jim Conklin as a Christ figure.
- The portrayal of nature as hostile and/or indifferent.
- The transition in Henry's identity from outsider to leader.
- The irony of Henry's ideas about courage.
- The change in Wilson's personality.

- The novel as a reworking of the classic "voyage of the hero" structure.

KEY CHARACTERS

Henry Fleming, the youth: The principal character. An introspective, confused private in the Union Army. The process by which he gains and maintains his courage creates the main conflict of the novel.

Jim Conklin, the tall soldier: A friend of Henry's who seems comfortable with the idea of fighting. His courage and death are symbolic.

Wilson, the loud soldier: Also a friend of Henry's, both in the beginning and, even more, at the end of the book. He is brash and overconfident before the first battle, humble and calm afterwards.

Henry's mother: A strong farm woman and a widow. She accepts Henry's enlisting even though she needs Henry and feels he would be more useful on the farm than on the battlefield.

The tattered man: A wounded soldier. He accompanies Henry and Jim Conklin for a short time and upsets Henry by asking about his wounds. Henry's eventual abandonment of him is symbolic.

The cheery-voiced man: A mysterious character who guides Henry back to his regiment's camp. Henry never sees his face.

ESSAY IDEAS

- How does Crane's use of color help support the themes of the novel?
- Describe and explain the change in Henry Fleming over the course of the novel.
- Discuss the different types of conflict in the novel: man vs. man, man vs. nature, man vs. himself.
- Discuss the use of religious imagery in the novel.
- Do you feel this book is relevant to contemporary times? Why or why not?
- Discuss the character of Wilson and his function in the novel.
- Consider Crane's use of adjectives in place of names. How does this affect the themes of the novel?

A SAMPLE ESSAY IN OUTLINE FORM

Discuss the development of Henry Fleming's identity.
- He initially views himself as an individual:
  - He feels alternately superior and inferior to the other soldiers, but never equal to them.
  - He is more concerned with his own performance than the regiment's. While separated from his fellow soldiers, Henry enters a "dreamlike state" where he questions his place in the army.
  - He feels he is "one small piece of the larger whole" that must protect itself.
- His experiences away from his regiment bring him to understand and better accept his place as a soldier:
  - The dead soldier and the squirrel.
  - The procession of the wounded, the tattered man, and Jim Conklin.
  - His own wound.
- He returns to his regiment and to battle changed and better prepared:
  - n the next battle, he fights well and is highly praised.
  - As he leaves the battle, he feels strong and sure of himself for the first time.

PLOT SUMMARY

Chapter 1 The novel takes place during the American Civil War. It opens in the camp of an anonymous regiment in the Union Army. On this morning a tall soldier reports a rumor that the regiment is going to move and attack the enemy from behind. A loud soldier disputes the validity of the information and a fight breaks out. This news sparks a train of thought in a young private, Henry Fleming, the novel's main character.

The youth returns to his tent. Bathed by the sun, the tent takes on a yellow tone, symbolic of the youth's fear. He recalls his last days at home and his mother's reaction to his enlistment. He lies on his bunk trying to convince himself that he will not flee from the battle. Finally, he asks the tall soldier, Jim Conklin, whether he would run. Jim replies that he might run or he might stand and fight, depending on what the men around him were doing. This reassures the youth that he is not the only soldier with doubts about himself.

Chapter 2 Although the regiment does not move right away, they do move a few mornings later with the intent of coming around behind the enemy. Because of the delay, the youth is anxious for an opportunity to test himself. The day of the march, the soldiers' uniforms appear to have a "deep, purple hue," symbolic of the royal, heroic impression the youth has of the Army. He also sees the "red eyes" of battle peering from across the river. The Army is described as "one of those moving monsters wending with many feet." Even though Henry Fleming is part of this creature, he feels separated from it by his doubts.

Chapter 3 The regiment continues its move to the place of battle. The men begin to leave behind anything that is not necessary. "You can eat now and shoot," says the tall soldier to the youth. "That's all you want to do." The youth notices how out of place their uniforms look against the soft greens and browns of nature.

Henry starts to feel paranoid, expecting to see his death coming. He sees a soldier's corpse, foreshadowing the many deaths that he will witness that day. As the regiment is shuttled over the back of the battlefield, the youth questions the intelligence of the commanding officers. But suddenly, the brigades near his regiment go into action. Wilson, the loud soldier, approaches Henry and gives him a packet of letters. He is afraid he is going to die and he wants Henry to give the packet to his family.

Chapter 4 As the fight goes on, Henry's brigade remains still and watchful. The lieutenant of their company is shot in the hand and swears so colorfully that it seems almost funny. A regiment nearby begins to flee despite the curses of its commanding officers. This onslaught of terrified men tempts Henry and his companions to run as well. The frozen nature of this chapter emphasizes the uncertainty of war and the lack of control over his personal destiny that Henry feels.

Chapter 5 Someone shouts, "Here they come!" A general gallops by and orders the brigade to hold the enemy back. Crane places the reader in the midst of the battle scene by describing the yells, the sound of guns, the cries of the wounded, the smell of gunpowder and sweat, and the intense heat. This technique is particularly effective because Henry himself becomes lost in the fight. He feels so strongly connected to the battle that he cannot flee, but must remain and fight. As he fights, Henry realizes that none of the soldiers are heroes, just men fighting the best they can.

When a brief interval comes in the shooting, Henry notices the many dead and wounded men nearby. He also sees a small group of injured soldiers shuffling towards the rear. It astonishes him that the sky is still so blue and the sun is still shining in the midst of such pain and suffering.

Chapter 6 After a few moments, the Rebel Army begins another attack. Henry feels that the enemy soldiers must be a great deal stronger than he if they can continue to fight with so much intensity. In the smoke of the battle, Henry sees a nearby man run madly away. He panics, feeling he has been left to fight the enemy alone.

Henry throws down his gun and begins to run "like a rabbit," feeling threatened on all sides. He slows his pace only when the noises have died down and he has regained his sense of direction. At this point he hears some commanding officers recounting how the regiment Henry belongs to has held its position. Henry realizes his grave error. He has run from the battle without reason, confirming his worst fears about himself.

Chapters 7-8 This is one of the novel's more surreal chapters as Henry begins to experience himself away from the Army and within the larger context of nature. He tries to justify his own cowardice by being angry at the soldiers who stayed to fight. The "yellow fog" he sees hovering over the battlefield is symbolic of these thoughts. He feels completely alienated and the landscape appears harsh and indifferent. This is the beginning of Henry's personal change.

In the woods, he encounters a squirrel. When he throws a pine cone at it, it runs away. Henry sees this as a direct parallel to his escape from the battlefield. In a clearing further on, he finds a soldier's corpse sitting against a tree. He runs away, imagining that the corpse is pursuing him.

Ironically, the youth finds himself running back toward the battle. Nature seems to be more hostile than ever; his path is constantly blocked by trees and brambles. Closer to the fighting, he encounters a group of injured soldiers moving to the rear. He begins walking with them. A tattered man, trying to be friendly, asks Henry where he's been wounded. The youth panics and moves away from the tattered soldier, hoping to hide his shame.

Chapter 9 Henry, walking with the injured men, feels jealous and wishes that he had his own wound, his own "red badge of courage." A gesture of one of the men near him distracts him from his thoughts. He realizes that the man is Jim Conklin. Jim has a fatal wound in the side, but is still walking. Henry offers to help him along. Jim accepts only because he is afraid he might fall down in the road and be run over by wagons.

To prevent this, Henry and the tattered man direct Jim into the fields nearby to die. At this point, the character of Jim Conklin takes on metaphoric qualities. Crane seems to be using him to represent all the men who have sacrificed themselves to the gods of war. The religious overtones of this scene also set up Jim as a potential Christ figure.

Chapter 10 While moving away from Jim's body, the tattered man mentions that he is beginning to feel badly himself. He asks Henry again about his wound, telling him to take particular care if it is internal. He is correct in assuming the youth's wound is internal, but he does not realize it is mental, not physical pain that Henry suffers. Henry is so upset by the tattered man's inquiry that he runs away from him in the field. In leaving behind the tattered man, Henry leaves behind his ideal of the noble, wounded soldier. He moves on, envying the solders who are lucky enough to be dead.

Chapter 11 Henry wanders gloomily in the direction of the battlefield. He sees a large group of soldiers and wagons retreating and begins to feel a little better about himself. Unfortunately, a fresh group of infantrymen appears and pushes its way through the retreating soldiers toward the front. This conflict in the road is symbolic of Henry's current internal conflict: to return to the battle and fight, or to keep retreating.

Although he at first wants to return to his company, he realizes how tired and thirsty he is. He also does not have a gun. He knows the only way his friends will respect him now is if the Union Army loses the battle and everyone else has to retreat. Then, Henry thinks, the other soldiers will consider him a prophet. But if the Army wins the battle, he will be mocked and ostracized for his cowardice, "the sore badge of his dishonor."

Chapter 12 All this time, Henry has been in the area just behind the battle because he wants to find out who is winning. Suddenly, another wave of retreating soldiers comes rushing out of the forest, indicating to Henry that the Union Army has definitely lost. He tries to ask the hurrying men what is going on but they are all too nervous and afraid to answer. Finally, he grabs one man by the arm, determined to discover what has happened. The man is so panic-stricken that he hits Henry over the head with his rifle. Henry is dazed but tries to keep walking so that he won't fall in the road.

As the struggle with his body gets more difficult, a cheery-voiced stranger comes along and offers to bring him back to his regiment. The cheery-voiced man is a difficult character to explain because Henry never sees his face. He may be some sort of guide, or he may not be a "real" character at all. He may simply be a symbol of Henry's wound and the way it gives him acceptable passage back to his fellow soldiers.

Chapter 13 Wilson and the corporal are very glad to see Henry because they both thought he had died. Henry doesn't really have to explain himself because Wilson starts fussing over his wound. Later, he has some coffee and has his head bandaged. Henry goes to sleep in Wilson's blankets feeling, for the first time, "like his comrades." Crane uses color heavily in this chapter to set the scene around the campfire and describe the solders and the temporary peacefulness of nature.

Chapter 14 Henry wakes up in a pale morning light that makes his comrades look like corpses. The pain in his head distracts him from this vision, however, and he gets up to have breakfast. At this point Henry notices the change in Wilson; he has grown from a young soldier, brash and loud, to a person of quiet confidence. Wilson's change foreshadows the change Henry will undergo later. Wilson is referred to as "the friend" from this point on in the novel.

Chapter 15 Later that morning, as the troops are waiting for their marching orders, Henry remembers the packet of letters Wilson gave him the day before. He decides to keep it as a weapon in case Wilson starts asking any questions about what really happened to his head. Henry begins to feel very superior to Wilson and the other solders because no one has discovered how cowardly he acted the day before.

As Henry stands there congratulating himself, Wilson approaches him about the letters. Henry is too surprised to make a rude or condescending remark. He thinks Wilson is foolish for openly acknowledging his cowardly thoughts.

Chapters 16-17 Battle sounds surround the regiment, which is stationed in some trenches. Henry gets very annoyed when, after a short time, they have to retreat away from the battle. He begins to criticize the commander of the forces for his poor planning but is silenced by a sarcastic man who says, "Mebbe yeh think yeh fit the hull battle yesterday, Fleming." As they turn to fight, Henry begins to wonder aloud what they are doing and why. Wilson is much more complacent and reassures him that everything will be fine, even as the enemy opens fire again.

As the battle begins, Henry resents the enemy's persistence, feeling that he has earned a day's rest after his troubles the day before. He directs his anger at the Rebel Army and goes into a dreamlike state of rage that keeps him loading and firing his rifle even when there is a brief stop in the action. The rifle is used here and in the previous chapters as a symbol for power.

The lieutenant praises Henry for fighting like a "wildcat." The other soldiers are in awe of him. Henry feels dazed and surprised at his own behavior; he has become a hero without realizing it.

Chapter 18 During a pause in the battle, Henry and Wilson get permission to get water from a stream Wilson thinks is nearby. Although the stream is not actually there, they do get a good view of the battlefield. A general and his staff approach to have a conference. The general asks the officer what troops he can spare for a charge.

After a moment of thought, the officer volunteers the 304th regiment, the one which Henry and Wilson belong to. The officer says they "fight like a lot a mule drivers." The general replies that he does not think many of the "mule drivers" will make it back. This is an important conversation for Henry because it makes him realize his lack of importance as one individual in one regiment of a gigantic army.

The two men take the news of the charge back to their regiment. As the officers come to rally the regiment, Henry and Wilson exchange a glance acknowledging their fear as well as their decision to fight.

Chapter 19 Henry unconsciously begins to lead the charge. At first, the regiment does quite well, but as they tire they begin to slow down. Wilson fires a shot to renew the attack, and the troops begin to move forward again. The regiment moves on until it comes to a clearing. There is so much smoke in the air that no one is sure what is going on.

Henry, the lieutenant, and Wilson surge to the front of the group trying to persuade the men to cross the clearing. Henry's attention is suddenly drawn to the Union flag carried by the color sergeant. He sees all the things it represents to him—virtue and invulnerability. At that moment, the color sergeant is shot. As he falls, Henry and Wilson both dive to keep their flag upright.

Chapter 20 Turning, both holding the flag, Henry and Wilson see how depleted the ranks of the regiment are. Although each wants to bear the flag, Henry gains possession of it. He is intensely disappointed when the men begin to retreat toward the officer who called them "mule drivers," and feels great shame knowing the regiment has done nothing to prove the officer wrong. He and the lieutenant try to encourage the men to fight, but they are all run down.

Through the smoke Henry sees a mass of troops, but he cannot tell if they belong to the Union or the Rebel Army. His question is answered when his retreating regiment is attacked from behind. Henry moves quickly to the midst of the soldiers and plants the flag. He holds his ground, even when the Rebel soldiers come so close that he can see their faces and the newness of their uniforms.

The firing slows and the smoke clears to reveal a few corpses lying on the ground. The men in the regiment look around at each other, sharing their pride in themselves and their weapons.

Chapter 21 As the regiment hurries back toward the lines, the older soldiers tease them for turning back too quickly. The same officer that had called them mule drivers gallops up suddenly and begins yelling at the regiment for not fighting hard enough. Henry decides the officer must not have seen the fight to be carrying on that way.

After the officers leave, several men come up to Henry saying they heard the general talking about him. They say the general called Henry "a jimhickey" and said that both he and Wilson "deserve to be major generals." At this point Henry has nearly formed a new identity for himself within the regiment, in contrast to his earlier confusion regarding his place in the Army.

Chapter 22 Quickly, the Rebel soldiers begin another attack. As the color bearer,

Henry feels deeply involved in the fight but only as a "spectator." He sees the two armies as two waves crashing into each other, with the blue uniforms sweeping away the gray. His own regiment fights bitterly again, trying to prove the insulting officers wrong. But for all their efforts, they lose quite a few men in the battle.

Chapter 23 A colonel tries to rally the men to push forward despite their casualties. Henry sees the hope in pushing the Rebel soldiers back from the fence behind which they have retreated. He feels daring and exalted as he rushes ahead. He fixes his attention on the Rebel flag, determined to capture it. Suddenly, someone shoots the Rebel color bearer and as he falls, Wilson leaps the fence to grab the flag out of the dying soldier's hands. The men are jubilant; not only has the charge been successful, they have also captured four prisoners. Henry notices again that up close the Rebel soldiers seem much like himself.

Chapter 24 On the march back to camp, Henry reviews the events of the past several days. He feels very proud of all his accomplishments. But his flight from the first battle and his desertion of the tattered man haunt him and remind him of where he has been. He realizes his mistakes; he also realizes that his experiences will keep him from repeating them. He has gained a new perspective that enables him to forgive himself and to go on with his life.

THE REPUBLIC

See PLATO'S REPUBLIC.

ROMEO AND JULIET

ABOUT THE AUTHOR

See page 111.

THE BIG PICTURE

Romeo and Juliet is perhaps the best-known and most imitated piece of literature in modern history. It tells the story of Romeo and Juliet, young lovers torn asunder by the feud between their two families. This theme of "star-crossed lovers" is prominent throughout all literature, from Shake-speare to *West Side Story*.

Why you're reading this book:
- Shakespeare is considered to be history's foremost playwright, and *Romeo and Juliet* one of his most famed plays.
- It is a classic tragedy.
- Its plot—that of star-crossed lovers—is found in many works of all eras.
- t raises crucial questions about duty, honor, and filial responsibility.
- It depicts the age-old conflict between the older generation and the younger generation.
- Shakespeare's language is beautiful and full of imagery.

Your teachers are looking for:
- The play's central conflicts: age vs. youth; night vs. day; honor vs. love; law vs. nature.
- Imagery and Symbolism:
  - The sun as metaphor.
  - Mercutio's Queen Mab speech
  - The way characters are used to represent traits or themes (i.e., Capulet as tradition and order; Juliet as natural emotion and true love).
- The tragic mistakes, or plot twists, in the play.
- The comic elements and amusing characters that Shakespeare often includes in his tragedies (i.e., the Nurse; Mercutio's speeches).

KEY CHARACTERS

Romeo: Lover of Juliet, he is passionate and, at times, rash in his decisions. He is a member of the Montague clan, who are in a bitter feud with the Capulets.

Juliet: A Capulet, lover of Romeo. She is a thirteen-year-old girl about to become a woman. She is strong-willed, and, like Romeo, passionate.

Mercutio: Romeo's best friend and one of the play's most comic characters. He does not regard love in the same romantic light as Romeo. Killed by Tybalt.

The Nurse: Juliet's nurse. She is very fond of Juliet. She is a comic element in the play, and although only a nurse, she is often insightful and wise.

Benvolio: Friend to Romeo.

Tybalt: A Capulet (Juliet's cousin), he kills Mercutio.

Friar Laurence: Tries to help Romeo and Juliet, but only serves to complicate matters further.

Montague/Lady Montague: Heads of the Montague family.

Capulet/Lady Capulet: Heads of Capulet family.

Prince Escalus: The Prince of Verona, he is responsible for banishing Romeo.

Paris: Juliet's suitor, he is the Capulets' choice for their daughter. Related to Prince Escalus.

Rosaline: The woman Romeo thinks he is in love with until he meets Juliet.

ESSAY IDEAS

- What are the key symbols in the play?
- Identify the key mistakes made by the characters in the play. Could the final tragic ending have been avoided?
- Compare/contrast Mercutio and Romeo.
- Discuss Juliet's rebellion against her family and what it shows about her character as well as the rules of Verona's society.
- What does Romeo and Juliet's relationship symbolize, and what forces is it going against?
- At what point do you think the play takes a tragic turn?

A SAMPLE ESSAY IN OUTLINE FORM

Compare Mercutio and Romeo.
- Mercutio:
  - Bawdy, loud, and satirical; a public figure.
  - Regards love more as a conquest than as an emotional involvement.
  - Appreciates fighting, drinking, and the company of men.
  - Emotionally immature; inexperienced in love.
- Romeo:
  - Quiet and emotional.
  - Much more of a romantic.
  - Strives for love and companionship constantly (i.e., his effort to give Rosaline goddess-like qualities).
  - His passionate love for Juliet is beyond Mercutio's understanding.

Mercutio is eloquent, outspoken, and comical, but lacks an understanding of the emotional issues that eventually become the focus of Romeo's life, and of the play as a whole. While Mercutio dies by the sword in a public argument, Romeo dies by his own hand to be with his love, Juliet. Shakespeare often uses two characters in this way to serve as contrasts—foils—to one another.

PLOT SUMMARY

Act I, Prologue The prologue summarizes the plot of Romeo and Juliet. It prepares us for the tragedy we are about to see.

Act I, Scene i The play begins with an argument between servants of the Capulet and Montague households in the square of Verona. It quickly develops into a battle, involving Benvolio and Tybalt as well as most of the Montague and Capulet households. The battle is interrupted by the Prince, who threatens both Capulet and Montague with death if the two families fight again. Everyone except Montague, Lady Montague, and Benvolio exit.

The three talk about how Romeo has seemed very low in spirit lately. The Montagues exit with the entrance of Romeo, who then talks with Benvolio. It seems that Romeo has been rejected by the woman he loves, Rosaline. Benvolio tries to cheer up his downcast friend, but is unsuccessful.

Act I, Scene ii Paris has asked Capulet for Juliet's hand in marriage. Capulet says he will only agree if Juliet wants to marry Paris as well. He invites Paris to the Capulet house that evening for their feast.

Later, in the streets of Verona, a Capulet servant meets up with Romeo and Benvolio. The servant has the guest list for the Capulets' party, but cannot read it. He asks Romeo for assistance, and Romeo learns that Rosaline will be there. He and Benvolio make plans to go that evening to the

Capulets.

Act I, Scene iii Lady Capulet discusses marriage with Juliet and urges her to consider Paris. Juliet does not protest against her mother. The nurse, in the first of her comic scenes, babbles on about love and marriage and the finer attributes of Paris.

Act I, Scene iv Mercutio, Romeo, and Benvolio are on their way to the Capulets' house. This is one of Mercutio's finest scenes, in which he delivers a long and animated monologue on Queen Mab. Romeo, however, is in no mood for Mercutio's antics and remains downcast.

Act I, Scene v At the party, the trio, disguised in masks, quickly blend in with the festivities. Suddenly, Romeo sees Juliet. In an instant, he falls deeply in love with her. His reverie is interrupted by Tybalt, who has recognized him as a Montague. He tries to engage Romeo in combat, but is severely reprimanded by Capulet and is told to leave the party.

Romeo speaks with the Nurse and finds out Juliet's name, and that she is a Capulet. When Romeo leaves the party, Juliet sends the Nurse after him. The Nurse learns his name and that he is a Montague.

Act II, Scene i Mercutio and Benvolio have lost Romeo on the way home. Mercutio tries to "conjure" Romeo in another comic scene. Benvolio finally pulls Mercutio home. Romeo has hidden in the Capulets' garden, hoping for another glimpse of Juliet.

Act II, Scene ii In the window under which Romeo hides, Juliet delivers a soliloquy about her love for Romeo. Romeo comes out of hiding and, professing his love, asks her to marry him. This is one of Shakespeare's most well-known and loved

scenes due to its romance and beautiful language. The two are forced to part at daybreak when the Nurse calls to Juliet from inside.

Act II, Scene iii The setting shifts to Friar Laurence's garden, where he is early in the morning. Romeo enters, fresh from his encounter with Juliet. He asks the Friar to marry them. In hopes that the marriage will heal the rift between the Montagues and the Capulets, Friar Laurence agrees.

Act II, Scene iv We learn from a conversation between Mercutio and Benvolio that Tybalt has challenged Romeo to a duel. Romeo enters, and he and Mercutio banter. The nurse enters on an errand to Romeo. Her mission is interrupted by Mercutio, who teases her to distraction until his exit with Benvolio. Romeo then gives the nurse a message for Juliet: he wants to be married that afternoon at Friar Laurence's.

Act II, Scene v The nurse returns to Juliet, but does not give her the message from Romeo immediately. Instead, she teases Juliet and plays on her impatience by complaining at length about her health. Juliet finally gets the message from her and the plan is made; she will meet Romeo at the Friar's.

Act II, Scene vi Romeo and Friar Laurence wait for Juliet. Foreshadowing the tragedy to come, the Friar expresses his worry that Romeo may be acting too quickly; however, Romeo is too love-stricken to feel cautious. Juliet arrives, and the pair are married.

Act III, Scene i Tybalt, his temper ablaze, searches for Romeo. He runs into Mercutio in the town square, and the two are almost at one another when Romeo appears. Tybalt tries to engage Romeo in a duel, but Romeo refuses. Mercutio attacks Tybalt and is killed. Romeo, in retribution, kills Tybalt. The people of Verona, including the Prince, are now crowded in the square. When the Prince hears the details of the fight, he exiles the newly married Romeo.

Act III, Scene ii The Nurse tells Juliet of Tybalt's death and Romeo's subsequent banishment. Juliet gives her ring to the Nurse and orders her to go to Romeo and tell him to meet her that night. Romeo is hiding out at Friar Laurence's.

Act III, Scene iii At the Friar's, Romeo has worked himself into a frenzy of grief that is not helped by the message from the Nurse. The Friar tells Romeo to get a hold of himself and proposes a plan: Romeo will see Juliet that night, then go to the city of Mantua until Verona is safe for him.

Act III, Scene iv Paris, Lady Capulet, and Capulet discuss Paris' plans to marry Juliet. While the Capulets are at first reluctant to give their approval so soon after Tybalt's death, Lord Capulet decides that the marriage shall take place in three days.

Act III, Scene v It is morning in Juliet's bedroom. Romeo and Juliet spend their last time together, enjoying the dawn. The Nurse rushes in to warn them of Lady Capulet's arrival. Romeo hurries off.

Lady Capulet enters and tells Juliet of her father's plans for her to wed Paris. Capulet enters and is shocked when Juliet refuses to agree to his plan. He becomes enraged and threatens to throw her out. When he exits, Juliet turns to her mother, then the Nurse, for comfort. Both refuse, and Juliet decides to turn to Friar Laurence for help.

Act IV, Scene i Before Juliet gets to the Friar's, Paris arrives and tells the Friar of his imminent wedding to Juliet. The Friar tries to get Paris to put the marriage off, but to no avail.

Juliet enters and is complimented at length by Paris. She manages to maintain her composure until he leaves, then she breaks down to the Friar. The Friar again proposes a plan: he will give Juliet a potion to take on her wedding night. It will make her appear to be dead for two days, after which she will reawaken. He says he will get word of the plan to Romeo, and Juliet agrees to it.

Act IV, Scene ii When Juliet returns to her household, she apologizes to her father for her previous disobedience and tells him she will marry Paris. Her father, excited by her agreement, decides to make the wedding date one day earlier.

Act IV, Scene iii In Juliet's bedroom that evening, the Nurse and Lady Capulet help prepare her for her wedding. Juliet finally gets them both to leave and is left alone.

She readies herself to take the drug. Suddenly, doubts flash before her. What if the potion is truly poison? What if she awakens in the family tomb before Romeo finds her? Finally, after seeing what appears to be the ghost of Tybalt, she drinks the Friar's potion.

Act IV, Scene iv The potion works. As the Capulets prepare for the wedding early that morning, Juliet lies "dead" in her bedroom.

Act IV, Scene v It is the Nurse who discovers Juliet. She screams for help, and the Capulets, with Paris and the Friar in tow, rush in. Their grief overwhelms them. The Friar tries to ease their pain by saying it is God's will, and that she will be at peace in Heaven. The household now prepares for a funeral.

Act V, Scene i Romeo's servant meets him in Mantua and tells him news of Juliet's "death." Romeo, who has not been informed of the plan for reasons we will discover later, believes her to be truly dead. He sends his servant away and goes to an apothecary, from whom he buys a vial of poison.

Act V, Scene ii Friar Laurence has learned that his letter informing Romeo of the plan never reached Mantua. Realizing the potentially dire consequences of the miscommunication, he sets off for Juliet's tomb.

Act V, Scene iii Paris is at the Capulet tomb, mourning the loss of Juliet. Romeo enters, and Paris quickly hides and spies on him. Romeo, meaning to open the tomb, sends his servant away with a letter to his father. The servant, however, stays to spy on Romeo as well. As Romeo opens the tomb, Paris jumps out of hiding. Thinking that Romeo has come to vandalize the tomb of the Capulets, he challenges him to a duel. In the fight, Romeo kills Paris.

Romeo then sees the still body of his love, Juliet. He delivers his final soliloquy, pledging his immortal love for her. He then drinks his vial of poison and dies.

The Friar enters the tomb and sees the bodies Romeo and Paris. Juliet awakes, and he tries to shield her from the sight of her dead lover. She sees Romeo, however, and will not leave the tomb despite the Friar's urging. The Friar then runs from the tomb, leaving her alone.

Juliet sees the bottle of poison in Romeo's hand, but there is none left. Outside, people are approaching. She takes Romeo's dagger and stabs herself.

The Montagues, the Capulets, and the Prince enter. We learn that Lady Montague has died from the pain of her son's fate. The Friar steps forward and tells the story of Romeo and Juliet's death, including his own part in their demise. Servants, as well as Romeo's letter, verify his story. The Prince, however, does not blame Friar Laurence; he instead blames the feud between the Capulets and the Montagues. Capulet and Montague decide to end the bloody feud and erect statues of Romeo and Juliet in honor of each other's families.

ABOUT THE AUTHOR

Nathaniel Hawthorne (1804–1864) was raised by his mother in Salem, Massachusetts. His father, a sea captain, died when he was very young. As a child, he felt isolated from other children. His mother's family was antisocial, and he had a leg injury that generally kept him indoors.

He graduated from Bowdoin College in 1825. After college, he set out to become a writer. He worked for twelve years, mainly contributing to magazines. Although he was so dissatisfied with much of his writing that he burned it, it attracted enough attention that his first book of short stories, *Twice Told Tales*, was published in 1837. *Twice Told Tales* earned Hawthorne many favorable reviews.

A year later, he married, but even with the success of tales like "Rappaccini's Daughter," he soon needed more money than his writing could bring in. His politically influential friends in the Democratic Party got him a job as Surveyor of the Port of Salem, Massachusetts. He lost the job three years later when the Whigs won the election and removed him from office. The following summer, his beloved mother died.

Despite all these problems, Hawthorne was able to find inspiration to write *The Scarlet Letter*. Along with its long introduction, "The Custom House," it was originally intended to be published as part of another collection of short stories, but was printed alone in 1850. *The Scarlet Letter* was an instant success in both Great Britain and America.

In 1852, he wrote another famous work, *House of Seven Gables*, also set in Salem.

But again, he was unable to support his family, so he accepted an overseas appointment from old friend President Pierce as American consul in Liverpool, England. He continued to write, but did not produce anything as widely successful as his earlier works. When he returned to America, his growing physical weakness led to his death in 1864.

THE BIG PICTURE

The Scarlet Letter is the story of Hester Prynne, an adulteress who is punished severely by her small, New England Puritan town for her actions. She endures, however, through her own courage, strength, and dignity.

Why you're reading this book:
- Its timeless themes: justice; forgiveness; the validity of law; and the hollowness and hypocrisy of society's standards.
- ts historical value as a depiction of Puritan society.
- It is considered by many scholars to mark the beginning of the American literary tradition, the first "truly American novel."

Your teachers are looking for:
- Symbolism:
  - Most obviously, the letter "A" and the different meanings that are attached to it.
  - The rosebush as hope.
  - Hester's daughter, Pearl, as an embodiment and reflection of her mother's passions.
  - The scaffold as truth.
  - The contrast between sunshine and darkness.

- The contrast between Hester's and Dimmesdale's ability to cope with their adulterous act.
- The meanings of the characters' names (Pearl, Dimmesdale, Hester Prynne, and Chillingworth) and how they relate to the actual characters.
- The rules of the Puritan society, and how they differ from Hester's rules.
- The way the author treats the issues of justice and hypocrisy.

This book can be difficult to read at first because of the confusing relationship between "The Custom House" and the rest of the book. It may help to think of it, along with the conclusion, as an explanation of how the story was created. Here the narrator of the story speaks directly to you, the reader.

KEY CHARACTERS

Hester Prynne: The woman who wears the scarlet letter "A" as a punishment for her adultery with Dimmesdale. The way she conducts her life gives the scarlet letter positive meaning later. She is beautiful, proud, and industrious.

Reverend Arthur Dimmesdale: Hester's pastor and the father of Pearl. Although young, he is a talented and beloved minister. He shows that anyone can be a sinner, and that if one does not confess a sin, it will eat away at the person.

Pearl: The daughter of Hester and Dimmesdale. She behaves lawlessly and reflects what Hester is feeling. She also acts as the conscience of Hester and Dimmesdale.

Roger Chillingworth: A doctor, his name is an alias; he is really Hester's husband. His goal in life is to find out who fathered Pearl, and his lust for vengeance makes him evil.

ESSAY IDEAS

- How and why does the meaning of the scarlet "A" change throughout the story?
- How does Pearl act as an indicator of Hester's feelings?
- How are Hester and Dimmesdale alike/different? Dimmesdale and Chillingworth?
- How do "The Custom House" and the conclusion relate to the rest of the book?
- f Hester, Dimmesdale, and/or Chillingworth had told the truth, how would the story have turned out differently?

A SAMPLE ESSAY IN OUTLINE FORM

Compare Dimmesdale and Chillingworth.
- Both men have secrets that dictate their actions and shape their characters:
  - Rev. Dimmesdale's secret from society that he committed adultery and is the father of Pearl.
  - Chillingworth's secret from both Dimmesdale and society that he is Hester's husband and has come to seek revenge on Dimmesdale.
- The two men's reactions to their respective secrets show them to be very different:
  - Chillingworth turns into an evil person driven by revenge; he is finally unable to forgive.
  - Dimmesdale becomes sick and weak from the moral burden of his secret; he eventually confesses his sin and purges himself of it.

Both Dimmesdale and Chillingworth are sinful and therefore have secrets to keep. But while Dimmesdale committed one sinful act in the past and is an otherwise good man, Chillingworth is inherently sinful and deceitful; his secret hides not just one act, but his ongoing evil character.

PLOT SUMMARY

The Custom House This chapter serves as an introduction to the book, explaining how the narrator discovered the original story of Hester Prynne. It directly refers to many of Hawthorne's own experiences, and starts out by speaking of "the autobiographical impulse." Hawthorne's detailed description of the Salem Custom House scene is characteristic of his work.

The narrator reminisces about his hometown of Salem. Recalling that his ancestors were Puritans who executed many people because they thought they were witches, he says that he is ashamed for them. His tone suggests that the Puritans were a very strict people that did not always do the right thing.

One day, the narrator explains, while looking through some records on an idle and rainy day, he discovered documents written by another Surveyor, Jonathan Pue. Wrapped in these, he found "the scarlet letter," faded and worn. Pue's documents contained the story behind the letter, which was worn by one Hester Prynne, a woman living in Massachusetts in the late 1600s. She seemed to be very respected as a nurse and especially helpful in affairs of the heart.

The narrator tells us this is the source the story came from; and although "The Custom House" is a fictitious tale told by a fictitious narrator—Hawthorne wrote *The Scarlet Letter* without any such documents—it establishes a kind of legitimacy for the story that follows. The narrator closes the essay with a good-bye to Salem and his old life.

Chapter 1—The Prison-Door The people of Boston are standing before the prison, which is next to a cemetery site. This initial focus on the prison and cemetery foreshadows that punishment and death will be important themes in the story.

The atmosphere is very dark and somber, but there is a rosebush blooming at the doorway of the prison. The narrator says that this rosebush has been surrounded by myth and so has been kept alive through history. He then tells us that the roses may mean that the tale to follow has a good moral, or that their beauty will lighten the sad end "of a tale of human frailty and sorrow."

Chapter 2—The Market Place We are told that the time is June, sometime during the seventeenth century. The Bostonians standing in front of the prison appear to be anticipating an execution. The narrator reminds us that crime was much different back then, that people were severely punished for acts that we may not even consider crimes today. But for these people, "religion and law were almost identical," so any kind of transgression was very public.

The women seem especially interested in this case. From their talk, we learn that the criminal is Hester Prynne, and that her crime is adultery. Hester is important to them because her act shamed all the women in the town. We also hear that her Pastor, Master Dimmesdale, takes her scandal to heart, as she is part of his congregation.

Hester then comes out of the prison carrying a three-month-old baby. She is wearing the red letter "A," which is more finely decorated than anything the Puritans would usually wear. Hester is tall, with lustrous brown hair; despite her misfortune, she is very dignified and beautiful.

She is led to the scaffold, where she is to stand on display. The solemn scrutiny of the onlookers' eyes is very difficult to bear, so to keep herself from screaming, she thinks of her past. She remembers her upbringing in England, thinking particularly of an older, scholarly man who was "slightly deformed," his left shoulder higher than the right. But her thoughts bring her back to Boston. The staring faces remind her of her present reality of punishment and shame, and she realizes things will never be as they were in the past.

Chapter 3—The Recognition Hester sees an outsider in the crowd, an Indian, who is accompanied by another man. With a start that makes her grab her baby Pearl tightly to her, she realizes that one of the man's shoulders is higher than the other. This is the man she had been thinking of before. The man also suddenly realizes that he knows Hester, and he is horrified. Their eyes meet, and he warns her with a gesture to be silent.

He then turns to inquire about the case, since he is a stranger to the area, having just been released by the Indians. This is when we get Hester's complete background. She came to Boston two years ago to be met later by her husband, but he never sent any word. So obviously, her husband could not have fathered this child, and Hester refuses to tell who the father is. She was spared execution because of the possibility that her husband may be dead. So her penalty is to stand on the scaffold for three hours and to wear the letter on her chest for the rest of her life.

The stranger (who is Hester's husband, Roger Prynne) agrees that this is a fair sentence, as "she will be a living sermon against sin," but he is very upset that the father is not on the scaffold with her. He vehemently swears that "He will be known!"

Then the Reverend John Wilson speaks

to Hester, standing in the same "unadulterated sunshine" as she and her child. He asks the Reverend Dimmesdale, as her pastor, to see if he can get her to reveal who her partner was.

Dimmesdale is a young minister who has already earned great distinction in the church. He is very scholarly, yet he also seems to be a bit unsure that he is treading the correct moral path. The irony of this scene is that he is the father of Hester's baby, but he does not speak up himself. He begs her to reveal the name so that he will not "hide a guilty heart" throughout his life.

Hester refuses to tell, even when Rev. Wilson says that if she does, she can remove the scarlet letter. Hester tells him it can never be removed, as it is branded on her heart. Someone from the crowd demands that she give her child a father, and Hester replies that her child will only have a heavenly father—"she shall never know an earthly one."

Finally, the ordeal is over, and an exhausted Hester returns to her cell. We have now met all the major characters of the book—Hester, Rev. Dimmesdale, Roger Prynne, and Pearl.

Chapter 4—The Interview That night, Hester is upset because Pearl is sick. The jailer brings a doctor, whose name is Roger Chillingworth. At the sight of him, Hester is terrified: It is her husband, who has adopted a false name.

He swears that he will not hurt the child, so despite her fears Hester allows him to administer to Pearl some medicine that puts her to sleep. Chillingworth says that he will bring Hester no harm either, because if he did she would no longer be able to act as an example for her sin. He then blames himself for her sin because their marriage was unmatched, he being old and deformed, and she being young and beautiful. Hester reminds him that she never loved or pretended to love him, unlike her "partner in crime;" but she admits that she has "greatly wronged" her husband.

Chillingworth asks for the name of the father, which she refuses to reveal. He makes her swear that as long as she keeps that name a secret, she can never reveal his identity to anyone, either. Before he leaves, he taunts her about the letter, and she asks him if he is a devil that has bound her to an oath that will ruin her soul. He answers ominously, "Not thine."

Chapter 5—Hester at Her Needle Hester's prison term has ended, and she steps out into the sunshine. She knows she is no longer an individual, but a symbol of the reality of sin. She chooses to stay in Boston; her love for Dimmesdale, the only other person in the world joined to her in this sin, holds her.

Hester stays in a remote cottage by the sea, supporting herself with her fine needlework, as seen on the decoration of the letter. The fact that she is "the sinner" seems to balance the vanity of the decorations she makes. Her work appears everywhere, although she is never allowed to ornament a bride's dress. While she dresses herself plainly, the clothes she makes for Pearl are fantastic creations. The narrator points out that this has a deeper meaning, that it is a reflection of something inside Hester that is not seen otherwise.

Hester is shunned by society, especially women and children. Even the poor, whom she helps as a self-chosen penance, insult her. Inwardly, she resents this treatment.

The letter seems to give her a new sense of the hidden sin within people's hearts. She dismisses this notion as a delusion, thinking that no other person could have sinned as she did. But she is, of course,

wrong; in fact, the reason why everyone hates her so much is that her presence reminds them that they, too, are sinners.

Chapter 6—Pearl This chapter depicts Pearl as an expression of her mother's emotions. Her name does not describe her personality, which is rather wild and impish, but it does reflect the fact that she is something of "great price, purchased with everything her mother had." However, Hester worries because Pearl is the result of adultery, and cannot see how her daughter can turn out to be good, even though she is a beautiful, healthy child.

It seems as if the turmoil that Hester felt during her pregnancy was transferred to her child. Hester and Pearl are always together and isolated from everyone else. Pearl does not get along with other children; she attacks those who taunt her and her mother in a way that Hester never would. Pearl's playmates exist only in her imagination; she only makes herself enemies, as if she recognizes that the whole world is against her and her mother.

Pearl also makes Hester nervous with her fascination with the scarlet letter. Pearl asks who sent her to Hester. When Hester replies, "thy heavenly Father," Pearl denies having one, saying that Hester must tell her who her real father is.

Chapter 7—The Governor's Hall Because she needs to deliver a pair of gloves to Governor Bellingham, Hester uses the visit as an excuse to plead her case: rumors are flying that Pearl will be taken away from her.

As they walk to the house, Pearl demands that Hester give her the sunshine that lies on it, and Hester tells her that she must gather her own. In the house, Pearl sees her mother reflected in a mirror, her image distorted in such a way that the "A" has become huge, overwhelming Hester.

This is how everyone sees her, with the "A," her sin, more central to her identity than her own face. Pearl also notices a rosebush in the Governor's garden, a symbol of hope for the mother and daughter.

Chapter 8—The Elf-Child and the Minister

It seems that Hester's ulterior motive has been suspected, as she is met not only by Governor Bellingham, but also by Rev. Wilson, Rev. Dimmesdale, and Chillingworth, who has become Dimmesdale's doctor and friend. They remark upon Pearl's unusual dress and directly question Hester as to whether she is morally fit to raise a Christian child.

Hester tells them that she can teach her daughter the lessons she has learned from the scarlet letter. The men then ask Pearl the fateful question, "Who made thee?," to which she should reply, "my heavenly father." Pearl, now three, has been taught this response by Hester, but she does not speak. At this moment, Hester notices how much uglier Chillingworth has become, an outward sign, like Dimmesdale's sickness, that all is not well with their souls.

Hester then entreats Dimmesdale to speak for her and explain why she must be allowed to keep Pearl, the child God has given her. This, of course, is a loaded question since he is the father. Dimmesdale points out that Pearl is a reminder of Hester's sin that is before her always, as the letter is before everyone else. This was God's purpose for her. Pearl will keep her mother from slipping to blacker sin, because through the child, there is hope for Hester to go to heaven. Dimmesdale's strong argument convinces his elders that Hester should keep Pearl.

At the end of his speech, we get our first inkling that Dimmesdale is Pearl's father, and that Chillingworth suspects him. On their way to leave, Pearl takes Dimmesdale's hand, and he kisses her on the head in a fatherly gesture. Chillingworth then asks if one can tell the father of a child by the way the child looks and acts.

Pearl's role as the safeguard of Hester's soul is illustrated when the two are leaving. Hester is asked by Mistress Hibbins, a witch, if she will join the devil worship that night. Hester refuses, but says that if they had taken Pearl away from her, she would have gladly gone.

Chapter 9—The Leech

"Leech" is an earlier word for doctor, and "to leech" also means to forcefully drain something out, so the word is an appropriate title for Chillingworth. He has set himself up in Boston as a physician. Since Dimmesdale's health is failing, the people are happy he is attending him.

It's important to note that Dimmesdale's so-called ailment often causes him to put his hand over his heart. He isn't physically ill, but rather morally plagued. Chillingworth strives to find the spiritual nature of Dimmesdale's illness. At his prompting, Dimmesdale's friends decided that the two should live together.

The town is happy about this arrangement, but they do notice that Chillingworth's face seemed to be becoming evil, as if he were working in witchcraft. But the people have so much faith in their minister that they are sure that even if he is sick, he could overcome Satan himself.

Chapter 10—The Leech and His Patient

In conversation, Chillingworth asks why some men carry their sins to the grave without confessing, and Dimmesdale answers that once people admit to sin, they are labeled as sinners and no longer seen as capable of doing good works. Chillingworth tells him that such people deceive themselves. Seeing Pearl and Hester playing outside on the tombstones of the cemetery, Dimmesdale changes the subject.

Seeing them leads Chillingworth to ask

Dimmesdale a central question of the novel: is Hester the less miserable than the father because she wears the scarlet letter? Dimmesdale replies yes, because she can show her pain. Chillingworth then asks him if there is anything he has been keeping from him. Dimmesdale admits that his sickness concerns his soul, something which Chillingworth has no right to meddle with.

When Dimmesdale is asleep, Chillingworth sneaks in and looks at his chest, which until now had always been covered. What he sees makes him ecstatic, and he dances around devilishly.

Chapter 11—The Interior of a Heart Chillingworth now knows Dimmesdale's secret and begins to toy with him. Dimmesdale senses this, but unable to pinpoint what the doctor is doing, he disregards his own instincts.

As Dimmesdale becomes weaker, his congregation loves him more. He is tempted to tell them the truth and expose what a hypocrite he is. When he implies his guilt, the people think that he is just being humble. The end result is that he hates himself.

Since he cannot say anything publicly, he tries to purify himself with fasts and scourges. During one all-night vigil, he thinks he has discovered a way to find a moment's peace. He dresses himself as if for public worship and goes out into the night.

Chapter 12—The Minister's Vigil Dimmesdale has climbed onto the scaffold in an imitation of Hester's public punishment seven years earlier. But no one is around, and even if they were, they could not see him. Realizing this is just a mockery, Dimmesdale cries out in self-hatred.

He thinks of what would happen if he stayed there until morning and laughs out loud. His laugh is answered by that of Pearl, who is walking with Hester. Pearl and Hester join him on the scaffold, holding hands. Pearl asks him to stand with them there the next day, and he replies that he will stand with them on the great judgment day. As he says this, a red light gleams in the sky. While the narrator tells us it was probably a meteor, this one seemed to look like the letter "A."

At the same time, Pearl notices Chillingworth. Dimmesdale, terrified, asks Hester who Chillingworth is, but Hester will not reveal the truth. Chillingworth teases him about his behavior and takes him home.

The next day, the old sexton returns a glove of Dimmesdale's that was found on the scaffold, thinking it was put there as a jest by the devil. The sexton also tells him that an "A" was seen in the sky the previous night, and was taken to mean "angel," because of the death the previous night of Governor Winthrop. Dimmesdale denies having seen it.

Chapter 13—Another View of Hester Frightened by the change in Dimmesdale, Hester resolves to do something. Hester now has a new place in society. With the passage of time and all her good deeds, people have begun to interpret the "A" not to mean "Adulteress," but "Able." The letter has become magical—it is said that an arrow once bounced off it. This change is accompanied by physical changes in Hester. No longer does one see her vitality and beauty, as when she first stepped out of the prison. Her appearance is now somber, as if love and passion have left her.

But her realization that she must help Dimmesdale shows that this is changing. She realizes that her oath to Chillingworth was an error, as it did not help Dimmesdale at all. So she decides to speak first to Chillingworth, when he is out gathering herbs near her house.

Chapter 14—Hester and the Physician

Hester puts her plan into action. When they meet, Chillingworth tells her that there is talk of allowing her to remove the letter. Hester says that it is not for men to decide; if it were meant to happen the letter would simply fall from her. As she speaks to Chillingworth, she realizes that his evil transformation is complete.

Hester then begins to discuss Dimmesdale and how Chillingworth has treated Dimmesdale as his "patient." Chillingworth admits that he has been torturing Dimmesdale's soul while pretending to be his caring doctor. Chillingworth's work has made him into something wretched. Hester tells him that she is going to reveal his identity to Dimmesdale. After an argument, he states that she can do as she wishes.

Chapter 15—Hester and Pearl Hester, watching Chillingworth leave, questions how sunlight can fall on someone so evil. Although she knows it is wrong, she hates him. She feels that her marriage to this man she did not love was a greater crime than the one for which she is being punished.

She returns to find Pearl playing in the water. Pearl has fashioned a typical Puritan garb for herself out of seaweed, with the addition of an "A" on her chest. Hester asks her if she knows why her mother wears an "A." Pearl is perceptive enough to say that it is for the same reason the minister keeps his hand over his heart. Hester thinks of clarifying this for her, but thinking that Pearl may still be too young, she for the first time lies about the letter's meaning.

Chapter 16—A Forest Walk Hester decides to meet with Dimmesdale while he is out walking. When she hears that he is heading to an Indian village, she plans to meet him on his way back. She and Pearl go to wait in the woods.

Pearl asks about the Black Man, the Devil, and Hester tells her that the scarlet letter is the mark he left on her the one time she met him. Hearing Dimmesdale approach, Pearl asks why the minister does not wear his mark on his chest, too. Hester, unable to answer, sends her off to play. Dimmesdale approaches her, walking slowly and alone, with a staff for support.

Chapter 17—The Pastor and His Parishioner Hester calls to him, using his first name. He recognizes her from the scarlet letter, and both are relieved that the other is real. They begin to talk and discover that neither has made peace with him or herself. Dimmesdale tells her how miserable he is. The fact that his congregation loves him while he is a hypocrite tortures him.

He tells her that it's a relief to be with someone who recognizes him for what he is, and wishes for either a friend or an enemy to talk to about it. Hester tells him that Chillingworth is just such an enemy. Realizing the part she has played in Dimmesdale's destruction, she reveals Chillingworth's true identity and her lie that concealed it.

Dimmesdale's emotions quickly pass from rage to sorrow, and he forgives her. He then says that Chillingworth is a worse sinner than they. Thinking death his only escape, he asks Hester to give him her strength. She suggests that he leave Boston and travel far away, taking on a new identity. Being as physically and mentally weak as he is, he does not think he can do it alone, so she decides to go with him.

Chapter 18—A Flood Of Sunshine Hester's life has made her an outsider, so her decision to leave the community is not hard. For Dimmesdale, however, who is the center of the community's life, the decision is very difficult. However, knowing that Hester will be with him, he consents.

The two are happy for the first time in seven years. Hester then takes off the scarlet letter and throws it away, feeling and looking again like a beautiful woman. Hester realizes that Dimmesdale must get to know his daughter, and calls Pearl to them.

Chapter 19—The Child at the Brookside As Pearl approaches them, adorned with flowers, both remark how much she looks like Dimmesdale, and are surprised that the resemblance didn't give them away. Pearl does not cross the brook and come to them, though. Instead, she points at her mother's chest. Hester realizes that Pearl misses the "A," and she asks Pearl to bring the letter to her. Pearl refuses to do it herself, and forces her mother to get it. As Hester puts it back on, her mood becomes somber again.

Pearl then accepts her mother, but shows no favor to Dimmesdale. She wants to walk hand in hand into town, and Hester tells her that they will walk together soon. Dimmesdale kisses Pearl, who then washes his kiss off in the brook. She stays apart from them as he and Hester speak of their future plans.

Chapter 20—The Minister in a Maze Dimmesdale goes ahead of Pearl and Hester and leaves the forest. He then reviews their plan: they will head back to the Old World on a ship that is to leave in four days. This will leave enough time for him to preach the Election Sermon, one of the most important of the year.

Upon entering the town, everything seems to Dimmesdale to have changed. As people come up to speak to him, he has trouble keeping himself from saying blasphemous things.

When Dimmesdale gets home, he settles down to write his sermon. Chillingworth comes in and seems somehow to know what is going on. When left alone, Dimmesdale stays up all night to write his sermon.

Chapter 21—The New England Holiday As the new Governor is being elected today, Hester and Pearl go into town. Pearl asks if Dimmesdale will be there, and if they will hold hands. She cannot understand why he can be with them in the dark on the scaffold, or in the woods, but not here in town on a sunny day.

The sailors from the boat have also come into town for the occasion, and Hester sees Chillingworth speaking to the commander of the ship. The commander then comes to speak to Hester and tells her that Chillingworth will be joining them on their voyage. Seeing this exchange, Chillingworth smiles at her across the marketplace. Hester has no time to warn Dimmesdale that Chillingworth knows of their plans.

Chapter 22—The Procession In shock, Hester watches the procession of citizens to the meeting-house. Dimmesdale follows the military and other authorities. He appears to have more energy and is no longer the sad, weak man he was. He looks so different that Hester feels she does not know him, and Pearl does not recognize him.

Mistress Hibbins finds Hester and tells her how the Black Man has marked Rev. Dimmesdale on his chest, and that it will soon be shown to the world. Dimmesdale then delivers his sermon, and although Hester remains outside by the scaffold, she can hear him speak. The commander sends word through Pearl that Chillingworth will bring Dimmesdale on board, and that Hester need only worry about herself and Pearl. This message only agitates Hester further.

Chapter 23—The Revelation of the Scarlet Letter The people leave the meeting-house and assemble in the square, praising Dimmesdale. As he leaves, it seems that the energy he had earlier has entirely left him. Rev. Wilson tries to help him, but he refuses, finding Hester and Pearl instead. He asks them to join him up on the scaffold.

Chillingworth tries to stop him, but Dimmesdale turns him away, telling him his hold over him is gone. Hester helps him onto the scaffold, and he tells her that he is dying. He then confesses to all the people that he was the one who should have stood with Hester seven years ago. He pulls his garment open, and reveals what is on his chest. Chillingworth, kneeling beside him, is upset because Dimmesdale has now escaped his revenge.

Pearl kisses him on the lips and promises to grow up as a good person. He says goodbye to Hester, who asks him if they will spend their immortal life together. He tells her that happiness will not be theirs, because their act was against each other's souls. His dying words are that all the agonies of his life have saved his soul.

Chapter 24—Conclusion This chapter is much like the opening essay, tying up the loose ends and revealing more of the book's meaning. It seems that there are several versions of Rev. Dimmesdale's death, some saying there was no mark on his flesh at all, and some saying that he never admitted any guilt. The narrator expresses the story's main moral that one should always show one's true self to the world.

Chillingworth dies soon after Dimmesdale; without his quest for revenge, there is nothing left for him to do. Pearl is named the heiress of his estate, including the properties in England. She and Hester travel there for a while, but Hester returns to her old cottage after several years. Hester is treated with a kind of reverence, and many people, especially women, come to her with their problems. When she dies, she is buried near Dimmesdale. One tombstone, engraved with an "A," serves for both.

SILAS MARNER

ABOUT THE AUTHOR

George Eliot (1819–1880), born Mary Ann Evans, spent her life in England. Her interests while growing up included philosophy, religion, and writing. She is considered one of the foremost writers of the Victorian period in England.

Before her career as a fiction writer, Eliot worked as a writer and editor for a radical newspaper, *The Westminster Review*. Finding little happiness there, her interests shifted, and she began translating religious and philosophical works.

Her decision to become a novelist was inspired by George Henry, a journalist from London. Henry strongly encouraged and supported Eliot's interest in writing fiction. Their relationship was also a romantic one; Henry's inability to obtain a divorce from his wife did not prevent him and Eliot from living together openly.

Eliot's major works include *Adam Bede*, *The Mill on the Floss*, *Silas Marner*, *Middlemarch*, and *Daniel Deronda*. Her work was extremely popular and established her as one of the leading novelists of her day. Before her death, she was recognized as one of the great writers of English fiction and remains so today.

THE BIG PICTURE

Silas Marner tells the story of a lonely weaver, a man devoted only to gold, who regains his love for life through his relationship with an abandoned child. It is a realistically written but beautiful story of redemption and rebirth.

Why you're reading this book:
- Its depiction of the life of the lower class is striking and authentic.
- It offers a realistic portrayal of nineteenth-century British life and society.
- The author's manipulation of time is remarkably effective.
- *Silas Marner* is a very easy book to read. The language is simple and the descriptions are not overwhelming, yet the characters and the plot are compelling.

Your teachers are looking for:
- Imagery:
  - References to ghosts throughout the book.
  - Gold.
  - Doors.
  - Animals.
  - Personification of Chance, Opium, Anxiety, etc.
  - Nature: the weather, gardens.
- The symmetrical time construct of the story:
  - The reader meets Silas Marner fifteen years after his departure from Lantern Yard.
  - Part II of the book takes place sixteen years after Silas has found Eppie.
- The illustration of the lower-class townspeople: their dignity and kindness as well as their flaws.
- The way the author alternates the main characters every few chapters (Godfrey Cass/Silas Marner and the Squire/the townspeople). In seeing both classes, we get a more balanced story.
- Themes of secrecy, deception, and fate.

KEY CHARACTERS

Silas Marner: A weaver who, deceived by his lover and friend, moves to the town of Raveloe. Ostracized and treated as a hermit, he learns the value of life by losing one treasure and gaining another.

Godfrey Cass: The eldest son of an upper-class family, he is secretly married and has a child. He fears anyone discovering the truth, because it may threaten his life with Nancy.

Dunstan Cass: Godfrey's brother, the antagonist. He represents the evil forces of greed and deception. Dunstan pays with his life for stealing Silas Marner's gold.

Eppie: Found by Silas Marner after she has been left to freeze in the snow. Her most striking feature is her golden locks. She is the biological daughter of Godfrey Cass, but is raised by Marner.

Nancy Lammeter/Cass: Beautiful daughter of a wealthy landowner in Raveloe. She is a true product of her class. Courted by Godfrey Cass, she later marries him. Ironically, she is unable to conceive children.

Dolly Winthrop: A married woman in the town whom Marner befriends after he finds Eppie. Gentle and kind, Dolly offers advice to the new father about children and religion. She is one of the most fully developed characters of all the villagers.

Mr. Macey: The parish clerk, another vividly portrayed townsperson. Macey is aware of the goings-on of the town. He believes in Marner even when the entire town regards him as strange.

ESSAY IDEAS

- Discuss some of the important symbols or images in the story (e.g., ghosts, gold).
- What is the significance of the loom and the garden?
- Discuss the role fate plays in this story.
- Does this story have a hero? Explain.
- What might this book reveal about the author's ideas concerning religion? What do we make of the pressure for Silas to attend church? And of the I.H.S. cakes of Mrs. Winthrop?
- How does the novel's time symmetry enhance the story?
- Explain the significance of the scene at the Rainbow with the villagers.
- ilas Marner is a moral allegory. Examine good vs. evil in the story.

A SAMPLE ESSAY IN OUTLINE FORM

Ghost images in *Silas Marner*
- Some haunting or ghostlike images in the novel:
  - Godfrey haunted by his secret wife and child.
  - Description of Molly.
  - Silas Marner:
    - His past from which he has run away.
    - The gold treasure he hoards in his floor vault.
    - At the Rainbow, Silas is referred to as a ghost.
    - Eppie comes into Silas Marner's life from out of thin air.
  - Dunstan's strange disappearance.
  - The villagers discuss the ghost horses living in Mr. Lammeter's stables.

Silas Marner himself is a ghost. His life is hollow, empty, and distant from others. It is only through discovering love—through his adopted daughter Eppie—that he is able to rejoin the living.

PLOT SUMMARY

PART I

Chapter 1 The novel is set in the small English town of Raveloe in the 1800s. Its first pages introduce us to Silas Marner from the townspeople's perspective. He is spoken of as one of a "disinherited race." Every town has its own Silas Marner—the man who appears out of nowhere and, surrounded by strange and mysterious ways, does not seem to fit into village life.

The reader then learns of the misfortune that has brought Marner to Raveloe. In his old town of Lantern Yard, Marner was a very religious man. However, his best friend, William Dane, framed him for a robbery against a dying deacon. Marner was unable to prove his innocence. Left by his lover and suspended by the church, Marner departed from his home.

By showing Silas Marner from these two different perspectives, Eliot causes us to pity Marner because of his history, but at the same time be wary of him because of the townspeople's uncertain view of him.

Eliot makes her first reference to the concept of Fate. She explains Marner's troubles as having been declared by "lots." Some Higher Force has the power to predetermine events. This theme will reappear at other points in the story.

Chapter 2 This chapter elaborates on the background information that Eliot introduced in the first chapter. Eliot contrasts Silas Marner's old home, Lantern Yard, with the new, still unfamiliar territory of Raveloe. Much of the description is of Raveloe's physical setting, but, the strangeness of Raveloe goes much deeper. Marner is lost and alone amongst his new neighbors: he does not share their lives, their ideas, or their history.

Silas gains a reputation for having magical powers when he helps to cure Sally Oates. The townspeople come to him for all sorts of illnesses, but Marner knows he cannot cure them. He refuses to help, and the villagers isolate him further.

Marner's disappointment in love and friendship carry over to his feelings about religion. In Raveloe, his interest in church and prayer disintegrates. His faith disappears as feelings of betrayal allow him to trust no one, even God.

Marner turns to his occupation, weaving, for solace. His loom becomes his only companion. But unlike in Lantern Yard, Silas gains little satisfaction from creating on the loom. Instead, he finds satisfaction in hoarding his money. He finds an iron pot and builds a vault in the floor in which to store his gold. The pot becomes his friend, and for fifteen years Silas Marner lived this lifestyle of "weaving and hoarding."

Eliot uses the time span of fifteen years to create a time symmetry. At the end of Chapter 2, she hints of a change that will significantly change Silas' life after fifteen solitary years. Until Christmas of that fifteenth year, he is just a simple weaver, or at most, a "doctor" of sorts. Now, his life will change completely.

Chapter 3 Eliot brings the reader fifteen years into the present and shifts the character emphasis. In Chapter 3, we meet the family of Squire Cass, the richest man in Raveloe. A widowed landowner, the Squire is held in high regard in the village. Though the family is of upper-class status and wealth, we learn that the Casses are neither the happiest nor the most moral family.

We are introduced to Godfrey and Dunstan Cass, the sons of the Squire, whose relationship sets the course of events in the story. Godfrey, the eldest, stands to inherit the Squire's property. Though he does have some wild tendencies, he generally is a good young man. He is very involved in courting Nancy Lammeter. Dunstan, the evil son, is spiteful and greedy. His irresponsible traits include drinking and gambling, and he seems to live in the shadow of his older sibling.

Money reappears as a central theme in the story. Godfrey owes his father money that he collected from one of the family's tenants. Godfrey loaned Dunstan the money; Dunstan lost every penny of it, and he now refuses to pay it back. Instead, he is blackmailing Godfrey, threatening to expose to the Squire and Nancy his brother's secret marriage to a drunkard, Molly. Godfrey, caught in a trap, is forced to sell his horse, Wildfire, for the money. At the end of the chapter, Dunstan leaves to sell his horse for him.

Chapter 4 On his way to find a buyer for his horse, Dunstan passes the home of Silas Marner near the Stone Pits. He wonders if there is any truth to all the rumors surrounding the mysterious weaver and his wealth, and if he could ever get his hands on any of the money.

Dunstan then meets with Bryce and arranges the sale of the horse with him. Bryce plans to purchase Wildfire later in the day at the Batherley Stables. Dunstan, happy with the deal, takes the horse out for one final run. However, he takes the horse over one too many fences and the horse, falling over one of the stakes, dies.

Dunstan, without the horse or the money, walks aimlessly until he again comes upon the home of Silas Marner. Caught in the dark, Dunstan hopes the weaver might have a lantern that he can borrow. Seeing that no one is home, he enters the cottage. He discovers the money in the floor vault and robs Marner.

Chapter 5 In this brief chapter, Marner returns home from a rare trip away from his cottage to deliver a piece of linen. Marner is excited at the prospect of eating a pork dinner, then counting his gold. When he discovers that his gold is missing, Silas panics. He cannot imagine who could have committed such a crime. He can think of only one villager, Jem Rodney, who may have stolen the money—he sometimes joked with Marner about his money.

Silas, his only purpose in life having been taken away, becomes a pathetic character here. He does not care if the crime goes unpunished; his only concern is that his gold be returned to him. Silas runs off to find the "great people in the village," the clergyman, the constable, and the Squire, who would have the power to remedy the situation. He heads for the Rainbow, the social center for the important townspeople. Yet, he finds that the upper-class folk are attending a birthday party and that the Rainbow is occupied only by the lower-class villagers.

Chapter 6 The next two chapters show Eliot's vivid realism at work. She powerfully evokes the scenes at the Rainbow through her vivid portraits of the villagers. The common people of the story are natural and real rather than stereotypes. Eliot portrays them as multi-dimensional people, revealing their strengths as well as their flaws.

Silas Marner steps into the Rainbow amidst a din of conversation. The butcher and the farrier are discussing buying and selling cows for meat, and the Lammeter family name is brought into the conversation. Eliot focuses here on the town gossip. We hear the history of the Lammeters from way up North. Mr. Macey, the parish clerk, gives a first-hand account of when young Lammeter and Miss Osgood got married. He frequently repeats this story and proudly claims himself an authority when he reveals that their child was conceived out of wedlock.

The conversation shifts from the marriage to the Lammeters' land. It seems that Mr. Lammeter does not use his stables, called Charity Land. Most of the men of the town agree that they are haunted and that one can hear the stomping and whipping of horses to this day. The farrier cannot believe that ghosts truly exist. The discussion of ghosts continues until the end of the chapter.

Chapter 7 During this conversation about ghosts, Silas Marner enters the room, and all eyes are upon him. Eliot ties the talk of ghosts together with Silas' ghost-like image.

Silas, frantic, announces the robbery and accuses Jem of the crime. The villagers calm him down and ask for the full story. For the first time, Silas is forced to open up to the townspeople. They quickly assure the weaver that Jem has been drinking at the Rainbow all night. They decide to visit the constable to swear a deputy. Mr. Macey and the farrier decide to help Marner to find the culprit and accompany him to the constable's home.

Chapter 8 The novel's focus shifts once again to the Cass family. Godfrey returns from the birthday party and is relieved by Dunstan's absence. He can turn his thoughts upon Nancy Lammeter, the love of his life, and temporarily forget about his brother and his secrets.

The next morning the entire town is talking about the robbery. Outside the Rainbow, all the common men discuss the situation. The rain has erased any footprints that might have been left by the thief, but a tinder box owned by a local peddler was found in the area. Though Dunstan disappeared at the same time the robbery occurred, no one suspects him because he is from an upper-class family.

Godfrey has little interest in the robbery; he is set on finding his brother and the horse. He imagines that his brother has run off with Wildfire. However, in an encounter with Bryce, the supposed buyer of the horse, Godfrey learns that the horse has been found dead.

Bryce explains the deal he negotiated with Dunstan. Meanwhile, Godfrey determines to reveal the truth to his father; he cannot keep the secret any longer. He decides to wait until morning to make his confession.

Chapter 9 Though Chapter 9 is brief, it is important in the development of the characters. We learn about the Squire and Godfrey and the Cass family. Eliot points out that the "Squire's life was quite as idle as his sons', but it was a fiction...." At breakfast the following morning, Godfrey tells the Squire about the horse and the money. Yet, he doesn't reveal his secret marriage. Not only is the Squire furious at his sons' misbehavior and deception, but he also ironically chooses this time to pressure Godfrey into asking Nancy Lammeter to marry him. Godfrey offers some feeble excuses and changes the subject.

The Squire also demands to speak to Dunstan. When Godfrey explains that he cannot find his younger brother, Squire Cass foreshadows Dunstan's tragic downfall by wondering if he has broken his neck or been hurt. The Squire declares that Dunstan is prohibited from returning home. This scene reveals that the Casses have little sense of family and no sense of order.

In the final paragraphs of the chapter, the theme of fate is brought into the story. Godfrey struggles with the events that have occurred and wonders if he has brought them upon himself or if Chance has played the important role.

Chapter 10 The scene shifts back to Silas Marner and the robbery. After several weeks, the peddler, the only suspect, cannot be found and the case is forgotten. Dunstan still has not returned, and his disappearance has gone practically unnoticed.

Meanwhile, Silas is devastated. His loss of the gold is as earth-shattering to him as was his betrayal by his friend and lover in Lantern Yard. Eliot delves deep into his pain; Silas feels his loss both emotionally and physically.

The townspeople slightly change their attitude toward the unfortunate weaver. As in the Rainbow scene, Eliot offers portraits of some of the common townspeople, for example Mr. Macey and Mrs. Winthrop. Mr. Macey amuses us with his opinions and advice, while Dolly Winthrop is charming and heartwarming.

Mr. Macey and Dolly Winthrop offer Silas much advice about religion. They each try to persuade Marner to attend church, especially since Christmas is coming up. Dolly goes so far as to bake Silas cakes with religious letters carved on top, and has her son, Aaron, perform a Christmas carol.

Silas, having lost sight of the concepts of love and faith, spends the holiday season alone. The rest of Raveloe, however, is caught up in Christmas festivities. At the Cass household, Christmas is merry. Dunstan's absence is still not considered unusual.

The Squire throws a big party on New Year's Eve. But Godfrey is unable to relax because of his father's pressure to marry Nancy and his fear of Dunstan's return.

Chapter 11 In this chapter, we meet the Lammeter family and get another view of upper-class Raveloe. We learn that Nancy Lammeter finds Godfrey's gestures unattractive to her. She has made it perfectly clear that she is not interested in marrying him, yet he continues to pursue her.

We are also introduced to Nancy's sister Priscilla. Though the two young women seem very different (Nancy is the beauty while Priscilla is seen as the "rougher" sister), they are very close to one another. Priscilla is very good-natured, but Nancy receives all the attention. Their sibling relationship is an interesting contrast to that of the Cass brothers. The Lammeter ladies, though part of the upper class, are rather simple and uneducated.

After dinner, we see Nancy and Godfrey interact for the first time. They dance, but young Nancy rips her dress and Priscilla runs off for needle and thread. Meanwhile, Godfrey tries very hard to appeal to Nancy. For the most part, she rejects his words. However, we learn from her thoughts that she is not totally opposed to Godfrey and his intentions.

Chapter 12 Chapter 12 is full of plot development and action. We finally meet the people in Godfrey's secret life. Molly, Godfrey's wife, is on her way with her young child to the New Year's Eve party at the Red House, where she plans to reveal her identity to everyone. She is dressed in rags much like the clothes that Silas wears. The party dresses of the high-class Lammeter ladies form a sharp contrast with the clothing of the poor and unfortunate.

Molly takes opium along the snowy roads. The addicting drug is described as a lifelike demon that is eating her inside out. The drug becomes so powerful that Molly becomes numb and falls asleep on the side of the road with her baby. The child wakes up from her sleep and, seeing light from a house, follows the brightness. She arrives at the open door of Silas Marner's cottage. Entranced by the warmth of the fire, she falls back asleep at the hearth.

The weaver, still caught up in memories of his gold, is unaware of the child's entrance. Breaking out of his daze, he turns to the fire and interprets the golden locks of the child's head as his missing money. In this scene, Eliot brings together the ideas of the gold as treasure and the child as treasure. The appearance of the child is as strange to Silas as the disappearance of the gold.

Marner feeds and comforts the crying child. In holding her, he feels strong sensations of tenderness and warmth. Some of his emotions, deadened by the incident in Lantern Yard, are brought back to life. Confused, Silas goes outside and follows the child's tracks from the house to the bushes by the Stone Pits. There, he finds a frozen woman covered in snow.

Chapter 13 The setting returns to the party at the Squire's home. Silas enters with the child and announces his discovery of the woman, possibly dead, in the snow. Eliot again uses ghost imagery in describing the entrance of the weaver. Godfrey, seeing Marner with his child, stands in shock.

The guests look on with astonishment, and the men rush out to where Silas claims the woman is lying. The women offer to care for the child, but Silas feels too strong a bond with the child to let go.

Godfrey, trembling, accompanies the men to the Stone Pits; it is determined that Molly is dead. Silas wants to keep the abandoned child, while Godfrey is relieved that his secret marriage is over. He no longer has to lie and feel guilty; he has no need to confess. He doesn't want the child, but promises himself that he will make sure it is cared for. Silas' feelings of responsibility toward the child greatly contrast with Godfrey's attitude.

Chapter 14 Molly is buried and Silas keeps the child. The softening in his manner is noticeable and the townspeople, particularly mothers, empathize with him.

Specifically, Dolly Winthrop becomes close with Marner. She gives him clothing for the child and advice about parenting and punishing misbehavior. She points out to Silas that now that he has a child, he must certainly attend church and christen the child. Silas agrees to the christening and decides to name the child Eppie. Here we see that the importance of religion in Raveloe is in the ceremonies and not in the meaning.

Eliot then contrasts the meaning of the gold with that of the child for Silas. While the gold was kept inside and hidden, Eppie is full of life and turns the weaver's thoughts outward. For the first time, Silas has the joy of experiencing nature and life with someone he cares for and loves.

Because of Eppie, Silas is no longer isolated from the people of Raveloe. People stop him on the street to admire the child and have a friendly chat. Villagers began to forget all the suspicions and fears they had about the "strange" weaver.

Chapter 15 Godfrey watches the weaver and Eppie with deep interest. He feels an eternal responsibility to keep an eye on his daughter and to make sure she is cared for properly. No one thinks Dunstan will come back, and Godfrey looks ahead to his ideal life with Nancy and the children they will have together.

PART II

Chapter 16 For the second time in the novel, Eliot makes an important shift in time. As the scene opens sixteen years later, the people of Raveloe are leaving church. First, we meet Mr. and Mrs. Cass. Now approaching his fortieth year, Godfrey is still the same. Nancy, while having matured a great deal, still possesses a youthful quality.

Following the Cass family, Silas Marner exits with his charming daughter, Eppie. Silas looks physically aged, but his contented eyes tell otherwise. Eppie has grown and matured into a beautiful young woman of whom the entire town is aware. A few steps behind her is Aaron, the son of Dolly Winthrop. Dolly has remained a true friend to the weaver throughout the years and her son seems quite taken with Eppie.

Silas and Eppie have an extensive discussion about planting a garden. Imagery of gardens and nature reflects the way Silas and Eppie have grown together.

Godfrey continues to keep an eye on Eppie, holding true to his word. He has contributed to the upkeep of Silas' cottage by donating furniture. His actions are not viewed by the townspeople as unusual, only generous.

By now, Silas has become a well-respected man of the town. He has even gone so far as to take up pipe smoking as a sign of status. His churchgoing shows his worthiness to the villagers. Over the years, his friendship with Dolly has strengthened. He has opened up and shared the painful memories of his past with her. Dolly and Silas have an exchange about Fate. Silas believes Fate took away his money and brought Eppie to him. Dolly informs Silas that Fate is tied to religion: drawing lots originated in the Bible.

At the end of the chapter, Eppie and Silas discuss her marriage to Aaron. This conversation between father and daughter is important because it focuses on the idea of change. Eppie doesn't want her life to be affected by her marriage: she wants Silas to live with her and Aaron, and promises never to leave her father alone. His comments reflect his previous dialogue with Dolly about Fate. He agrees to her conditions, but explains that it is not in her power to decide whether or not her life will change.

Chapter 17 This chapter is set in the home of Godfrey and Nancy. Mr. Lammeter and Priscilla, still unmarried, are visiting after church. Priscilla has been living with her father and managing the farm. The two sisters, still close, take a walk in the garden. Again, garden imagery appears.

Two important points arise from the sisters' conversation. Godfrey, wanting to purchase a dairy, has not changed in his ways; he always wants more. We also learn that Nancy cannot bear children. Her childlessness seems to be Fate's punishment for Godfrey's past actions.

After Priscilla and Mr. Lammeter leave, Godfrey goes for a drive near the Stone Pits. Nancy thinks he is mulling over farming ideas, but we are drawn to think that his motive is to catch a glimpse of Eppie.

Nancy, alone, contemplates her own destiny. Her deepest wound stems from her inability to have children. She wonders if she has done everything in her power to change her circumstances. Why is she denied such a blessing? Godfrey had wanted desperately to adopt a child, but she had refused, believing that she had no right to cross Fate's path. A servant, Jane, interrupts Nancy's solitude. She informs Nancy that something unusual has happened and all the town is in an uproar.

Chapter 18 Chapter 18 is the climax of the novel. Godfrey returns to his worried wife to report that Dunstan's skeleton has been found wedged beneath two stones as the Stone Pits were being drained. Silas Marner's stolen money has been uncovered along with the body.

Godfrey takes this moment to reveal to his wife the secrets that he has kept from her for so long. With no more threats of blackmail by Dunstan, Godfrey can atone for his lies on his own terms. He confesses to his marriage to Molly and his real relationship with Eppie. Nancy forgives him and Godfrey announces that he still wants Eppie as his own. They plan to visit Silas that evening.

Chapter 19 Back at the cottage, Silas and Eppie review the day's events. Though Silas is pleased by the return of the gold, his happiness centers around Eppie. The money is for her, he decides. His obsession with the gold has been completely replaced by his love for his daughter; Eppie and her happiness are his only priorities.

The Casses call at the cottage and ask to adopt Eppie. They insist that they could provide her with a more respectable lifestyle that is more suited for a lady. Silas leaves the decision to Eppie, who politely refuses the offer. She is more than content with her life with Silas.

In frustration and anger, Godfrey reveals Eppie as his child. He acts selfishly and conceitedly. When Silas questions Godfrey's ethics, the scene becomes somewhat heated. Here, the class conflict in the novel comes to a head. The Casses wish to win Eppie's affections with material possessions. However, the lower class, and a strong belief in family, prevails. Silas knows that trust and love go hand in hand and, again, leaves the choice up to Eppie. Eppie believes that though Godfrey may be her biological father, Silas is her real father. Godfrey has great difficulty accepting this decision and departs abruptly.

Chapter 20 Godfrey and Nancy return from the cottage. At home, Godfrey reevaluates his life. He finally accepts his "punishment," or Fate. He realizes that it is too late to raise Eppie, and that not having a child of his own is a small price to pay for what he has done. He decides to continue to help Eppie financially and to put her in his will.

Godfrey's reevaluation also includes his immediate family. He realizes the impor-

tance of Nancy in his life and promises to improve the marriage. He and Nancy decide not to reveal all the circumstances and events of Godfrey's past publicly; there is no point in dredging up the past.

Chapter 21 Silas, an aged man, finally settles his past. He and Eppie take a trip back to Lantern Yard to visit the pastor and find out about the outcome of the robbery for which he was framed. Upon his arrival there, he finds everything he once knew falling apart or gone entirely.

The weaver's dismal and unhappy past is powerfully evoked. Lantern Yard itself has gone to ruin: the whole area smells and has become dark and cramped. Just as Raveloe was on Silas' initial arrival there, Lantern Yard is strange and unfriendly. The chapel has been replaced by a factory and Silas cannot even find the pastor. He returns to Raveloe with the knowledge that his past is finally closed and can no longer haunt him. Through the love of his daughter, Silas has emerged from the dark into the light.

Conclusion Time is shifted forward once again. Eppie and Aaron are getting married. Nancy Cass has given Eppie a wedding dress. Following the wedding, Silas will live with the young couple at the cottage, showing that the strength of family has triumphed. The Lammeters watch the procession beyond the Red House to the humbler part of the village, once again contrasting the two classes that live side by side in Raveloe.

The celebration following the wedding ceremony takes place at the Rainbow, and we are reminded of the earlier illustrations of the commoners. Their lives, too, are not to be forgotten. Eliot's final image is of a huge garden, signifying growth and life, planted all around the house.

THE SUN ALSO RISES

ABOUT THE AUTHOR

See page 200.

THE BIG PICTURE

Hemingway's *The Sun Also Rises* is a bleak tale, accurately reflecting the spirit of the post-World War I "lost generation." Jake Barnes tells the story of his frustrated relationship with Lady Brett Ashley with a sharp wit and cynical humor. Like many of Hemingway's novels, this is a story of human emptiness and decay.

Why you're reading this book:
- It is one of the classic novels of one of the most celebrated American writers.
- Hemingway's spare and direct writing style complements the story that he tells.
- It poignantly depicts the moral emptiness and lack of direction that characterized a particular generation of Americans ("the lost generation").

Your teachers are looking for:
- How the pure and vital landscape becomes a depressing wasteland.
- Church and spirituality: in this novel, they are traditional anchors for personal values and morality.
- Class and ethnicity: the way the characters use racial or ethnic slurs and class labels to belittle others.
- How alcoholism is used to fill the moral void.
- Sickness and injury, i.e. Jake's impotency; Georgette's saying "everyone's sick"; the goring of the bull runners.
- The role money plays in this society.
- Humor and wit: Jake's ability to mask his depression with humor; Bill's relaxing and strangely insightful nonsense.

KEY CHARACTERS

Jake Barnes: The narrator and central figure in the story. Jake lives in Paris as a reporter for the *Herald Tribune*. His war injury has left him impotent. Has a frustrated relationship with Lady Brett Ashley.

Robert Cohn: The child of a wealthy Jewish New York family and a Princeton graduate. Cohn relies on athletic ability to ease his ethnic insecurity. He is a writer living in Paris. He is a hanger-on, both a pathetic and tragic character.

Frances: Cohn's lover, she is dominating and self centered. Her suffocating control over Cohn reveals his pathetic side.

Bill Gorton: Jake's witty traveling companion. As Bill has no roots to speak of, he does not weigh Jake down with his troubles. His lighthearted wordplay and refreshing perspective ease Jake's troubled spirit.

Michael Campbell: Brett's fiancé, Mike is an upper-class Scotchman. Although he has no money and many creditors, he lives the carefree life of the idle rich.

Count Mippipopulos: An older man, the count is a wealthy and idle visitor to Paris. Brett uses him for money, drinks, and entertainment. Though he is not malicious, the count's moral values are virtually nonexistent.

Pedro Romero: An up-and-coming young bullfighter. Romero's incredible good looks and natural bullfighting skill make him the perfect target for Brett's lust and destruction.

Montoya: The owner and namesake of the Hotel Montoya in Pamplona. A bullfight aficionado, and thus a friend of Jake's. He loses respect for Jake when Jake allows Brett to corrupt the bullfighter Romero.

ESSAY IDEAS

- Compare the landscape of Paris with that of San Sebastian and Pamplona. How does the landscape reflect the mood and events of the story?
- *The Sun Also Rises* has been said to speak for a "lost generation." What do you think is the general philosophy of the book?
- Is the narrator's attitude the same as the author's?
- Should we feel sorry for Cohn? Should we blame him, his friends or his society for the way he acts? Explain.
- Explore the role of drinking in the novel.
- How does Jake Barnes deal emotionally and physically with his injury?

A SAMPLE ESSAY IN OUTLINE FORM

In what ways does the book highlight Jake's impotence?
- Relationships:
  - With women:
    - On a literal level, he cannot make love to them.
    - He cannot make Brett stop her destructive behavior.
  - With men:
    - Robert Cohn:

- He can never get angry at him; only feels sorry for him.
- Rarely shows what he truly feels toward Robert.
- Tendency to isolate himself:
  - Constantly finds himself alone.
  - Drinks as a means of isolating himself from others.
- Jake's role as narrator:
  - He is always an observer, never an active participant.

Jake's impotence is most obvious in his relationships with women. However, his impotence goes further than this. In Jake, Hemingway gives us a picture of a man frustrated by his own inability to act on all levels. Jake's impotence is characteristic of the general lack of meaning and fulfillment among the novel's characters.

PLOT SUMMARY

BOOK ONE

(Set entirely in Paris)

Chapter I The narrator, Jake Barnes, gives a brief and extremely cynical description of Robert Cohn. Cohn is insecure and overly defensive; Jake's description suggests that Cohn will be an important but unpopular character.

Jake tells a story of Cohn in Paris. Cohn, embarrassed because Jake had mentioned another woman in front of his lover Frances, kicks him under the table. Jake finds Cohn pathetic and Frances petty and overbearing.

Chapter II Cohn visits Jake Barnes at his newspaper office in Paris—a regular inconvenience to Jake. Jake declines Cohn's ridiculous invitation to travel in South America and Africa. Cohn is immature but earnest, and we get the sense that Jake feels some sympathy for him.

He invites Cohn out for a drink, then artfully ditches him. He returns later to his office to find Cohn there, asleep. The two go out to a cafe, and Cohn explains the reason for his exhaustion: he and Frances were up late talking the previous night. Jake can picture the pathetic bedroom scene. This is typical of Jake: he can picture things, but he cannot live them.

Chapter III Alone now at the cafe, Jake invites a passing woman, Georgette, for a drink. She accepts and asks for dinner. As they talk, she becomes less and less attractive. Jake invited her to sit down out of boredom but soon finds himself regretting the company. It is possible that she is a prostitute.

Jake shies away from her kisses in the taxi, saying that he is "sick." She replies that everyone is sick. Over dinner, Georgette presses him more about his "illness." Jake says that he was injured in World War I. We later find out that his wounds have made him impotent.

At dinner, Jake becomes bored to the point of disgust with Georgette. They are invited to a table of "writers and artists," including Cohn and Frances. Jake makes a little sport by introducing Georgette as his fiancée.

The entire group goes to a rustic dance hall. Lady Brett Ashley walks into the room, surrounded by her usual swarm of pretty-boy suitors. Jake joins her at the bar, and the two complain about the boring evening and their friends. Deciding to leave, Jake gives the owner of the dance hall money for Georgette, and he and Lady Brett hail a taxi. In the taxi, Brett confesses to Jake that she is miserable. She calls him "darling," a sign that Brett and Jake were once lovers.

Chapter IV Brett manages to get a kiss out of Jake. She stops the kiss, however; because of Jake's impotence, the physical contact only frustrates them. They talk briefly of their past relationship before heading to another bar.

At the bar, the Cafe Select, they find most of the crowd from the dance hall, including Count Mippipopulos. The count takes an immediate fancy to Lady Brett. Jake quickly tires of watching the count's advances and leaves for his apartment.

At his apartment, Jake tries in vain to push Lady Brett out of his thoughts, but cannot. He curses Brett; it is his love for her that makes his impotence unbearable. He examines his injury in the mirror. He curses his fate, wondering what became of others in the war who received similar injuries.

Brett shows up at Jake's apartment with the count downstairs, waiting in his car. She is using his attraction to her to get free dinner and drinks, and invites Jake along. Jake refuses, although he does make plans to see her for dinner the next day. Brett leaves him alone.

Chapter V The next day, a walk around Paris with his coffee and cigarettes lifts Jake's spirits slightly. He goes to his office for a morning of work, then out with a fellow newspaperman for a drink. Upon returning to his office, he finds Cohn, who invites him for yet another lunch. Cohn, who noticed Lady Brett the evening before, questions Jake about her. He is unaware of Jake's and Brett's history.

Jake at first grudgingly answers Cohn's questions. Cohn continues to push, however, and Jake finally tells him to "go to hell." Cohn, far too insensitive to realize that he has hit a nerve in his friend, is deeply offended. He acts so hurt and pathetic that Jake once again feels sorry for him.

Chapter VI While waiting for Brett to arrive for dinner that night, Jake writes letters to pass the time. She does not show, but Jake is not greatly affected; he has been stood up by her many times before. He just sits on his own and enjoys the Parisian landscape.

He decides to move to the Cafe Select, where he meets up with a friend, Harvey Stone. Stone has obviously been at the bar all day, perhaps for a few days, drinking heavily. Jake, while realizing that Stone is a leech, kindly buys him a drink. Cohn approaches their table. Jake, as usual, is tactful, but the drunk Stone is annoyed by Cohn. He asks Cohn where he'd rather be. When Cohn replies that he'd rather be reliving his college football glory days, Stone insults him, calling him immature. Cohn, offended, threatens Stone, and Jake tries to placate Cohn. Frances arrives. She, too, is very insulting to Cohn, talking about him as if he weren't there.

At her request, Jake follows Frances to a cafe across the street. There, she confides in him that she is worried that Cohn might leave her, which will ruin her plans for wealth and a family. When Cohn rejoins them, she treats him like a child. Jake finally becomes disgusted with this display and leaves for his apartment.

Chapter VII Upon returning to his apartment, however, Jake finds Brett. She once again invites him to join her and the count. When Jake hedges, she sends the count out to buy champagne so that she can talk alone with Jake.

Brett tells Jake that she will be traveling to San Sebastian, Spain. Upon her return, her fiancé Michael will join her in Paris. Before the two can talk further, the count returns with champagne and takes the group out for dancing and drinks. The count is shown to be a pathetic character: He tries to use his money to buy friends and happiness.

At the end of the evening, Jake returns home alone.

BOOK II

Chapter VIII Brett and her fiancé are in Spain, and Cohn has not been around for a little while. But Jake's hilarious friend Bill Gorton is in Paris, and Jake enjoys his company tremendously. Lady Brett returns from Spain with her fiancé, and the group meet up over food and drinks. Brett's fiancé Michael gets extremely drunk and cannot keep his hands off of her, but the comic influence of Bill keeps tensions between Brett and Jake under control. After a while, Jake and Bill go off on their own to a boxing match.

Chapter IX The following day, Jake gets a letter from Cohn. He has been vacationing and wants to know if Jake wants to meet him to take a fishing trip in Spain. Jake agrees, writing Cohn that he will meet him in the South of France. The two will then continue on to Pamplona.

Later on, Jake sees Brett and Michael at the Cafe Select and invites them along. Brett seems hesitant. When Michael leaves, she tells Jake that she once went to Spain to have an affair with Cohn, and is afraid that meeting him with her fiancé would be uncomfortable.

Jake goes with Bill to meet Cohn. Both travelers are in a high-spirited mood when they meet him, and the three men check into a hotel.

Chapter X In the morning, Jake, Cohn, and Bill buy fishing gear and hire a car to Pamplona. The scenery on the ride to Spain is both beautiful and strangely new.

Upon arriving in Pamplona, they check into the Hotel Montoya, named after a famous bullfighter friend of Jake's. After a good meal, the trio are well-fed and well-rested.

The tension quickly rises again, however. Brett and Michael have promised to meet the group at a specific time, and Bill makes a bet with Cohn that they will not make it. Cohn takes the bet far too seriously. In addition, he constantly complains about needing a shave and a haircut.

Jake receives a telegram from Brett saying that she is in San Sebastian with Michael and will be late meeting the trio. The next morning, Cohn leaves, saying that Brett asked him to meet her in San Sebastian. While Cohn is lying, Jake and Bill couldn't care less; his absence has made their trip enjoyable again.

Chapter XI Jake and Bill take a trip to a small town, drinking wine and talking with the Spanish peasants on the bus with them. A waitress brings back Jake's tip, assuming he had made some error. These people, simple and honest, are a perfect antidote to Jake's morally bankrupt crowd of friends. That night, the two men check into a quaint hotel, happy and rejuvenated by life's simple pleasures.

Chapter XII The next day, the men awake to a beautiful day. They go out walking, and Bill jokes good-naturedly with Jake about his job and the literary pretensions of "irony and pity" that are in fashion at the time. They fish, nap, eat, talk, and drink wine.

The two friends, sometimes joined by a third, Harris, enjoy this relaxed lifestyle for five days. Nothing is heard of Brett, Michael, or Cohn.

Chapter XIII One morning, Jake receives a letter from Brett and a telegram from Cohn, saying that all will meet in Pamplona. Bill and Jake spend one more drunken night with Harris and are on their way. Harris is sad to see them go and gives them parting gifts.

Back in Pamplona, Bill and Jake check back into their hotel and meet up with Montoya, the bullfighter. He asks whether or not Jake's friends are lovers of bullfighting like themselves. Jake, Bill, Brett, Cohn, and Michael are reunited in the hotel. After an awkward few minutes, they all decide to go into town for the running of the bulls.

Before every bullfight, the bulls run through barricaded streets to the bullring. The Spaniards run with them to show their bravery; some are badly hurt during the run. The group, most of them drunk, look on. Michael, who is far drunker than everyone else, begins to make fun of Cohn for following Brett around San Sebastian. Bill takes Cohn away from Michael and buys him a drink.

Chapter XIV Jake, by now totally drunk, leaves his friends in disgust and returns to his hotel room. There he tries to read but can only think of Brett. The next morning, Brett offers to go to confession with Jake. Jake refuses her company. Brett goes to get her palm read instead. The town of Pamplona is beginning to swell with people and excitement—the bullfighting festival is at hand.

Chapter XV The fiesta begins with an explosion of mass drunkenness. Brett is barred from entering the church because of her hat and is danced around like an idol by the revelers. The group of friends spend the day participating in the town's drunken celebration. Cohn, as usual, cannot keep up and passes out.

At the bullfights, Jake and Bill sit with Montoya. Jake gets extremely annoyed with Cohn, who seems completely bored by the fighting. Brett, however, is fascinated with the gory spectacle, as well as the handsome, talented bullfighter Pedro Romero.

Chapter XVI The following day, the bullfights are canceled due to rain. Jake and Montoya meet with Romero in a cafe. At an adjacent table, Brett, sitting with Michael and Cohn, lusts after Romero. Michael, noticing his wife's attention to Romero, yells drunkenly to the young bullfighter that Brett wants him. He then starts in on Cohn. This time, Cohn has had enough, and challenges Michael to a fight. The crowd quickly breaks up to avoid the hostilities.

Brett leaves the cafe with Jake. While walking through town, she confesses to him that she is miserable with Michael. Brett looks to Jake for comfort and support. However, the two come upon Romero, and Brett's unhappiness is soon forgotten. Jake introduces Brett to Romero and leaves.

Chapter XVII Mike and Bill have been thrown out of the hotel for starting fights. When Cohn finds out that Jake has introduced Brett to Romero, another fight breaks out and Cohn beats both Jake and Michael up. A sobbing Cohn later tries to make amends, but Jake's pity for him is finally exhausted; he feels only disgust for Cohn.

Watching the running bulls, Jake sees a man gored. The newspaper account, as well as the stories of the death throughout town, makes the death seem horrible and personal. The bull is later killed in a fight by Romero, who gives its ear to Brett. Brett, once again proving her insensitivity, loses it. We later find out that Cohn has tried unsuccessfully to beat up Romero.

Chapter XVIII At lunch the next day, Michael finally shows disgust for his fiancée's numerous sexual encounters. Brett tries to defend herself to Jake, claiming that she is a changed woman. Judging from her past, we suspect otherwise.

Jake, Brett, and Bill watch Romero that afternoon at the bullfights. He fights skillfully and courageously, besting even the most difficult bull. He presents its ear to Brett, and the two leave on a train to Madrid. Jake tries in vain to drown his sorrows in drink with Bill.

BOOK III

Chapter XIX Jake, Michael, and Bill travel to France, where they go their separate ways. Jake stays in France because there he can tip the waiters. To Jake's way of thinking, tipping someone means making a friend—the easiest, simplest relationship there is. Jake then returns to San Sebastian and lives a simple, quiet life, swimming and reading for several days.

His peace is interrupted yet again by Brett, who sends him a telegram from Madrid asking him to come to her. In Madrid, she once again cries on his ever-ready shoulder. She has sent Romero back to Pamplona, knowing that their happiness could not last, and has resigned herself once again to her previous decadent lifestyle. The two talk of their own relationship; Brett suggests that sex between them, if it were possible, would be great. They get drunk late into the night.

A TALE OF TWO CITIES

ABOUT THE AUTHOR

See page 85

THE BIG PICTURE

A Tale of Two Cities, Dickens' most heavily historical novel, takes place in Paris and London during the French Revolution. The novel is centered around one family, the Manettes, and what happens to them during this period; but in characteristic Dickensian style, the plot is intricate and there are several subplots.

Why you're reading this book:
- It offers colorful, dramatic insight into the French Revolution.
- Of all of Dickens' works, it is one of the most accessible.

Your teachers are looking for:
- Themes:
  - Imprisonment—real or imagined.
  - Death and rebirth.
  - Isolation.
  - Love and hate.
- The comparisons between London and Paris.
- The evolution of Sidney Carton as a character.
- Images carried throughout the book:
  - Blood/wine.
  - Hunger.
  - Water.
  - Roads.
- The division of classes, both English and French.
- The significance and role of Madame Defarge.
- The concept and execution of justice.

KEY CHARACTERS

Jarvis Lorry: An employee of the venerable Tellson's bank. True to his profession, he is a neat, methodical man, although his bright eyes at times betray a heart more generous than that of the average banker.

Lucie Manette: A pretty young woman, about seventeen years old. She is described most often by her golden hair and her forehead that is the barometer of all her feelings. Living in England at the time her father is discovered in the Bastille, she brings him to London to help him regain his health.

Dr. Alexandre Manette: A man held prisoner without cause in the Bastille for many years. He is a brilliant doctor who has suffered amnesia and strives to regain his health for his daughter Lucie's sake.

Monsieur Defarge: The owner of the wine shop in St. Antoine. With his wife, he becomes one of the leaders of the French Revolution.

Madame Defarge: A strong woman whose driving passion is to seek revenge against the Evremondes and all French aristocrats. Her hatred fuels the Revolution.

Jerry Cruncher: The odd job man/messenger for Tellson's who moonlights as a grave-robber. He is one of the few comic characters in the book, along with his wife and son.

Charles Darnay: A young, "modern" gentleman who is an emigrant from France. He is earnest and intelligent and well-

Sidney Carton: Dickens describes him as "the idlest and most unpromising of men." Yet he works very hard (when he wants to) and loves very deeply (when he cares to admit it).

Miss Pross: The personal servant of Lucie Manette whom Dickens characterizes as a "wild red woman, strong of hand." She is a rather comic representation of the English lower class.

ESSAY IDEAS

- How does the opening paragraph create a theme and a mood that continue throughout the novel?
- Describe the juxtaposition of wine and blood in the novel. How is it effective?
- What do you think is the overriding theme of the novel? Why?
- Discuss the idea of imprisonment as it relates to Dr. Manette.
- According to Dickens, is the English social system of his time similar to the French system before the Revolution? Explain.
- Discuss Madame Defarge and her role in the Revolution. Do you agree with her thinking? Her methods for revenge?
- Compare/contrast Charles Darnay and Sidney Carton. How are they both heroic? What are their faults?

A SAMPLE ESSAY IN OUTLINE FORM

Counterparts/doubling in *A Tale of Two Cities*
- Each character has a counterpart:
  - Sidney Carton/Charles Darnay.
  - Madame Defarge/Lucie Manette.
  - Miss Pross/Jerry Cruncher.
- The book is divided evenly between events in London and events in Paris.
- Many occurrences in one city have

counterparts/parallels in the other:
- The echoes of footsteps in the Manettes' courtyard in Soho/the actual gathering of people in their courtyard in Paris.
- The English mob surrounding the spy's funeral/the French mob in Saint Antoine.
- The conflict between the upper class and the lower class in both cities.

From the novel's opening paragraph, Dickens creates a sense of twos, of contrasts. The use of doubles functions on several different levels—thematically, symbolically, and as a plot device—thereby strengthening the coherence of the novel's overall structure.

PLOT SUMMARY

BOOK I: RECALLED TO LIFE

Chapter 1—The Period "It was the best of times, it was the worst of times...in short, the period was so far like the present period, that some of its noisiest authorities insisted on its being received, for good or for evil, in the superlative degree of comparison only." So reads one of the most famous introductions in all of literature. Dickens is describing the year 1775, a time of turmoil for both England and France, as the differences between the rich and the poor grew increasingly severe.

Chapter 2—The Mail On a cold Friday evening in November 1775, the Dover Mail, the coach that carries the mail to Dover, labors up Shooter's Hill. A messenger hails the coach and asks for a passenger by the name of Jarvis Lorry. The message for Mr. Lorry reads, "Wait at Dover for Mam'selle." Lorry's cryptic answer is, "Recalled to life." The messenger, Jerry Cruncher, rides off, muttering to himself that it is a "blazing strange message."

Chapter 3—The Night Shadows Dickens opens this chapter with the speculation "...that every human creature is constituted to be that profound secret and mystery to every other." Jarvis Lorry dozes in the coach and dreams of digging up a man who has been buried for eighteen years.

Chapter 4—The Preparation By morning, the coach delivers Mr. Lorry to the Royal George Hotel. Lucie Manette arrives soon thereafter. Mr. Lorry tells her that her father has been found alive, living in the home of an old servant in France. As the accounts of Dr. Manette have always been under the care of Tellson's bank, it is Mr. Lorry's duty to take Lucie to him. They must travel in secret, however, because the reason for Dr. Manette's long imprisonment is unknown. After a few moments Lucie faints, and her nurse, the wild Miss Pross, rushes in to care for her and scold Mr. Lorry.

Chapter 5—The Wine Shop Dickens opens this chapter with a word-picture that is characteristic of his style. Mr. Lorry and Lucie Manette have traveled to the St. Antoine district of Paris. He describes the men, women, and children of Saint Antoine greedily drinking wine spilled out of a broken cask. The moment goes as quickly as the wine, the only reminder being the word BLOOD scrawled on a wall. The people of Saint Antoine are starving.

The keeper of the wine shop, Monsieur Defarge, scolds the man who drew on the wall and returns to his shop. His wife calls his attention to the strangers on the premises, Mr. Lorry and Lucie Manette. Before attending to them, he pauses to speak with three men, all of whom call each other Jacques. He then turns to escort the strangers out into a rear courtyard and up a few flights of stairs. At the top of the stairs, Monsieur Defarge unlocks a door to reveal a white-haired man busily making shoes.

Chapter 6—The Shoemaker Defarge approaches the man and asks him his name. The faint reply is "One hundred and five, North Tower." Lucie moves quietly to his side and sits next to him on the bench. He is startled by her presence but the shining radiance of her hair distracts him. He touches it gingerly and then pulls a little bag on a string out from his shirt. In the bag are three golden hairs that match Lucie's. He wonderingly asks her who she is. She pulls him to her and comforts him.

The two are left alone while Mr. Lorry and Defarge prepare for a speedy departure from Paris. Dr. Manette acts lost and confused to be leaving his garret and asks to take his shoemaking tools and supplies with him.

BOOK II—THE GOLDEN THREAD

Chapter 1—Five Years Later Dickens opens this book with a description of Tellson's Bank, a cramped, dusty place that considers its very inconvenience to be part of its eminence and respectability. He compares Tellson's establishment to Eng-land: any suggestion of change, no matter how reasonable, is considered blasphemy at the least and treason at the worst.

He describes the home of Jerry Cruncher, the odd job man for Tellson's, where the basic interactions are always the same. Apparently, Mrs. Cruncher is a very religious woman and often prays on her knees. In a highly comic scene, Jerry refers to her praying as "flopping" and is convinced that she prays against him and his good fortune as an "honest tradesman."

Chapter 2—A Sight Jerry takes a message to Mr. Lorry at the Old Bailey, the courthouse next to Newgate prison. Gossiping with the gatekeeper, Jerry discovers that a trial for treason is going on. If the man is found guilty, he will be executed in the most horrible way imaginable.

The defendant's name is Charles Darnay. As Jerry enters the courtroom, Darnay is being sworn in on the witness stand. On the other side of the room, he sees Dr. and Lucie Manette, who are to be witnesses for Darnay.

Chapter 3—A Disappointment The Attorney-General opens his argument by describing the evidence he has accumulated against Charles Darnay. He gives a rousing speech commending the patriotism of his chief witness. Mr. Lorry and Lucie both testify that they saw and spoke to Darnay aboard the packet-ship that travels between Dover, England and "Keelless" (Calais), France.

The Attorney-General's case hinges on the testimony of a witness who claims to have seen Darnay at a certain hotel waiting to collect military information. The testimony is undermined by the fact that the witness is not entirely sure it was Darnay he saw. Sidney Carton, another lawyer in the courthouse, goes to stand next to Darnay. The physical likeness between this man and Charles Darnay is incredible to everyone. The jury finds Darnay not guilty.

Chapter 4—Congratulatory The Manettes, Darnay, Carton, Mr. Lorry, Jerry, and the defense lawyer, Mr. Stryver, are gathered outside the courthouse. They all agree that they are quite worn out from the day, with the exception of Mr. Stryver, who insists that he and Carton have much work to do later on that night. As everyone is leaving, Carton invites Darnay to dine with him at a nearby tavern. After dinner, Carton drinks alone and mutters to himself, wishing he could trade places with Darnay so that he might have a chance with Lucie.

Chapter 5—The Jackal Here the reader discovers how Mr. Stryver has become so successful. He spends every night with Sidney Carton, drinking and giving him his most difficult problems to solve. Carton allows himself to be used as Stryver's "jackal" because he is unambitious. They work until the early hours of the morning. Before Carton departs, the two men drink a toast to Lucie Manette.

Chapter 6—Hundreds of People Four months after the trial, Mr. Lorry goes to visit the Manettes in their apartment in the London suburb of Soho. They are out when he arrives, however, so he chats briefly with Miss Pross. She lets him know that the Doctor still keeps his shoemaker's bench and tools in his room and that at times he has very strange moods.

She also complains that "hundreds of people" have been calling on Lucie, but only Mr. Darnay and Mr. Carton come to call before Lucie returns. Darnay tells a story of a prisoner who had buried a medical bag; the story upsets Dr. Manette a great deal, although he tries to hide it. Eventually, the group sits still for a while and listens to the echoing footsteps and the falling rain.

Chapter 7—Monseigneur in Town This chapter, set in Paris, shows the excessive lifestyle of the French aristocracy. Monseigneur, a particularly high-ranking aristocrat, has four elaborately clad men working as a team to serve him his morning chocolate: "one lackey carried the chocolate-pot into the sacred presence; a second, milled and frothed the chocolate with the little instrument he bore for that function; a third, presented the favoured napkin; a fourth..., poured the chocolate out."

It is a ludicrous scene, particularly in contrast to that of the starving people of Saint Antoine scooping wine out of the street. The morning ritual finished, Monseigneur deigns to view the people who have come to see him. He is generally rude to most of them, as is his custom.

One man, the Marquis St. Evremonde, leaves in a huff, his carriage hurtling through the streets. One of its wheels hits something. A cry goes up from the bystanders as a man comes forward to gather a bundle from under the carriage. It is the body of a child. The man begins to scream "Dead!" and to cry. Defarge tries to comfort him. The Marquis tosses a gold coin at each of them. As he is driving away, one of the coins is thrown back in his carriage window.

Chapter 8—Monseigneur in the Country

As Dickens paints the countryside surrounding Monsieur the Marquis' estate, it is obvious that the people and the land are being worked to death. At one point the carriage stops and a mender of roads is questioned as to why he was staring at the Marquis. He replies that he was staring at a man hanging onto the back of the carriage. The Marquis sends him away.

Chapter 9—The Gorgon's Head

The nephew of the Marquis, expected for dinner, has not yet arrived. The Marquis decides to begin alone. Halfway through, the nephew appears, and he is none other than Charles Darnay. Darnay is a kind man despite his relation to the Marquis, and earnestly argues with his uncle that the aristocracy's treatment of the poor is wrong. He renounces his property and title.

The next morning, the Marquis is found stabbed in his bed, the note on the knife reading, "Drive him fast to his tomb. This, from the Jaquerie."

Chapter 10—Two Promises

A year later Darnay has become an established French tutor. He has fallen in love with Lucie and goes to Dr. Manette to speak of his intentions. Dr. Manette is touched by his consideration. To encourage the doctor's trust in him, Darnay begins to reveal his true identity and reason for being in England. Strangely distressed, the doctor orders him to stop and to tell him on the morning of the wedding. When Lucie returns home later that evening, she hears her father working at the shoemaking bench that he has not approached in so long.

Chapter 11—A Companion Picture

Mr. Stryver and Sidney Carton are working and drinking late at night. Mr. Stryver announces his intention to propose to Lucy, which he thinks, will be a "piece of good fortune for her." He asks Carton for approval but doesn't get it.

Chapter 12—The Fellow of Delicacy

On his way to propose to Lucy, Mr. Stryver stops by Tellson's to tell Mr. Lorry of his plan. As a tactful man of business, Mr. Lorry suggests that Mr. Stryver should not venture the proposal at all, as it might be difficult for Dr. Manette or Lucie to be "explicit" with him. Mr. Lorry offers to go to the house instead, and to inquire into the situation. After doing so, he again tries to discourage Stryver from his marriage hopes.

Chapter 13—The Fellow of No Delicacy

Stryver's talk of marriage finally drives Sidney Carton to confess himself to Lucie. Finding her alone one day, he shakily admits that she alone has had the power to make him reconsider his wasted life. He is speaking to her to stir pity, not love, in her heart. He simply wants her to know of his devotion to her, however unworthy. As Lucie weeps for the man Carton could have become, he asks for her secrecy. In parting, he makes a statement whose great significance will become clear at the end of the novel. He tells her, "think now and then that there is a man who would give his life, to keep a life you love beside you!"

Chapter 14—The Honest Tradesman
As Jerry sits at his post outside Tellson's, a funeral procession approaches. He is interested because the hearse is surrounded by a mob rather than mourners. From a man in the crowd, Jerry finds out that this is the funeral of Roger Cly, the Old Bailey spy, and the former key witness in the Darnay trial. The crowd's general hatred of spies incites them to hijack the hearse and rejoice loudly as they take the coffin to the cemetery.

Later that night, Jerry goes out "fishing"; that is, meeting a few of his friends to dig up the newly buried body. Young Jerry, Jerry's son, follows them to the cemetery. He gets so frightened watching them, however, that he runs home imagining a coffin is chasing him.

Chapter 15—Knitting
The scene returns to the Paris wine shop where the revolutionaries have been gathering as early as six in the morning. Defarge has brought the mender of roads to tell the story of the man accused of killing the Marquis. He relates vividly how the man was tortured and thrown in jail and how the King's soldiers came to build a forty-foot gallows next to the fountain at the center of the village. After the man is hung, his body is left hanging over the fountain, poisoning the water. The Jaquerie—as the band of revolutionaries is called—decide to register the crime with Madame Defarge. Every crime committed against the people and every person causing these injuries is recorded

in Madame Defarge's knitting.

Chapter 16—Still Knitting
The Defarges are alerted by a compatriot in the police force that an English spy from Old Bailey named John Barsad has been sent to their quarter. The next day he stops by the wine shop and attempts to converse with Madame Defarge. She knits him into her register as he compliments her on the pattern. When Monsieur Defarge enters, Barsad greets him with "Good day, Jacques." Defarge replies that the gentleman must be mistaken, as his name is Ernest Defarge.

Not put off, the spy refers to Defarge's connection to Dr. Manette. He asks if the Defarges have heard the news that Lucie is to be married. He informs them that she is to marry a native Frenchman, none other than the Marquis de Evremonde's nephew, a man who in England calls himself Charles Darnay. After Barsad leaves, Defarge expresses his hope that Darnay's destiny will keep him out of France.

Chapter 17—One Night
The night before Lucie's wedding to Darnay, she and her father sit quietly. She assures her father that he will always have her love and support. Dr. Manette replies that he is happy for her and relieved that she is going on with her life instead of wasting it caring for him. He then talks for the first time about his experiences in prison and how he dreamed of having a daughter.

Chapter 18—Nine Days
As promised, Darnay and Dr. Manette meet on the morning of the wedding. Dr. Manette emerges from the study looking extremely pale. No one comments on it, and the wedding goes as planned. That night, however, the Doctor reverts entirely to his shoemaker's persona and will not snap out of it. Miss Pross and Mr. Lorry decide to keep this development a secret from Lucie, who is on her honey-

moon. As the chapter ends, Dr. Manette has been cobbling for nine days.

Chapter 19—An Opinion On the tenth morning, Dr. Manette appears to have returned to normal. He seems uneasy but unsure that anything has happened. To be tactful, Mr. Lorry asks Dr. Manette for some medical advice. Mr. Lorry proceeds to tell of a "friend" whom he is very close to and about whom he is very concerned. In this manner, he is able to relate Manette's behavior of the past nine days. Mr. Lorry asks Manette if perhaps this friend might be prevented from his behavior if the tools were taken from him. Dr. Manette keeps up the pretense of giving advice and agrees that it should be done, although not in the gentleman's presence.

Chapter 20—A Plea When Mr. and Mrs. Darnay return from their honeymoon, the first person to greet them is Sidney Carton. He takes Darnay aside to ask if he might be considered a friend, welcome in their house. Darnay agrees; Carton has always been a frequent guest, and Darnay has not forgotten the service that Carton did for him during his trial for treason. Later that evening, however, Darnay remarks on Carton's pitiable state and how little he makes of himself. The remarks trouble Lucie, and she makes a point of asking her husband to always have compassion in his heart for Carton.

Chapter 21—Echoing Footsteps This chapter summarizes the events of the past eight years and bring the story to the first year of the French Revolution, 1789. The title of the chapter works in two ways: the echoes refer to the comings and goings of the past years but also serve to foreshadow the action that is to come.

During this time, both Darnay and Dr. Manette have been reasonably successful and prosperous. Lucie has given birth to two children, a son and a daughter, but the son has passed away. Sidney Carton only comes to see the little family about six times a year, but little Lucie, the Darnays' daughter, loves him dearly.

Finally, Dickens brings the reader to the hot, wild night in July on which the Revolution began. First he shows the Darnays, Dr. Manette, and Mr. Lorry listening to the echoes as they did one night long ago (see Book II, Chapter 6). Using the sound of footsteps as a transition, he plunges the reader into the storming of the Bastille.

When the waves of mad peasants finally overpower the fortress, Defarge grabs a prison officer and forces him to show him 105 North Tower, the words that Dr. Manette had uttered when he first saw him after his imprisonment. Darnay searches the cell and finds the initials A. M. carved into the wall.

Chapter 22—The Sea Still Rises Once the violence has begun, the people of Saint Antoine are all the more ready to strike against the enemies of the people. The Defarges find out that an old aristocrat named Foulon, who had told the poor people to eat grass, is nearby. It takes only a few minutes to rouse a mob to seize him, hang him, and place his head (with grass in its mouth) on a pike.

Chapter 23—Fire Rises One night soon thereafter, the Jaquerie sets fire to the chateau once occupied by the Marquis de Evremonde. With the fire as inspiration, the people also decide that Monsieur Gabelle, though the lowliest of state officials (a tax collector), should be duly punished for his crimes. He barricades himself in his house, however, and avoids death at least for that night.

Chapter 24—Drawn to the Loadstone Rock Three years after the storming of the

Bastille, the climate in France is still tumultuous and very hostile to members of the aristocracy. The members of the upper class who survived the early purges and fled to England congregate at the Paris branch of Tellson's bank.

One afternoon as Charles Darnay is visiting Mr. Lorry, a letter arrives addressed to Monsieur heretofore the Marquis de Evremonde. This person, of course, is Charles Darnay, although no one save Dr. Manette is aware of his true French name. The letter is from Monsieur Gabelle, who has suffered much trying to help the Evremonde family and is currently in prison awaiting death. Darnay decides, despite the strong possibility of danger to himself, to journey to Paris to try and help Gabelle. Thinking it will cause Lucie and her father the least distress, he writes them letters to inform them of his intentions and leaves the next day.

BOOK III—THE TRACK OF A STORM

Chapter 1—In Secret Naive about the "new order" in France, Charles Darnay/Evremonde walks directly into the arms of the peasant law enforcement. It is only the tone and address of his letter from Gabelle which enables him to begin his journey inland to Paris. He is eventually told that he must have an escort to protect himself, and must pay for it as well. Darnay is escorted to Paris, but before he can do anything to help Gabelle, he is sentenced to prison. Apparently new laws have been made condemning all French emigrants as traitors.

Although Darnay is welcomed by the other aristocratic prisoners in La Force, his imprisonment is "in secret" so he is not allowed in the prison's common rooms. Darnay's captivity directly parallels Dr. Manette's: it is for a crime he has no knowledge of, and he has no way to communicate his plight to his family.

Chapter 2—The Grindstone Tellson's bank in France is quite a bit different than its British counterpart. Not only does Mr. Lorry (who has traveled to Paris to aid Dr. Manette and Lucie with Darnay) find the lavish interior of the bank disturbing; there is a large grindstone placed in the courtyard where the revolutionaries come to sharpen their already bloody weapons.

Lucie and Dr. Manette enter. On reading Charles' letters, they rushed to Paris to find him and have discovered that he is in prison. They have had no difficulty traveling because Dr. Manette's history as a Bastille prisoner gives him extremely high status. Once Lucie and her daughter are safe with Miss Pross and Mr. Lorry, Dr. Manette goes out into the crowd and asks for their help. They receive him with great shouts of approval and move off toward La Force.

Chapter 3—The Shadow Mr. Lorry feels it is irresponsible of him to shelter Lucie, an emigrant's wife, under the bank roof. However, he helps her and her father to find alternate lodgings nearby. Soon after, the Defarges pay them a call to bring notes from Dr. Manette and Charles. Both messages are reassurances that Charles is fine and that the Doctor has enough influence to help him. The Defarges' visit is eerie, however, as they are leaders of the revolutionaries who have imprisoned Charles. Madame Defarge behaves very coldly to Lucie and knits her and her daughter into the register "for their safety."

Chapter 4—Calm in Storm Four days after his departure with the crowd, Dr. Manette returns full of the horrors he has seen. He reports Charles to be safe for the time being, but that he can do nothing until

Charles is brought before the tribunal of the new republic of "Liberty, Equality, Fraternity or Death." In the meantime, Dr. Manette secures a position as a prison doctor, making rounds daily through several prisons, including La Force.

The chapter closes with images of La Guillotine, the "sharp female newly-born." It is a popular subject for jokes and models of it are worn around people's necks in the place of crosses.

Chapter 5—The Wood-sawyer Early in Charles' captivity, Dr. Manette shows Lucie a certain place where her husband may be able to see her from a window he gains access to around three in the afternoon. For the following year and three months, Lucie goes to the indicated spot every day, regardless of the weather. The Doctor finds her in this spot one afternoon to tell her that Charles has finally been summoned to trial.

Chapter 6—Triumph The next day, Charles Darnay stands accused of being an emigrant whose life is forfeit to the Republic, "...under the decree which banished all emigrants on pain of Death." Charles, following careful instructions given him by Dr. Manette, slowly outlines his defense. He states that he married a French woman, renounced his aristocratic uncle long ago, and had been tried in England as an enemy to England due to his French citizenship. In short, although not living in France, Charles claims that he has always been loyal to the people of France. On the strength of Dr. Manette's testimony, Charles is acquitted.

Chapter 7—A Knock at the Door Darnay is reunited with his family, although both he and Lucie are apprehensive about remaining in France. That same night, Charles is arrested again and told that he will stand trial again the next day. The only explanation given is that Charles has been denounced by the Defarges and one other anonymous party.

Chapter 8—A Hand at Cards Back in England, Miss Pross and Jerry Cruncher are out shopping and encounter her long lost brother Solomon. Miss Pross nearly blows her brother's cover by screaming when she sees him. He drags her out of the shop and into the street, where Jerry realizes that he also recognizes this man. He begins trying to guess the man's name when, out of nowhere, Sidney Carton appears and identifies the man as John Barsad, one of the spies of the Old Bailey in London. Carton also knows that Barsad is a prison spy and may be able to help them save Darnay. Carton decides that the four of them should go to Mr. Lorry's house to consider these events and perhaps coerce Mr. Barsad to use his knowledge to help them.

As he is laying out the "cards" he can use to blackmail Barsad into helping him, Sidney Carton pauses to inquire about the man he saw Barsad with earlier. Coincidentally, the companion was Roger Cly, the spy whose funeral was celebrated near Tellson's. Barsad protests that Cly is dead, but Jerry Cruncher interjects that there was nothing in the coffin but rocks and dirt. With so much information gathered against him, Barsad finally agrees to help Carton gain access to La Force prison.

Chapter 9—The Game Made Barsad leaves, and Carton reports that the spy has granted access to Darnay but only once, to be used if he is sentenced to death. Carton asks Mr. Lorry to say nothing of his presence or activities in London to Lucie. After speaking with Mr. Lorry, Carton goes out and makes a mysterious purchase from a pharmacist.

The next day, Alexandre Manette is called as the third denouncer of Charles Darnay/Evremonde. Of course, everyone is shocked and confused. Defarge reveals a paper he found hidden in 105 North Tower. It is written in Dr. Manette's hand, describing the reasons and circumstances of his imprisonment.

Chapter 10—The Substance of the Shadow This chapter tells Dr. Manette's story. It begins in 1757, when Dr. Manette was called on an emergency in the middle of the night. He was taken to the Evremonde chateau and instructed by the elder of the two Evremonde brothers to try to save a dying peasant girl and her brother, both victims of the younger Evremonde brother's violence. Both peasants died.

Horrified by the careless cruelty of the aristocrats, Dr. Manette sent a letter to a court authority reporting the incident and bitterly denouncing the Evremondes. Around the same time, he was visited by the wife of the older brother and her young son (Charles Darnay). She told the doctor that the peasant girl had a surviving sister and that she wanted to contact her, for she was committed to trying to make amends to the family for her brother-in-law's conduct. The Evremonde brothers learned of Dr. Manette's letter, however, and had him thrown in the Bastille.

Within minutes, Darnay (the son of the elder Evremonde brother) is found guilty and sentenced to death the next day.

Chapter 11—Dusk As the sentence is pronounced, Lucie asks permission to embrace her husband once more. Dr. Manette tries to apologize to them but is so overcome by the situation that he begins tearing at his hair and shrieking. When the jailers separate Charles from her, Lucie faints. Sidney Carton carries her unconscious form to the carriage, rides along to their apartment, and carries her upstairs. As he turns to leave, he kisses her cheek and whispers, "a life you love," echoing what he said to her years ago as he confessed his love to her (see Book II, Chapter 13).

Chapter 12—Darkness That afternoon, Carton pays a visit to the wine shop in Saint Antoine. Madame Defarge is startled to see someone who so closely resembles Charles Darnay, but on discovering he is an Englishman, she dismisses him. Because Carton is speaking French very poorly, the Defarges feel comfortable fighting in front of him. Carton actually speaks fluent French, however, and overhears Madame Defarge arguing that Lucie and her daughter should be killed as well for their relation to Charles Darnay/Evremonde. Madame Defarge reveals that she was the surviving sister of the peasant girl and boy killed by the Evremonde brothers. This is the driving force behind her hatred and her revolutionary fervor.

At Mr. Lorry's lodgings Dr. Manette wanders in from the street, having again assumed his shoemaker persona. Carton and Lorry agree that he should be taken to Lucie. In Dr. Manette's coat, Carton finds the papers that will enable Dr. Manette, Lucie, and her daughter to pass safely over the border. He entrusts these to Mr. Lorry along with his own pass. He also confides what he has overheard in the wine shop; Lucie and her daughter, and perhaps Dr. Manette as well, are in danger of being denounced by Madame Defarge. He impresses on Mr. Lorry the importance of their fleeing from Paris as soon as possible. Finally, Mr. Lorry and Carton agree to meet in the courtyard of Tellson's the following day.

Chapter 13—Fifty-two On the day of his execution, Charles Darnay writes several letters in an effort to put his heart and mind at ease. Sidney Carton enters the cell and urgently requests Darnay to switch clothes with him. As Darnay is doing this, Carton drugs him so that he falls unconscious. Barsad enters with two prison guards, and promises to convey Darnay to Mr. Lorry.

As the prisoners are called out to the carts which carry them to the Guillotine, Carton is befriended by a young seamstress. She immediately realizes that he is not Darnay/Evremonde. She asks him if he is dying for Darnay and his wife and child and he urges her to "Hush!" She asks if she can hold his hand. As these two move towards death, Dickens shows the Manettes, Lorry, and Darnay all being carried to safety and life.

Chapter 14—Knitting Done As Miss Pross and Jerry Cruncher finish preparing to leave, Jerry goes out to fetch a carriage. Madame Defarge appears at the apartment expecting to find a grief-stricken Lucie. Instead, she is received by a defiant Miss Pross. Thinking Pross is hiding Lucie in one of the inner rooms, Madame Defarge threatens her with a pistol. The two women struggle but "Miss Pross [fights] with the vigorous tenacity of love, always so much stronger than hate." Madame Defarge fires the pistol but is thrown off balance and falls on the shot. The blast from the gun blows Miss Pross' eardrums but she is sensible enough to get out of the apartment. She and Jerry meet and make their escape.

Chapter 15—The Footsteps Die Out Forever In the opening paragraphs of this final chapter, Dickens sums up his feelings about the French Revolution. "Crush humanity out of shape once more, under similar hammers, and it will twist itself into the same tortured forms. Sow the same seed of rapacious licence and oppression over again, and it will surely yield the same fruit according to its kind."

At the execution, Carton bears the taunts of the crowd calmly and turns his attention to comfort the seamstress. She kisses him and goes to the Guillotine directly before him. He repeats the words from his father's funeral service once more and dies, number twenty-three of the fifty-two enemies of the Republic slotted to die that day. "They said of him, about the city that night, that it was the most peaceful man's face ever beheld there. Many added that he looked sublime and prophetic."

The book closes by returning to Carton's last thoughts. He visualizes a new and better world and the Darnays happy at last. He imagines they have a son whom they name Sidney, who may become a judge. He hopes that when they tell his namesake the story, they will express his final thought: "It is a far, far better thing that I do, than I have ever done; it is a far, far better rest that I go to than I have ever known.

TO KILL A MOCKINGBIRD

ABOUT THE AUTHOR

Nelle Harper Lee (1926–) was born in Monroesville, Alabama, the daughter of a lawyer. She attended Huntington College, studied law at the University of Alabama, and attended Oxford in England for a year. During the 1950s she worked as an airline reservation clerk, but left to devote her time to writing.

Her first and only book, *To Kill a Mockingbird*, received high critical acclaim, winning not only the 1961 Pulitzer Prize for Literature but several other important awards as well. The book, which Ms. Lee thinks of as a "love story," has been translated into many foreign languages and in 1962 was adapted for the screen.

THE BIG PICTURE

To Kill a Mockingbird is a first-person account of a young child coming to terms with racism and intolerance in a Southern town. On a larger scale, it is a condemnation of the injustice of prejudice and a plea for greater understanding and tolerance between races.

Why you're reading this book:
- It explores ideas about "difference" and prejudice, and why people think the way they do.
- It is a moving call for justice and tolerance.
- It illustrates how a spare and efficient writing style can still create powerful emotions.
- It realistically portrays the observations of a sensitive and intelligent child growing up.

Your teachers are looking for:
- How the book deals with race relations in the Deep South.
- How Lee blends the different strands of her story into a coherent whole.
- The eccentricities of the characters.
- How the perspective of a young child affects the way the story gets told.

KEY CHARACTERS

Scout (Jean Louise) Finch: The narrator. Her story covers her childhood in Maycomb from ages six to nine. Scout is bright, sensitive, and tomboyish—a strong-willed and irrepressible character.

Jem (Jeremy Atticus) Finch: Scout's brother, four years her elder. He tends to act as a check on Scout.

Dill (Charles Bakes) Harris: Scout and Jem's friend and Scout's "fiancé." He visits Maycomb every summer and is the instigator of many pranks.

Atticus Finch: Scout and Jem's father and the town lawyer. He is well-respected, well-liked and highly moral.

Calpurnia: A black woman who is the Finches' cook and de facto governess. She is considered "part of the family."

Miss Maudie Atkinson: Scout's neighbor. She loves gardens and bakes the best cake in Maycomb. She knows how to treat children like people.

Mrs. Henry Lafayette Dubose: A mean old woman who lives down the street and is a neighborhood terror. Jem crosses her path and the kids learn a lesson about bravery.

Aunt Alexandra: Atticus' sister. She is

determined to make Scout a lady and Jem a gentleman.

Robinson: A black man falsely accused of raping a white woman. He is a good man, respected and liked.

Bob Ewell: The town parasite and a drunk. He and his family live on the dump and live off the bounty of the county. The father of the woman who accuses Tom.

Mayella Ewell: The oldest child of Ewell, she is shy and very lonely.

Heck Tate: The town sheriff.

Boo (Arthur) Radley: A recluse who lives on the Finches' street. Possibly deranged, possibly dangerous, and possibly just shy.

ESSAY IDEAS

- What is the significance of the title? How does it work with the rest of the book?
- Describe how Scout and Jem mature throughout the novel.
- Discuss the different ideas in the book of what it means to be "fine folk," to "have background," or to be a "lady" or "gentleman."
- Examine the meaning of "bravery" in the novel.
- Discuss "difference" as it pertains to one or more of the following areas: race, sex, class, sanity, intelligence, lifestyle.

A SAMPLE ESSAY IN OUTLINE FORM

Discuss the relationship between racism and class prejudice in *To Kill a Mockingbird*.
- Racism:
  - It is all-pervasive; bigotry is shared by almost all the whites in Maycomb.
  - Being born with black skin is an insurmountable obstacle:

  - Tom Robinson, despite being a good man, is found guilty of a crime he didn't commit.
  - One can never transcend race.
- Class prejudice:
  - Also very prevalent, but unlike race, class does not doom someone:
  - Lower-class whites can transcend class: even "white trash" like Bob Ewell can reap the benefits of society.

The town of Maycomb is guilty of both class prejudice and racism in the novel. The members of this society constantly categorize others, and define themselves, according to both race and class. However, it is racism that runs the deepest. Racism blinds the jurors in Tom's trial, resulting in his death. In the end we see that neither race nor class, but actions, determine the worth of a man.

PLOT SUMMARY

Chapter One The opening chapter places us in Maycomb, the seat of Maycomb County in Alabama. The town and its history are described with feeling and detail, as are the characters that are introduced to us. The narrator, Scout, shows us the world around her. It is summertime, before she starts school. Scout tells us the story of Arthur "Boo" Radley, who lives three houses down and is regarded as a dangerous, crazy person. The kids (Scout, Jem, and Dill) are afraid of him but delight in talking about him, making up games about him, and trying to get up the courage to prank the Radley house.

Chapter Two Dill goes back to school at Meridian, and Scout goes into the first grade. The teacher of Scout's class does not know how to handle the children of Maycomb, least of all Scout, and the morning is a disaster for both of them. The children don't know what to make of their new teacher, either. Scout gets a light whipping from the teacher, and learns that not everyone understands Maycomb's ways.

Chapter Three   Scout starts to fight Walter, the boy who caused the misunderstanding that earned Scout the whipping, but Jem stops her. They all go to the Finches' for lunch. Back in school that afternoon, the teacher continues to mishandle her first graders, who decide to take pity on her. We are also introduced to the Ewell clan, the lowest of Maycomb's low. We will meet them again later on.

Chapter Four   Scout is still bored by school, but summer is on the way. Walking home from school she finds some wrapped gum that was left in the knot-hole of a tree on the Radley property. That summer, we are told, Jem, Dill, and Scout will play a variety of games involving Boo Radley.

Chapter Five   Wounded because Jem and Dill exclude her from playing a game, Scout befriends Miss Maudie Atkinson, one of the neighbors. On the porch one evening, Miss Maudie and Scout talk about good people and bad Christians. This exchange is important in establishing the morality of the novel. Jem, Scout, and Dill try to prank Boo Radley and get caught by a furious Atticus, who forbids them to bother Boo again.

Chapter Six   The children have grown bolder. This time they sneak into the Radleys' collard patch and have to run away under shotgun fire. Escaping, Jem leaves his pants caught on the fence. That night Jem goes back for his pants despite Scout's protests. He returns safely, although Scout hears his cot "trembling" beneath him.

Chapter Seven   Jem, after being silent and moody for a week, finally reveals to Scout that his pants had been detached from the fence, sewn up, and folded when he retrieved them. A series of gifts begin showing up in the Radley tree, mystifying the children. Then one day the knot is cemented up, supposedly because the tree is diseased. It looks perfectly healthy, however.

Chapter Eight   Scout sees her first snow. School is cancelled, and the siblings build a snowman of sorts: a caricature of one of the neighbors. In the middle of the night Miss Maudie's house catches on fire. As the fire is fought, Scout and Jem stand outside, freezing, and Scout receives a strange visit from Boo.

Chapter Nine   This chapter shows Scout growing, changing, learning, and questioning her assumptions. First, she fights a boy for saying that Atticus (her father) is defending a "nigger." During Christmas, she ends up fighting her cousin Francis and gets unfairly whipped by her uncle. She teaches her uncle a few things about children, and about fairness as well.

Later, listening in on Atticus and Uncle Jack, Scout and the reader find out what the trial is all about. A black man, Tom Robinson, has been accused of raping a white woman; it is a case which Atticus, as the black man's lawyer, has no hope of winning.

Chapter Ten   Scout and Jem think that Atticus, who is nearly fifty, is less impressive than other dads, despite Miss Maudie's assurances. When a rabid dog stalks the neighborhood, Atticus shoots it square in the head with one perfect shot. The children are awed to discover that their father is the famous "one-Eyed Finch," and Atticus' character gains more depth.

Chapter Eleven We are introduced to a new character, Mrs. Henry Lafayette Dubose, a mean-tempered, "wrathful" old woman. Following Atticus' advice, the children try to be polite. But Jem's temper gets the better of him, and one day he ruins her garden in a fit of anger. As punishment, Jem and Scout must go to read to Mrs. Dubose every day after school for a month. They find it a horrible experience: Mrs. Dubose is mean and tends to fall asleep during the reading. They realize that she keeps them there a little longer every afternoon. Soon after, the children are released forever, when Mrs. Dubose dies. This chapter examines "what real courage is."

Chapter Twelve This summer, Dill doesn't come back, and Atticus goes away to the legislature. Jem is growing up fast and has "acquired a maddening air of wisdom." Calpurnia takes Scout and Jem to the First Purchase African M.E. Church, where Scout notices many differences between black people's and white people's customs. Scout also notices that all churches seem to preach the "Impurity of Women" doctrine. Calpurnia, one of the few literate blacks in the community, is found to have a "double life," and she and the Finches contemplate differences between blacks and whites.

Chapter Thirteen Aunt Alexandra comes to live with the Finches in Maycomb, to Scout's dismay. Aunty likes to talk about other people, and about her ideas on "background" and "fine folk" as opposed to "trash." Some people, however, have other ideas.

Chapter Fourteen Dill runs away from his parents to stay in Maycomb, causing Scout to think about what makes good parents.

Chapter Fifteen Atticus' case starts to cause real trouble. Tom Robinson is moved into the Maycomb jail, and the night before the trial Atticus keeps watch over him. Jem, Scout, and Dill sneak into town and watch as a group of white men arrive, demanding that Atticus hand Tom over to them. Atticus refuses, and the scene becomes increasingly ugly until the kids interrupt.

Chapter Sixteen It is the day of Tom Robinson's trial. The kids stand outside and watch the procession; it seems that everybody in Maycomb County has come to town. Jem tells Scout and Dill about the people. The dialogue serves to heighten the sense that everybody knows everybody in small towns and that there are few secrets.

Harper Lee tells the story of Mr. Dolphus Raymond. He is a rich man from an old family; however, he is always half-drunk in public and has a common-law marriage to a black woman. He and this woman have several mixed-race children who "don't belong anywhere." Through Raymond's story and the way he is perceived by others, the author illustrates ideas about difference; this theme is further enforced as Scout wonders about what makes a person black.

The court convenes and the kids can't get seats until Reverend Sykes brings them into the Colored balcony. From there Scout looks down on Judge Taylor, who "kept a firm grip on any proceedings," although he looks as if he is sleeping.

Chapter Seventeen The first witness in the trial is Mr. Heck Tate, the town sheriff. His story, briefly, is that Mr. Bob Ewell called him when his daughter, Mayella, was raped. Atticus, on cross-examination, finds out that Mayella's right eye was blackened, and that there were finger-marks all around her throat from being choked. The next witness is Bob Ewell. He is a "redneck," a local good-for-nothing. He is rude and crude, and accuses Tom Robinson of raping his daughter in an obscene way, causing a court uproar. Atticus also finds out that Bob Ewell is left-handed.

Chapter Eighteen Mayella Ewell is "a thick bodied girl accustomed to strenuous labor." Although uneducated, she is "stealthy" and "has enough sense" to make the jury sympathetic. She accuses Tom of attacking and raping her. But on Atticus' cross-examination, a different picture emerges. Atticus has Mayella talk about her pitiable home life, how she has no friends, and how her father is abusive and an alcoholic. He confuses her in her story about the rape.

She again accuses Tom, and when he stands to meet her accusation, everyone sees that his left arm is crippled and is completely useless. Although Mayella is clearly in the wrong, the author portrays her with some sympathy as a lonely, abused, neglected young girl who in turn abuses her privileged position as a white woman. Like the mixed children of Mr. Dolphus, Mayella doesn't belong anywhere.

Chapter Nineteen Atticus calls his only witness, the accused, Tom Robinson. Tom gives a completely different story than Mayella's. He says that Mayella was always asking him to do little chores for her, and that he did them because she had no other help. On the day in question Mayella asked him inside to do a chore. Then she grabbed him, hugged him, and kissed the side of his face.

Bob Ewell, says Tom, saw this through the window and started screaming at Mayella. Tom took the opportunity to run. Lee illustrates the "subtlety of Tom's predicament." To repel Mayella, a white woman, would have been a certain death sentence. On the other hand, actually kiss-ing her, or doing anything else with her, would have doomed him as well. Running away makes him look guilty; but when he defends himself verbally, he is interpreted as calling white people liars. Such are the intricacies of racism.

Mr. Gilmer, the attorney for the prosecution, cross-examines Tom, who makes the mistake of saying that he, a black man, "felt sorry" for Mayella, a white woman. Gilmer's cross examination is racist in tone: he plays on the jury's prejudices. This so upsets Dill that Scout has to take him outside.

Chapter Twenty Dill is crying because Gilmer is not treating Tom like a human being. The children are overheard by Mr. Dolphus Raymond. He teaches them a valuable lesson on prejudice and attitudes, and the children learn his big secret. Dill and Scout return to the courtroom in time to hear Atticus' closing statement.

Chapter Twenty-One The verdict is in after a lengthy deliberation by the jury. Tom Robinson is found guilty.

Chapter Twenty-Two The kids and Miss Maudie muse over the trial and human nature. Then they hear the news: Mr. Ewell "stopped Atticus...and told him he'd get him if it took the rest of his life."

Chapter Twenty-Three Tom has been transferred to another prison. The Finches talk about the courtroom, about fairness and juries. Aunt Alexandra gives a lecture about "fine folk," and what it means to have background. The society in which the book is set is a sharply divided one, and issues of social class and caste are important. Later, Jem and Scout exchange their own ideas on "background."

Chapter Twenty-Four It is the end of August, and Aunty is giving a reception for the ladies of Maycomb. Scout has to act like a "little lady," and although she isn't too pleased at first, she finds out that maybe it is not all bad. This part of the chapter explores the ideas of hypocrisy, trust, and background. We learn also that Tom is dead. He was shot when he tried to escape from prison.

Chapter Twenty-Five Atticus and Calpurnia take Jem and Dill to break the news of Tom's death to his wife, Helen. The town hardly reacts to Tom's death—after two days, interest has waned.

Chapter Twenty-Six Scout starts the third grade, not much happier than she was in the first. Hitler is persecuting the Jews in Germany, and the children discuss it during Current Events. This prompts another musing on the meaning of "fine folk," as Scout wonders how people that condemn Hitler for his persecution of the Jews can turn around and persecute blacks in their own town.

Chapter Twenty-Seven Bob Ewell is causing trouble in Maycomb, harassing Tom Robinson's widow and accusing Atticus of getting him fired from his job. Scout, meanwhile, is cast in the school Halloween pageant as "Pork," with a costume making her look "exactly like a ham with legs." Atticus gracefully bows out of having to go watch the pageant, so Jem walks Scout the short distance to the school.

Chapter Twenty-Eight The pageant begins with a salute to Maycomb's history. Scout, listening underneath her Pork costume backstage, falls asleep and misses her entrance. To cover her chagrin, she leaves her costume on for the walk home with

Jem. It is very dark, and they have to walk slowly through the woods. They notice that someone is following them.

The attack that follows is confusing because Scout cannot see well from under her costume. Scout is attacked, but someone saves her. She feels an unidentified body under the tree, then notices a man carrying an unconscious Jem up to the Finch house and runs after him. The doctor and the sheriff are both called, and Scout notices but does not recognize Jem's savior, standing in the corner. Heck Tate has news: Bob Ewell is dead, "lyin' on the ground under that tree down yonder with a kitchen knife stuck up under his ribs." It becomes clear that Ewell was the attacker, and that the person who saved Scout and Jem must have killed him.

Chapter Twenty-Nine Scout recounts the story to Atticus and Sheriff Tate. She identifies the man standing in the corner of the room as the fourth person in the fracas, the man who carried Jem home. It is Boo Radley.

Chapter Thirty Atticus and Heck Tate argue about Ewell's death. Heck insists that Ewell killed himself, falling on his own knife. This reasoning upsets Atticus, but Scout understands it perfectly: even though it is a lie, to tell the truth—that Boo Radley killed Bob Ewell—would "be sort of like shootin' a mockingbird."

Chapter Thirty-One Scout accompanies Boo, now called Mr. Arthur, back home. In her mind, she reviews the last few years of her life and, upon returning to her own house, lets Atticus read her to sleep.

WUTHERING HEIGHTS

ABOUT THE AUTHOR

Emily Brontë (1818–1848) was born in Yorkshire, England, the fifth child of Reverend Patrick Brontë and Maria Branwell Brontë. Mrs. Brontë died of cancer in 1821, leaving her six children in their father's care. In 1824, the four daughters were sent to the Cowan Bridge School, a school for the children of clergymen. The conditions were terrible; Maria and Elizabeth, the two oldest daughters, died, and Charlotte, another daughter, became very sick.

When *Wuthering Heights* was published, no one in the publishing world took much notice of it. Brutal and violent, wild and passionate, it was very different from most of the work that was being published at the time

Wuthering Heights was Emily Brontë's only novel; she also published some poetry. When she died at age thirty, she knew nothing of the great praise *Wuthering Heights* would later receive.

THE BIG PICTURE

"*Wuthering Heights* was hewn in a rough workshop, with simple tools, out of homely materials." These words from the foreword to the second publication of the book very accurately describe *Wuthering Heights*—it is a wild and coarse tale of unfulfilled passion and seething hatred. Its raw emotional power, rare in works of its time, makes it one of the most-read novels of the nineteenth century.

Why you're reading this book:
- It is an engaging, tragic tale of love and hate, and good versus evil.
- A brutal, sometimes revolting story of

characters who seem truly cursed, it is unlike anything that came before it.
- Brontë's writing style is eloquent, rich, and dense with meaning and imagery.
- Brontë uses an interesting method of narration, with two different people explaining events and the histories of the characters.

Your teachers are looking for:
- Examples of Brontë's "wild" and "simple" style.
- Brontë's development of the conflicts between the characters so that the tension builds throughout the novel.
- Spiritual imagery throughout the novel.
- The time structure of the novel—how it jumps back and forth rather than following a straight line, and how this is significant.

KEY CHARACTERS

Lockwood: A relatively insignificant character in the action of the book, he serves as the narrator for the first four chapters of the novel.

Mr. Earnshaw: He brings home a young orphan from Liverpool named Heathcliff. He takes a genuine liking to Heathcliff, making his own son (Hind-ley) very jealous.

Mrs. Earnshaw: She does not appreciate her husband's taking in Heathcliff.

Hindley Earnshaw: Earnshaw's son. He hates Heathcliff and is jealous of the attention his father lavishes on him.

Catherine Earnshaw: Hindley's sister. She is arrogant and wild. Although she loves Heathcliff, she marries Edgar Linton.

Frances Earnshaw: Hindley's wife. She dies after her son, Hareton, is born.

Hareton Earnshaw: Hindley and Frances' son. He begins the story as a somewhat cruel person, but later tries to be more affectionate and warm.

Heathcliff: The boy whom Mr. Earnshaw brings home to live with his family. He is a sulky child, and grows to be a cruel adult. He loves Catherine and is devastated when she marries Edgar Linton. He is married to Isabella Linton.

Linton Heathcliff: The sickly son of Heathcliff and Isabella Linton.

Edgar Linton: Catherine's husband. After her death, he becomes a recluse.

Cathy Linton: Edgar and Catherine's daughter. She has a happy marriage with Hareton. Heathcliff tries to make her suffer and pay for the heartbreak her mother caused him.

Isabella Linton: Edgar Linton's sister. She marries Heathcliff.

Nelly Dean: The servant at the Grange.

Joseph: A companion and servant of Heathcliff.

Zillah: A woman of questionable morals who takes Nelly's job at Wuthering Heights.

ESSAY IDEAS

- Is this story so farfetched as to be unbelievable? Can people like its characters really exist? Why or why not?
- Whom are you more sympathetic toward, Heathcliff or Hindley? Make a case for either one, using as many examples from the story as you can to back up your argument.
- Do you think this story is trying to make a statement? If so, what is it and how does the author go about making it? If not, why not?
- What is the purpose of having Mr. Lockwood telling any part of this story?

- Find examples of events happening more than once in the novel. What do you think is the significance of recurring events?

A SAMPLE ESSAY IN OUTLINE FORM

Discuss Brontë's use of setting to illustrate characters.

- Brontë uses different settings for different characters in order to reflect their contrasting personalities and values:
  - Wuthering Heights/Heathcliff:
    - Both are dark, brooding, and forbidding.
    - Wuthering Heights is unclean and ill-kept—reflects Heathcliff's uncivilized nature.
    - Both Heathcliff and Wuthering Heights have a powerful, threatening presence.
  - Thrushcross Grange/Edgar:
    - Lighter, more open than Wuthering Heights.
    - More civilized.
    - Everything is neat and in order.
    - Calming, gentle.
  - Catherine spends time in both places; she is a mixture of the two:
    - Has a darker side that draws her to Heathcliff /Wuthering Heights.
    - Aspires to life at the Grange but is bored by it.
    - Torn between the two settings as she is torn between Edgar and Heathcliff.

Brontë's use of setting in *Wuthering Heights* helps to enhance our understanding of the characters as well as heighten the tension between them. The contrast between Heathcliff and Edgar—as well as Catherine's dilemma—is made vividly clear by their respective environments.

PLOT SUMMARY

Chapter 1 The year is 1801. The narrator, Mr. Lockwood, is visiting with his new landlord, Mr. Heathcliff, at Wuthering Heights. Heathcliff seems less than eager to rent out any part of his estate. Joseph, a servant, is summoned to bring wine. Lockwood gives a detailed description of the interior of the house and Heathcliff's own appearance. He then talks of why Heathcliff has earned himself the reputation of being coldhearted. When Heathcliff and Joseph leave the dining room, Lockwood teases Heathcliff's dogs into a state of frenzy. Heathcliff returns and gives Lockwood some wine. The two men visit briefly.

Chapter 2 Looking around Wuthering Heights, Lockwood finds a woman sitting at Heathcliff's table, whom he assumes to be Mrs. Heathcliff. She is very cold to Mr. Lockwood. Heathcliff enters, and Mr. Lockwood asks if he can borrow one of Heathcliff's men to help him back to the Grange, his home on the estate. Heathcliff refuses his request. Mr. Lockwood makes a reference to Heathcliff's "lady." Heathcliff bitterly replies that Mr. Lockwood mocks him—his "lady" is gone. Lockwood guesses that the woman is Heathcliff's daughter-in-law. She is Catherine Linton, Hareton Earnshaw's wife.

Joseph enters the room, cursing Lockwood for his idleness. Mrs. Heathcliff shuts the old man up, and Lockwood asks her for help in finding his way home in the storm. While all in the house are bickering, Lockwood attempts to make his way back home but is stopped by Joseph and the dogs. He is ushered back inside and into a bed.

Chapter 3 Zillah leads Mr. Lockwood to his room. She tells him to make no noise, as no one is supposed to be staying in this room. He sees the names Catherine Earn-shaw, Catherine Heathcliff, and Cath-erine Linton etched into the wood paneling. He falls asleep, but wakes up when he hears a knock on the window. He falls back to sleep and dreams that he is again awakened by the sound of tapping on the window.

He tries to open the window and break off a branch of a tree that he thinks is making the noise on the glass. He instead grabs a hand and hears a small voice crying to let her in. Lockwood asks who it is and the voice says that it is Catherine Linton. As he wakes from his nightmare, Heathcliff bursts into the room demanding to know why Lockwood was asked to sleep in this room. Thinking that the house is haunted, Lockwood decides to leave. Heathcliff opens the window and calls out for Cathy.

Lockwood goes down to the kitchen and sees Joseph. Hareton shows him into the living room, where Heathcliff and his daughter-in-law are having a quarrel. Lockwood leaves and makes his way back to the Grange.

Chapter 4 When Mr. Lockwood gets home, he asks his housekeeper, Nelly Dean, about the Heathcliff household. Nelly Dean has known the family for eighteen years. At this point, she takes over the narration and the story goes back in time to when Mr. Earnshaw first brings Heathcliff home and Hindley hates him. Nelly puts him at the bottom of the stairs hoping that he will leave, and Mr. Earnshaw fires Nelly because of the incident.

Heathcliff is named after another child of the Earnshaws' who died. Catherine Earnshaw, Mr. Earnshaw's daughter, comes to love Heathcliff. After Mrs. Earnshaw dies, Hindley only grows more jealous of Heathcliff's relationship with his father.

Chapter 5 Finally, the jealous Hindley is sent away to school. Catherine and Joseph are now fighting; the servant is taking advantage of Mr. Earnshaw, who is very ill. The night Earnshaw dies, Joseph tries to hide his death and tells the children to go to bed. Catherine goes to hug her father and screams that he is dead. She and Heathcliff comfort each other.

Chapter 6 Hindley returns for his father's funeral with a wife, Frances. Hindley is now very bitter and turns Nelly and Joseph into true slaves. When Frances tells Hindley she does not like Heathcliff, he is banished to the servants' quarters. When Catherine and Heathcliff go out of the house, Hindley locks the door behind them so that they cannot get back in. Nelly sits up and waits for them to let them in.

Heathcliff comes home alone one of these nights, saying that Catherine is staying at Thrushcross Grange, the home of the Lintons. They had gone to see how the Lintons live and were disgusted by the children's spoiled ways. The Linton children saw the two looking into their windows and sent their dog after them. The dog bit Catherine on the ankle and she fainted. A servant carried her into the house and Heathcliff was told to go back home.

Catherine is treated like a queen at the Grange, and Hindley is scolded by Mr. Linton for not watching out for his sister. Hindley is now incensed at Heathcliff and plans to throw him out. He tells Frances to watch Catherine for fear that she might rebel.

Chapter 7 Catherine stays at the Grange for five weeks. She returns home looking groomed and clean. She is overjoyed to see Heathcliff, but tells him to clean himself up, comparing him to the clean and handsome Edgar Linton. Heathcliff runs from the room, embarrassed.

When the Lintons come over, Edgar Linton baits Heathcliff, insulting him. In retali-ation, Heathcliff throws hot applesauce in his face. The rivalry between them is established.

Chapter 8 Frances has given birth to a son; however, complications during child-birth result in her death a week later. The baby, Hareton, is taken care of by Nelly. Hindley, unbearably depressed by his wife's death, treats Heathcliff cruelly.

Edgar Linton courts Cathy occasionally. The rivalry begins to intensify when Heath-cliff invites Catherine to take a holiday break with him but she prefers to spend her time with the Lintons. Furthermore, she tells Heathcliff that he bores her.

Chapter 9 That night, Hindley returns home drunk. In a stupor, he picks up his son Hareton and accidentally drops him over the stairs. Luckily, Heathcliff is there and catches him. Nelly takes the baby to the kitchen. Heathcliff follows, sitting in a corner.

Catherine comes in to tell Nelly that Edgar has proposed and that she means to accept. Not realizing that Heathcliff is sitting in the kitchen, she says that Hindley has degraded Heathcliff so much that there is no possible way she could marry him. Heath-cliff leaves the house, missing Catherine's conclusion, that she loves him.

Catherine gets a fever waiting up for Heathcliff to return, but he is nowhere to be found. The Lintons have Catherine to their estate to rest and recuperate; how-ever, they catch her fever as well and much of the family dies. Catherine then returns to Wuthering Heights.

Heathcliff is gone for the next three years. During that time, Catherine and Edgar are married. Nelly leaves Wuthering Heights to live with Catherine at Thrush-cross Grange.

Chapter 10 Relative peace prevails for a

few years. Then, on an evening in September, Heathcliff arrives at the Grange. Nelly is utterly shocked at his appearance: Heathcliff looks like a gentleman. Nelly announces the visitor without giving his name.

Heathcliff enters and Catherine is surprised and very pleased to see him. Edgar, however, is greatly displeased by their obvious affection for each other. Heathcliff tells Catherine that he will not leave again.

Heathcliff quickly attracts the attention of Isabella Linton. Edgar is now even more worried: the Grange could now go to Heathcliff, as Isabella is Edgar's heir.

Chapter 11 Nelly goes to visit Wuthering Heights and Hareton is outside. When she tells him who she is he throws stones at her, not realizing that she was once his nurse. He says that his "Devil Daddy" taught him to do that. Heathcliff appears, and Hareton tells Nelly that he loves Heathcliff. She leaves, confused and scared.

The next day Heathcliff and Isabella are seen hugging at the Grange. When Edgar tells Heathcliff to leave the Grange, he refuses. Edgar is furious. He punches Heathcliff and runs out. Heathcliff says he will "crush his ribs."

When Edgar returns, he tells Catherine she must choose between him and Heathcliff. She runs to her room, locks herself in, and stays there for two days, eating nothing. Edgar orders Isabella not to go near Heathcliff, or he will disown her.

Chapter 12 After three days, Catherine asks for some water and food, saying that she is dying. At first, Nelly does not believe her. However, Catherine begins to have strange hallucinations and Nelly begins to fear for her safety. Edgar enters the room and is horrified by Catherine's appearance. Nelly goes to get medical help.

The doctor examines Catherine, and he says he does not think that she will survive. The next morning, Isabella runs away with Heathcliff. Edgar states that Isabella is no longer his sister.

Chapter 13 Catherine's health improves, but she will remain sick for the rest of her days. We learn that she is pregnant. Heathcliff and Isabella have been gone for two weeks.

Isabella writes to Edgar from Wuthering Heights some weeks after her elopement with Heathcliff. He refuses to answer her letter. She then writes to Nelly, telling her that she thinks Heathcliff may be the Devil. Now living at Wuthering Heights with Heathcliff, she has met the now-disgusting Hindley, who locked her in his room for a few hours and told her of his desire to kill Heathcliff. Joseph then threatened to walk out when she wanted to cook a meal.

Heathcliff has told her that Edgar made Catherine sick, and that he would take revenge on Isabella until he could take revenge on Edgar. Isabella says in her letter that she hates Heathcliff and was a fool to marry him.

Chapter 14 Nelly visits Wuthering Heights and is appalled. Isabella is disheveled, while Heathcliff looks well-kempt. He asks of Catherine and is greatly angered when Nelly refuses to let him meet her.

Heathcliff begins to taunt Isabella. She fights back, saying that his plans to gain power over Edgar will be thwarted. Nelly tries to leave, but Heathcliff won't let her until she says she will bring Catherine a note telling her of his desire to see her.

Chapter 15 Four days after her encounter with Heathcliff, Nelly gives Catherine the note while Edgar is at church. Before Catherine can read it, however, Heathcliff rushes into the room. He grabs Catherine and hugs her. She at first tells him she does not pity him in his grief for her. Eventually, the two reconcile and embrace passionately. They are still hugging when Edgar returns. Heathcliff leaves and wanders around the garden, hoping to hear news of Catherine.

Chapter 16 Catherine dies that night after giving birth to a girl, Cathy. Nelly goes outside to tell Heathcliff the news. He asks if Catherine said his name as she was dying. She did not, and he curses Catherine not to rest in her grave. A few days later, Catherine is buried.

Chapter 17 Isabella has run away from Heathcliff. Hindley had locked Heathcliff outside the house and tried to enlist Isabella's help in killing him. At the very last second, she ran and told Heathcliff of the plan. Heathcliff fought the weapon out of Hindley's hand and then threw a dinner knife at Isabella. As she fled Wuthering Heights, Heathcliff and Hindley were fighting and Hareton was hanging a litter of puppies.

Isabella moves to a suburb of London where she gives birth to a sickly son, whom she names Linton. Isabella dies when Linton is twelve years old; Hindley dies six months after Isabella. Because Edgar is Linton's uncle, he is now his guardian. Hareton has become a beggar because his father, Hindley, has gambled away his estate. Heathcliff now owns Wuthering Heights and Hindley's son, Hareton.

Chapter 18 When Edgar goes to London to claim Linton Heathcliff, Nelly is left to take care of Cathy. Cathy takes a ride on her pony with her dogs, and as she passes Wuthering Heights, Hareton's dogs attack hers.

Worried when Cathy does not return,

Nelly searches and finds her in the kitchen of Wuthering Heights, talking to Hareton. Nelly tells Cathy not to tell her father about being at Wuthering Heights.

Chapter 19 Cathy is excited by the prospect of her cousin Linton staying with them, but Linton seems small and sickly compared to Cathy. Joseph later arrives to claim Linton as Heathcliff's son. Edgar insists that his sister provided for him to take care of the boy, but Joseph threatens to have Heathcliff come and claim him. This sways Edgar, and he says he will send the boy in the morning.

Chapter 20 The next morning Nelly takes Linton to Wuthering Heights. Linton does not believe that his father is alive because his mother never even mentioned him. He does not want to leave the Grange.

Heathcliff is cruel to Linton the moment he meets him, bringing the boy to tears. Heathcliff's only interest in Linton is that he will one day inherit the Grange. He is disappointed in the appearance of his pasty-faced weakling of a son.

Chapter 21 With Linton living away from the Grange, Cathy doesn't remember her cousin by the time she turns sixteen. One day while Cathy and Nelly are walking near Wuthering Heights, Heathcliff sees them and pretends he does not know who Cathy is. He asks her who her father is and she says Edgar. She asks if Hareton is his son and he tells her that he is not, but that he does have a son whom he will introduce her to. Heathcliff wants Linton and Cathy to marry.

The two are introduced. Linton is attracted to Cathy and she invites him to the Grange. Nelly later warns Cathy against having anything to do with Wuthering Heights. When Cathy tells her father of her visit to the estate, he tells her that Heathcliff is a murderer and forbids her to go there again. Despite all this, Nelly finds notes that Cathy and Linton write to each other. Nelly burns the notes and sends a letter to Linton telling him not to write anymore.

Chapter 22 Edgar gets very sick and is confined to the house. Cathy and Nelly go for a walk and Cathy's hat blows over a wall. Again, Heathcliff mysteriously appears and tells Cathy that Linton is quite upset over their break in communication. He says that he is leaving for a week and he hopes Cathy will visit soon. Nelly later tells Cathy that she is sure Heathcliff is lying. The next day, Cathy and Nelly ride to Wuthering Heights.

Chapter 23 Cathy and Nelly arrive at Wuthering Heights and they give Linton some water and wine. Linton asks Cathy to spend some time with him. However, the two get into an argument about their parents and she pushes his chair. When Nelly and Cathy go to leave, Linton throws a temper tantrum. Nelly and Cathy reconcile with Linton, but Nelly tells Cathy she cannot visit him again.

Nelly gets sick and is in bed for the next few weeks. Cathy cares for her father and Nelly, sneaking away to the Heights at night.

Chapter 24 Cathy confesses to Nelly that she has been visiting the Heights every day, and tells her that she and Linton have been getting along very well. However, one day when she visited, Hareton answered the door. When she told him she had come to see Linton, he left, embarrassed.

As Linton and Cathy were sitting and talking, Hareton stormed in. He threw Linton from his chair and he raised his hand to Cathy as if to strike her. Hareton threw

the pair out of the room. The fight brought on a coughing spasm for the sickly Linton. Nelly tells Edgar of this incident, and he again forbids Cathy to go the Heights. He will, however, allow Linton to visit the Grange.

Chapter 25 Edgar tells Nelly he would not mind if Cathy wanted to marry Linton, as long as it made her happy. He writes to Linton, telling him that he can visit the Grange. Linton replies that his father will not let him, so Edgar lets Cathy and Nelly go to the Heights to visit Linton. Both Edgar's and Linton's health are deteriorating at the same fast pace.

Chapter 26 Cathy and Nelly meet Linton and he is a self-pitying mess. When they say that they will leave, he becomes very upset. He dozes for a while, dreaming that his father is calling him. Cathy finally says that she should leave if she cannot divert his attention from his ailing health. She makes plans to visit next Thursday.

Chapter 27 Edgar is dying and wants Cathy to visit with Linton so that she will not be alone. She meets him in the moors near Wuthering Heights. Linton makes a characteristically self-pitying speech about his worthlessness. When Cathy gets ready to leave, Linton throws himself on the ground. He begs for her help, saying that if she leaves his father will kill him.

Heathcliff enters. He asks Nelly if Edgar is dying. Heathcliff hopes that Edgar will die before Linton. He asks Cathy to walk home with her cousin. Cathy tells Linton that she has been forbidden to visit Wuthering Heights. However, mindful of Heathcliff's temper, Linton, Cathy, and Nelly agree to go with him.

Once they are inside the Heights, Heathcliff locks the door. He offers Linton to Cathy as a present. Cathy tries to get the key from him, biting his hand, but Heathcliff hits her and threatens Nelly for intervening. Cathy and Nelly try to escape when he goes to find their horses, but they are unsuccessful.

Heathcliff returns and tells them that their horses have left. He sends Linton to bed. He then gives Cathy his ultimatum: she must marry Linton or stay locked up until her father dies. He takes Cathy, leaving Nelly locked in a bedroom.

Chapter 28 After five days, Zillah finds Nelly. She lets her go, telling her that it was rumored that she and Cathy were lost in the marsh land. Nelly finds Linton downstairs. He tells her that Cathy is locked upstairs and can do nothing but cry. Nelly asks for the key to set Cathy free, but Linton refuses. Nelly goes to the Grange to seek help.

Edgar is extremely ill. When she tells him of their kidnapping at the Heights, Edgar decides to change his will quickly so nothing will fall into the hands of Heathcliff if Linton should die.

Cathy finally escapes from the Heights and returns to the Grange. Edgar dies happily, thinking that Cathy will be well taken care of. However, the lawyer does not appear until after Edgar's death—he was under orders from Heathcliff not to come. The lawyer orders Edgar not be buried next to his wife Catherine, but Nelly knows that Edgar's last will must be carried out.

Chapter 29 Heathcliff comes to pick up Cathy from the Grange. He has tortured Linton for two hours because he let Cathy escape. Nelly begs for Linton and Cathy to stay at the Grange. Heathcliff, however, has a different plan: he now wants to rent the Grange and have Cathy work for her room and board at Wuthering Heights. Cathy prepares to leave and Nelly begs to come along as housekeeper. Heathcliff

won't hear of it; he forbids Nelly even to visit.

Chapter 30 Nelly tries to visit the Heights but isn't allowed to see Cathy. Linton has died. Heathcliff showed Cathy the will that he claims Linton signed before he passed away. It leaves Cathy with nothing. Nelly wants to get a cottage and live with Cathy, but she knows that Heathcliff won't allow it.

The story has now come to the present day. After hearing this ghastly tale, Lockwood wants to tell Heathcliff that he will be leaving for London and that Heathcliff should find another tenant.

Chapter 31 Mr. Lockwood goes to the Heights, and Hareton lets him in. He brings a note to Cathy from Nelly. Lockwood asks if she has a message to be brought back. Heathcliff enters and asks Lockwood why he is visiting. When Lockwood tells him of his plans to stay in London, Heathcliff tells Lockwood that he will still have to pay the rent even though he is leaving. Lockwood stays for dinner. Cathy is ordered by Heathcliff to eat alone in the kitchen.

Chapter 32 Six months later, Lockwood comes back and visits the Grange. He also visits the Heights. Nelly is now the housekeeper at the Heights. Hareton and Cathy are in the kitchen, both looking healthy and bright. Heathcliff died three months ago. Nelly tells the story of Heathcliff's "queer death," and how Cathy and Hareton have grown so fond of each other that they are planning to marry.

Chapter 33 Nelly tells the story of how before his death, Heathcliff grabbed Cathy by the hair, enraged. He screamed that she would destroy Hareton. Finally he calmed down enough to let go of her. Later on, Heathcliff saw the pair together and was reminded of Catherine, Cathy's mother. Here Heathcliff seems a more sympathetic character, a man forever haunted by his lost love.

Chapter 34 Nelly finishes her story. Heathcliff spent the rest of his days in a trance-like state, barely speaking to anyone. One night, he spoke of plans for his funeral. The following morning Nelly found him in his room dead. Nelly tells Lockwood of the rumors that Heathcliff's spirit had been seen with that of a woman. One shepherd said that his sheep wouldn't cross a path because they saw the two spirits together. Lockwood leaves and walks to the three gravestones of Edgar, Catherine, and Heathcliff. He wonders how any of the spirits could not be resting peacefully.

ABOUT THE AUTHORS

Tufts Student Resources (TSR), founded at Tufts University in 1980 by Tom Alperin, Nancy Gibson, Steve Dennis, and Seth Godin, started out as a temporary employment agency. It soon became the largest student-run business in the nation.

Often employing more than 400 students at a time (out of a total enrollment of 4,400), TSR has provided travel services, promoted concerts, and run a catering and snack food delivery company, among other things. At one time, TSR had translators on staff capable of translating 30 different languages.

Today, TSR is still entirely student-run. Housed in its own building, the organization runs several businesses and exclusively employs Tufts students, helping them to earn money to pay for tuition.

TSR managers have gone on to pursue successful careers in business and education, with more than a few using their experiences at TSR to help them succeed.

This guide was written by a team of students working for TSR, most of them juniors and seniors majoring in English or Political Science.

Seth Godin, editor of *Quick Lit*, is president of Seth Godin Productions, Inc., creator and packager of books, videotapes, and videotex. He wishes he had had a copy of this book when he was in high school.